Medieval Boundaries

THE MIDDLE AGES SERIES

Ruth Mazo Karras, Series Editor

Edward Peters, Founding Editor

A complete list of books in the series is available from the publisher.

Medieval Boundaries

Rethinking Difference in
Old French Literature

Sharon Kinoshita

PENN

UNIVERSITY OF PENNSYLVANIA PRESS

PHILADELPHIA

10 9 8 7 6 5 4 3 2 1

Published by
University of Pennsylvania Press
Philadelphia, Pennsylvania 19104-4112

Library of Congress Cataloging-in-Publication Data

Kinoshita, Sharon.
    Medieval boundaries : rethinking difference in Old French literature /
Sharon Kinoshita.
        p. cm. — (The Middle Ages series)
    Includes bibliographical references and index.
    ISBN-13: 978-0-8122-3919-5
    ISBN-10: 0-8122-3919-9 cloth : alk. paper
    1. French literature—To 1500—History and criticism.   I. Title.
II. Series.
PQ151.K56 2006
840.9'001—dc22   2005052724

In memory of my parents,
Koujiro "Koko" Kinoshita
and Haruno Ogawa Kinoshita

Contents

Introduction

Medieval Boundaries began with the curious realization that many of the best-known works of medieval French literature take place on or beyond the borders of "France" or even the French-speaking world: the *Chanson de Roland*, the *Lais* of Marie de France, Chrétien de Troyes's *Cligès*, *Aucassin et Nicolette*, and a host of others. Capitalizing on this insight, *Medieval Boundaries* sets out to rethink Old French literary production (circa 1150–1225) through the thematics of cultural interaction. The inaugural phase of vernacular French literature, I will argue, is inextricably linked to historical situations of contact between French-speaking nobles and peoples they perceived as their linguistic, religious, and cultural others.

Like much recent work in the emerging field of "postcolonial medievalism," *Medieval Boundaries* is animated by theoretical problematics derived from Edward Said's *Orientalism* and postcolonial theory: the representation of the other, the dynamics of cross-cultural contact, the question of the crusades as a proto-colonial enterprise. To date, much of the work in postcolonial medievalism has focused on late medieval England in the age of Chaucer and after. The cultural and temporal specificity of this focus has important consequences. In late medieval England, as critics like Jeffrey Jerome Cohen, Geraldine Heng, Suzanne Conklin Akbari, and others have shown, it is possible to identify elements of the discourses of Orientalism and nationalism in nascent but clearly recognizable forms.[1] Such exercises in postcolonial medievalism thus tend, implicitly or explicitly, to make an argument for continuity, construing the Middle Ages as the site of the origin, or at least the consolidation, of the emergent ideologies of European colonial expansionism.

Medieval Boundaries seeks to complicate this understanding by delineating the specificity of a representative range of medieval texts along three critical axes: periodization, geography, and vernacularization. We will begin with periodization. In her synthetic study *Strong of Body, Brave and Noble*, Constance Brittain Bouchard cautions against the dangers of reading history "backward," of assuming that a phenomenon or attitude found in the fourteenth or fifteenth century must also have existed in the twelfth.[2] *Medieval Boundaries* explicitly casts the early thirteenth century as a moment of epistemic rupture, in which several key twelfth-century institutions, practices, and mentalities were, in relatively short order, re-organized, challenged, or abolished. The Fourth Crusaders' sack of Con-stantinople (1204) and the Albigensian Crusade (1209–29) marked a turning inward of the violence Pope Urban II had unleashed in 1095 with his famous cry, "Deus lo volt!" (God wills it!), while Philip Augustus's victory over the Angevin-Flemish coalition at the battle of Bouvines (1214) assured the ascendancy of the French monarchy over the great feu-dal lords—many of whom had, at the time of Philip's accession (1180), commanded greater wealth and power than the king himself.[3] But it was the Fourth Lateran Council (convened in Rome in November 1215) that most ominously augured some of the changes to come. Most particularly, the attention devoted to identifying and regulating internal others—Jews, heretics, and lepers—gestures toward the increasingly disciplinary tax-onomies of the thirteenth and fourteenth centuries, part of an epistemic will toward totalization also manifest in the encyclopedic impulse preva-lent in Latin and vernacular culture alike.[4] Whatever the causes of this epistemic shift, medievalists working in a wide range of specializations agree on its effects. For R. R. Davies, the thirteenth century brought a new tone to the Anglo-Norman colonization of Wales: "racial distinctions became sharper and more abrasive," accompanied by "notions . . . of legal and even moral uniformity" that would have been alien to early twelfth-century Normans—"motivated by greed and power, not by racial or 'na-tional' animus."[5] For Geraldine Heng, the long thirteenth century is one of the policing of internal and external boundaries, of "interiors turned inside out for inspection," of an impulse toward containment, assimila-tion, and regulation; not coincidentally, it is also the century of the rise of medieval nationalism, built on "*a racializing discourse* of biological and spiritual difference, posited on religion, color, and physiognomy."[6] David Abulafia likewise identifies the late Middle Ages with "the hardening of the external boundaries" between Christianity, Judaism, and Islam in a process linked to the "wider process of state-building"; by the fourteenth century, "even the Muslim kingdom of Granada . . . had become staunchly Islamic in identity" while the Christian kingdoms "increasingly legislated to separate their Jewish and Muslim subjects from the rest of civil society, even if the new laws were often honoured in the breach." The "fuzzy and foggy" religious frontiers of earlier times gave way to "mental barricades," sometimes "translated into real, physical walls, dividing the *judería* or *morería* from Christian society and from the nation state of which they could not be members."[7]

My second critical axis concerns the geography of medieval French literature. Geography, Franco Moretti has argued, shapes narrative structure: "Placing a literary phenomenon in its specific space—mapping it"—can thus be a powerful tool of analysis, "bringing to light relations that would otherwise remain hidden."[8] Approaching medieval texts in this way requires, however, an initial effort of defamiliarization. In the twelfth century, the national borders we today take for granted were far from inevitable. Henry II and Richard I of England ruled an "Angevin empire" stretching from the Scottish border in the north to Aquitaine in the south, while the count-kings of Aragon were assembling a trans-Pyrenean empire wrapping around the Mediterranean from Barcelona to Marseilles. This means that the nationalist paradigms that have traditionally shaped our understanding of the Middle Ages are frequently ill-suited to the objects they purport to explain.[9] In our period, to take one example, it is impossible to correlate language with nation: by the late twelfth century, Old French was spoken in England, Norman Sicily, Lusignan Cyprus, and the crusader states of Outremer, but not in the area today known as southern France. One of postcolonial medievalism's most significant contributions has been to analyze the emergence of nationalism in the fourteenth and fifteenth centuries in the context of England's Hundred Years War against France and the consolidation of English as a literary and national language.[10] Conversely, one of the goals of *Medieval Boundaries* is to *de*link our readings of twelfth- and early thirteenth-century French texts from the teleology of the modern nation, making visible alternate histories not defined by the borders of the modern Hexagon.[11] As we will see, the interests and imagination of the crusaders, mercenaries, pilgrims, merchants, and settlers who constituted the audience of Old French epic and romance were not limited to the frontiers of twelfth-century—let alone twenty-first-century—France. A fundamental thesis of this book is that medieval French speakers had a much greater degree of involvement in and knowledge of the cultures of the Iberian peninsula and the Mediterranean than modern readers generally credit.

The third critical axis *Medieval Boundaries* seeks to make visible is the distinction between Latinate and vernacular culture. Against a trickle-down theory of medieval culture, in which Old French literature is presumed to mirror the ideologies and concerns of official and learned texts of the day, I believe, with Peter Haidu, that vernacular texts of the twelfth and thirteenth centuries "constitute a new cultural territorialization, best identified as that of a 'minor literature': one in which a subordinate group—minor at least within the sphere of culture and ideology—constructs its own textuality, as against an official and formally institutionalized culture (that of the Church), a construction in which everything is to be read politically, as implying collective values. In this context, the reading of medieval textuality as representing a closed ideological and semiotic monophony is as gross a travesty of historicism as one can find!"[12] The long twelfth century, between the Council of Clermont (where Pope Urban II preached the "armed pilgrimage" that would become the First Crusade) and Bouvines, was a moment of *prise de conscience* for the feudal nobility for (and, in some cases, by) whom the earliest surviving examples of Old French and Occitan literature were composed. This was the age of great turf battles between the church and feudal kings and princes, exemplified in flashpoints like the Investiture Controversy, the assassination of Thomas Becket, and (in a case we will examine at length) the Albigensian crusades. In the ways they conducted their wars and contracted their marriages, colorful figures like Guilhem IX of Aquitaine and even staid ones like French king Philip Augustus repeatedly ran afoul of papal policies that sought to bring all areas of secular life under ecclesiastical control. In such circumstances, as Jeffrey Kittay and Wlad Godzich write, "The very decision to write in a vernacular tongue grants that tongue a status that bears at least some analogy to that of Latin. . . . It reflects a perception of the social and communicative importance of the tongue and inevitably raises issues of hegemony of one tongue over others."[13]

Nowhere is the intersection of periodicity, geography, and vernacularization more important than in representations of Latin Europe's interactions with its religious and cultural others. Bracketed by the conquest of Jerusalem in 1099 and the conquest of Constantinople in 1204, the twelfth century is, indisputably, a century of crusade. It is certainly possible to construct a history of Christian-Muslim hostility running in a straight line from the council of Clermont in 1095 to our own present moment. My argument in *Medieval Boundaries*, however, is that postcolonial medievalism's disproportionate focus on the English fourteenth century has produced a skewed impression of a proto-modern Middle

Ages in which nascent phases of nationalism, colonialism, and Orientalism are always already visible. In part, this has to do with another problem of periodization: the divide between the late Middle Ages and early modernity.[14] In a sense, claims for the medieval roots of early modern racism or colonialism may be seen as the dark side of claims for a twelfth-century "Renaissance" and discovery of the individual: a subaltern attempt to overturn the binary "othering" of the Middle Ages imposed by the discourse of early modernity.[15]

But, as Ania Loomba writes, "any meaningful discussion of colonial or post-colonial hybridities demands close attention to the specificities of location."[16] Rather than attempting to trace the continuities between medieval and modern intolerance, *Medieval Boundaries* tries to bring into focus the messier, less codified age before the early thirteenth-century epistemic divide, a world less riven by fixed perceptions of difference. "Nation" was an unstable category that could be defined neither linguistically nor territorially, marking anything from regional feudal affiliations (*gens Normannorum*) to a nascent sense of Latin—opposed to Orthodox—Christianity (*gens latina*). Representations of alterity were notably more fluid and less marked by the racializing discourses typical of later centuries than we sometimes assume.

It is particularly in analyzing the relationship between medieval Christians and Muslims that the focus on vernacular literature *as such* can make a difference. This is a topic that has, of course, been treated by many eminent medievalists: Norman Daniel, for example, in *Islam and the West: The Making of an Image* (1960), and R. W. Southern in *Western Views of Islam in the Middle Ages* (1962). Revisiting these classic essays in the wake of Edward Said, however, we cannot help but be struck by the incommensurability underpinning both titles: an abstract, geographically defined culture, "the West," on the one hand, and a world religion, "Islam," on the other.[17] For the Middle Ages, it would surely make better sense to speak of "*Christian* views of Islam" (Daniel's chapter headings include "The Early History of Christian Anti-Islamic Polemic," "Revelation: Christian Understanding of Islamic Belief," and "The Relation between Islam and Christianity") or even "*Latin Christian* views of Islam," since Southern repeatedly underscores the distinction between Latin Europe and the Byzantine East. Both titles, moreover, cast Islam as an object, created by Western representational machinery and offered up to the Western gaze.[18] The focus on Islam (rather than on Muslims or the Islamic world) reflects the tendency of many modern studies to privilege medieval anti-Muslim polemic. Containing "much that is appalling to the [modern] reader: crude insults to the Prophet, gross caricatures of Muslim ritual, deliberate deformation of passages of the Koran, degrading portrayals of Muslims as libidinous, gluttonous, semihuman barbarians," medieval treatises furnish vivid and copious material to those interested in tracing the long genealogy of Christian hostility toward Islam.[19] Obscured in the process, however, are medieval Christians' lived reactions to and interactions with Muslims and the Islamic world—interactions much more complex and multifaceted than implied in the demonizing depictions by Norman Daniel or Edward Said himself.

Composed in a milieu often at odds with the "official culture" of Latin clerics, vernacular French literature offers a peek at this other Middle Ages, often lost beneath the radar of ideological polemic. An emblematic object here is the so-called Eleanor vase, a luminous honeycombed rock crystal vessel (today displayed in the Louvre) that Eleanor of Aquitaine brought north with her in 1137 when she married the French king Louis VII. There Abbot Suger—the king's minister and architect of the new "Gothic" style—had it fitted with a precious metal frame bearing the following inscription: "Hoc vas sponsa *dedit* Alienor Regi Ludovico Mitadolus avo mihi rex sanctis que Suger" (As a bride, Eleanor gave this vase to King Louis, Mitadolus to her grandfather, the King to me, and Suger to the Saints). The vase (originally carved in pre-Islamic Sassanian Persia) had first come into Eleanor's family as a gift to her grandfather, the troubadour-duke Guilhem IX. The giver, Mitadolus, has been identified as ʿImād al-Dawla (the last *ṭāʾifa* king of Saragossa), deposed in 1110 by the Almoravids, his Muslim co-religionists from North Africa. After losing his kingdom, ʿImād al-Dawla made common cause *with* the Christian king of Aragon, Alfonso I, *against* the Almoravids at the battle of Cutanda in 1120. Since Guilhem was there, too, it may have been on this occasion that he received the vase: a token of friendship between two political allies, one Muslim and one Christian. In Suger's inscription, a single verb, *dedit*, governs four acts of giving: ʿImād al-Dawla's to Guilhem IX, Eleanor's to Louis, Louis's to Suger, and Suger's to his spiritual patron, Saint Denis. The original act of giving, by the Muslim king to the Christian duke, is part of the vase's proud pedigree, syntactically indistinguishable from the abbot's donation to the saints.[20] Both in its hybridity and in its migration across the Christian-Muslim "divide," the "Eleanor vase" materializes the very kind of cross-confessional dealings that would have surprised no one in medieval Iberia (where, for one brief moment in the early eleventh century, the Christian king of Navarre was a first cousin of the Muslim ruler of Cordoba). Such material traces of cross-cultural commodities and practices cede nothing to the postmodern hybridities chronicled by the likes of Pico Iyer or Néstor García Canclini.[21]

Of course, this does not mean that Christian-Muslim relations were consistently peaceful; this was a violent age.[22] But it does means that religion was never the only—and sometimes not even the dominant—criterion in the determination of difference. Even in the fourteenth century— "among the most violent of centuries" for minorities—"violence across religious boundaries was relatively rare. The majority of altercations took place within religious communities, not across them."[23] This also means that amid crusades and polemics there was an almost continuous history of political accommodation, commercial exchange, and cultural negotiation across the Muslim-Christian divide. Though the details of such non-hostile interactions are too often known only to specialists, a good deal circulates as common knowledge: that much medieval and early modern scientific inquiry was catalyzed by the "recovery" of ancient Greek texts filtered through Arabic translations and commentary; that the wealth of the Venetian empire was built on trade for Eastern luxury goods like silk and spices; that the nickname of the Spanish "national" hero, the Cid, derived from an Arabic word (sidi) meaning "my lord." Yet somehow, by a logic of denial—"Je sais bien, mais quand même"—such insights rarely come together in a critical mass sufficient to overturn the master narrative of the clash of civilizations.

Medieval Boundaries thus seeks to recast the contours of some of our most familiar images of the period, to see Henry II not only as the English king responsible for the Assize of Clarendon or the martyrdom of Thomas Becket but also as the king whom Adelard of Bath praised as a "philosopher-prince" with a passion for Arabic science and who dispatched his youngest daughter, Joan, to distant Palermo to marry the Norman king, William II;[24] to see Eleanor of Aquitaine not only as the queen who brought a taste for Provençal poetry to the French and English courts but also as the princess whose grandfather (closely related to the kings of Aragon and Castile) exchanged gifts with the deposed Muslim king of Saragossa; and to see their son, Richard the Lionheart—the English king who, notoriously, spent only six months of his ten-year reign in England— as the prince who composed lyric verse in both Old French and Occitan, who conquered Cyprus and sold it to his Poitevin vassal Guy de Lusignan, and reputedly offered his sister Joan (now the widowed queen of Sicily) in marriage to Saladin's brother, al-ᶜĀdil.[25]

Displacing the crusades as the privileged model of medieval Christian-Muslim interaction also allows the internal complexities among both Christians and Muslims to emerge. Robert Bartlett has reconceptualized Europe not as an essentialized geographical entity given in advance but as a culture of shared practices, overlapping with but not identical to Latin Christendom. First crystallizing in the heartland of the former Carolingian empire, this culture subsequently spread through conquest, colonization, and acculturation. For our purposes, his work not only gives us better purchase on the collective identity emerging among the crusaders and others actively engaged in the "expansion of Europe" but throws light on the anomalous position occupied by peoples who are indisputably Christian but not always treated as completely European, living in areas where Europe and Latin Christendom did not fully coincide. The clearest example is that of medieval Wales and Ireland—the so-called Celtic fringe—whose inhabitants were often depicted as savage and intractable others.[26] A more complex case is that of Spain. Even aside from the centuries-long tradition of coexistence between Muslims, Christians, and Jews, Christian Iberia (with the exception of Barcelona) was set off from the emerging culture of Europe by its Visigothic past and its isolation from programs of standardization characterizing Carolingian and post-Carolingian society. Thus the culture encountered by northerners who began crossing the Pyrenees in the mid-eleventh century, though Christian, bore traces of difference: its distinctive "Mozarabic" liturgy (officially replaced by the Roman rite in 1080 but persisting well into the thirteenth century and beyond), its Visigothic (rather than Carolingian) hand, as well as its easy assimilation of many forms and aspects of Arabic culture. It is, I suggest, French contact with these lands—familiar yet foreign, where the boundary between self and other was not always self-evident—that underlies many vernacular texts of the twelfth and early thirteenth centuries.

By returning medieval French and Occitanian literature to this historical context, *Medieval Boundaries* seeks to produce new perspectives on well-known texts like the *Chanson de Roland* and the *Lais* of Marie de France, as well as to argue for the historico-thematic relevance of lesser-known texts like *La Fille du comte de Pontieu* or *La Chanson de la Croisade Albigeoise*. Part I, "Epic Revisions," examines literary representations of conquest and colonization in twelfth-century *chansons de geste*. Chapter 1 focuses on *La Chanson de Roland*, canonized as *the* foundational text of the French Middle Ages. Typically taken as a precocious expression of French national sentiment, the *Roland* has more recently been seen as a locus classicus for the medieval expression of Christian-Muslim antagonism. This chapter seeks simultaneously to contest these readings and to complicate the vision of the Middle Ages on which they are built by unpacking the opening scene of the poem, in which the pagan king Marsile offers Charlemagne vast wealth if only he will lift his siege of Saragossa and go home. Rather than skimming over this episode as a plot device designed to set Roland's heroic death in motion, I consider it against the contemporary Iberian institution of *parias*: the payment of tribute money by the Muslim *ṭāʾifa* kings to the Christian rulers of Castile and Aragon. After showing how many Normans and other northerners had intimate, firsthand experience of Iberian politics, I argue that the *Roland* does not so much reflect a preexisting ideology of crusade as actively work to construct it, precisely by taking on the Realpolitik clearly governing Christian-"Saracen" relations at the poem's outset.

Chapter 2, "The Politics of Courtly Love," focuses on *La Prise d'Orange*, the best-known example of the stock epic motif of the Saracen princess who converts to Christianity for love of a brave Christian warrior. Contesting traditional assumptions that this theme (and the comic notes accompanying it) represent a "contamination" of epic seriousness by the thematics of romance, I argue that Guillaume Fierebrace's seduction of the Saracen queen Orable literalizes the courtly trope of love-as-siege while exporting the dubious morality surrounding adulterous love into a context, the crusades, in which all moral qualms are erased. The second part of the chapter demonstrates this "epic" theme's wide dissemination, showing it at work in highly disparate texts where it has not previously been recognized: the *Chanson de Roland* (where the conversion of the Saracen queen Bramimonde constitutes a condensed and de-eroticized version of the same motif), the *Pèlerinage de Charlemagne* (where Oliver's seduction of the emperor of Constantinople's daughter parodically situates the motif in a situation where the princess, already Christian, is *not* available for conversion), and *Aucassin et Nicolette* (where the foreign-born Christian convert must return to her roots as a Saracen princess in order to bring the text to proper closure).

Part II, "Romances of Assimilation," examines representations of nonmilitary contact on the southern and northern frontiers of Latin

Christendom. Chapter 3 analyzes the mid-twelfth-century romance *Floire et Blancheflor* in its Mediterranean setting, reading the uncanny physical resemblance between the titular protagonists—one a Saracen prince, the other a Christian slave—as an allegory for the intense interconnection between medieval Islamic and Latin Christian cultures. Floire's pursuit of Blancheflor (who had been sold as a slave) from their home in Muslim Spain eastward to "Babylon" (Cairo) constitutes, I suggest, an important reterritorialization of the medieval Mediterranean: formerly cast as the space of *translatio*—the historical migration of political and cultural hegemony from Greece to Rome to France (exemplified in the *Roman d'Enéas* and the prologue to Chrétien de Troyes's *Cligès*)—it is remapped as a space of commerce and interconfessional exchange, concluding with the conversion not of the Saracen *queen* (as in chapter 2) but of the Saracen *king*.

Chapter 4, "Colonial Possessions: Wales and the Anglo-Norman Imaginary in the *Lais* of Marie de France," turns to the northwestern border of the feudal world, where post-Carolingian Europe met the so-called Celtic fringe. Its point of departure is the common ground shared by Marie de France's *lais* "Yonec" and "Milun": both are set in Wales and both, exceptionally, feature the birth of an illegitimate son. These two facts, I posit, are not unrelated, for one of the things distinguishing Welsh society from the emerging European norm was its attitude toward illegitimate children. The chapter goes on to read the differences between the two plots as divergent takes on the Anglo-Norman colonization of Wales: in "Yonec," the heroine's secret love affair with the king of an occluded kingdom bespeaks a sympathy for the indigenous past, while in "Milun" the chivalric successes of the titular protagonist and his illegitimate son exemplify the integration of Cambro-Norman Wales into the normative world of European chivalry.

Part III, "Crisis and Change in the Thirteenth Century," argues for seeing the two decades following 1200 as a moment of epistemic rupture, in which events like the Fourth Crusaders' sack of Constantinople (1204), the Albigensian Crusade (beginning in 1209), and the Fourth Lateran Council (1215) both precipitate and exemplify a wide-ranging reorganization of politics and the imaginary. In literature, this perturbation is marked by the disruption of the dominant generic forms of epic and romance, producing curious hybrid forms—as in *Aucassin et Nicolette* and *Le Roman de la Rose ou de Guillaume de Dole*—that constitute a transition between twelfth-century literature and the new modes of dream vision and allegory (as in *Le Roman de la Rose* and *La Queste dou Saint Graal*) that will come to typify the late Middle Ages. One of the most striking developments is the sudden emergence, in the first years of the century, of vernacular prose, which has been analyzed as a response to a perceived crisis in the "truth value" of verse, linked to the shifing fortunes of the great feudal nobility.

Chapter 5, "Brave New Worlds," is the first of two chapters devoted to early vernacular prose. One of two Old French chronicles of the Fourth Crusade, Robert de Clari's *La Conquête de Constantinople* is typically ignored in favor of the more "authoritative" account of Geoffroy de Villehardouin, one of the crusade's organizers. This chapter focuses precisely on the moments of the *Conquête* usually dismissed as the most problematic: the colorful "digressions" describing Robert's encounters with the wonders of Constantinople. Far from exemplifying the author's naïveté, I argue, these episodes underscore the havoc the experience of the Fourth Crusade wrought with the basic categories of the Western mentality: Christianity, chivalry, lineage, feudal hierarchies, and East-West difference.

Chapter 6, "The Romance of MiscegeNation," takes up a prose romance considered the first Old French "nouvelle," *La Fille du comte de Pontieu* (c. 1220). Like *Floire et Blancheflor*, *La Fille* begins on the Santiago trail and features a romance between a Christian woman and a Saracen prince. Both texts, moreover, purport to supply the genealogy of a famous historical figure: Charlemagne in the first instance, Saladin in the second. In this text, however, the lines between Christian and Saracen culture are even more radically scrambled and revalued than in the former. Pontieu—and Christian Europe more generally—is posited as the site of genealogical failure: the count's barren daughter is raped on the way to Santiago de Compostela to pray for an heir, then cast adrift by her father for attempting to kill her husband. This failure is redeemed in Almería, where the count's daughter converts to marry the sultan—becoming, in effect, the paradigmatic Saracen queen of our Chapter 2. The disparate fates of the two children she bears the sultan before returning to Christendom make visible the contradictions in the imaginative politics of lineage and conversion—here represented as less unproblematically regenerative than in the twelfth-century texts examined in Part I.

Medieval Boundaries concludes in Chapter 7 with *La Chanson de la Croisade Albigeoise*, a curious Occitan text that pours one of the Middle Ages' most traumatic events—famously described by Ernest Renan as one that all Frenchmen "must have forgotten"—into the form of a vernacular epic. The first part of this hybrid text, composed by a Navarrese cleric named Guilhem de Tudela, narrates the start of the war from the perspective of the predominantly northern French invaders. My reading focuses on the Anonymous Continuation, tracing the emergence, in response to the war itself, of a *regional* Occitanian consciousness distinct from the Cathar (Albigensian) cause and built around a vocabulary of chivalry and feudal values of precisely the kind undermined in the texts examined in chapters 5 and 6. The chapter concludes by returning to the generically idiosyncratic *chantefable Aucassin et Nicolette*. Composed in Picard (the Old French dialect associated with the same cultural milieu as Clari's *Conquête de Constantinople* and *La Fille du comte de Pontieu*) and set in Beaucaire (the site of one of the most decisive sieges of the Albigensian Crusade), this hybrid verse-prose text systematically inverts the norms of feudal and courtly society—another reaction to the ways the Occitanian wars strained the values of the twelfth-century "culture of fidelity" past their limit.

The payoff of these readings is, I hope, at least twofold. First, *Medieval Boundaries* seeks, quite simply, to give students of medieval French literature a stronger sense of the historical context grounding the works we study. In contrast to poststructuralist-inflected readings from the 1980s forward, my focus is less on textual, intellectual history (reading vernacular texts in relationship to contemporary works in Latin philosophy and theology) than on political, economic, and sociocultural interactions: the practices and lived experiences that would, I think, have been more immediate to the feudal nobility for whom this literature was composed.[27] More ambitiously, through its detailed unpacking of medieval representations of cross-cultural contact, *Medieval Boundaries* seeks to highlight the specificity of *modern* notions of alterity and cultural difference. Examining the variety, complexity, and reversability of cultural contact in the twelfth and thirteenth centuries problematizes oversimplified postcolonial genealogies of ideologies like nationalism, Orientalism, and colonialism, underscoring the need for alternate genealogies of a medieval West that can no longer simplistically be adduced as the moment of origins of a "clash of civilizations."

PART I

EPIC REVISIONS

I

"Pagans Are Wrong and Christians Are Right"

From Parias *to Crusade in the* Chanson de Roland

To be a medievalist, Bernard Cerquiglini has written, is to take a stand on the *Chanson de Roland*.[1] In the song's long critical history, this has meant taking sides on questions such as Roland's heroism or his *démesure*, on the poem's composition by a poet of genius or a singer of tales. Two things, at least, seemed beyond debate: first, that the poem casts the Saracens as a fierce and intractable Other, as epitomized in Roland's unforgettable rallying cry, "Pagans are wrong and Christians are right" (1015) (Paien unt tort e crestïens unt dreit); and second, that women have little place in this stark celebration of military valor, as evidenced in the scant thirty lines devoted to the death of Roland's fiancée, Aude.[2] Recent metahistories of our discipline, however, have revealed how strongly the *Roland*'s canonization as the preeminent French epic was linked to late nineteenth-century historical exigencies. Prized as a precocious assertion of French national sentiment, it performed important cultural work as the Third Republic strove to overcome the humiliation of the Franco-Prussian War and formalize its colonization of Algeria.[3] At this crucial moment in the history of medieval French studies, epic was defined as the perfect expression of a feudal, Christian, nationalist ethos in which women played little part.

In this chapter, I examine what it might mean to disengage our understanding of Old French texts from these nineteenth-century paradigms. Rather than casting the *Roland* as a fixed expression of medieval proto-national and proto-Orientalist ideologies, I argue that the crusading ethos presumed to permeate the poem from the outset is, instead, produced during the course of it. This difference, however small, opens a critical space for historicizing—for revealing the constructedness of—the "clash of civilizations" model that dominates so much of our thinking about medieval Christian-Muslim relations.[4] In fact, beneath the stark simplicity of Roland's declaration that "Pagans are wrong and Christians are right" lies a complex nexus of historical ambiguities, literary conventions, and ideological reformulations. The opening scene of the poem, I will show, represents an Iberian culture of *parias*—the tribute money Christian and Muslim rulers exchanged as part of a negotiated accommodation of mutual advantage. When the pagan king of Saragossa offers Charlemagne a rich treasure to lift his siege and go home, it would have seemed perfectly familiar to a contemporary audience; this accommodationism was the status quo that needed to be set aside for the mentality of crusade to emerge. And the figure who brings this politics of intransigence into being is Roland.

Medieval constructions of alterity are trickier than they first appear. The parallelism structuring the *Roland*'s representation of pagans and Christians is a case in point: the shared values that on the one hand make the Saracens likely prospects for conversion on the other raise the spectre of a crisis of differentiation. At the same time, the unity of Charlemagne's empire is disrupted by the layering underlying the historical process Robert Bartlett has memorably called the "europeanization of Europe." As if in compensation, the *Roland* works to produce "Frank" as a new collective identity, recoding Roland's *feudal* intransigence as a clash of civilizations based on *religious* difference. In the poem's concluding episodes, this newly founded dualism is reinforced through the strategic deployment of gender: far from being marginal to this feudal Christian epic, Aude (Roland's fiancée) and Bramimonde (the poem's lone Saracen woman, situated at the intersection of the medieval problematics of gender and culture) are central to its construction of difference.

*   *   *

As is well-known, the distant historical event underlying the Roland legend was an ambush suffered by the rearguard of Charlemagne's army in 778.[5] Far from an apocalyptic crusade between Muslims and Christians, this campaign began as one of those alliances, so frequent in the history of the Middle Ages, across confessional lines. In 778, Ibn al-ʿArabī, the Muslim governor of Barcelona, had come to Paderborn seeking Charlemagne's aid in his revolt against ʿAbd al-Raḥmān I, the Umayyad emir of Cordoba.[6] The campaign started well but stalled outside the gates of

Saragossa when one of Ibn al-ʿArabī's co-conspirators proved unreliable; meanwhile, news of a Saxon revolt made Charlemagne turn for home. High in the Pyrenees, his army was attacked—its baggage train looted and its rearguard massacred—not by "Saracens" but by a contingent of Basques. In the following centuries, this incident (unrecorded in Charlemagne's lifetime) assumed the proportions of legend. Of the changes wrought by time and the poetic process, two stand out: the elevation of Roland (who appears in Einhart's ninth-century *Vita Karoli Magni* simply as "count of the Breton march") into the poem's martyr and central hero, and the transformation of the perfidious Wascones into Saracens. What had begun as local power struggle opposing "not two religions, still less two States, the Franks and the Umayyads, but Carolingian power on the one hand and, on the other, rival powers divided among themselves by religious, ethnic and political differences" was transformed into the song we know as the *Chanson de Roland*, "a great epic of treachery and loyalty, and this humiliating defeat at the hands of unknown brigands transformed into a holy crusade, a glorious martyrdom, a great apocalyptic victory ordained by God."[7]

In *Roland*'s opening scene, Marsile, the Saracen king of Saragossa, convenes his council of barons to ask their advice. Emperor Charles of France has come to harass them, and their army is no match for the Franks. How, he asks, is he to avoid death and shame? In response, Blancandrin, a pagan leader known for his wisdom and loyalty, makes a momentous proposition: let Marsile offer Charlemagne his loyal service and great friendship, accompanied by an impressive array of wild animals and treasures; let him promise to follow the Frankish emperor to Aix, where he will convert to Christianity and become Charlemagne's vassal; finally, let them send their own sons as hostages to guarantee the peace, for it is better they should lose their heads than for the Saracens to lose both honor and possessions. We, of course, know that the pagans are not to be trusted: the fact that they are willing to sacrifice their sons in order to buy peace is simply a measure of their depravity. The poem's ideological parameters are set in the opening *laisse*, which definitively states that Marsile will come to a bad end because "he does not love God" (7) (Deu nen aimet)—a worldview later epitomized by Roland's battlefield cry, "Pagans are wrong and Christians are right!" and reinforced by our own understanding of epic as the genre of heroism and fixed moral values.[8]

In the eleventh and twelfth centuries, however, many contemporary "Franks" would have recognized Marsile's message as an offer of *parias*, the tribute money the politically weak *ṭā'ifa* kings of Muslim Iberia paid to their Christian neighbors.[9] These payments, which historian Angus McKay has likened to a "protection racket," attest to the Christian kings' growing military power. Originally,

Christian rulers had contracted to supply Muslim princes with specific military support in return for cash. But they were soon to step up their demands and, using the threat of war, they forced treaties on the Muslim rulers which stipulated the surrender of fixed amounts of cash, known as *parias*, which were to be paid annually and at regular intervals. These *parias* came to form an essential part of the regular income of Christian rulers who, although short of manpower for reconquest, could use warfare as a lever to induce the Muslim payers of *parias* to increase the sums involved.[10]

The first Christian king to collect *parias* on a grand scale was Fernando I of León-Castile (1035–65). The *Historia Silense* recounts one typical exchange between Fernando and the *ṭā'ifa* king of Toledo. This king

gathered together an immense amount of gold and silver coin and of precious textiles. Under safe conduct he made his way very humbly to the king's presence and steadfastly besought his excellency to accept gifts and desist from laying waste his marches. He said furthermore that both he and his kingdom were commended to Fernando's lordship. Now indeed King Fernando, *though he thought that the barbarian king spoke insincerely, and though he himself was entertaining designs of a far different nature, nevertheless for the time being* accepted the treasure and called off his campaign against the province of Carthaginensis. Laden with much booty he returned to the Tierra de Campos.[11]

Part of such income Fernando I donated to the monastic order of Cluny, in sums so enormous they helped finance the construction of Cluny III, the largest building in Latin Christendom.[12] *Parias* were so central to the king's power that he included them in his will: to his eldest son, Sancho II, went the kingdom of Castile and the *parias* of Saragossa; to García, Galicia and the *parias* of Seville and Badajoz; and to Alfonso VI, Fernando's favorite, León and the *parias* of Toledo. As Alfonso's power expanded, he imposed tribute payments on Granada as well. As the deposed *ṭā'ifa* king ʿAbd-Allāh later recalled in his memoirs,

he fixed the annual tribute at 10,000 mitqals. He spoke to me softly, saying: ". . . I will not subject you to anything else except the payment of the tribute, which you will send to me each year without delay. If you hold back payment, you will receive the visit of my ambassador and his stay will occasion you some expenses! It is better for you, therefore, to hurry up and hand over the money!" I accepted his words since I knew that the payment of 10,000 mitqals per year protected me from his misdeeds and was better than Muslim losses and the ravaging of the country.[13]

Though based on the threat of force, *parias* were part of a larger culture of opportunism that included frequent alliances across religious lines. For both Christians and Muslims, this was an age of fratricidal violence: rulers readily conspired with their confessional others against their own brothers. In 1072, when Sancho II of Castile seized his lands, Alfonso took refuge at the court of al-Maʾmūn, the *ṭāʾifa* king of Toledo.[14] A few years later, Alfonso in turn supported al-Maʾmūn's grandson al-Qādir against the *ṭāʾifa* king of Badajoz in exchange for both *parias* and control of castles guarding the road to Toledo.[15]

No figure better exemplifies the accommodationism of eleventh-century Iberia than Alfonso's most famous vassal—the Cid, Rodrigo Díaz de Vivar. Exiled on suspicion of having embezzled the *parias* of Seville, the Cid fled to Muslim Saragossa, fighting for the *ṭāʾifa* king al-Muʿtamin against both Christian foes like Count Ramon Berenguer II of Barcelona (who had earlier declined the Cid's services) and Sancho I of Aragon, and Muslim foes like al-Muʿtamin's own brother al-Mundhir, ruler of Lleida and Tortosa.[16] Eventually, this Castilian adventurer with the Arabic nickname established his own short-lived *ṭāʾifa* kingdom of Valencia, a Christian enclave in Muslim lands. This "truly remarkable career" was made possible by the "distinctive circumstances" of the age: "the acceptability of tribute-taking as the primary mode of Christian-Islamic relationship in Spain; the ease of crossing cultural frontiers; [and] the absence of any ideology of crusade."[17] Even when an ideology of crusade did emerge in the twelfth century, adventurers continued to cross the confessional divide; Christian mercenaries served Muslim rulers, and vice versa, for the next several centuries.[18]

So it was that in 1118, when King Alfonso I "the Battler" of Aragon conquered Saragossa in fact rather than fiction, he showed a restraint completely at odds with the violence unleashed by Charlemagne in the *Chanson de Roland*. Though Pope Gelasius II had declared this campaign a crusade, it—like many in the so-called Spanish Reconquest—was waged with an eye toward minimizing the toll of death and destruction.[19] Late eleventh-century Saragossa was one of the most brilliant successor states to emerge from the dissolution of the caliphate of

Cordoba.[20] Like many *ṭā'ifa* rulers, its Banū Hūd kings compensated for their lack of real political power with lavish displays of cultural refinement. Aḥmad al-Muqtadir (1046–81), a great patron of letters, assembled a vast library and sponsored *majālis* (sing. *majlis*)—stylized aesthetic gatherings devoted to conversation, poetry, and wine; his son al-Muᶜtamin (1081–85) was a scientist who authored a famous mathematical treatise.[21] Saragossa's court culture was centered in the Aljafería, a jewel-like summer palace situated just west of the city whose fortress-like exterior, reflecting the political turbulence of the age, concealed a wondrous interior exemplifying the refinement of *ṭā'ifa* palace architecture (of which it is today the "best preserved and most beautiful" surviving example).[22] After his conquest, Alfonso made the Aljafería his seat of government, perhaps conducting business in its central patio, graced by an arcade of interlacing, polylobed arches.[23] Far from forcing the city's Muslims to convert, Alfonso encouraged them to remain: they would be allowed to keep their own officials and to move freely within his realm. Those wishing to leave could emigrate with all their possessions. In the late twelfth-century, the Muslim historian Ibn al-Kardabus reported that as they vacated the city, Alfonso stopped them and demanded to see their wealth. "If I had not asked you to show me the riches that each of you is carrying with him, you would have been able to say: 'The king didn't know what we had; otherwise, he would not have let us leave so easily.' Now you can go wherever you like, in complete safety," he said, providing them with an escort to the border of his realm.[24] Such negotiated surrenders, meant to ensure a peaceful transition of power, were common practice in medieval Iberia: the treaty of Saragossa served as the model for later surrenders at Tudela (1119) and Tortosa. Its success in preserving the land's Muslim population may be measured by the persistence of Arabic-speaking Muslim communities in the Ebro valley over the next several centuries.[25]

It may be argued that the Frenchmen who composed *Roland*'s prime audience were far removed from such accommodationism; to the extent that they thought about Muslims at all, it was as adversaries to be extirpated from the Holy Land because—in the words of the crusading pope Urban II—"Deus lo volt!" (God wills it). Conventional wisdom has it that when the French began crossing the Pyrenees in large numbers, they brought with them a Cluny-inspired politics of intransigence that fired the spirit of Reconquest and hardened the lines between confessional

TABLE 1.1.   Lineage of Alfonso I of Aragon

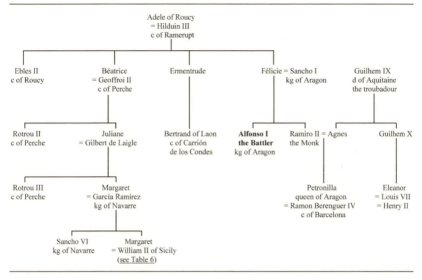

communities. In 1064, French and Occitanian lords at the conquest of Barbastro slaughtered its defenders in violation of the terms of the negotiated peace, demonstrating what one historian calls "the difference in the attitudes of those Christians who had continual contact with Muslims and those who did not. The zeal and fanaticism displayed by the latter contrasted sharply with the comparative tolerance of the former."[26]

Yet surely it is possible to imagine lines of assimilation running in the opposite direction as well: French and Occitanian lords taking up not just the luxurious trappings of Muslim culture but also the accommodationism and laissez-faire politics of coexistence that constituted business as usual throughout Christian and Muslim Iberia. Around 1100, when the *Roland* was likely composed, Normans in whose dialect the song was being sung began streaming across the Pyrenees, along with other French and Occitanian adventurers. Through his mother, the Aragonese king Alfonso the Battler was the nephew of Count Ebles II of Roucy in Champagne (Table 1.1),[27] and several of his northern cousins played important roles in the early twelfth-century Reconquest.[28]

In Alfonso's service they would have met with some surprising companions. Among his allies at the battle of Cutanda in 1120 was ᶜImad al-Dawla, the last *ṭāʾifa* king of Saragossa whom the Almoravids (his coreligionists from North Africa) had deposed ten years before[29]—and inverse example of the scenario of the Christian in the service of a Muslim lord that we noted above.[30] By the mid-twelfth century, when the Oxford *Roland* was set down in writing, significant numbers of Normans and other northerners had directly experienced Iberian modes of coexistence, perhaps even in Saragossa itself.[31]

Under these circumstances, it is not far-fetched to read the beginning of the *Roland* as textualizing not an ideology of crusades but a culture of *parias*. Here are the terms of the peace Blancandrin proposes:

"Don't worry! Send Charles (the haughty and proud) an offer of loyal service and very great friendship. Say you'll give him bears, lions, and dogs, seven hundred camels and molted hawks, 400 mules laden with gold and silver, and fifty carts to bear it all away: he can well use it to hire soldiers. He's made war in this land long enough: he should go back to France, to Aix. Say you'll follow him there by the feast of Saint Michael and will receive the Christian faith: you will be his man in honor and in goods. If he wants hostages, say you'll send him some: ten or twenty, to reassure him. We'll send our legitimate sons: were he to be killed I will send my own. Better that they should lose their heads than that we should lose honor and possessions, or be reduced to mendacity." (27–46)

("Ore ne vus esmaiez!
Mandez Carlun, a l'orguillus, al fier,
Fedeilz servises e mult granz amistez:
Vos li durrez urs e lëons e chens,
Set cenz camelz e mil hosturs müers,
D'or e d'argent quatre cenz muls cargez,
Cinquante carre qu'en ferat carïer;
Ben en purrat lüer ses soldeiers.
En ceste tere ad asez osteiét:
En France, ad Ais, s'en deit ben repairer.
Vos le sivrez a feste seint Michel,
Si recevrez la lei de chrestïens:
Serez ses hom par honur e par ben.
S'en volt ostages, e vos l'en enveiez,
U dis u vint pur lui afïancer.
Enveiuns i les filz de noz muillers:
Par num d'ocire i enveierai le men.
Asez est melz qu'il i perdent lé chefs

Que nus perduns l'onur ne la deintét,
Ne nus seiuns cunduiz a mendeier!")

Even with 700 camels and other assorted beasts for extra color, the similarities between this scene and the *Historia Silense*'s account of the *ṭāʾifa* king
of Toledo's embassy to Fernando I are unmistakable. In each, a Muslim
king offers his Christian besieger vast wealth and the promise of feudal loyalty if only he will call off his attack and go home. Significantly, both peti-
tions are successful: the Christian folds up his tents and leaves his Muslim
adversary in peace, receiving a fortune in gold and silver in return.

In the *Roland*, the pagans have no reason to doubt that the Franks
are motivated by the desire for material gain. Earlier, the poet had characterized Charlemagne's conquest of Cordoba by the quantity of treasure
seized: "His knights got great booty [grant eschech] in gold, silver, and
expensive equipment" (99–100). Now Ganelon explicitly attributes Roland's
popularity among the Franks to his ability to assure them wealth and profit,
telling Marsile: "They love him so much they will never fail him: he procures them so much gold and silver, mules, warhorses, silks, and equipment. He has the emperor himself in his sway; he'll lead him from here to
the East" (397–401) (Il l'aiment tant ne li faldrunt nïent; / Or e argent lur
met tant en present, / Muls e destrers, palies e guarnemenz; / L'empereür
tient tut a sun talent; / Cunduirat lui d'ici qu'en Orïent). Before battle is
joined, Roland inspires his men with thoughts of booty: "We'll have a fair
and noble take: no king of France ever had such a bold one" (1167–68)
(Encoi avrum un eschec bel e gent: / Nuls reis de France n'out unkes si
vaillant).[32] Later, when Charles exacts vengeance from the pagans responsible for Roland's death, his revenge is inseparable from the raw economics
of war: "Mult grant eschec en unt si chevaler" (2478).

During his embassy to the pagans, Ganelon warns Marsile that the
Franks cannot be defeated in battle and advises him to overwhelm them
with treasure instead: "Give the emperor enough wealth to amaze all the
Franks" (570–71) (L'empereür tant li dunez aveir / N'i ait Franceis ki tot
ne s'en merveilt). Indeed, back in the Frankish camp, tribute is exactly
what Charles is expecting: "the king awaits news of Ganelon *and the tribute* from the great land of Spain" (665–66, emphasis added) (De Guenelun
atent li reis nuveles / E le *treüd* d'Espaigne la grant tere). When Ganelon
returns, the Franks are suspicious of the offer he brings—"We should be
on our guard" (192) (Il nus i cuvent guarde)—but they are war weary
and sorely tempted by Marsile's proposition. Ganelon dismisses Roland's

opposition as "brash counsel" (228) (Cunseill d'orguill), telling the emperor: "Whoever advises you that we should reject this plea doesn't care, lord, what kind of death we die" (226–27) (Ki ço vos lodet que cest plait degetuns, / Ne li chalt, sire, de quel mort nus murjuns). Though the Franks are initially reluctant to endorse Ganelon's advice, when Charlemagne's trusted counselor Naimes notes that in light of Marsile's losses his offer is credible and should be accepted—"This great war should not go on" (242) (Ceste grant guerre ne deit munter a plus)—they second his speech with an almost palpable sense of relief: "The Franks say: 'The duke has spoken well'" (243) (Ben ad parlét li dux). For the moment, the tribute culture of *parias* wins out over the culture of feudal war.

*   *   *

It is precisely to counter the temptation of such practices of coexistence and accommodation that the poem must construct a politics of intransigence, and the agent of this transformation is Roland. Throughout the poem, as Eugene Vance has shown, Roland incarnates the principle of memory.[33] In the first Frankish council scene, he opposes Marsile's offer by evoking the history everyone else seems willfully to have forgotten:

Unwilling to countenance it, Count Roland rises to his feet to speak against it. He says to the king: "Don't dare believe Marsile! It was seven full years ago that we came to Spain; I have conquered Noples and Commibles for you; I've taken Valterne and the land of Pine, Balaguer and Tudela and Sezille. King Marsile behaved very treacherously. He sent fifteen of his pagans, each bearing an olive branch: they spoke to you in these very same words. You took counsel from your Franks, who advised you rather foolishly. You sent two of your counts to the pagan: one was Basan and the other Basile; he took their heads under Haltilie. Carry out the war you started; lead your army to Saragossa; besiege it for the rest of your life, and avenge those the felon has killed!" (194–213)

(Li quens Rollant, ki ne l'otriet mie,
En piez se drecet, si li vint cuntredire.
Il dist al rei: "Ja mar crerez Marsilie!
Set anz ad pleins qu'en Espaigne venimes.
Je vos cunquis e Noples e Commibles;
Pris ai Valterne e la tere de Pine
E Balasguéd e Tüele e Sebilie:[34]

Li reis Marsilie i fist mult que traïtre:
De ses paiens vos en enveiat quinze—
Chascuns portout une branche d'olive—
Nuncerent vos cez paroles meïsmes.
A voz Franceis un cunseill en presistes,
Loërent vos alques de legerie.
Dous de voz cuntes al paien tramesistes:
L'un fut Basan e li altres Basilies;
Les chefs en prist es puis desuz Haltilie.
Faites la guerre cum vos l'avez enprise,
En Sarraguce menez vostre ost banie,
Metez le sege a tute vostre vie,
Si vengez cels que li fels fist ocire!")

In the poem's opening lines, which Roland's speech closely echoes, the Franks' victories are clearly attributed to the king: "Charles the king, our great emperor, has been in Spain seven full years. He conquered the proud land as far as the sea" (1–3) (Carles li reis, nostre emperere magnes, / Set anz tuz pleins ad estét en Espaigne. / Tresqu'en la mer cunquist la tere altaigne). Here, in contrast, Roland takes personal credit for the success: "*I* conquered *for you* . . ." (198) (*Je vos* cunquis . . .) Curiously, the place-names he cites strongly evoke the historical conquests of Alfonso the Battler: Valtierra (1110) and Balaguer (1103), taken from the Banū Hūd rulers of Saragossa, and Tudela (1119), placed under the governorship of Rotrou of Perche.[35] Roland's speech, in other words, transforms *Aragonese* victories into *Frankish* military triumphs that underwrite his counsel to reject the pagan offer of peace. Marsile, he reminds his uncle, has done this before; to listen to him now would mean not just being duped for a second time but shrugging off the murder of the hapless ambassadors, Basan and Basile. Where Naimes and the other Franks long to return to *douce France*, Roland demands feudal vengeance, urging Charlemagne to commit himself to *clere Espaigne* and the path of perpetual war: "Metez le sege a tute vostre vie!"

"Pagans are wrong and Christians are right": the difference is foundational. Marsile is predestined to come to a bad end *because* "he serves Mahumet and prays to Apollin" (8) (Mahumet sert e Apollin recleimet). Yet at the same time, both sides are orderly feudal hierarchies, each a mirror image of the other. Like opposing kings on a chessboard, Charlemagne and Marsile/Baligant convoke their barons to council, array their troops, and carry personal standards into battle.[36] Moreover, Christians and pagans speak the same language: whether exchanging ambassadors or haranguing each other in formulaic displays of bravado, they have no need of interpreters.[37] This will toward parallelism accounts for the poem's most notorious "inaccuracy": the Saracen "trinity" of Mahumet, Apollin, and Tervagant. Both sides imagine their gods as feudal overlords, expected to dispense favors and miracles commensurate with the devotion they are offered. Similar in language and custom, the two sides arguably differ in religion *and nothing more.*

This play of similarity-in-difference produces some oddly contradictory moments, as when King Corsablis, described as "a Berber, expert in evil arts," nevertheless speaks "like a good vassal: 'For all God's gold I will not be a coward'" (886–88) (Barbarins est e mult de males arz. / Cil ad parlét a lei de bon vassal: / "Pur tut l'or Deu ne voill estre cuard"). Exploiting the *Roland*'s paratactic logic (with each line functioning as an autonomous unit), this passage condemns Corsablis's evil ways even as it praises him as a worthy vassal.[38] Now since good vassalage is a defining value of Frankish Christendom and since to be Christian is inseparable from being Charlemagne's vassal, it logically follows that a chivalrous pagan like Corsalis or Margariz of Seville (960) would need only swear loyalty to the Frankish emperor to become a valorous Christian.

This possibility of conversion is explicitly broached in the description of another of Marsile's lieutenants:

There is an emir from Balaguer. He has a noble appearance and a proud, bright countenance. When mounted on his horse, he bears his arms proudly. He is well known for his vassalage: *were he a Christian, he would be a worthy baron.*[39] (894–99, emphasis added)

> (Uns amurafles i ad de Balaguez:
> Cors ad mult gent e le vis fier e cler;
> Puis quë il est sur sun cheval muntét,
> Mult se fait fiers de ses armes porter.
> De vasselage est il ben alosez:
> *Fust chrestiens, asez oüst barnet.*)

Imperceptibly, the demarcation between Christian and pagan drawn in Roland's battlefield cry, "Pagans are wrong and Christians are right," begins to seem less intransigent. Roland's cry, after all, is part of his exhortation on the duties of a good vassal:

For his lord one should suffer handships, endure both great heat and great cold, and be willing to lose one's hide and hair. Now let each man strike great blows. Let no bad song be sung about us! Pagans are wrong and Christians are right! (1010–15)

(Pur sun seignor deit hom susfrir destreiz
E endurer e granz chalz et granz freiz,
Si'n deit hom perdre e del quir e del peil.
Or guart chascuns que granz colps i empleit,
Male cançun de nus chantét ne seit!
Paien unt tort e chrestiens unt dreit.)

If the perfect vassal is defined by his readiness to suffer *destreiz* for his lord, then stout pagans like Margariz of Seville or the emir of Balaguer are ideal candidates for conversion. Equal to their Frankish counterparts in all but religion, they need only accept Christianity to become exemplary barons.[40]

In the *Roland*, however, such potential is never realized. Although in later *chansons de geste* it is not unusual for praiseworthy pagans to convert, here, with the single exception of Bramimonde, Charlemagne shows no interest in winning the hearts and minds of the enemy. Indeed, conversion is viewed with suspicion: Marsile's scheme to rid himself of the Franks turns, after all, on his false promise to embrace Christianity. He accepts Blancandrin's counsel—"Say you'll follow him [to Aix] by the feast of Saint Michael and will receive the Christian faith"—without ever seriously entertaining the possibility of conversion. At the height of his battle against Baligant, Charles exhorts the pagan to convert—an idea the emir summarily dismisses:

"Receive the law that God proffers us—Christianity—and I will love you forever; serve and believe in the Almighty King!" Baligant says: "You preach a bad sermon." Then they strike with their girded swords. (3597–3601)

("Receif la lei que Deus nos apresentet,
Chrestïentét, e puis t'amerai sempres;
Puis serf e crei le rei omnipotente!"

Dist Baligant: "Malvais sermun cumences!"
Puis vunt ferir des espees qu'unt ceintes.)

The poem's lack of interest in conversion reflects historical reality: not until
the emergence of the mendicant orders in the thirteenth century did the
Latin church make concerted attempts at missions.[41] More fundamentally,
it points to an impending crisis of nondifferentiation: as long as the possibility of conversion is held open, any sense of identity built on the opposition between self and other remains intrinsically unstable.

At the turn of the twelfth century, the designation "Christian" was in
fact proving more problematic than anyone could have predicted. In
1096, westerners responding to Urban II's call to liberate the Holy Land
set out for Jerusalem in the certainty they were going to protect fellow
Christians. Their enthusiasm simultaneously derived from and contributed to the idea of a unified Christendom—as in this passage by First
Crusade chronicler Fulcher of Chartres:

Who ever heard of such a mixture of languages in one army, since there were
French, Flemings, Frisians, Gauls, Allogroges, Lotharingians, Allemani, Bavarians,
Normans, English, Scots, Aquitainians, Italians, Dacians, Apulians, Iberians, Bretons, Greeks, and Armenians? If any Breton or Teuton wished to question me,
I could neither understand nor answer. But we who were diverse in languages,
nevertheless seemed to be brothers in the love of God and very close to being of
one mind.[42]

In Fulcher's utopian vision, the linguistic and cultural differences between these diverse nations were easily subsumed in their common faith.
Reality fell somewhat short of this ideal. Once in the East, the crusaders'
relations with the Byzantine emperor quickly deteriorated into a mix of
suspicion, resentment, and outright hostility. The reasons were political:
alarmed by the zealous masses who had responded to his appeal for military assistance, Alexios I showed no compunction in undermining their
campaign. But they were also cultural: in their dealings with Greeks and
Armenians, crusaders were often less struck by their common faith than
by their cultural differences. Some westerners found their eastern coreligionists as strange as the Muslim enemy they had come to fight. Soon,
crusade leaders were openly negotiating with their Seljuk Turkish "enemies" against their Byzantine "allies." Western resentment against the
Greeks continued to grow throughout the twelfth century, culminating in
1204 in the crusader sack of Constantinople.[43]

Even as the experience of the crusades fractured the myth of a unified Christendom, it spawned a sense of common identity among *Latin* Christians. Once in the eastern Mediterranean, men who defined themselves as Normans or Angevins, Flemings or Champenois gradually became conscious of a shared culture distinguishing them not only from Muslims from Greeks and other eastern Christians as well. Westerners first expressed this newly perceived commonality by referring to themselves as *Latins*.[44] Soon, however, they adopted a new designation: *Frank*. Originally a quasi-ethnic term used in the narrow sense of "men from northern France," it became the Greek and Muslim name for all westerners—a usage the westerners soon borrowed for themselves. Though largely synonymous with "Latin Christian," it was not identical to it. In the twelfth and thirteenth centuries the designation *Frank*, as historian Robert Bartlett puts it, "implied modernity and power." It came to refer to men from the "core" of the former Carolingian empire, agents of the expansion of a cluster of institutions and practices eventually identified with "European" culture. The term, Bartlett writes, was shorthand for "aggressive westerner" far from home.[45]

At the turn of the twelfth century, this collective identity was still in formation. In the *Chanson de Roland*, the word *Franc* and its derivatives appear over one hundred times; as a designation for Charlemagne's troops, it functions in specular relation to the term *gent paienor*,[46] falling somewhere between the narrow sense of "men from northern France" and the broad sense of "aggressive western Christian." While all Charlemagne's men seem haunted by the memory and the promise of *douce France*, their imagined community is a fragile one. In the catalogue of troops preceding the poem's final battle, for example, "Franks" fill the first, second, and tenth of Charlemagne's divisions. The remaining battalions are composed of distinct "nations" retaining their regional identities: Bavarians, Alemanni, Normans, Bretons, Poitevins and Auvergnats, Flemings, Lorrainers and Burgundians (laisses 218–25).[47] The differences between this list and Fulcher's are striking: Greeks are conspicuously absent, even though Roland boasts of having conquered Constantinople. Armenians (eastern Christians with whom the crusaders contracted numerous political and marital alliances) and Slavs and Hungarians (peoples converted to Christianity two centuries *after* the time of the historical Charlemagne) are excised from Christendom altogether and shown as part of Baligant's pagan army.[48] Registering the haziness of Western conceptions of religious and cultural difference, these omissions reveal the contingency of Frankish-Christian identity even as the poem purports to construct it.

These slippages in the poem's representational economy become especially interesting in light of Roland's death speech at the end of the battle of Roncevaux, commemorating the victories won with the aid of his sword, Durendal:

With this [sword] I conquered Anjou and Brittany for him; with it I also conquered Poitou and Le Maine for him; with it I conquered Normandy the free for him; with it I also conquered Provence and Aquitaine for him, and Lombardy and all Romagna; with it I conquered Bavaria and all Flanders for him, and Bulgaria and all Poland; Constantinople (which pledged him loyalty), and Saxony, where he does as he wills; with it I conquered Scotland and Ireland for him, and England, his private domain. (2322–32)

> (Jo l'en cunquis e Anjou e Bretaigne,
> Si l'en cunquis e Peitou e le Maine;
> Jo l'en cunquis Normendie la franche,
> Si l'en cunquis Provence e Equitaigne
> E Lumbardie e trestute Romaine,
> Jo l'en cunquis Baiver e tute Flandres
> E Buguerie e trestute Puillanie,
> Costentinnoble, dunt il out la fiance,
> E en Saisonie fait il ço qu'il demandet;
> Jo l'en cunquis e Escose e Irlande,
> E Engletere, que il teneit sa cambre.)

As highlighted by the obsessive anaphora, the very nations now composing Charlemagne's army are themselves recent conquests. In this light the catalogue of troops cited above does not so much *describe* Frankish unity as *perform* it, assimilating former enemy tribes like the Bavarians or the Saxons into the imagined community of *douce France*. From this perspective, Roland *must* die so that his re-collection of the historical layering underlying the nascent Frankish state—the memory of the violence that has gone into the formation of Charlemagne's empire—may die with him.[49] Charlemagne's annihilation of the Saracens to avenge Roland's death is a ritual forging the various peoples composing his army into a new *Frankish* nation—subjects of a *douce France* symbolically demarcated from Marsile's *clere Espaigne* by the high peaks and dark valleys of the Pyrenees.

In this sense, the battle of Roncevaux matters less for the pagan defeat than for the creation of a new Frankish-Christian community. This would explain the poem's lack of interest in conversion: Saracens must remain Saracens so that the Christians may become Franks. Ganelon's treason bespeaks the fragility of a polity bound only by its individual members' allegiance to Charlemagne. When Marsile tenders his (false) promise to embrace "Christian law" (39), he threatens to disrupt the precarious binarism through which Charlemagne's empire has hitherto been defined. Even in Roland's resounding assertion that "Pagans are wrong and Christians are right," the militant declaration of Carolingian superiority conceals an anxiety born of a crisis of differentiation.

Constructed as parallel in all but religion, the Franks and pagans differ only in one other respect: the role accorded their women. The instauration of difference begun by Roland's death and Charlemagne's revenge reaches its culmination back home in Aix, in the twinned drama of Aude's death and Bramimonde's conversion.

* * *

For Roland, the ordeal at Roncevaux has less to do with extending Christian rule than with demonstrating his own feudal rectitude. His dispute with Oliver over whether or not to sound the olifant to recall Charlemagne's troops is ultimately a disagreement over good vassalhood. For Roland, doing one's duty means holding nothing back. On taking charge of the rearguard, he had assured the emperor that he would not lose a single palfrey or warhorse "not first purchased by the sword" (759); even his assertion "Pagans are wrong and Christians are right" comes, as we have noted, at the end of a long harangue on the hardships a vassal must willingly suffer for his lord. For Oliver, on the other hand, being a good vassal means guaranteeing the well-being of the emperor's men so that they might live to serve him another day; whence his insistence that they sound the olifant when they *first* perceive Ganelon's betrayal, not *after* the battle, when it is, in his terms, too late.

For both Christians and pagans, Roncevaux functions as a referendum on Charlemagne's lordship. As king, he is obligated to protect the vassals who render him *auxilium* and *consilium*; the ambush of his rearguard thus exposes him to the accusation of having abandoned his men. It is this charge that Oliver explicitly seeks to deflect by laying responsibility for the battle squarely on Roland: "You did not deign to sound your olifant; therefore you have no [help] from Charles. He doesn't know a thing about it. The noble one bears no blame; those [with him] there are

not to blame" (1171–74) (Vostre olifan ne deignastes suner, / Ne de Carlun mie vos nen avez; / Il n'en set mot, n'i ad culpes li bers; / Cil ki la
sunt ne funt mie a blasmer). By the same token, it is no accident that the
pagans taunt the Franks by impugning Charlemagne's lordship, as in this
speech by Marsile's nephew Aëlroth:

"Felonious Franks, today you will fight us. The one who should have protected
you has betrayed you: rash is the king who left you in these passes . . ." When
Roland heard this, God! he was greatly pained . . . "Vile wretch! Charles is not at
all rash, and never embraces treason. He did the valiant thing in leaving us in the
passes." (1191–93, 1196, 1207–9)

> ("Feluns Franceis, hoi justerez as noz.
> Traït vos ad ki a guarder vos out:
> Fols est li reis ki vos laissat as porz! . . ."
> Quant l'ot Rollant, Deus! si grant doel en out . . .
> "Ultre culvert! Carles n'est mie fol,
> Ne traïsun unkes amer ne volt.
> Il fist que proz qu'il nus laisad as porz.")

The best way to demoralize the Franks, as Aëlroth recognizes, is to assail
the integrity of their lord.

Roland's decision *not* to sound the olifant at the crucial moment before battle is thus not an expression of *démesure* but a principled stance
and a reasoned strategy.[50] He has already made clear that to him, proper
vassalage means the willingness to suffer any hardship for one's lord. In
committing himself and his men to certain death, Roland is keeping his
word while at the same time staging a mass sacrifice that, unlike the loss of
Basan and Basile, will be impossible for Charlemagne to ignore. Like the
martyrs of Cordoba—that small group of militant Christians who in the
mid-ninth century intentionally courted the death penalty by publicly re-
viling Islam[51]—Roland seeks to interrupt what he perceives as a reprehen-
sible slide toward lax accommodationism. The turning point occurs just
before the battle is joined. Archbishop Turpin blesses the troops, absolving
them of their sins and assuring them that if they die they will be holy martyrs (Se vos murez, esterez seinz martirs [1134])—recognizably a crusade indulgence like the one issued by Urban II at the Council of Clermont in
1095. Roland, who had earlier silenced Oliver for calling Ganelon a traitor,[52]
now turns to him and says, "Lord companion, as you clearly recognized,

Ganelon has betrayed all of us in exchange for gold, silver, and treasure. The emperor will very well have to avenge us" (1146–49) (Sire cumpainz, mult ben le savïez / Que Guenelun nos ad tuz espïez: / Pris en ad or e aveir e deners. / Li emperere nos devreit ben venger). The treasure mentioned here refers not to the gold and silver sent in tribute to Charlemagne but to Ganelon's personal take: "ten mules laden with the purest Arabian gold" (652) (Dis muls cargez del plus fin or d'Arabe), together with the rich gifts that sealed his pact with Marsile. In this instant, the *parias* and precious objects of exchange central to the tributary culture of empire are recoded as blood money—the material evidence of Ganelon's betrayal.[53] Feudal and Christian right are made to trump pagan wealth: the sword Valdabrun gives Ganelon may contain the equivalent of "over a thousand gold coins" (621) (plus de mil manguns), but Roland's Durendal, encrusted with some of the finest relics in all Christendom, is "worth more than pure gold" (1540) (plus valt que fin or).

This purposeful construction of a politics of intransigence comes to a head in the Baligant episode, a late addition to the *Roland* legend narrating the apocalyptic battle between Charles and the emir of Babylon-across-the-sea.[54] Borrowing from classical discourses of the "monstrous races," this episode contains most of the descriptions modern critics cite to exemplify the poem's demonization of the Islamic other: the fearful squadrons of Occians, with "hides hard as iron" (3249), or the "big-headed Micenes, covered with thick bristles like pigs all down their spines" (3221–23).[55] Not coincidentally, this is also the episode that presents crusading fervor at its most explicit. Returning to Roncevaux to avenge Roland's death, Charlemagne abandons the accommodationism of *parias* culture. The battle pits the Christian emperor against the Saracen emir in single combat. Each exhorts the other to surrender, with Baligant offering Charles a place in the pagan feudal order, and Charles defending Christianity as the price of his feudal love:

The emir said: "Charles, think! be advised to ask my forgiveness. You killed my son, by my word, and you unlawfully dispute me for my own land. Become my man: I want to give you the land in fief. Come serve me, from here to the East." Charles replies: "How vile that sounds to me—that I should grant a pagan peace or love! Receive the law that God offers us—Christianity—and I will love you forever more. Believe in Him, serve the Almighty King!" (3589–99)

(Dist l'amiraill: "Carles, kar te purpenses,
Si pren cunseill que vers mei te repentes!

Mort as mun filz, par le men escïentre,
A mult grant tort mun païs me calenges;
Deven mes hom; en fiét le te voeill rendre;
Ven mei servir d'ici qu'en Orïente!"
Carles respunt: "Mult grant viltét me semblet:
Pais në amor ne dei a paien rendre.
Receif la lei que Deus nos apresentet,
Chrestïentét, e puis t'amerai sempres;
Puis serf e crei le rei omnipotente!")

Baligant, as we have seen, categorically rejects Charlemagne's offer, his intransigence—like Roland's—helping to reinstate difference between the two camps. With Saint Gabriel's encouragement, Charles cleaves his opponent in two, bringing the battle to an abrupt end. With Baligant's death, his men scatter in confusion: "Pagans flee, as *God wills it*" (3625, emphasis added) (Paien s'en fuient, cum *Damnesdeus le voelt*)—an obvious echo of the famous cry, "Deus lo volt!" with which Pope Urban II launched the First Crusade. The Baligant episode completes the Christianization of the Frankish campaign.

*   *   *

In 1870, during the Prussian siege of Paris, the medievalist Gaston Paris delivered his inaugural lecture at the Collège de France titled "*La Chanson de Roland* et la nationalité française." At this moment of crisis, the poem's incantatory evocation of "sweet France" and its examples of heroism and sacrifice provided historical roots for the French sense of national identity. Eleven years later, Paris published two articles on Chrétien de Troyes that established "courtly love" as the predominant theme of medieval French romance.[56] To a surprising degree, these two interventions have set the agenda for discussions of gender and genre ever since. Accorded pride of place for its role in the emerging ideology of nationalism, the *Chanson de Roland* came to determine what counted as epic. Its battlefield ethos and its representation of Christians and pagans were taken as normative of the genre. More subtlely, its "marginalization" of Aude and Bramimonde seemed to establish the epic as a masculine genre, devoted to the enculturation of a warrior class.[57] In one recent assessment, "Women barely feature in this masculine world. Aude and Bramimonde,

the only two female characters in the text, mediate male relations: Aude
represents the bond between Oliver and Roland and Oliver's threat not
to allow Roland to marry her (1719–21) signals the tension between them,
whilst the conversion of Bramimonde symbolizes Charlemagne's victory
over Marsilie."[58] Romance, on the other hand, was designated the genre of
the knight's encounter with woman. Extricated from her place in feudal
society, the courtly lady (exemplified by Guenevere in Chrétien de
Troyes's *Le Chevalier de la Charrete*) was mystified as the necessarily elusive object of male chivalric desire. As long as this binary opposition between the masculine world of the *chanson de geste* and the feminine world
of the romance remained unexamined, women's roles in epic—and in the
historical and ideological contexts which produced it—were bound to
remain invisible.

Feminist medievalists have begun to question this monological construction of epic, most significantly in Sarah Kay's critique of the automatic dismissal of female epic characters as a sign of "romance influence."
The disproportionate importance accorded the *Roland*, she argues, leads
critics to take *its* treatment of gender as normative and therefore unduly
to disregard the much greater degree of female presence in other poems
as the product of generic "contamination." Recoding the *Roland*'s "preeminence" as "eccentricity," Kay illuminates the integral roles women
play in other *chansons de geste* in matters pertaining to warfare, lineage,
feudal loyalty, and crusade—the central preoccupations of epic.[59]

The same is true of the *Roland* itself: Aude and Bramimonde are
central to this "masculine" drama of Ganelon's betrayal, Roland's death,
and Charlemagne's revenge. The smallness of the roles accorded them (in
comparison to women in other *chansons de geste*) merely serves to concentrate and, paradoxically, magnify their ideological significance. Given the
crisis of nondifferentiation lurking behind Roland's bold declaration that
"Pagans are wrong and Christians are right," it is the opposition between the vociferously dissenting queen and the quiet Christian maid that
finally secures the difference between pagans and Franks. Bramimonde,
the Saracen queen who embraces the Christian God "for love," is the site
where alterity is both articulated and overcome. Her ideological significance is obscured when analyzed in terms of *either* race *or* gender, for
then she is marginalized as a subset ("woman") in the larger category of
pagan, or as a subset ("Saracen") of that already marginalized category,
"women." Located at the confluence of the two groups against which

Frankish masculinity defines itself, the Saracen queen cannot be reduced to one or the other but signifies in the text as a *female* pagan.

As the figure through whom the *Roland* engenders its politics of difference, Bramimonde becomes increasingly important as the story unfolds. She first appears during Ganelon's embassy to Marsile, in the ritual presentation of gifts sealing their treacherous pact. Stepping forward after Valdabrun and Climorin, she welcomes the renegade Frank in the language of feudal love. Her greeting, "I love you *well*" (635) (Jo vos aim *mult*), pointedly inverts the defiant challenge, "I have *no* love for you *at all*" (306) (Jo ne vus aim *nïent*), Ganelon had hurled at Roland during the Franks' council.[60] She then gives Ganelon two precious necklaces for his wife—fleetingly alluding to the sorority of Frankish women into which she will be absorbed at the end of the poem and explicitly evoking the absent woman who, as Roland's mother, Charlemagne's sister, and Ganelon's wife, binds the text's three male protagonists together in feudal-familial allegiance and conflict.

In subsequent scenes, Bramimonde increasingly embodies the stock character of the Saracen princess—the young foreign woman who converts to Christianity, often for love of a strong Frankish warrior. This common epic motif was an ideologically satisfying way of representing contact with Muslims, who (unlike the pagans on Latin Christendom's northern and eastern frontiers) had few cultural incentives for conversion: they could be seduced only in the imagination, in the figure of the bold princess ready to exchange a royal Saracen husband for an intrepid Christian count.[61] In stories like that of Orable, the beautiful queen who delivers her city into the hands of the doughty Guillaume Fierebrace, accepts baptism, and marries him, erotic fantasy and political victory meet.[62]

Stripped of the heady eroticism surrounding a figure like Orable, Bramimonde demystifies the function of the Saracen princess: to abandon religion, family, and culture to embrace Frankish Christianity. When Marsile retreats to Saragossa, his hand severed by Roland, the queen takes in at a glance the enormity of the pagans' loss and leads an extraordinary revolt against their gods:

In front of him was his wife Bramimonde—crying, shouting, strongly lamenting. There are more than 20,000 men with her. They curse Charles and fair France. They run off to Apollin's crypt and rail against him, foully abusing him. "*Hey! bad god! why have you brought us such shame? Why have you let our king be defeated?* What a poor reward you give to one who serves you!" Then they snatch away his sceptre and crown and hang him by his hands from a pillar. Then they topple him to the ground between their feet, beating him and smashing him to pieces with big sticks. And they snatch Tervagant's bright jewel and push Mahumet into a ditch. Pigs and dogs bite and trample him. (2576–91, emphasis added)

(Dedevant lui sa muiller, Bramimunde
Pluret e crïet, mult forment se doluset,
Ensembl'od li plus de trente mil humes
Ki tuit maldïent Carlun e France dulce.
Ad Apolin en curent en une crute,
Tencent a lui, laidement despersunent:
"E! malvais deus, porquei nus fais tel hunte?
Cest nostre rei porquei lessas cunfundre?
Ki mult te sert, malvais lüer l'en dunes!"
Puis si li tolent sun sceptre e sa curune,
Par mains le pendent sur une culumbe,
Entre lur piez a tere le tresturnent,
A granz bastuns le batent e defruisent.
E Tervagan tolent sun escarbuncle,
E Mahumet enz en un fossét butent,
E porc e chen le mordent e defulent.)

Though Bramimonde's role is partially subsumed in the plural verbs *maldïent, tencent,* and *despersunent,* she is unmistakably in charge: the formulaic line "Ensembl'od li plus de trente mil humes" (2578) echoes an earlier description of Marsile amid *his* assembly of barons: "Envirun lui plus de vint milië humes" (13).[63] Stepping into the place of her maimed husband, Bramimonde leads a revolt of the kind usually attributed to male Saracens, who wreak punishment upon their gods "in a futile rage at the inefficacy of their . . . protection."[64] When Emir Baligant's ambassadors greet her in the name of the Saracen gods, Bramimonde excoriates them for a breach of feudal contract:

Bramimonde said: "Now I hear great madness! *These gods of ours are vanquished!* At Rencesvals they performed miserably: they allowed our knights to be killed there; they failed my lord in battle. He's lost his right hand: the noble Count Roland cut it off. Charles will have all of Spain in his power; what will become of me, a miserable and wretched captive? Oh, alas! that I have no man to kill me." (2714–23)

(Dist Bramimunde: "Or oi mult grant folie!
Cist nostre deu sunt en recrëantise;
En Rencesvals malvaises vertuz firent:
Noz chevalers i unt lessét ocire,
Cest mien seignur en bataille faillirent;
Le destre poign ad perdut, n'en ad mie,
Si li trenchat li quens Rollant, li riches.
Trestute Espaigne avrat Carles en baillie.
Que devendrai, duluruse, caitive?
Lasse! que n'ai un hume ki m'ocïet!")

For a society that articulated faith and feudal loyalty in the same discourse, nothing could be more damning than Bramimonde's accusation of *recreantise*. Mahumet, Apollin, Tervagant, she is saying, are bad lords: their weak showing (*malvaises vertuz*) in allowing the pagans to perish at Roncevaux contrasts miserably with the "great miracles" (2458) (*vertuz mult granz*) the Christian God had performed at Charlemagne's behest, stopping the sun so the emperor could pursue Roland's killers. Her allusion to Marsile's severed hand calls attention to the symbolic castration of the entire political order, while her woeful lament over her own future points to the dire fate awaiting female enemy captives. In reciting this litany of misfortune, Bramimonde builds an unimpeachable case for the indefensibility of the pagans' spiritual system.

Having denounced her gods, Bramimonde next targets her feudal superiors. When Baligant's ambassadors assure her that the emir will pursue the Franks all the way to France, she turns on them with cutting sarcasm: "He needn't go so far! You'll be able find the Franks closer by. He's already been in this land seven years. The emperor is valiant and a fighter: he would sooner die than flee the field. There's no king on earth he ranks as more than a child. Charles fears no man alive" (2734–40) (Mar en irat itant! / Plus prés d'ici purrez truver les Francs: / En ceste tere ad estét ja set anz. / Li emperere est ber e cumbatant, / Meilz voelt murir que ja fuiet de camp; / Suz ciel n'ad rei qu'il prist a un enfant, / Carles ne creint hom ki seit vivant). Wresting the initiative from her incapacitated husband, the indignant queen exposes the bankruptcy of the pagan political order: her allusion to the Franks' seven-year siege of Saragossa impugns Baligant's failure as a feudal lord to come to the aid of his vassal; her insistence that Charlemagne would never flee the field calls attention to Marsile's own flight. In strategically praising the Christian emperor, she signals her contempt for all of pagan society. Belatedly, her hapless husband rouses himself to speech: " 'Drop it,' said King Marsile. To the messengers, he said: 'Lords, speak *to me!*' " (2741–42, emphasis added) ("Laissez ç'ester!" dist Marsilies li reis. / Dist a messages: "Seignurs, parlez *a mei!*").

It would be easy to hail Bramimonde's unruly speech as a positive example of female agency: the Saracen princess "does not merely ventriloquize a controlling masculine fantasy: she helps to shape it, and thereby disrupts assumed hierarchies."[65] As postcolonial feminism has taught us, however, the construction of gender cannot be separated from the construction of cultural difference. The ideological work Bramimonde performs depends on the "strategic deployment of sexual difference" within a larger narrative of cultural encounter.[66] Her brazenness disrupts not *all* hierarchies in general but the pagan religious and social order in particular. For the Franks, therefore, her outspokenness is not merely acceptable but desirable. Her dissent exposes the failures of the Saracen system, while her aggressiveness (unthinkable in a proper Christian wife) instantiates pagan deviance and prepares the way for her conversion. Whatever feminist edge her words contain works in the interest of Frankish Christendom: she *must* speak, for she is the site where pagan society turns against itself.

Not surprisingly, then, after Charlemagne's rout of Baligant's army, it is Bramimonde who delivers the city into the emperor's hands:

Charles has won his battle. He has knocked down the gate of Saragossa. . . . He takes the city; his people entered and, by virtue of his power, slept there that night. Proud is this white-bearded king. Bramimonde has surrendered the towers to him—ten big ones and 50 little ones. (3649–51, 3653–56)

(E Carles ad sa bataille vencue.
De Sarraguce ad la porte abatue . . .
Prent la citet, sa gent i est venue;
Par poëstét icele noit i jurent.
Fiers est li reis a la barbe canue,
E Bramimunde les turs li ad rendues:
Les dis sunt grandes, les cinquante menues.)

Now the stakes of the *Roland*'s poetics of conquest become visible: Charlemagne's troops occupy Saragossa, wreaking havoc in its mosques and synagogues and forcibly baptizing more than 100,000 pagans:

The emperor has taken Saragossa. He sends a thousand French to search the city, the synagogues, and the mosques. With iron mauls and hatchets in their hands, they shatter the image of Mohammed and all the idols: there will be no more magic or fraud. The king believes in God, and wants to serve him. So bishops bless the waters and lead the pagans to the baptismal font. If anyone refuses Charles, he has that man imprisoned, or burned, or killed. (3660–70)

> (Li emperere ad Sarraguce prise,
> A mil Franceis fait ben cercer la vile,
> Les sinagoges e les mahumeries;
> A mailz de fer e a cuignees qu'il tindrent
> Fruissent Mahum e trestutes les ydeles;
> N'i remeindrat ne sorz ne falserie.
> Li reis creit Deu, faire voelt sun servise,
> E si evesque les eves beneïssent,
> Meinent paiens entresqu'al baptistirie.
> S'or i ad cel qui Carle cuntredie,
> Il le fait prendre[67] o ardeir ou ocire.)

This commitment to the total extirpation of Islam comes as no surprise, given the emperor's earlier conquest of Cordoba: "The emperor rejoices and is happy: he has taken Cordoba and demolished its walls and knocked down its towers with his catapults. . . . In the inner city no pagan was left who was not killed or converted to Christianity" (96–98, 101–2) (Li empereres se fait e balz e liez: / Cordres ad prise e les murs peceiez, / Od ses cadables les turs en abatiéd. . . . / En la citét nen ad remés paien / Ne seit ocis u devient chrestïen). This image of total war is, as we have seen, completely contrary to the course of Alfonso the Battler's historical conquest of Saragossa, managed with a restraint meant to assure the prosperity of Muslim lands newly brought under Christian rule.[68] My purpose is not to impugn the *Roland*'s historical "accuracy" but to emphasize the degree of ideological distortion involved in crafting such a vision for an Anglo-Norman audience whose fathers and grandfathers may have been veterans of Alfonso the Battler's Ebro valley campaigns.

Amid the slaughter and forced conversions, the only pagan Charlemagne spares is Bramimonde, for whom he has something quite different in mind: "More than a hundred thousand are baptized true Christians, but not the queen: she will be taken to sweet France, a captive: the king wants her to convert *for love*" (3671–74) (Baptizét sunt asez plus de cent milie, / Veir chrestïen, ne mais sul la reïne: / En France dulce iert menee caitive, / Ço voelt li reis, *par amur* cunvertisset). Learning of Charlemagne's annihilation of Marsile's army, Bramimonde had lamented that she had no one to slay her, yet with the conquest of her city, she is the only survivor not immediately forced to choose between conversion and death. Instead, she is to be taken back to Aix-la-Chapelle and instructed in the Christian faith so that she might actively choose it. No trace of the carnal compromises Charlemagne's plan: the phrase *par amur* signals not romantic desire but the *voluntary* nature of her conversion. The narrator forestalls any suspicion to the contrary: "The king and his men all mount their horses, along with Bramimonde, whom he leads into captivity. But he wishes only to do good by her" (3679–81) (Muntet li reis e si hume trestuz, / E Bramimunde meinet en sa prisun; / Mais n'ad talent li facet se bien nun). For untold thousands of Saracens, refusal to convert meant instant death; their queen, however, is taken to the heart of Charlemagne's empire so that she might embrace his God as actively as she has denounced her own.

*   *   *

In symbolic terms, the convert is the obverse of the traitor: Bramimonde's baptism, signaling her acceptance of both Christianity and the feudal Frankish world it entails, sutures the breach opened by Ganelon's treasonous commerce with Marsile.[69] Previously, Bramimonde has functioned as the site of disruption: denouncing Saracen culture from within, her unruly speech reinstates difference between the two barely distinguishable camps. Now, as the scene shifts to Aix, Bramimonde—the text's lone Saracen woman—is implicitly paired and compared with the poem's other female figure, belle Aude. However small their place in the *Roland* as a whole, the two women are prominent at its end. Their appearances bracket the climactic episode of Ganelon's trial, Aude's preceding it (laisses 268–69) and Bramimonde's immediately following (laisse 290). The contrast between the visions they present of Frankish and Saracen femininity is crucial to the *Roland*'s resolution. Reversing the binarism of later colonial discourse, it is the foreign woman who displays a new feminine agency while the Frankish woman is consigned to passivity and silence.

Returning to his capital, Charlemagne is met by Roland's fiancée, Aude. Though this is her first appearance in the text, her name has come up before: during the battle at Roncevaux, Oliver, angry at Roland for sounding the olifant, threatens to break off his friend's engagement to his sister (1719–21). Once the two patch up their differences, however, Aude is forgotten—an object of exchange less important, it seems, in forging the homosocial bond than in threatening to disrupt it. Now, given the chance to speak for herself, her only thought is for Roland:

The emperor has returned from Spain and comes to Aix, the best seat in France. He climbs the palace stairs and enters the room. See Aude, a beautiful girl who came to him. She said to the king: "Where is Roland the captain, who swore to take me as his spouse?" Charles is grieved and distressed; he weeps and pulls his white beard: "Sister, dear friend, you're asking me about a dead man." (3705–13)

> (Li empereres est repairét d'Espaigne
> E vient a Ais, al meillor siéd de France,
> Munte el palais, est venut en la chambre.
> As li venue Alde, une bele dame.
> Ço dist al rei: "O 'st Rollant le catanie,
> Ki me jurat cume sa per a prendre?"
> Carles en ad e dulor e pesance,
> Pluret des oilz, tiret sa barbe blance:
> "Soer, cher' amie, d'hume mort me demandes.")

Through his grief, Charlemagne struggles to imagine a new future for himself, for the Franks, and for Aude: "I shall give you a worthy replacement—Louis. I can't do better than that: he is my son and he will hold my kingdom" (3714–16) (Jo t'en durai mult esforcét eschange: / C'est Loëwis; mielz ne sai jo a render; / Il est mes filz, si tendrat mun reialme).[70] Aude immediately rejects the proffered exchange—not because she objects to Louis (though he is destined to cut a poor figure in the epic tradition) but because her love is nontransferable. *Preux* like her fiancé rather than *sage* like her brother, she drops dead at the emperor's feet.[71] Refusing her prescribed role in the feudal politics of lineage, she elects the dramatic gesture of absolute devotion over the option of a measured, longer-term advantage.[72]

Aude replies: "These words are strange to me. May it not please God, his saints, or his angels, that I should remain alive after Roland!" She pales and falls at Charlemagne's feet, already dead. May God have mercy on her soul! Noble Frenchmen weep for her and lament her. (3717–22)

(Alde respunt: "Cest mot mei est estrange.
Ne place Deu ne ses seinz ne ses angles
Aprés Rollant que jo vive remaigne!"
Pert la culor, chet as piez Carlemagne,
Sempres est mort; Deus ait mercit de l'anme!
Franceis barons en plurent si la pleignent.)

In feudal terms, Aude's decision is shortsighted: in dismissing as *mot estrange* Charles's offer to exchange a dead Roland for a live Louis, she rejects the opportunity to join her lineage to the emperor's direct line. But in dying, she demonstrates a loyalty to Roland that equals Roland's to Charles. Taciturn where Bramimonde is vociferous, intransigent where the pagan queen is mutable, she exemplifies the fixity of a feudal-Christian order heretofore threatened by instability and fragmentation. The very *briefness* of the episode concentrates its effect: with drama and pathos, this scene conjures the enormity of Charlemagne's loss and adds to the tally for which Ganelon must pay.[73]

If Aude's ideological task is to refuse all exchange, Bramimonde's is to embrace it. Having denounced her husband, his overlord, and their gods, she has been brought to Aix further to renounce her homeland, her name, and her religion. She is baptized in the poem's penultimate laisse, just after Ganelon's execution. Paradoxically, it is the conversion of the Saracen queen and her integration into Frankish society that provide closure to this song of feudal loyalty and heroic sacrifice.[74] No male pagan of stature remains alive: offered a chance at conversion, Baligant has categorically refused, while those like the emir of Balaguer who would have made good Christians have been slain with the rest.[75] Only Bramimonde survives, her conversion *par amur* bearing witness to the superiority of Frankish Christianity. That she converts for love, but not for love of Charles, has sometimes been perceived as a lack.[76] But the fact that she is *not* Charlemagne's romantic interest is crucial: her love is not for a man but for an entire religious and social order.

This is not to say that Bramimonde can be recuperated as a feminist subject. Her display of self-determination is less an act of feminist agency than part of a scripted role in the construction of Frankish Christianity. For Bramimonde, conversion means submitting both to the Christian God and to a discursive regime that demands women's silent acquiescence. As Saracen queen, she enjoyed the prerogative of strong speech. Her rebelliousness against the pagan gods distinguished her from her husband (predestined

for a bad end) as well as from Aude, who rejects marriage to a future emperor in favor of immediate death. As a Christian, however, she must relinquish the defiant spirit that has defined her. Although she elects Christianity
par amur as Charlemagne intended, he is the one to articulate her will:

When the emperor has taken his revenge, he summoned the bishops of France,
Bavaria and Germany. "In my house there is a noble captive; she has heard so
many sermons and parables that she wishes to believe in God and seeks Christianity. Baptize her, so that her soul may belong to God." They reply: "Let the god-
mothers do it, trustworthy and high-born ladies!" At the baths at Aix there is a
huge crowd. There they baptize the queen of Spain. They found for her the name
of Juliane: she is Christian *through true understanding*. (3975–87, emphasis added)

> (Quant l'emperere ad faite sa venjance,
> Si'n apelat ses evesques de France,
> Cels de Baviere e icels d'Alemaigne:
> "En maisun ai une caitive franche;[77]
> Tant ad oït e sermuns e essamples,
> Creire voelt Deu, chrestïentét demandet.
> Baptizez la, pur quei Deu en ait l'anme!"
> Cil li respundent: "Or seit fait par marrenes
> Asez creües e haltes nëes dames!"
> As bainz ad Ais mult sunt granz les cumpaignes;
> La baptizerent la reïne d'Espaigne;
> Truvét li unt le num de Juliane.
> Chrestïene est *par veire conoisance*.)

In giving Ganelon gifts for his wife, Bramimonde had momentarily
made visible the otherwise neglected world of Frankish women. Now she
is silently absorbed into the gyneceum of *marrenes* waiting to oversee her
baptism in the waters of Aix.

Despite the enormity of Charlemagne's losses at Roncevaux, his symbolic victory over the Saracens is complete. The bankruptcy of pagan society has been revealed not only in the failure of its kings and *recreantise* of its
gods but in the unruliness of the woman willing to denounce them. Bramimonde's dissent shores up the distinction between Saracens and Christians
at a crucial moment of the threat of nondifferentiation. Brought from Spain
to the heart of the Frankish empire, she is like the saint choosing *translatio*:
her successful removal from Saragossa to Aix vindicates Charlemagne's
cause.[78] The olifant and the bodies of Roland, Oliver, and Turpin have been

deposed along the way in the churches of Bordeaux and Blaye, objects of veneration to serve as *lieux de mémoire* of Charlemagne's loss and sacrifice.[79] Bramimonde, in contrast, survives as the living tribute to the Franks' victory. Brought to the center of empire, her conversion and lapse into silence punctuate Charlemagne's Spanish campaign and definitively substantiate Roland's vision of the world: *Pagans are wrong and Christians are right.*

* * *

The case of the *Chanson de Roland* reveals how powerfully our *lieux de mémoire* both determine and are determined by the ongoing process of interpretation. It reveals how strongly the male homosociality that has haunted the discipline of medieval studies from its inception has inflected our vision of feudal society. It reveals the specificity of modern notions of alterity, often rooted in unexamined assumptions of racial or biological difference. In *The Subject of Violence*, Peter Haidu observes that to date nearly all work on the *Roland*'s "historical contextualization" or "hidden historical meaning" has been done by foreign scholars, while studies undertaken in France remain dominated by "traditional French ideological values of nationalism and superficial religiosity."[80] For the past century and more, medievalists have cultivated the *Chanson de Roland* as a *lieu de mémoire* of the origin of a precocious French national sentiment. Unpacking that site reveals the poem's critical history to be inseparable from a history of Franco-German conflict and colonial ideology. Disengaging the *Roland* from this colonial context, in which alterity is implicitly or explicitly cast in the taxonomic categories of racialized difference, reveals surprising histories of accommodationism and exchange and brings into focus the fluidity characterizing medieval notions of difference. This in turn reveals "France" and "Europe" to be not geographical entities given in advance but ideological constructs with their own deeply complicated history of conquest, colonization, and acculturation in ways that continue to resonate, for example, in political debates on multiculturalism in France or in the emergence of the European Community.[81] The *Roland*, it turns out, *is* an exemplary text—not for its depiction of heroic sacrifice or its articulation of a precocious national sentiment but for the way it concentrates and imbricates questions of self and other, gender and genre, history and ideology.

That is why, for each generation, to be a medievalist has meant taking a stand on the *Chanson de Roland*.

2

The Politics of Courtly Love

La Prise d'Orange *and the Conversion of the Saracen Queen*

In Chapter 1 we read the *Chanson de Roland* as a text transforming the culture of *parias* into a culture of crusade, fixing the binary opposition between Christians and Saracens through its differential deployment of the female characters Bramimonde and Aude. In this chapter, we turn to *La Prise d'Orange*, the most fully elaborated version of the epic of the Saracen queen. Ostensibly set during the reign of Charlemagne's son Louis the Pious, it recounts epic hero Guillaume Fierebrace's conquest of the city, giving him the name by which he is known to literary history: Guillaume d'Orange. A pivotal part of this adventure is his amorous siege and conquest of the superb queen Orable, wife of the Saracen emir Tiebaud and the stepmother of Arragon, who holds Orange in fief from his father. Like Bramimonde, she abandons husband and faith in order to deliver the city to its Frankish invaders, accepting baptism at their hands. Unlike the queen of Saragossa, however, she is motivated not by disillusionment with the efficacy of the pagan order but by her love for the handsome conqueror, Guillaume Fierebrace. This love plot and the comedic elements it entails have proven an embarrassment for critics concerned that they compromise the poem's seriousness and generic coherence. In many ways, Guillaume Fierebrace is an ideal "epic" hero, extending the borders of the Frankish kingdom (coextensive with Christendom itself) through his military valor; like the heroes of romance, however, he frequently appears ridiculous in the process of wooing and winning the highborn lady whom he desperately loves. "Half way between epic and courtly romance," write its modern translators: "an ambiguous, contrastive position propitious to comedy."[1]

Until recently, surprisingly little attention has been paid to Orable, the poem's idealized, feminized Other. Interested in questions of form and genre (and guided, perhaps, by presuppositions of what María Rosa

Menocal has called "a medieval Europe of simple paternity and unambiguous truths and meanings"), early critics took an interest in the motif of the Saracen queen largely for the way it revealed lines of influence among *chansons de geste* and between Old French epics and other oral and textual traditions.[2] Still, the omission is curious, for Guillaume's fascination with Orable is key to his conquest of Orange, jewel in the crown of Emir Tiebaud's magnificent empire. He first formulates his plan after hearing reports of Orable's superlative beauty; taken captive inside Orange by her stepson Arragon, he procures weapons through his budding friendship with the enemy queen. Finally, her conversion to Christianity and her marriage to Guillaume serve symbolically to legitimate the count's military conquest of the Islamic south. Recent work has begun to redress this imbalance—particularly, as we have seen, in Sarah Kay's important reassessment of the place of women in epic.[3] If, in 1989, María Rosa Menocal could still characterize modern readings as dismissing the foreignness of non-Christian elements as exotic but ultimately irrelevant, the late 1990s saw at least one study questioning the erasure of race in the poem's representation of Orable—who, as a Saracen, was presumed to be black.[4]

What are the ideological stakes of *La Prise d'Orange*'s representation of conquest-by-seduction? The identification of a foreign land with its women was destined to become a common political trope, particularly in the French colonization of North Africa, whose relevance to the "birth" of medieval studies in late nineteenth century we alluded to in Chapter 1. Symbolically, women "have long been at the center of the conflict between East and West . . . as phantasmic representations of Western designs on the Orient. . . . Possession of Arab women came to serve as a surrogate for and means to the political and military conquest of the Arab world."[5] "For the French colonizers who conquer[ed] them militarily, control[led] them administratively, stud[ied] them as sociologists, ethnographers, and historians, and represent[ed] them in both high and popular forms of art and literature," women embodied Algeria. "In the colonialist fantasy, to possess Algeria's women is to possess Algeria."[6] Mutatis mutandis, this formulation exactly captures the intrigue of *La Prise d'Orange*: to seduce Orable and to convert her to Christianity is to assimilate Orange to Frankish Christendom, under the tutelage of the intrepid Count Guillaume.

Focused on the Saracen woman, the poem functions not in spite of its generic hybridity but because of it. Rather than casting love and war as antithetical activities reified in the binary opposition of epic and romance, it emphasizes the congruence of love-as-war and war-as-seduction. Far from some unwonted intrusion of courtly thematics into the stark masculine-militaristic mode of the epic, Guillaume's infatuation with and seduction of the foreign and female Other constitute a quintessential scenario of desire, crusade, and conquest. In Guillaume's pursuit of the proud Saracen queen, the politically troubling or inconvenient aspects of medieval social practices and literary discourses are brilliantly recuperated, projected onto the Saracen Other or mobilized to the benefit of Guillaume's amorous crusade in the service of Christendom. And the key to this ideologically satisfying gendered representation of medieval colonialism is the conversion of Orable, whose seduction makes standard tales of courtly love seem like stylized, depoliticized repetitions.

*   *   *

From the beginning of the *Prise d'Orange*, women and war are inseparable. The poem opens in the month of May amid blooming fields, softly flowing waters, and sweetly singing birds recalling the conventional prerequisites of love in countless troubadour lyrics. But the same spring thaw that inspires the lover's passion also signals the season of military campaigns. Cooling their heels amid the splendors of the recently conquered Saracen stronghold of Nîmes, Guillaume and his vassals fidget in unaccustomed inactivity. Without new cities to conquer or ladies and jongleurs to relieve his boredom, Guillaume even curses the pagans for their effrontery in *not* launching a new invasion.[7] Nîmes, so recently the scene of his triumph, now assumes the aspect of a prison: "I'm too bored staying here; we're shut up inside here like prisoners" (67–69) (Que trop m'enuist ici a sejorner; / Ensement somes ça dedenz enserré / Com li hom qui est enprisonné).[8]

The remedy for Guillaume's ennui takes the form of Guibert, a knight newly escaped from Saracen captivity who brings word of just the sort of adventure the Franks have been craving: the nearby city of Orange and its superb queen, Orable:

There's no fortress like it from here to the Jordan River. Its walls are high, the tower large and wide, as well as the palace and lookouts. Inside there are 20,000 pagan lancers and seven score Turks, bearing precious standards, who guard this city of Orange very well and very much fear that Louis will take it—along with you, fair lord, and the barons of France. Then there's Arragon, a rich Saracen king, son of Tiebaut, from the land of Spain, and Lady Orable, a noble queen: there's none as beautiful between here and the East. She is beautiful: slender and noble, her skin as white as a flower on the branch. God! what good are her body or her youth, since she doesn't believe in God, the almighty father. (192–207)

(Tel forteresce n'a trusqu'au flun Jordane,
Hauz sont les murs et la tor grant et ample,
Et le palés et les reconoissances.
La dedenz a .XX.M. paiens a lances
Et .VII.XX. Turs qui ont chieres ensaignes,
Qui mout bien gardent cele cité d'Orenge,
Qui mout redoutent Looÿs ne la praigne
Et vos, beau sire, et les barons de France;
Et Arragons, uns riches rois aufaigne,
Filz est Tiebaut de la terre d'Espaigne;
Et dame Orable, une roïne gente,
Il n'a si bele desi en Oriënte,
Bel a le cors, eschevie est et gente,
Blanche la char comme la flor en l'ente.
Dex! mar i fu ses cors et sa jovente,
Quant Dex ne croit, le pere omnipotente!)

Guillaume's boredom instantly evaporates. Impatient at Guibert's long account of his captivity and escape, he prods him to say more about the marvelous city. "Is Orange really as you've described it? . . . Friend, fair brother, is Orange that rich?" (240, 267), he queries in two successive similar laisses. Guibert reiterates the beauty of the city and its queen, with Orable assuming a greater and greater place with each repetition.[9] By the time he is done, Guillaume's incredulity and curiosity have turned to desire—for the city of Orange, but more acutely for its pagan queen, with whom he declares himself hopelessly, desperately in love: "My love for her so binds and dominates me that I can neither understand nor describe it; if I don't have her soon, I'll die" (290–92). Roused to action, he makes this rash vow: he will neither bear arms (262–66) nor take nourishment (283–91) until he has seen Orange and taken the woman he loves but has never laid eyes on.

Both the fugitive Guibert and Guillaume's own nephew Bertrand are horrified, protesting the folly of his plan. Evoking the magnitude of the pagan forces, Guibert begs him to desist: "Forget it: what you're thinking is madness" (316) (Lessiez ester, folie avez pensee). Bertrand more somberly

warns his uncle he will be caught, extradited to Persia, and cast into Emir
Tiebaut's prison. But Guillaume brushes their protests aside, justifying his
determination as a lover's madness: "A man in love is full of folly" (360)
(Home qui aime est plains de desverie); "A man in love is completely mad"
(366) (Hom qui bien aime est trestoz enragiez). Guillaume's passion has a
celebrated literary precedent: the *amor de lonh* thematized in troubadour
Jaufre Rudel's poem, "Lanquan li jorn son lonc en mai," in which distant
love is explicitly associated with Saracen lands.[10] Unlike the object of
Jaufre's desire, however, Guillaume's distant love resides not across the sea
in Tripoli but little more than a stone's throw across the Rhone River. What
makes Orange—or, for that matter, Orable—so special is precisely the indissoluble link between them. Each a metonym for the other, the city and
its queen are virtually indistinguishable: each is superlative, unmatched. Of
Orable, Guibert avers: "there's none so fair that can be found in all Christendom or pagandom" (254–55) (Il n'a si bele en la crestïenté / N'en paienie
qu'en i sache trover); and Orange is desirable, in Guillaume's eyes, precisely
because "no count or king possesses its like" (319) (tele n'a nule ne cuens ne
rois). Overtly, it closely resembles Nîmes. Each is a *locus amoenus* of beautiful gardens, singing birds, and blooming flowers. In comparison with the
more pedestrian flora of Nîmes—flowering woods and meadows, fresh
grass, and rosebushes (40, 50)—the profusion of spices in Orable's garden
explicitly evokes the exoticism of the east: "Spices, cinnamon, galingale, and
incense, sweet fragrances, of hyssop and allspice" (658–59) (Pitre et canele,
garingal et encens / Flere soëf et ysope et piment).[11] Her palace, designed
by Grifonnez d'Aumarice, captures the beauty of nature through the artifice
of culture: "There's no flower growing from here to Pavia that isn't artfully
painted in gold" (273–74) (Il ne croist fleur desi que en Pavie / Qui n'i soit
painte a or et par mestrie). Still, the main thing Orange has that Nîmes lacks
is Orable. From the moment she is introduced, the Saracen queen becomes
the focus of Guillaume's desire. In declaring his passion and vowing to possess her and her city together, he disengages the courtly lover's extravagant
obsession from the discourse of pilgrimage underlying much troubadour
lyric and links it instead to the military fervor of the would-be crusader.[12]

*   *   *

La Prise d'Orange, critics aver, has little basis in history. The character Guillaume is loosely based on a count of Toulouse who, in the time of
Charlemagne, helped repel Saracen incursions along the Mediterranean

coast.[13] Otherwise, the representation of history in *La Prise* is "rather hazy," with remains of the past "lying around here and there, pell-mell."[14] This lack of historicity is reflected in the incongruity of the text's proper names: Tiebaut, the pagan emir with the decidedly French name, and Arragon, whose name recalls the kingdom that played such a central role in the Iberian Reconquest.[15] The poem's political geography is equally confusing: Bertrand's evocation of "the thirty kings born in Spain" (1686; compare 1718) seems to allude to the numerous short-lived *ṭāʾifa* kingdoms of eleventh-century Iberia, but the description of Tiebaut's capital, Almería (1303) (Aumarie), as an "African city" (1302) (cité d'Aufrique) across the sea seems to betray a hopeless ignorance of Mediterranean geography and culture.

Yet this ignorance is curious, for northern French-speaking audiences of *chansons* like the *Prise d'Orange* had every reason to be closely interested in the turbulent politics of the region.[16] For the kings, counts, and viscounts scrambling to snatch up heiresses to increase their own landed power, Guillaume's obsession with the beautiful pagan queen Orable would have seemed perfectly natural.[17] Both Louis VII of France and Henry II of England cultivated claims to the countship of Toulouse, based on their respective marriages to Eleanor of Aquitaine, granddaughter of Philippa of Toulouse (see Table 2.1). In 1154, after divorcing Eleanor

TABLE 2.1. The Comital Houses of Toulouse and Barcelona

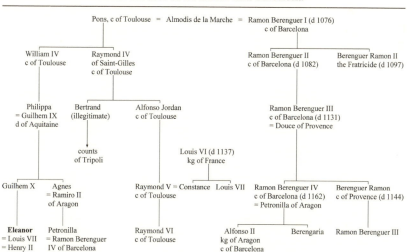

and thus losing his claims to her lands, Louis gave his sister Constance to Raymond V of Toulouse—part of a political realignment designed to forestall the expansion of Angevin power in the south. Henry countered by cultivating an alliance with Raymond's great nemesis Count Ramon Berenguer IV of Barcelona, son of Count Ramon Berenguer III, whose marriage (1112) to Douce of Provence had given the counts of Barcelona a power base east of the Rhone—bringing them into direct conflict with the counts of Toulouse.[18] In 1158, Henry betrothed his infant son Richard (the future Lionheart) to Ramon Berenguer's daughter, Berengaria; in 1162, when the count was on his deathbed, Henry took the count's wife, sons, and lands under his protection.[19]

And what of Orange? Located on the east bank of the Rhone, in 1129 it had come under the control of Guillaume d'Omelas (younger brother of Count Guillaume VI of Montpellier), who married its heiress, Tiburge. This "Guillaume d'Orange" and his wife had two sons, Guillaume and Raimbaut (the troubadour Raimbaut d'Aurenga), and two daughters, Tiburge and Tiburgette, whose nearly identical names, if nothing else, call attention to this family's fondness for onomastic play (Table 2.2).[20]

This being the case, it is striking that Tiebaut, the French name of the Saracen emir, may be derived by combining the first syllable of *Ti*burge and the second of Raim*baut*: the two names (feminine and masculine, respectively) associated with the native dynasty of Orange.[21] In turn, Orable's baptismal name Guiborc closely resembles an amalgam of the first syllable of *Gui*llaume (as in both Guillaume d'Omelas and Guillaume Fierebrace) with the second syllable of Ti*burge*. This linguistic play alone seems openly to proclaim *La Prise*'s connection to the twelfth-century politics of Occitania and Provence. Moreover, like all the feudal nobles in

TABLE 2.2.   The Houses of Montpellier-Orange

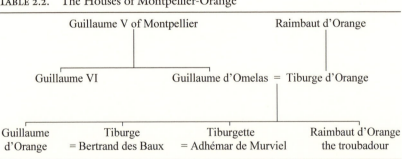

the great arc stretching from Barcelona to Provence, the lords of Montpellier, Omelas, and Orange could not help but be caught up in the political rivalry between the houses of Barcelona and Toulouse. When Count Ramon Berenguer III of Provence died without a direct heir in 1166, his cousin Alfonso II of Aragon assumed the title marquis of Provence—in opposition to Raymond V of Toulouse, who (having repudiated Constance of France) laid claim to Provence by marrying the late count's widow. The upshot is that from the towers of Omelas (situated on a mountain top twenty-four kilometers west of Montpellier), the lords of Orange "could actually see the territories of Aragon."[22] Though Guillaume d'Orange (son of Guillaume d'Omelas and Tiburge d'Orange) mysteriously disappears from the historical record, his brother, Raimbaut the troubadour, lived until 1173. At his death, his lands were divided between his two sisters—those east of the Rhone (presumably including Orange) to the elder, Tiburge, and those west of the Rhone to the younger, Tiburgette.[23]

* * *

In the age of imperialism, the female objects of Orientalist desire—from Ingres's odalisques to Delacroix's "Femmes d'Alger dans leur appartement"—fascinate precisely by their alterity. Glittering surfaces and barriers of language and culture create an incomprehension that excites. In comparison, the *Prise d'Orange* is strikingly devoid of topoi like the harem and the veil that dominate later Orientalist discourse.[24] Like her Saracen sisters Bramimonde and Nicolette, Orable compels Guillaume's attention less because she is Other than because she is superlative. With her dazzling complexion as white as hawthorn (279) or as shining snow (666), she is indistinguishable from French Christian beauties in everything but degree. Fairer than any other woman to be found in either Christendom or pagandom, she is the site of excess that effaces the opposition between them.

Throughout the *Prise d'Orange*, cultural difference serves only to further the intrigue or to produce the comic effects that make the poem famous. Occasionally, the descriptions of the pagans recall those of the *Chanson de Roland*: Orable's stepson Arragon is "large and heavy and strong and tall, his head broad and his brow bound with iron, his nails long and pointed and sharp" (231–33). In general, however, the *Prise* casts alterity in a more pragmatic mode, as when Guillaume forces a reluctant Guibert to accompany him back to the city he has just fled on account of the linguistic expertise in "Turkish and African, Bedouin and Basque" (327–28) (turquois / Et aufriquant, bedoïn et basclois) he has acquired during his three years' captivity.[25] At the gates of the city, Guillaume himself talks his way past the guard "in his language" (420) (en son langaige); having darkened his skin with botanical dyes, he claims to be a translator bearing a message from King Tiebaut (reprising the talent for disguise so successfully deployed in the *Charroi de Nîmes*, when he posed as a merchant from Canterbury). Once inside Arragon's palace, the count keeps his wonder at its riches and marvels to himself and courteously salutes the enemy king in the name of Mohammed and Tervagant (477). As in the *Charroi de Nîmes*, Guillaume's success is predicated on his skill at passing— at trading on the *interchangeability* of identities (Christian and pagan, Frank and Turk, noble and servant) whose difference feudal society otherwise took for granted.[26]

This reminds us once again that medieval concepts of alterity were less fixed than has sometimes been supposed. In the Middle Ages, as Robert Bartlett has shown, terms like "race" and "nation" referred not to biology but to customs, language, and law—features that could be transformed from one generation to the next, or even within a single lifetime.[27] Religious conversion, of course, offers an exemplary case of the instantaneous assimilation of the Other to the same. Thus when the *Roland* laments the fact that the otherwise admirable emir of Balaguer is not Christian or when Guibert regrets the surpassing beauty of the Saracen queen—"Dex! mar i fu ses cors et sa jovente, / Quant Dex ne croit, le pere omnipotente!" (206–7)—their expressions are not merely formulaic.[28] For Orable as for Bramimonde, "love" is the means to conversion. In the *Roland*, as we have seen, this means feudal love, inseparable from the love of Charlemagne's God. The *Prise*, on the other hand, capitalizes on the isomorphism of feudal and erotic love, reaching both narrative and ideological consummation in the erstwhile pagan queen's marriage to the intrepid Christian, Guillaume Fierebrace.[29]

The frequency of such interfaith marriages is a matter of some historical controversy. In the crusader states, "intermarriages" generally involved Latin Christian men and native, eastern Christian women.[30] Marriages to converted Muslims, though rarer, did occur, as shown in Fulcher of Chartres's famous description of the rapid acculturation of the first generation of crusaders: "we who were Occidentals now have been made Orientals . . . Some have taken wives not merely of their own people, but Syrians, or Armenians, *or even Saracens who have received the grace of baptism*."[31]

Whatever the historical reality, the *representation* of such relationships became a commonplace of medieval epic—the "theme of the Saracen princess," first identified by Joseph Bédier and given literary-historical roots by F. M. Warren in a 1914 article. Among the antecedents Warren identifies are an exemplum from Seneca, three tales from the Arabic version of the *Arabian Nights*, and an episode in Orderic Vital's chronicle of the First Crusade—the apocryphal tale of Bohemond of Antioch's escape from a Saracen prison with the help of his captor's daughter, Melaz. (Melaz and her father convert to Christianity, and she marries not Bohemond but his cousin Roger.) What the heroines of these generically diverse texts all share is a boldness that, in Warren's eyes, clearly marked them as foreign: "The masterful nature of these women, foreign to France and to the feminine ideal of the French, would therefore be ancestral, inherited. It would have been bequeathed to them by their virile progenitor of classical antiquity."[32] In songs such as *Mainet* and *Fierabrace*, where the heroines (Galienne and Floripas) are unmarried, they are "flirty" and "immodest," but their roles in the overall plot remain fairly minor. In *La Prise d'Orange*, on the other hand, Orable is a serious and dignified Saracen queen, and the significance of her conversion correspondingly greater.[33]

Far from remaining the passive object of Guillaume's desire, Orable actively initiates the amorous exchange when the bold Frankish count suddenly turns shy and awkward in her presence. Eventually, trading arms for love, she—like Bramimonde—delivers her homeland into the hands of the Franks, abandoning her husband and religion in the process.[34] But where Bramimonde embraces Christianity only after the pagans' utter defeat, Orable enables Guillaume's conquest of Orange through the aid and counsel she gives to the Frankish intruders.

In the *Chanson de Roland*, Charlemagne's desire to convert Bramimonde *par amur* contained little trace of the carnal or profane; in that context, "love," I suggested, was meant to underscore the voluntary nature of her conversion.[35] Conversely, the plot of the *Prise* turns precisely on the motif's eroticization. The story of Guillaume and Orable's reciprocal love personalizes the Saracen queen's motivations in actively rejecting husband, family, and religion in order to embrace Christianity—and feudal Christian society—in their place. At the same time, it cannily recuperates courtly motifs of adulterous passion, putting them to work as symbolic resolutions of political crises internal to Frankish society and effacing the taint of immorality through the religious and ideological victory of Orable's conversion.

* * *

Like the *mal-mariée* of courtly tradition, Orable is the young, beautiful bride of a much older man. This situation, common in an age when marriages were contracted for political and familial interests, is (from the Provençal lyric to Chaucer) a staple of the medieval literature of adultery. Sequestered by their jealous old husbands, young wives find solace with handsome young lovers who help them forget their virtual imprisonment.[36] Even as a literary theme, however, adultery poses something of a moral dilemma. Even in the relatively secularized world of the twelfth-century vernacular, representations of extramarital passion are largely limited to short, hypostasized moments of lyric effusion. Translating illicit sexual relations into narrative proved more problematic: the fragmentation of the Tristan corpus and the "unfinished" state of Chrétien de Troyes's *Chevalier de la Charrete* attest, if only anecdotally, the difficulties of bringing such tales to successful narrative closure.

The opening of *La Prise d'Orange* reads like a variation on the story of Tristan and Iseut. Comfortably ensconced in her tower Gloriete, Orable is married to the aged Tiebaut, far-off in his African lands. Closer at hand is Arragon, Tiebaut's son and regent—a scenario that introduces the possibility (as in *Tristan*) of symbolically redressing the age discrepancy between husband and wife by substituting a young man of the king's own lineage in the queen's bed. This, however, is not to be: in fact, stepmother and stepson regard each other not with illicit passion but with mutual dislike and suspicion. When Guillaume inquires after the Saracen queen, Arragon condemns his father's folly and his stepmother's alleged betrayals:

"He's acting quite crazy, for he is old, with a white beard, and she's a young and beautiful girl: there's none so beautiful in all pagandom. In Gloriete she carries on her love affairs. She'd prefer Sorban of Venice—a young bachelor with his first beard, who can make his living from jousting—to Tiebaut of Slavonia. An old man who loves a young girl is too crazy: he's quickly cuckolded and driven mad." When Guillaume hears him, he begins to laugh. "Really," says Guillaume, "don't you like her at all?" "Not I, for sure! God curse her! I only wish she were in Africa, or in Baudas, in the kingdom of Almería."[37] (619–34)

("Il fet mout grant folie,
Quar il est vielz, s'a la barbe florie,
Et ceste est bele et juenete meschine,

Il n'a tant bele en tote paiennie.
En Glorïete mainne ses drüeries;
Mielz ameroit . . . Sorbant de Venice,
Un bacheler juene de barbe prime,
Qui de deport et d'armes set bien vivre,
Qu'el ne feroit Tiebaut d'Esclavonie.
Trop par est fox vielz hom qu'aime meschine,
Tost en est cous et tornez a folie."
Ot le Guillelmes, si commença a rire:
"Voir," dit Guillelmes, "or ne l'amez vos mie?"
"Ge non, por voir, Damedex la maudie!
Ge verroie ore qu'ele fust en Aufrique
Ou a Baudas, el regne d'Aumarie.")

Whether Arragon is tormented by his own desire for the queen (as Lachet suggests) or simply offended by the unnaturalness of this May-December marriage, from a dynastic standpoint his antipathy toward his stepmother is completely understandable.[38] Any children she bears will be potential rivals not just for his father's affection but presumably for the succession as well—a threat made all the more intolerable should Orable produce an illegitimate child passed off as her husband's own. In any event, despite their physical proximity, the Tristanesque plot remains but an unrealized temptation. Arragon is no Tristan; though "king" in his own right, he remains an ineffectual son in the shadow of an old but still powerful father, the magnificent emir. More important, Orable—her stepson's salacious innuendoes notwithstanding—is no Iseut: though bound in a marriage whose unnaturalness seems obvious to all, she never bemoans her fate or wishes for a lover to console her.

Never, that is, until the arrival of Guillaume Fierebrace. If Arragon is an unworthy object of desire, adventure provides a more attractive alternative in the form of the enemy count. When the Saracen queen is overcome by passion for the Frankish warrior who has come to woo her, the moral ambiguity attached to the conventional scenario of adultery is conveniently dispelled. Orable's willingness to accept Christianity to win Guillaume's heart distinguishes her love from the dangerous passion of the courtly adulteress. In turn the count, in seducing the Saracen queen, converts her to Christianity *par amur*. Moreover, his adultery—far from violating his faith to his feudal lord (as does Tristan's or Lancelot's)—in fact enhances it, by winning him a fief to compensate him for his sovereign's

neglect. In short, when the lady in question is a Saracen queen, adulterous love is no longer immoral or politically subversive but a strategic ideological solution.

The site of the mutual seduction of the Frankish warlord and the
Saracen queen is Gloriete. The imaginative geography of the text is mapped
in concentric circles around this magnificent tower, the innermost sanctum of Arragon's royal palace. As a symbolic space, Gloriete concretizes
the convergence of the two objects of Guillaume's campaign: "[i]n its
metonymical relation to both the city and the lady, the tower becomes an
apex of desire, a symbol of the goal in an ultimate quest."[39] Like the lover-
narrator of Guillaume de Lorris's *Roman de la Rose*, Guillaume Fierebrace must penetrate a concentric series of obstacles to reach his beloved:
the walls of Orange, of Arragon's stronghold, and finally of Gloriete itself.
The tower seems to be Orable's private domain, her own enclave at the
heart of Arragon's palace. The first time her stepson captures the Franks,
she curses him and orders him out of her tower: "Leave the tower immediately! If you stay longer you will regret it" (1242–43) (Isnelement issez
hors de la tor! / Ja plus ceanz mar seroiz a sejor). The second time the
Franks are captured, she helps them escape through a secret passage
known only to her: "Underneath us there's a tunnel. No man born of
mother knows of it, except my ancestor, who had it excavated: He had
the tunnel dug from here to the Rhone" (1398–1401) (Par desoz nos a une
bove tel / Nel set nus hom qui de mere soit nez, / Fors mes aieus qui la
fist enz chever; / Desi qu'au Rosne fist la bove percier).[40]

For the count and his followers, the tower represents, if not the
harem of the modern Orientalist imagination, then the temptation of
stasis and luxurious abandon: " 'God,' says Guillaume, 'This is paradise!'
Guïelin says, 'I've never seen anything nobler. I'd like to stay here my
whole life long; I wouldn't want to budge from here for anything' "
(676–79) ("Dex," dist Guillelmes, "Paradis est ceanz!" / Dist Guïelin:
"Onques ne vi tant gent. / Ge vorroie estre ici tot mon vivant; / Ne m'en
querroie movoir ne tant ne quant").[41] The Franks' unabashed wonder exemplifies the danger should the lure of Saracen exoticism become uncou-
pled from the ideology of crusade and conquest. Even near the end of the
poem, when Guillaume and his companions are under siege for the third
time, his nephew Guïelin is reluctant to abandon this heaven-on-earth:
"I would rather die in this lovely tower than in sweet France or at Aix-la-
Chapelle" (1419–20) (Mielz voil morir en iceste tor bele / Qu'en douce
France ne a Es la Chapele).[42] In the long run, Gloriete is the stage for

Orable's conversion, where she will exchange both family and faith for those of her lover; in the short run, it is the site where Guillaume's epic resolve is called into question, where all categories of identity must be set in motion as a prerequisite to the conversion of the Saracen queen.

Paradoxically, though the *Prise*'s ideological force derives from Orable's voluntary embrace of Guillaume and all he represents, to win her the count must momentarily relinquish the traits that most closely define him. Of course, mutability is nothing new to Guillaume Fierebrace. In *Le Charroi de Nîmes* he had proven himself a master of disguise capable of manipulating his outward appearance for military and political ends. Now, posing as an emissary from the Emir Tiebaut, he gains an audience first with Arragon, then with Orable. This strategy is not without its risks: during his discussion with the queen, he is recognized by a Saracen recently escaped from Frankish captivity who literally unmasks Guillaume by wiping the paint off his face. Onlookers are stunned to find themselves face-to-face with the mighty Guillaume Fierebrace: "His skin was as white as a flower in summer" (779) (Blanche ot la char comme flor en esté). Presumably, the resplendent white skin exposes him as a Frank and a Christian, but it is also, of course, an exemplary sign of feminine beauty, notably that of Orable herself: "Blanche [ot] la char comme la flor en l'ente" (205). In this one aspect, at least, the Frankish warrior and the Saracen queen are identical.[43] And, in a telling convergence of the martial and the erotic, the count's involuntary response at being unmasked as an intruder is identical to his reaction at first seeing Orable: "All the blood of his body stirred" (781) (Trestot le sanc del cors li est müé).[44]

Nor is exposure as an intruder the only risk Guillaume runs in the close confines of Gloriete. Now at Arragon's mercy, he must depend on Orable for salvation: having come to seduce the Saracen queen, he must now transform himself into the male object of female desire. The feminization implicit in this inversion of gendered hierarchies has ample precedent: standard courtly tropes draw their force, after all, from the incongruity of privileging the unforgiving *domna* over the supplicant lover.[45] Yet in the *Prise* this inversion is both comic and unsettling. Throughout the poem, the mighty Fierebrace is fetishized at least as much as Orable;[46] as a landless knight with no toponym to anchor his name, he must be identified by physical attributes instead: Guillaume "of the bold countenance" (21) (a la chiere hardie) or "with the short nose" (573) (au cort nes). Furthermore, the would-be conqueror is frequently reduced to a love-struck fool, as when his nephew Guïelin taunts him for

hesitating to make love to the lady he has come to woo, even as they fend
off Arragon's men: "You came inside here for love" (911) (Par amistiez
entrastes vos ceanz).

Whether because or in spite of these perturbations, Guillaume suc-
ceeds in winning Orable's favor. When the curious queen casually asks him
(still masquerading as her husband's ambassador), "So, what kind of man
is Guillaume Fierebrace?" (722) (Quiex hom est dont Guillelmes Fierebrace?), he seizes the chance to present himself in the best possible light:

"Truly," says the count, "he has a proud heart, huge fists and a wondrous pair of
arms. There isn't a man between here and Arabia that, if Guillaume were to
wound him with his sharp sword, wouldn't be all sliced up, body and arms: his
sharp sword cuts straight through to the earth. (725–30)

> ("Voir," dit li cuens, "mout a fier le corage
> Et gros les poinz et merveilleuse brace.
> N'a si grant home desi que en Arabe,
> Se il le fiert de l'espee qui taille,
> Que ne li tranche tot le cors et les armes:
> Desi en terre cort l'espee qui taille.")

Earlier, when Arragon had posed a similar question, Guillaume had em-
phasized Fierebrace's great wealth: "He is so rich in pride and possessions
that he cares nothing for pure gold or bright silver" (578–79) (Tant par est
riche, menanz et assazé / Que il n'a cure d'or fin ne d'argent cler); here,
to the lady, he emphasizes instead his bravery and physical strength. His
words do their work, for now it is the Saracen queen who begins to ex-
hibit signs of *amor de lonh*: "By Mohammed, he must be a fine border
lord. Happy the lady who has his heart" (732–33) (Par Mahomet, il doit
bien tenir marche; / Liee est la dame en cui est son coraige). Like Laudine in Chrétien de Troyes's *Chevalier au Lion*, Orable craves a warrior
strong enough to defend a lady's lands and sets her heart on Guillaume
without ever having seen him.

The strategy pays off handsomely shortly afterward when Guillaume—
bereft of the sword whose incomparable power he has just been describing—begs the Saracen queen to arm him: " 'My lady,' he says, 'give me
arms, *for the love of God*, who suffered on the cross; *by Saint Peter*, if I live
through this, you will be richly repaid' " (937–40; emphasis added).
("Dame," dist il, "garnemenz me donez, / *Por l'amor Deu*, qui en croiz fu

penez; / Que, *par saint Pere*, se ge vif par aé, / Mout richement vos iert guerredoné"). It is a turning point for both Guillaume and Orable: without a moment's hesistation, the Saracen queen rushes off to fetch hauberk, helmet, shield, and lance, each described by the narrator with blazon-like intensity. Pride of place goes to Tiebaut's sword, which she had withheld from everyone—even Arragon, "his legitimate son" (953) (ses filz de moillier espousé), who heartily coveted it. In conferring it on the Frankish intruder, Orable interrupts her husband's own line of succession, restoring a phallic power and dignity to the hapless Guillaume.

Not even this gesture, however, absolves the pagan queen of suspicion. When the Franks escape and are recaptured, Guïelin is sure Orable has betrayed them (1188–90); when she asks that the prisoners be consigned to her care, even Guillaume comes to believe in her treachery (1357–59). Guïelin throws himself on her mercy, pledging to become her vassal if she will secure their release: "I would become your sworn man; I would very willingly render you service whenever you wanted. Noble lady, have mercy!" (1354–56) (Vostre hom seroie et jurez et pleviz, / Mout volentiers en rendrai le servis, / Quant vos plera; gentill dame, merci!). However, having already armed the Franks *por l'amor Deu*, she will now intervene only for the love of Guillaume himself: " 'By my faith,' says Queen Orable, 'if I thought my efforts would be repaid—if Guillaume Fierebrace were to take me—I would free all three of you from prison and would quickly become Christian" (1374–78) ("En moie foi," dist la roïne Orable, / Se ge cuidoie que ma paine i fust sauve, / Que me preïst Guillelmes Fierebrace, / Ge vos metroie toz trois hors de la chartre, / Si me feroie crestïenner a haste"). Guillaume readily accepts; with Orable's help Guibert flees to Nîmes to bring Bertrand to their rescue. Though Guillaume, Guïelin, and Orable are recaptured in the meantime, Bertrand and his troops eventually arrive. In the poem's longest laisse, they rout the pagans of Orange and slay Arragon, preparing the way for Orable's absorption into Frankish-Christian society.

* * *

In the *Chanson de Roland*, Bramimonde is brought from Saragossa to Aix-la-Chapelle so that she may embrace Christianity, *par amur*, at the heart of Charlemagne's empire. In *La Prise d'Orange*, Orable stays in place: her conversion and marriage are inseparable from the Christianization of Orange and the investiture of Guillaume as its lord. Stripped of the rich clothes that marked her as exotic and foreign, the pagan queen is taken to a newly consecrated former mosque; there, under the auspices of the count's two nephews, Orable is christened Guiborc, thus passing (in accordance with the onomastic practices outlined earlier) from an identification with her city—*Orange*—to an identification with the lineage of *Gui*llaume and *Gui*elin:

> They have Orable's robes removed and baptize her to the honor of God. They divest her of her pagan name: Bertrand holds her, along with the noble *Guïelin* and *Gilbert*, the worthy and wise; according to our law, they name her *Guiborc*. In a church they had had consecrated (where before, Mohammed had been worshipped) Count *Guillaume* went to marry her. Bishop *Guimer* sings mass for them. (1867–76; emphasis added)

> (Orable firent de ses dras desnüer,
> Il la baptisent en l'enor Damedé,
> Le non li otent de la paieneté;
> Bertran la tint et *Guïelin* li ber
> Et *Guilebert*, le preux et le sené;
> A nostre loi la font *Guibor* nomer.
> A un mostier qu'eurent fet dedïer,
> La ou Mahom fu devant reclamé,
> L'ala li cuens *Guillelmes* espouser,
> Messe lor chante li evesque *Guimer*.)

Everyone returns to Gloriete, where the marriage is lavishly celebrated. The poem then concludes in a short, abrupt laisse: "Count Guillaume has married the lady; afterwards he remained in Orange some thirty years: no day went by without a challenge" (1886–88) (Li cuens Guillelmes ot espousé la dame; / Puis estut il tiex .xxx. anz en Orenge / C'onques un jor n'i estut sanz chalenge). Though Guillaume is credited with having "conquered" Orange "by force" (1863) (ot par force conquisse la cité), his rule, this epilogue suggests, is ultimately legitimized less by his conquest of Orange than by his marriage to its erstwhile queen.

In the *Roland*, love meant the perfect equivalency of divine love (the love of God) and feudal love (the reciprocal bond uniting lord and vassal). In the cycle of Guillaume d'Orange, on the other hand, it is the *failure* of feudal love—King Louis's failure to give Guillaume Fierebrace his due—that had brought the hero and his nephews south in the first place. Armed with an anticipatory grant from the king who had treated them so shabbily, they set off to carve out their own fiefdom through conquest.[47]

But as the Nîmes example demonstrates, military victory alone is insufficient. Despite their conquest of its Saracen prince, the Franks' hold on the city remains precarious; in moments of danger, they cannot help but think nostalgically back to the homeland: to Chartres and Blois (333), Paris and Sens (497), Reims or Laon (539).[48] In a sense, Guillaume's boredom at the beginning of the poem is the obverse of his expectation that Emir Tiebaut will reappear any day to challenge him. Later, his nephew Bertrand, left behind to garrison Nîmes, anxiously laments over the inevitability of a pagan reconquest (1676–90).

In the *Prise d'Orange*, the threat female inheritance posed to twelfth-century political stability is turned to the advantage of the Franks: intimately associated with Orange, Orable is implicitly acknowledged queen of the city so that, through her conversion and marriage, it might pass to her new husband, politically and symbolically legitimizing the Franks' military conquest.[49] Demoted from queen to countess but elevated from pagan to Christian, she is the means through which the landless Fiere-brace acquires feudal honor as Guillaume d'Orange. For the Franks, the romantic love of the Saracen queen not only fulfills the dearest desire of the lovesick count but provides a timely resolution of the internal problems besetting French feudal society, compensating the faithful vassal for the inadequate love of his feudal lord.

Not that Guillaume's tenure will be easy: his future as a frontline fighter for Christendom is guaranteed. Never again will he face the boredom (and the threat of the uselessness of the warrior class) that so eroded his morale at the beginning of the poem. But in this ongoing battle, he has a helpmeet without equal: Countess Guiborc, lauded in the *Chanson de Guillaume* (composed earlier than the *Prise* but recounting a subsequent phase of the hero's biography) in the following terms: "There was no woman like her in Christendom when it came to serving and honoring her lord or exalting holy Christianity or maintaining and protecting the faith" (1487–90) (Il n'i out tele femme en la crestienté / Pur sun seignur servir e honorer, / Ne pur eschalcer sainte crestienté, / Ne pur lei maintenir e garder). Having helped confirm Guillaume's dignity as a knight and a warrior, the proud pagan queen is destined to become the exemplary Christian wife—all thanks to the amatory prowess of the seductive Guillaume Fierebrace.

In the *Prise*, the thematics of courtly love are conscripted to the ideological project of conquest and crusade. Kathryn Gravdal has called attention to the frequency of rape as a central plot device in medieval

French literature.⁵⁰ Whether sublimated in a scenario of triangulated desire, with the knight "winning" the lady by defeating her lover (a practice
codified in the "Custom of Logres" in Chrétien de Troyes's *Chevalier de la
Charrete*), or made explicit in the knight's forcible "seduction" of the
peasant shepherdess, this conflation of eroticism and violence (with its
hint of class conflict and hierarchical differentiation) is symbolically deployed to do the work of *internal* colonization. The *Prise d'Orange*, on
the other hand, suggests that when the colonization in question is external, a different kind of represention may be called for—one that erases the
violence of military conquest in the Saracen woman's willing embrace of
the conqueror and his religious and political order. This emphasis on romance and seduction is all the more crucial when the Other at issue is
perceived as culturally superior, as in the case of the Islamic cultures of the
medieval Mediterranean. By recasting crusade in the form of an amorous
intrigue, tropes of "courtly love"—the siege that another Guillaume, de
Lorris, lays to the tower protecting the rose of his desire, the "warring" of
Yvain and Laudine for amorous hegemony—may be mobilized in the service of an ideology of expansion and conquest. Conversely, by casting the
amorous intrigue in the form of a crusade, the most subversive aspects of
medieval literary discourse are contained: the social instability provoked
by adulterous love is projected onto the pagans, making the seduction of
the king's wife a virtuous act contributing to the triumph of Christendom. When it is a Saracen woman who repudiates her Muslim lord and
chooses her own second husband *par amur*, the very elements susceptible
of arousing anxiety if attributed to her Christian sisters—her assertiveness,
her betrayal of family and faith, her implicit control of the land—work instead to the advantage of the feudal order they would otherwise threaten.

*   *   *

Paradoxically, the symbolic power of the motif of the Saracen queen
may be discerned in two cases where it fails: *Aucassin et Nicolette* and *Le
Pèlerinage de Charlemagne à Jérusalem et à Constantinople*. Each is sui
generis: the first the lone example of the Old French *chantefable*, striking
for its thoroughgoing inversion of the norms of both feudal society and
courtly literature, the second a parodic poem that, according to Alexandre
Leupin, corrodes the epic from within, exhausting the resources and possibilities of the genre. In this brief conclusion I would like to suggest that
the generic strangeness of each work derives from a strategic "misfire" in

the plot of the Saracen princess.[51] In each case, the "solution" the motif offers in adjudicating scenarios of cultural contact is blocked by the fact that the woman in question, however foreign, is *already* Christian.

Like *Floire et Blancheflor* (the subject of Chapter 3), *Aucassin et Nicolette* tells the story of two young would-be lovers divided by a parent's opposition.[52] Aucassin is the son of Count Garin of Beaucaire. Nicolette, as we are repeatedly told, is "a captive brought from a foreign land; the viscount of this city bought her from the Saracens and brought her to this city, raised and baptised her, and made her his goddaughter" (2.29–31) (une caitive qui fu amenee d'estrange terre, si l'acata li visquens de ceste vile as Sarasins, si l'amena en ceste vile, si l'a levee et bautisie et faite sa fillole)—all of which makes her an inappropriate object of Aucassin's desire. One day, her godfather, the viscount "will give her a young man who will earn an honorable living for her" (2.31–33) (li donra un . . . un baceler qui du pain li gaaignera par honor); meanwhile, if Aucassin wants to marry, his father would be happy to procure him "the daughter of a king or count," telling him, "there is no man in France so rich that you couldn't have his daughter, if you wanted her" (2.34–35) (le file a un roi u a un conte: il n'a si rice home en France, se tu vix sa fille avoir, que tu ne l'aies).

Why does Garin think Nicolette so unworthy? The most obvious answer is her Saracen birth, coupled with her lowly status as the ward of the count's feudal subordinate. As in *Floire et Blancheflor*, it is the death of the father—and by extension, of his regime of feudal and genealogical rectitude—that authorizes the son finally to marry the girl of his desires. At the same time, this happy ending depends on the revelation of Nicolette's identity when she is kidnaped by Saracen pirates and taken to the city of Cartage: "and when Nicolette saw the walls of the castle and the country, she recognized herself—that she had been brought up there and taken as a young child; but she was not too young to realize that she had been the daughter of the king of Cartage, and had been brought up in the city" (36.8–12) (et quant Nicolete vit les murs del castel et le païs, ele se reconut, qu'ele i avoit esté norie et pree petis enfes, mais ele ne fu mie si petis enfes que ne seust bien qu'ele evoit esté fille au roi de Cartage et qu'ele avoit esté norie en le cité). Nicolette, in other words, is a Saracen princess: reunited with her father and brothers, she is restored to the exalted rank she had forgotten. Yet royal blood, she soon learns, is as much a liability as a prerogative, subjecting her to the *pagan* version of the feudal politics of lineage: "They wanted to give her to a pagan king, but she didn't want to get married" (38.9–10) (Baron li vourent doner un roi de paiiens, mais ele n'avoit cure de marier). Determined to resist, Nicolette "learned to play the vielle" (s'aprist a vieler) and—like Guillaume Fierebrace—"took an herb, anointing her head and face so that she was all black and colored" (38.12, 15–16) (prist une herbe, si en oinst son cief et son visage, si qu'ele fu tote noire et tainte). Disguised as a jongleur, she takes ship for Beaucaire; there she finds Aucassin—now count (Garin having died), but still despondent over the loss of his Nicolette. Failing to recognize her, Aucassin listens to the jongleur's retelling of his love affair with Nicolette—learning from the song that Nicolette is the daughter of the king of Cartage, that "any day now, they want to marry her to one of the noblest kings of all Spain," but that "she would rather hang or burn than take any such [husband], no matter how rich" (40.9–12) (li veut on doner cascun jor baron un des plus haus rois de tote Espaigne; mais ele se lairoit ançois pendre u ardoir qu'ele en presist nul tant fust rices). Within a week, the two lovers are reunited. Nicolette's godmother, the viscountess (the viscount, like Aucassin's father, having died) brightens her skin again with an herb called "esclaire," dresses her in rich silks, and presents her to Aucassin, who promptly marries her, making her "lady" (41.19) (dame) of Beaucaire.

Within the text, this happily-ever-after ending represents the triumph of the festive, carnivalesque world of the son over the stern and hierarchical world of the father. Aucassin, after all, had previously averred he would rather go to hell (where one could find brave and handsome knights, beautiful ladies—each with two or three lovers—musicians, jongleurs, and kings) rather than to heaven (populated by cranky old priests, the lame, the poor, and the miserable). By the same token, in his eyes, Nicolette's luminiscent beauty marks her, regardless of her origins, as far superior to the world's most powerful empresses and queens. But what ultimately makes the resolution of *Aucassin et Nicolette* so symbolically satisfying, I suggest, is its intertextual evocation of the plot of the Saracen princess. At the beginning of the text, already Christian and the goddaughter of the count's feudal subordinate, Nicolette is of little ideological worth. Once revealed to be the daughter of the king of Cartage, however, Nicolette (like Orable) is made available for conversion. By rejecting marriage to a rich Saracen king in order actively to return to the Christian count of Beaucaire (just a stone's throw downstream from Guillaume's Orange), she not only vindicates Aucassin's devotion but recuperates the frivolity of the text's dangerously parodic inversions.

A more complex variation of the plot of the Saracen princess occurs in *Le Pèlerinage de Charlemagne*, in which a visit to Jerusalem provides the pretext for the Frankish emperor to take the measure of the king of Constantinople. The poem opens at the abbey of Saint Denis, center of the Capetian cult of monarchy, with Charlemagne celebrating his own majesty and loudly demanding to know if anyone has ever seen a more splendid ruler. His question is rhetorical, so he is astonished when his own queen suggests that the greatness of the Greek emperor, Hugh the Strong, far exceeds his own. When Charles turns on her, she swiftly backpedals, trying to nuance her claim: " 'Emperor,' she said, 'don't get angry! He is richer in wealth and gold and silver coin, but he is in no way as brave or as good a knight when it comes to striking blows in battle or pursuing an army' " (26–29) ("Emperere," dist ele, "ne vus en curucez! / Plus est riche d'aver e d'or e de deners, / Mais n'est mie si pruz ne si bon chevalers / Pur ferir en bataile ne pur ost encaucer!"). In this passage, as Eugene Vance points out, money rivals the sword as master signifier: with her "foolish speech," the queen opens the door to a confrontation between Frankish bravura, on the one hand, and Byzantine wealth and sophistication, on the other.[53]

Above I suggested that in scenarios of cultural contact, the emphasis on romance rather than military force becomes ideologically important when the Other in question is perceived as culturally superior. In *La Prise d'Orange*, Guillaume's seduction of Orable helps ease the Franks' humiliation at the Saracens' advanced artistic and technical skills, metonymically rendered by the splendors of Arragon's palace. The Byzantine Empire, on the other hand, presented a more difficult challenge. From approximately 1096, the experience of crusading had brought Latin Christians into close contact with their eastern coreligionists. Though ostensibly allied in a united Christian front against the Seljuk Turks, the Franks quickly came to distrust the Greeks, whom they accused of duplicity and political double-dealing. In contemporary literature, the Byzantine Empire becomes a disruptive force destabilizing the Christian-Saracen binary: unlike Baligant in the *Chanson de Roland*, Hugh the Strong cannot reassuringly be understood as Charlemagne's pagan counterpart in a cosmic chess game of good and evil.[54]

Requiring an alternate representational logic, the *Voyage de Charlemagne* borrows the *Chanson de Roland*'s strategy of gendering cultural difference through the contrastive juxtaposition of two women—one Frankish, the other foreign. As in *Aucassin*, however, the ideological "solution" offered by the motif of the Saracen queen is blocked by the fact that the foreign woman (in this case Hugh the Strong's daughter) is *already* Christian and therefore unavailable for conversion. Again as in *Aucassin*, this socio-narratological impasse produces a series of parodic inversions: Constantinople takes precedence over Jerusalem as the true goal of Charlemagne's journey to the East; Oliver, not Roland, plays the key role in the text's gendered resolution; and it is the Frankish woman who disrupts her society through her rebellious speech, while the foreign woman restores Frankish (male) dignity through her soft-spoken compliance. In the end, this contrast between the text's two women helps reinstate a reassuring binarism, redeeming western masculinity by the double humiliation of the Frankish queen and the Byzantine princess.

In Constantinople, the Franks are startled to find King Hugh tilling the fields from atop a golden plough and amazed by the splendors of his domed imperial palace. Intimidated by and aggressively defiant at the undeniable evidence of the Greeks' wealth and cultural refinement, Charlemagne and his "rude baronage" (657) (ruiste barnage)—including Guillaume d'Orange!—pass the evening in private, getting drunk and boasting one after the other of the extraordinary feats they will perform to vindicate their superiority over the Greeks. Several of these *gabs* showcase the Franks' strength and dexterity: bursting a suit of chain mail, catching apples while racing three horses at full speed, falling on upturned swords from the top of the town's highest tower; others, however, betray their propensity for destruction: toppling the columns supporting the emperor's palace, flooding the city by diverting a nearby river, smiting Hugh at his own dinner table. Roland vows to give a blast on his olifant mighty enough to knock down all the city gates and strip the hairs from the king's beard. This focus on the physical, meant to prove their superiority, only serves to confirm the contrast between Frankish force and Byzantine refinement. Most astonishing of all is Oliver's boast that he would "take" the emperor's daughter one hundred times: "Let the king take his daughter, whose skin is so blonde, and put us in her room in a bed all alone: if this very night I don't take her testimony a hundred times, let me lose my head tomorrow: I swear I will!" (486–89) (Prenget li reis sa fille, qui tant ad bloi le peil, / En sa cambre nus metet en un lit en requeit: / Si jo n'ai testimonie anut de li cent feiz, / Demain perde la teste, par covent li otrai!). In a way his choice is no surprise; at dinner he had already spotted the princess at her father's side, imagining to himself a quick sexual fling, inseparable from physical abduction: "Oliver looked and her and began to love her: 'May it please the glorious king of holy majesty, let me have her in France, or in the city of Dun. For I would completely have my will with her.' He said it between his teeth, so that no one could hear him" (404–8) (Oliver l'esgardat, si la prist a amer: / "Pluüst al rei de glorie de saincte majestet / Que la tenise en France, u a Dun la citet: / Kar jo'n fereie pus tutes mes voluntez!" / Entre ses denz le dist, qu'on nel pot escuter). Reduced to speaking sotto voce at the king's own table, Oliver now unleashes a sexual boast whose vulgarity crudely reasserts Frankish masculinity in the face of the Greeks' effete refinement.

The next day the Franks are horrified to learn that their *gabs* have been overheard by one of the emperor's spies and that they are being called on to make good on their drunken boasts. Desperate to save face, Charlemagne uses the relics he has brought from Jerusalem to invoke the intervention of God and His saints. In a deus ex machina resolution, an angel descends from the heavens and on God's behalf sternly admonishes the emperor against the misuse of relics even as he agrees, just this once, to bail the Franks out of their dilemma. Meanwhile, Hugh, falling prey to the same kind of sexual bravado shown by the Franks, selects Oliver as the first to be put to the test: "Here stands Oliver, who so madly said that he would have my daughter a hundred times in a single night. Let me be dishonored in all courts if I do not hand her over to him! If I don't let him, I'll lose my self-esteem. If, through his weakness, he fails a single time, I'll cut his head off with my gleaming sword: he and the twelve peers will be martyred!" (693–99) (Ci astat Oliver, qui dist si grant folie, / Que une sule nuit avreit cent feiz ma fille. / Fel seie en tutes curs, si jo ne li delivre! / Si ne li abandun, dunc ne me pris jo mie: / Faille une sule feiz par sa recreantise, / Trancherai lui la teste a m'aspee furbie! / Il e li duze per sunt livred a martirie!). The joke, of course, is on Hugh: whether Oliver "takes" his daughter one time or a hundred, her sexual honor will still be lost. The princess, for her part, maintains a poignant grace in the midst of her trepidation:

Oliver came in and started to laugh. When the maiden saw him, she was very afraid; still, she was courteous, speaking nobly: "My Lord, did you leave France in order to kill us women?" Oliver responds: "Don't be afraid, fair friend: *If you are willing to believe (in) me*, you will be safe/saved." (708–13, emphasis added)

(Oliver i entrat, si començat a rire.
Quant le vit la pucele, mult est aspoürie;

Purquant si fud curteise: gente parole ad dite:
"Sire, essistes de France pur nus, femmes, ocire?"
E respund Oliver: "Ne dutez, bele amie:
Si crere me volez, tute en serrez garie!")

Where Bramimonde, at the end of the *Roland*, affirms her belief in the
Christian God—"*Creire voelt Deu*, chrestientet demandet" (3980)—
Hugh's daughter is asked to believe in Oliver alone: "*Si crere me volez*,
tute en serrez garie!" Then, to assuage her fears, Olivier shifts to a more
courtly register:

"Lord," said the maiden, "have mercy on me: I'll never again be happy if you
shame me!" "Fair one," said Oliver, "I should be at your command, if you acquit
me of my vow to the king. *I'll make you my sweetheart*, I don't ever want anyone
else." The girl was very courteous, and pledged her faith that she would. (720–25)

("Sire," dist la pucele, "aiez merci de mei!
Jamès ne serrai lee, se vus me huniset!"
"Bele," dist Oliver, "al vostre cumant seit,
Mais que de men cuvent m'aquitiez vers lu rei.
De vus ferai ma drue: ja ne quier altre aveir."
Cele fud ben curteise, si l'en plevit sa fei.)

Despite her cooperation and the angel's intervention, however, "the
count, that night, didn't do her more than thirty times" (725a) (Li quens
ne li fist mes, la nuit, que .xxx. feiz).[55] Nevertheless, the next morning
Hugh's daughter delivers victory to the Franks by confirming Oliver's
virility: "In the morning, at dawn, the king came and called to his daughter, asking her in private: 'Tell me, fair daughter, did he do it to you
100 times?' And she replied, 'Yes, fair lord king!'" (726–29) (Al matin, par
sun l'albe, i est venuz li reis / E apelat sa fille, si li dist en requeit: /
"Dites mei, bele fille, ad le vus fait .c. feiz?" / E cele li respunt: "Oïl, bels
sire reis!").[56] Through his sexual potency—artificially enhanced by divine
intervention and through the princess's lie—Oliver vindicates Frankish
honor at the expense of the virgin princess's honor. His feat alone is not
decisive, however: Hugh demands satisfaction from two other Franks as
well. The first is our friend Guillaume d'Orange, who, "by a miracle of
God" (751) (par la Deu vertud), lifts a massive metal ball and tosses it, destroying the walls of Hugh's palace. The second is his brother Bernard,

who, again with God's help, diverts a river and floods the streets of Constantinople.[57] In *Le Voyage*, in other words, the seduction of the beautiful foreigner (paralleling Guillaume's of Orable) is attributed to Oliver, while the demolition of the foreign capital (like Charlemagne's of Saragossa) is displaced onto the lineage of Aymeri de Narbonne.[58]

In the *Roland*, Charlemagne makes a point of taking Bramimonde back to Aix so that her conversion might enhance Christendom at the heart of his empire. Once competition shifts from the battlefield to the bedchamber, toward a foe no longer Saracen but Greek, the foreign princess becomes expendable: already Christian, she cannot enhance feudal Christendom by her conversion. So as the Franks prepare to depart Constantinople, Oliver (despite his promise to the princess and his own previously expressed desire to "have" her in France) simply leaves her behind:

As soon as the French had finished eating, they started to leave. Their mules and pack animals were brought up to the porches. Happy to be leaving, the French mounted up. King Hugh's daughter rushes up. Seeing Oliver there, she seizes the hem of his cloak: "I've given you my friendship and love. Take me to France: I'll go with you!" "Fair one," said Oliver, "I leave you my love: I'm going back to France with my lord Charles!" (849–57)

> (Quant Franceis unt manget, des ore s'en irrunt.
> Les mulz e les sumers lur tint om as peruns:
> Si sunt muntez Franceis qui a joie s'en vunt.
> La fille al rei Hugun i curt tut a bandum:
> La u veit Oliver, sil prent part sun gerun:
> "A vus ai jo turnet m'amistet et m'amur!
> Car m'enportez en France: si m'en irrai od vus!"
> "Bele," dist Oliver, "m'amur vus abandon:
> Jo m'en irrai en France od mun seignur Carlun!")

Previously seduced by the language of romance, the princess is now victimized by the exigencies of epic—Oliver's shabby behavior completing the westerners' aggressive defiance of their rich and culturally refined coreligionists. Instead of being assimilated into Frankish Christendom, she is left behind to suffer the double humiliation of her seduction and abandonment.[59] If Bramimonde fulfills her ideological function by renouncing her husband, homeland, and faith, the nameless Byzantine princess serves hers by remaining behind as a living incarnation of her father's defeat and humiliation.

Chastened but victorious, Charlemagne returns to Saint Denis and, (in)secure in the knowledge of his proven superiority, deposes the relics responsible for his victory and tersely pardons his queen (in the final line of the poem) "for love of the Sepulcre at which he had prayed" (870) (Pur l'amur del sepulcre que il ad aüret). Despite the minimal critical attention accorded them, the text's two unnamed female characters both precipitate its action and permit its resolution—Charlemagne's wife through her "foolish" praise of Hugh the Strong, and Hugh's daughter through her verbal confirmation of Oliver's superhuman virility. The cost of this reaffirmation of Frankish masculine superiority, however, is the viability of epic discourse itself, distorted and "corroded" out of all recognition. Such is the price of the "misfire" of the plot of the conversion of the Saracen queen.

*   *   *

In the wake of Edward Said's *Orientalism*, critics sympathetic to his project nevertheless began to insist that representations of cultural difference were neither fixed nor singular but in fact heterogeneous and contradictory. Rather than focusing on simple binary oppositions between Occident and Orient, one must be attentive to the "heterogeneities, inconstancies, and slippages" specific to each individual case.[60] The extraordinary thing about *La Prise d'Orange* is the way it orchestrates the "heterogeneities, inconstancies, and slippages" to produce an ideologically powerful vindication of Frankish colonial expansion. Derided for its lack of narrative coherence, celebrated for its comic inversion of epic motifs, this poem functions not in spite of its crossing of discourses and genres but because of it.

At once representative of her people and utterly unique, Orable incarnates the very possibility of assilimilation through conversion. In some ways, she is the forerunner of la Malinche: the indigenous woman whose sexual liaison with the Christian intruder is a symbolically central betrayal leading to the conquest of her people. By gendering its politics of conquest, *La Prise d'Orange* anticipates the strategy of later colonial administrations that sought to collaborate with the women under the pretext of liberating them from oppression by their own men.[61] From the Frankish perspective, on the other hand, Orable is like the saint choosing *translatio*; the success of her conversion signals not simply her willingness but its rightness in the eyes of God.[62] In actively choosing feudal Frankish

Christianity, she confirms it. The result is an eroticized representation of Frankish aggression against the Saracens of Spain that, for all its comic inversions, vindicates the military and amatory prowess of a masculinized French feudal society. Ironically, however, in legitimizing the northern French conquest of southern France, the tales of Guillaume Fierebrace's expeditions to Nîmes and Orange inadvertently prepared the ideological ground not only for the crusades in Iberia and the Levant but for the northern French invasion of the south, soon to be realized, as we will see in Chapter 7, in the Albigensian crusades of the early thirteenth century.

PART II

ROMANCES OF ASSIMILATION

3

"In the Beginning Was the Road"

Floire et Blancheflor *in the Medieval Mediterranean*

"IN THE BEGINNING WAS THE ROAD."[1] With this one famous line, the eminent medievalist Joseph Bédier summed up his theory on the origins of the *Chanson de Roland*. The road was the pilgrimage trail to Santiago de Compostela and the theory was that the *Roland* was composed by a poet of genius—possibly a cleric from one of the monasteries on the trail—to popularize pilgrimage sites along the way. In Chapter 1, we examined the way the *Roland* negotiates the transition from a culture of *parias* to a culture of crusade. In this chapter we turn to another work set on the Santiago trail: *Floire et Blancheflor*, a curious text that, though contemporary with the first romances of antiquity and stylistically inspired by them, takes the medieval Mediterranean as the stage for a kind of crossconfessional understanding far outstripping the *parias* culture of the *Chanson de Roland*.[2]

The genre of romance appeared in the mid-twelfth century, designating texts in *romanz*—the vernacular tongue of the French feudal nobility—in contradistinction to the Latin of the clerics. The first generation of texts consisted of "translations" of the tales of antiquity that, together with Wace's *Brut* (a translation of Geoffrey of Monmouth's *Historia Regum Britanniae*), narrated a process of *translatio imperii*: the transfer of political hegemony from East to West. In the following generation (c. 1180), Chrétien de Troyes codified this ideological vision of history in the prologue to his "Byzantine" romance, *Cligès*, explicitly linking the twinned programs of *translatio studii* and *translatio imperii*. Both chivalry (*chevalerie*) and learning (*clergie*), he writes, flourished first in Greece, then in Rome, and now in France, their true home. As a result, the fame of the Greeks and Romans has been extinguished: no one, he continues, in an audacious bit of hyperbole, speaks of them any longer.[3] Like Bernard of Chartres's famous image of the *moderni* as dwarves

perched on the shoulders of giants, this formulation concedes the monu-
mentality of the old, all the better to assert the superiority of the new:
from its inception, medieval romance is linked to a declaration of the
West's double-barreled supercession of the East, anticipating later centuries' emplotment of civilization as the inexorable march of political and
cultural hegemony from Greece to Rome to the West.[4]

Floire et Blancheflor eludes conscription in this linear history of the
West. Reversing the flow of Eneas's east-to-west journey, it maps an alternate *translatio*: the genealogy of Latin Europe is rerouted through the
medieval Mediterranean, cast not as the uncharted space of exile and conquest but as a world of cross-confessional contact and long-distance
trade. Like *Aucassin et Nicolette* (which it strongly resembles), *Floire et
Blancheflor* builds on the familiar tale type of youthful lovers, separated by
force, who struggle against fate but are eventually happily reunited. A
French knight and his daughter on their way to Santiago de Compostela
are ambushed by Saracens. The knight is killed, but his pregnant, unmarried daughter is captured and taken to Naples, in Muslim Spain. Inserted
into the comfortable domesticity of the royal household, she becomes the
queen's servant and confidante; no attempt is made to convert her, and
she excites neither the king's desire nor the queen's jealousy. On Easter
Sunday, the queen gives birth to a son, Floire, and her handmaiden to a
daughter, Blancheflor. Reared together, the Saracen prince and the illegitimate Christian slave grow so inseparable that eventually the king, fearing
his son will refuse a proper political marriage for love for his companion,
sells Blancheflor to some itinerant merchants. Floire, disconsolate, dis-
guises himself as a merchant and tracks her to the harem of the emir of
Babylon; when they are discovered together, both are sentenced to die.
Their mutual love so amazes their captors, however, that the emir not
only spares them but presides over their marriage. When Floire's father
dies, the two return to Spain where Floire, now king, converts to Christianity for love of Blancheflor. Their daughter, Berthe aux Grands Pieds,
becomes the mother of the great emperor Charlemagne.[5]

Part of a complex textual tradition of multiple recensions and proliferating translations, *Floire et Blancheflor* seems to resist identification with
specific temporal or spatial coordinates.[6] Perhaps this explains why the
tale's historical "meaning" has so rarely been explored: its recirculation of
conventional motifs invites typological rather than historically situated readings.[7] Even the most conventional of tropes, however, signifies differently in
different historical contexts. In the aftermath of the Second Crusade, *Floire*

offers us a trace of Latin Europe's encounter with the Mediterranean world that the historian S. D. Goitein has reconstructed in such remarkable detail from the accidental archive of the Cairo Geniza.[8] In contrast to the clean lines of the *Chanson de Roland*, in which the high peaks and somber valleys of the Pyrenees symbolically demarcate Christian France from Saracen Spain and contact between Franks and pagans is limited to the field of battle, it is a world not riven by proto-national borders but crossed by political, economic, and phastasmatic flows. Swerving from the Santiago trail to "pagan" Spain to Egypt and back again, *Floire et Blancheflor* describes a trajectory of deviance that totally transforms the straight and narrow path of *translatio*.

*   *   *

Santiago de Compostela was one of the premier pilgrimage sites in medieval Christendom. The cult of the apostle Saint James dated to the early ninth century, when his remains were "revealed" to a monk named Pelagius. Credited with inspiring a Christian victory over the Muslims at the battle of Clavijo in 844, Santiago was given the epithet Matamoros (Moor killer) and made patron saint of the Spanish Reconquest. In 997 his church was destroyed in one of al-Manṣūr's seasonal raids on the Christian north. Quickly rebuilt, it was soon attracting pilgrims from throughout Latin Christendom and beyond. Over time, four distinct itineraries developed; originating in Tours, Vézelay, Le Puy, and Saint-Gilles, they converged in the Pyrenees and wended their way westward to Compostela.

The cult of Santiago proved a flashpoint in Christian Spain's relationship with the rest of Latin Europe. As the (reputed) evangelist of Spain, a rival to Saint Peter, Saint James was a symbol of Iberian exceptionalism. When he first came to the throne, Alfonso VI of León-Castile (whom we met in Chapter 1) openly defied papal opposition to the spread of the saint's cult by supporting the renovation of the pilgrimage church of Santiago. In 1080, this building program was suspended: having decided to cultivate Rome's favor (for example, by replacing the Iberian "Mozarabic" rite with the Roman liturgy common to most of the rest of Latin Europe), the king resumed his father's massive donations to Cluny, leaving little money for Santiago de Compostela.[9] By the turn of the twelfth century, however, a reshuffling of the balance of power in Iberian ecclesiastical politics brought Santiago and Cluny closer together.[10] During the next half century, the Santiago pilgrimage became a truly international phenomenon, attracting powerful penitents like the empress Mathilda (in

1125) and the troubadour-duke, Guilhem IX of Aquitaine (in 1137) as well
as flocks of common pilgrims bearing staffs and wearing distinctive cloaks
called *pèlerines*. By the late 1130s, the trail even had its own guidebook,
which dispensed travelers' advice and described the three-star attractions
to be found along the way.[11] By mid-twelfth century, the fictional characters
wending their way to Santiago de Compostela would have been treading a
path well-worn by their French-speaking compatriots.

Floire et Blancheflor opens on the Santiago trail with a nameless French
knight (93–94) (un François, / chevalier et preu et courtois) on his way
"to the lord Saint James" (95) (au baron Saint Jake). As in *La fille du comte
de Pontieu* (the prose romance we will take up in Chapter 6), the pilgrimage is linked to a scandalous breach in the feudal politics of lineage:

He was taking a daughter of his, who had dedicated herself to the apostle before
leaving her native land, on account of *her lover*, who was dead, and by whom she
was pregnant. (96–100, emphasis added)

> (une soie fille i menoit
> qui a l'apostle s'ert vouee
> ains qu'ele issist de sa contree,
> por *son ami* qui mors estoit,
> de cui remese ençainte estoit.)

The prologue had described the baby's father simply as "a Christian
count" (16) (uns cuens crestiiens). Now we learn he is dead. How did he
die? Gloriously, in battle, or ignominiously? We are not told. The text
seems to imply that he died before he could marry his sweetheart. Yet his
title leads us to suspect a larger scandal: after all, in contemporary feudal
society (as opposed to the compensatory world of romance), the daughter of a simple knight would hardly have made a suitable countess. Making a penitential pilgrimage to the ends of the earth in order to dedicate
herself "to the apostle," this disgraced single mother reveals the high price
of illicit passion.[12] As in *La Fille du comte de Pontieu*, the Santiago pilgrimage becomes a one-way journey into exile, a way of exporting problematic
wives and daughters to Saracen Spain where the sexual scandals they pose
can be reworked and resolved through linked strategies of conversion and
miscegenation.[13]

Their troubles begin when a Spanish Saracen king comes to ravage
the coast of Christian Iberia:

A king had come from Spain[14] with a great company of knights. In his ship he crossed the sea and arrived in Galicia. His name was Felix, and he was pagan. He had sailed against the Christians to take booty and to reduce the cities in the land to ashes. . . . He pillaged cities, took booty, and carried everything back to his ship. . . . Behold the ravaged countryside: the pagans took joy and delight in it. (57–64, 69–70, 75–76)

(Uns rois estoit issus d'Espaigne;
de chevaliers ot grant compaigne.
O sa nef ot la mer passee,
en Galisse fu arivee.
Felis ot non, si fu paiiens,
mer ot passé sor crestiiens
por el païs la proie prendre
et les viles livrer a cendre. . . .
Viles reuboit, avoirs praoit
et a ses nés tot conduisoit. . . .
Es vos le païs tout destruit,
paiien en ont joie et deduit.

In the twelfth century, a pagan attack on the Santiago trail would inevitably have evoked the *Chanson de Roland*, with its ambush high in the Pyrenees. Felix, however, is singularly uninterested in doing battle against Christians, preferring to ravage the countryside and devastate their settlements: "there remained neither steer nor cow / nor castle or city untouched" (72–73) (ne remest ainc ne bués ne vace, / ne castel ne vile en estant). A parodic recasting of the *Roland*'s opening description of Charlemagne's campaign— "No castle remained before him, no wall or citadel was left to be taken" (4–5) (N'i ad castel ki devant lui remaigne; / Mur ne citét n'i est remés a fraindre)—this incongruous emphasis on livestock marks Felix's expedition less as a crusade than as the kind of predatory raid the Cordoban general al-Manṣūr launched against Santiago de Compostela in 997. According to a contemporary Arab chronicler, "the Muslims seized all the booty they found there and knocked down the buildings, walls, and church so that no traces remained. Nevertheless, the guards al-Manṣūr assigned protected the tomb of the Saint and prevented anyone from harming it; but all those beautiful, solidly built palaces were reduced to dust: no one would have suspected their existence."[15] The booty seized included livestock, treasure, slaves, and bells from the cathedral.[16]

Such raids derived from the Arab tradition of *ghazw* (pl. *ghazawat*), an "expedition, usually of limited scope, conducted with the aim of gaining plunder."[17] In medieval Iberia, they had become part of a complex economy of predatory raids. In 1112, for example, the Galician coast was pillaged by English crusaders en route to Jerusalem, whose atrocities the *Historia Compostellana* likened to those of the Almoravids (the North African Berbers who had invaded the Iberian peninsula in 1086).[18] The same source reports that in 1113, Diego Gelmírez (the bishop of Santiago we met above) financed the construction of two Genoese biremes—the better to raid Muslim lands:

> They paid the Ismailites back their previous destruction and ill treatment, and more. They burned houses and harvests in the field (it was the season of battages), cut trees and vines, their sword sparing neither old nor young. They burned and destroyed their temples and did not blush to commit filthy acts. They seized their cargo or sailing ships, accustomed to carrying Christian captives, and destroyed and burned them. Finally, their sword sated and their ships loaded with gold, silver, and spoils, they returned home in joy, singing the praises of God and Saint James.[19]

Ostensibly, such episodes fit unproblematically within a narrative of Reconquest, the centuries-long struggle between Muslims and Christians. Like so much else in the history of medieval Iberia, however, al-Manṣūr's raid defies analysis along strict confessional lines. His forces, for example, included many Christian counts "who acknowledged his authority and appeared with their warriors with great pomp." Returning from the sack of Santiago, al-Manṣūr's troops ravaged territory belonging to the king of León but carefully ceased hostilities when traversing lands subject to "the confederated counts serving in his army." Upon taking leave of his Christian allies, al-Manṣūr "had them process in front of him, in order of rank, and distributed clothing to them and their soldiers."[20]

Among the most valuable commodities taken in *ghazawat* were the captives who could be sold as slaves.[21] Since female slaves were especially prized, the different fates *Floire* allots its fictional pilgrims make perfect historical sense: the knight is killed, while his daughter is reserved for the king:

> They gave her to King Felix. He looked at her closely: from her face, he could readily see that she was of high lineage; he says that, if he can, he will make a present of the girl to the queen. (105–10)

(Au roi Felis l'ont presentee
et il l'a forment esgardee.
Bien aperçoit a son visage
que ele estoit de grant parage,

et dist, s'il puet, a la roïne
fera present de la mescine.)

Like Bramimonde in the *Chanson de Roland*, the woman is destined for a
special place in the king's household. Unlike Charlemagne, however, Felix shows no interest in erasing his captive's religious and cultural difference: as the text takes pains to specify, "he let her keep her religion" (137)
(sa loi li laist molt bien garder). Here the *Roland*'s homosocial violence
gives way to the cross-confessional sorority of the two expectant mothers
who both give birth on Easter Sunday—the queen to a son named Floire
and her companion to a daughter, Blancheflor.

Linked by the harmony of their names and the coincidence of their
birth, the pagan prince and the Christian captive are diametrically opposed
in every way that matters to medieval society. In the prologue, for example,
the narrator emphatically underscores the religious difference dividing them:

Her friend Floire (whom I mentioned to you) was engendered by *a pagan king*,
and Blancheflor, who so loved him, was engendered by *a Christian count*. Floire
was born of *pagans* and Blancheflor of *Christians*. (13–18, emphasis added)

(Flores ses amis que vos di
uns rois paiiens l'engenuï,
et Blanceflor que tant ama
uns cuens crestiiens l'engenra.
Flores fut tos nés de *paiiens*
et Blanceflors de *crestiiens*.)

The text specifies that Floire has a pagan wet nurse—ostensibly for reasons
of religious purity, "for their faith [lor lois] forbade" it (184), but practi-
cally to keep his future love for Blancheflor from being incestuous. As the
romance progresses, the two grow to be inseparable and, increasingly, indistinguishable, sharing a reciprocal love born of their perfect resemblance:
"the two children *loved each other* very much, and *resembled each other* in
beauty" (223–24, emphasis added) (Li doi enfant molt *s'entramoient* / et de
biauté *s'entresambloient*). Later observers repeatedly note their resemblance,
one insisting that Blancheflor must be Floire's "twin sister" (1728) (suer
jumele), "for they are marvelously alike" (1732) (car a merveille sont sanlant). Mirror images of one another, Floire and Blancheflor problematize
feudal society's most basic categories of difference.[22]

This uncanny likeness has caused some critical consternation. Typically, Floire and Blancheflor's perfect resemblance is explained in terms of their youth, as "the conventionally androgynous beauty of literary medieval children."[23] This appeal to age conveniently resolves the poem's troubling collapse of gender distinctions (strongly hinted at here but explicitly foregrounded in Babylon when Floire is mistaken for a girl): masculinity (like kingship) is a role Floire will assume as he ages. Gender, in turn, becomes a strategy for the representation of religious difference, displacing "anxieties of conversion . . . by rendering Floire's masculinity, not his religion, the main obstacle to his love for Blancheflor." This reading of the poem's complex imbrication of age, religion, and gender opens the way for a satisfactorily teleological conclusion: "Masculinity provides a narrative trajectory . . . Christianity cannot offer."[24]

But what if we approach this slippery nexus of identity in terms of religious and cultural difference? From this perspective, the uncanny resemblance between the Saracen prince and his Christian companion—so alike they are easily mistaken for "close relatives" (1731) (proçain parent)—evokes a vision of medieval Christianity and Islam as "sibling societies," linked (as Richard Bulliet has recently proposed) by "common roots" and a long "shared history," holding sovereignty "in neighboring geographical regions and following parallel historical trajectories." Like "fraternal twins . . . almost indistinguishable in childhood" whose paths only later diverge, neither of which can adequately be understood without reference to the other, medieval Arabic and Latin traditions figure as the twin progeny of Mediterranean antiquity.[25]

This startling reconceptualization—so contrary to received ways of thinking medieval Islam and the West—lends new complexity to the scene in which a six-year-old Floire is put to school, with Blancheflor at his side. Sharing their lessons in the king's pleasure garden, the two make excellent progress, as their friendship assumes its first erotic edge:

They read *pagan books* in which they heard love spoken of. They took great pleasure in the love strategems they found there. . . . Together they read and learn and understand the joys of love. When they get back from school, one kisses and embraces the other. (231–34, 239–42, emphasis added)

> (*Livres* lisoient *paienors*
> u ooient parler d'amors.
> En çou forment se delitoient,

es engiens d'amor qu'il trovoient. . . .
Ensamle lisent et aprendent,
a la joie d'amor entendent.
Quant il repairent de l'escole,
li uns baise l'autre et acole.)

What are these "pagan books" that so enflame their imagination? An early thirteenth-century Anglo-Norman variant explicitly names Ovid[26]—a reasonable choice, since the *Ars Amatoria* was a popular medieval school text (despite the moral ambiguity of its subject matter) and since the protagonists' Latin, we are told, is quite proficient:

both were so well schooled that they could speak Latin well and write it on parchment, and converse; around other people, they could speak in Latin so that no one understood them. (268–72)

(furent andoi si bien apris
que bien sorent parler latin
et bien escrire en parkemin,
et consillier oiant la gent
en latin, que nus nes entent.)

Linguistic difference at this presumably Arabic-speaking court had been hinted at earlier, when the queen practices her French with her Christian servant: "she often plays and speaks with her, and learns French under her tutelage" (139–40) (o li sovent jue et parole / et françois aprent de s'escole).[27] In that context, the children's precocious use of Latin as a kind of private code may signal its foreignness. Conversely, it may simply allude to the cultural difference between vernacular-speaking nobles and Latin-speaking clergy (the very gap that occasioned the rise of romance in the first place) and the children's ability to bridge it.

The word "pagan," persistently used to describe Muslim Spain, collapses the distinction between Islam and classical antiquity. The connection between the two was never more explicit than in this period, when the intense traffic in Arabic translations helped catalyze the Latin West's rediscovery of Greek philosophy and science.[28] In his treatise on the astrolabe, *De opere astrolapsus* (c. 1150), Adelard of Bath describes himself as setting out to "write in Latin what I have learnt in Arabic" and praises the future Henry II of England as a "philosopher-prince" enamored of Arab astronomy.

Whether true or fanciful, this dedication both reveals the cultural prestige attached to Arabic learning and gives a surprising spin to the portrait of a prince closely associated with the romance project of *translatio*.[29]

Our ignorance of conditions of medieval literary production makes it difficult to say how much a work like *Floire* might owe to such transcultural exchanges. In our tale's second prologue, the narrator claims to have learned the young lovers' story from two sisters who heard it from a cleric, who in turn read it in a book (33–54). But as Adelard's treatise shows, in the twelfth-century West, such a book might conceivably have an Arabic provenance. It is a small step to imagining the *livres paienors* firing the young lovers' desire as an Arabic text like *The Neck Ring of the Dove* (a love treatise by the eleventh-century poet and polymath Ibn Ḥazm) or the tale of *Bayād and Riyād* (lavishly illustrated in a manuscript from late twelfth-century Seville), as well as Ovid's *Ars Amatoria*.[30]

Within the romance, such transgressional thinking is opposed by Felix himself. Guided by a sense of genealogical rectitude worthy of any feudal monarch, he is distressed by his son's unseemly attachment to Blancheflor and worried that it will interfere with a proper dynastic marriage to "the daughter of a king or an emir [aumachour]" (304). Felix's inability to imagine Blancheflor as Floire's bride, we should note, runs counter to the historical practices of medieval Iberia, where caliphs and emirs routinely took Christian wives and concubines of both high and low station.[31] Though the queen dissuades him from putting Blancheflor to death, he nevertheless devises a way to be rid of her—selling her to a group of "merchants from Babylon" (415–16) (marceans de / Babiloine) and commissioning a false tomb to convince Floire that his sweetheart is dead.

Described in a passage of over one hundred lines, this fabulous sepulchre in marble, gold, silver, and crystal recalling the monumental tombs of Pallas and Camilla in the *Roman d'Enéas* explicitly links *Floire* to the tradition of the *romans d'antiquité*.[32] Topped by twin statues of the two lovers that kiss and embrace with each passing breeze, it also evokes the Byzantine automata adorning King Hugh the Strong's palace in *Le Pèlerinage de Charlemagne*. It is inscribed, however, with an epitaph "carved in letters of Arabian gold" (662) (de l'or d'Arrabe bien letree)—an ambiguous formulation that, like the lovers' *livres paienors*, overlays the tomb's self-consciously classicizing form with a spectral Islamic presence. Ostensibly, only the gold is designated as Arabian. Yet given the popularity of Arabic or faux Arabic inscriptions even in the Latin West, it is easy to imagine the monument itself decorated in Arabic script.[33]

Felix's elaborate ruse is a failure: when a disconsolate Floire tries to kill himself, his parents reluctantly admit that Blancheflor is alive but has been sold as a slave. Their justification closely anticipates that offered by Count Garin of Beaucaire in *Aucassin et Nicolette*:

we wanted you to forget her and, with our advice, marry the daughter of some powerful king who would bring honor to us and to you. We wanted Blancheflor not to love you anymore, *for she was Christian—a poor creature of low station*. The merchants who bought her have taken her to another land. (1071–78, emphasis added)

(voliemes que tu l'oubliasses
et par no consel espousaisses
la fille d'aucun rice roi
qui honerast et nos et toi.
Nos voliemes que Blanceflor
n'eüst a toi plus nule amor,
por çou que crestiiene estoit,
povre cose de bas endroit.
En autre tere l'ont menee
marceant qui l'ont acatee.)

Like Aucassin, Floire wants nothing to do with his father's politics of lineage. Reanimated by the news that Blancheflor is alive, he sets out to find her in the mercantile world to which she has been consigned.

*   *   *

In the *Roman d'Enéas* as in the *Aeneid*, the Mediterranean is a space of desire and temptation, the danger one must overcome in order to get on with the business of *translatio*. *Floire*, in contrast, presents the Mediterranean as a site of possibility and transformation. This mercantile world in which identities, destinies, and cultural values may be weighed, negotiated, and exchanged first comes into view when Felix decides to dispose of Blancheflor. Working through a bourgeois intermediary "who knew a lot about markets and spoke many languages" (425–26) (qui de marcié estoit molt sages / et sot parler de mains langages), he trades her to some Cairene merchants in exchange for a rich treasure including "thirty gold and twenty silver marks, twenty Benevento silks, twenty variegated eastern cloaks, and twenty Indian purple tunics" (437–40) (.xxx.

mars d'or et .xx. d'argent / et .xx. pailes de Bonivent, / et .xx. mantiax
vairs osterins, / et .xx. bliaus indes porprins).

Unpacking this shipment places us squarely in the world of medieval
Mediterranean commerce, where the highly wrought rhetorical language
used to describe Blancheflor's tomb (555–666) gives way to a literal inven-
tory of her worth. Since twenty gold dinars was the standard price for
a female slave, the amount of coin alone here offered underscores her exceptional worth.[34] Yet the Benevento silks, oriental purple cloaks, and indigo tunics likely to mean little to the modern reader in fact all point with
great precision toward the polyglot, seafaring world in which "people and
goods, books and ideas travelled freely from one end of the Mediterranean to the other," where silks were the luxury commodity par excel-
lence and fine garments the symbolic objects in which "economies of
prestige value and market value converged."[35] High-grade indigo, to take
one example, originated in Persia or Afghanistan and was shipped west
through the great markets of Baghdad and Cairo, where it was one of the
commodities prized by Italian merchants.[36] Paradoxically, the descriptions
most opaque to us today would have read as a clear evocation of contemporary long-distance commerce to a medieval audience.

The centerpiece of the collection, however, is a priceless gold goblet
crafted by Vulcan himself, described in a passage of seventy lines. "Marvelously well-crafted and very subtlely adorned with fine niello" (447–49),
it is etched with scenes from the Trojan War, conjuring (like Blancheflor's
tomb) the literary-historical world of the *romans d'antiquité*.[37] This evocation of the thematics of *translatio* is confirmed by the goblet's own
travels: brought by Aeneas from Troy to Lombardy, given to Lavinia and
passed down to Julius Caesar, it materializes the first stage of *translatio*'s
westward migration. The story is disrupted, however, by two dissonant
details. First, the scenes decorating the cup are described in inverse
chronological order, beginning with the siege of Troy (451–56), spooling
backward to the abduction of Helen (457–64), and concluding with the
judgment of Paris (465–90). By reversing *translatio*'s unidirectional line,
Floire seems to call its historical inevitability into question. Second, the
goblet is hijacked from the second leg of the trajectory that should have
taken it north to Germany or France (the end point of *translatio* in
Otto of Freising's *Two Cities* and Chrétien's *Cligès*, respectively[38]), and—
having inexplicably fallen into the hands of some "Babylonian merchants"
(415–16) (marceans de Babiloine)—is now rerouted from Latin Europe to
pagan Spain.

In her study of the medieval Mediterranean, art historian Eva Hoffman suggests that portable objects like metalwork, ivories, and silks drawing on a visual vocabulary common to Fatimid Egypt, Byzantine Greece, Norman Sicily, and al-Andalus participated in a rivalry "played out through commerce and diplomacy" rather than military conflict. Identity and meaning were formed through "circulation and networks of connection rather than through singular sources of origin or singular identification." This "constant traffic of people and goods, at court level through gifts and at merchant-class level through trade, proved an effective recipe for sustaining a fragile co-existence and a delicate balance of power." This was "not cross-cultural exchange in the traditional sense" but "a discourse of portability that mapped a common visual language across cultural and religious boundaries."[39] The golden goblet, of course, is just such an artifact—its exquisite niellowork undoubtedly linking it, in twelfth-century eyes, with coveted objects produced in and circulating between Fatimid Egypt and al-Andalus.[40]

Blancheflor, too, is obviously just such an object. Felix sells her to the "merchants of Babylon" precisely because of his fixed sense of the limited worth of this "poor creature of low station" (1078) (povre cose de bas endroit). In the mercantile Mediterranean, however, all values are up for renegotiation. Separated from Floire and sold as a slave, Blancheflor's fortunes have never been lower. At the same time, the exorbitant price she commands overwhelmingly contests Felix's low estimation of her worth. At this moment, two contradictory systems converge: the feudal economy of lineage, in which the illegitimate daughter of a captive Christian slave counts for nothing, and a commercial economy that appraises her luminous beauty at "face" value. Trafficked across the sea and sold for a king's ransom in gold, Blancheflor becomes the site where value is delinked from family and birth, and the conflicting values of the feudal West and the caliphal East are put to the test.[41]

Blancheflor is not the only one transformed by the mercantile Mediterranean. To search for his beloved, Floire exchanges his royal identity for a commercial one:

I will seek her [disguised] as a merchant. I'll take seven pack animals with me: two loaded with gold and silver, and as many receptacles as I wish; the third loaded with deniers, which I'll need; and two with expensive textiles—the best you can find. (1142–48)

(comme marceans le querrai,
.VII. somiers avoec moi menrai,
les .II. cargiés d'or et d'argent
et de vaissiaus a mon talent,
le tiers de moneés deniers,
car tos jors me sera mestiers,
et les .II. . . . de ciers dras,
des millors que tu troveras.[42])

As a merchant, Floire proves less than convincing. Freely acknowledging his lack of commercial savvy (revealed in his "innumeracy" in accounting for only five of his seven pack animals), he willingly relies on the expertise of his father's chamberlain, who "is really good at selling and buying, and can give advice when it's needed" (1157–58) (bien set vendre et acater / et au besoing consel doner).[43] Even with assistance, however, Floire fools no one: "he's not a merchant," declares an innkeeper in the Spanish port where Floire takes ship, "he's a nobleman on a quest" (1287–88) (n'est pas marceans, / gentix hom est, el va querans). "I really think it would be a joke," echoes an Egyptian bridgekeeper, "for you to sell cloth at retail" (1722–23) (Molt me sanle que çou soit gas / que vos dras vendés a de-tail)—reacting, it seems, to Floire's endearing ineptitude.

However ineffectual Floire's disguise, his journey transforms the standard romance plot of abduction and rescue into "a quest based on trade"[44] and reterritorializes the Mediterranean as the space not of *trans-latio* but of trade circuits connecting Naples/Iberia and Babylon/Cairo. Floire sails on a ship whose voyage is timed to coincide with the emir of Babylon's annual gathering, for then, its captain confides, "I could maybe sell my wares, and, I think, make a profit" (1377–78) (mes toursiaus puet estre vendroie, / si cuit que jou i gaigneroie). Taking the "French road" across the sea, Floire crosses to Egypt in a remarkable nine days.[45] His ship makes landfall in Baudas, where all merchandise is subject to a 17 per-cent tax: "The port belonged to the emir; many men worked there. Whether rightly or wrongly, everyone had to give to the port a sixth of his wealth and swear that they were telling the truth" (1439–44) (Li pors es-toit a l'amirail; / maint home i a eü travail. / U soit a droit u soit a tort, / tot lor estuet doner au port / la siste part de lor avoir / et puis jurer qu'il dient voir).[46] Exchanging precious coin and commodities for information on Blancheflor as he goes, Floire plies one of the premier trade routes of the medieval Mediterranean.

* * *

Babylon, where much of the rest of the romance is set, was Latin Christendom's name for the great city of al-Qāhira (Cairo)—the city victorious. In the mid-twelfth century, Cairo was the capital of the Fatimids, Ismaili Shiites who ruled Egypt and surrounding lands from 969 to 1171.[47] At its heart lay a palatine complex composed of the Great Eastern palace (housing the caliph) and the Western palace (housing his harem).[48] It was an impressive spectacle, as attested by the eleventh-century Persian traveler Nāser-e Khosraw:

> Viewed from outside the city, the sultan's palace looks like a mountain because of all the different buildings and the great height. From inside the city, however, one can see nothing at all because the walls are so high. They say that twelve thousand hired servants work in this palace, in addition to the women and slavegirls, whose number no one knows. It is said, nonetheless, that there are thirty thousand individuals in the palace, which consists of twelve buildings.[49]

Even by Mediterranean standards, the Fatimid court was a rich one, populated by "princes from all over the world—the Maghreb, the Yemen, Byzantium, Slavia, Nubia, and Abyssinia . . . the sons of Georgian kings, Daylamite princes, the sons of the khaqan of Turkistan"—high-ranking stipendiaries, each with an assigned role in the scripted performance of ritual: "No aristocrat receives less than five hundred dinars, some drawing stipends of up to two thousand dinars. The only function they have to perform is to make a salaam to the grand vizier, when he sits in state, and then withdraw to their places."[50] It was a triumph of competitive display.[51] The palace treasury contained a staggering array of beautiful and expensive objects—part of a strategy of accumulation that, in the words of one tenth-century caliph, "should serve above all to compete with one's adversary in splendor and to display one's own magnificence."[52] These objects included gold and silver vessels, jewels, pearls, precious stones, carved rock crystal vases, ivories, ceremonial robes, linens and silks produced in special state factories, arms, spices, and "strange curiosities" like a miniature garden with silver trees bearing amber fruit or another with richly decorated pavilions.[53] Received as tribute or intended for use in court ceremonials, these objects were annually reviewed by the caliph himself in a ritual display of his great wealth and symbolic power.[54]

Even beyond the walls of the imperial compound, Cairo and the neighboring settlement of Fustat abounded in luxuries, reflecting the city's pivotal location in networks of East-West exchange. The rich dressed in silks or fine locally produced linens, used imported Tunisian soaps and drank from cups of Chinese porcelain.[55] The markets featured an astounding assemblage of goods from all parts of the Fatimid empire and beyond: tortoiseshell boxes, combs from Africa, etched Maghrebi crystal, elephant tusks from Zanzibar, leopard skin sandals from Abyssinia. By the eleventh century, merchants from Amalfi, Pisa, and Genoa—drawn to Egypt by these and other commodities from the rich India trade—were doing business in Old Cairo (Fustat) on such a large scale that any interruption in their trade risked triggering a recession.[56]

Highly conventionalized, *Floire et Blancheflor*'s description of "Babylon" draws on the same repertoire of tropes used for cities like Carthage in the *Roman d'Enéas* or Constantinople in the *Pèlerinage de Charlemagne*.[57] Nevertheless, several elements could easily pass for renditions of first- or secondhand accounts of medieval Cairo. The high wall encircling the city, pierced by 140 gates surmounted by "wide, strong towers" (1796), suggests the massive stone walls of the imperial Fatimid compound, "fortified at regular intervals by massive square bastions."[58] Inside, the "more than 700" towers (1800) recall the high-rises described by Nāṣer-e Khosraw. Even the variety of "pomegranates, figs, pears, and copious quantities of peaches and chestnuts" Floire finds in Babylon—"for they are plentiful in that kingdom" (1687, 1689–90)—evokes the bounty noticed by that eleventh-century traveler:

oranges, citrons, apples, jasmine, basil, quince, pomegranates, pears, melons, bananas, olives, myrobalan, fresh dates, grapes, sugarcane, eggplants, squash, turnips, radishes, cabbage, fresh beans, cucumbers, green onions, fresh garlic, carrots, and beets. No one would think all these fruits and vegetables could be had at one time . . . [but] since Egypt is quite expansive and has all kinds of climate . . . produce is brought to the city from everywhere and sold in the markets.[59]

Finally, like the Fatimid caliph, the emir of Babylon presides over a tributary court attended by myriad subject-princes: "The emir has imposed his rule over 150 kings. If he summons them to Babylon, all will come without delay" (1783–86) (Li amiraus a sa justise / sor .C. et .L. rois mise. / Se il les mande en Babiloine, / tot i venront sans nul essoine).

The centerpiece of *Floire*'s Babylon, however, is the fantastic Tower of Maidens (1896) (Tors as Puceles). Situated in a beautiful garden enclosed by a gold and azure wall and overflowing with fruit trees, sweet-smelling spices, flowers, and sweetly singing birds, this wondrous green marble building with marble pillars and a gold and azure ceiling (1871–72) recalls luxury structures across the Mediterranean.[60] Inside, crystalline pipes— "marbre cler comme cristal" (1847)—carry water to the third floor: an engineering marvel that conjoins the beauty of Fatimid rock crystal with the wonder of Islamic hydraulic technology.[61] An eastern version of the enchanted castles of romance, the tower is distinguished by the eunuchs in attendance: "The guards in the tower don't have their genitals" (1903–4) (Les gardes qui en la tor sont / les genitaires pas nen ont).[62]

Located (like Orable's Gloriete) at the concentric center of the emir's domains, the Tower of Maidens is home to one hundred and forty beautiful virgins—including, inexplicably, the German king's daughter Gloris. Even among this collection of beauties, Blancheflor quickly stands out from the rest—a prized new piece in the emir's human treasury. As he later describes: "I gave a good deal of gold for her: seven times her weight" (2716, 2718) (Grant masse d'or por li donai. . . . VII. fois son pois)—an exorbitant purchase price that leaves the Cairene merchants "completely happy, for they made much profit" (527–28) (tout lié, / car assés i ont gaaignié). Like the one-of-a-kind artifacts hoarded in the Fatimid treasury, Blancheflor's worth exceeds pure monetary calculation:

Her beauty stood out among all the others; that's why I held her so dear. In the tower among my 140 beautiful maidens, I had her served with honor. I held her dear above all the others. Such was my love for her that I wanted to make her my wife. Because she was both beautiful and noble, I had invested all my desire in her. (2719–28)

(Sa biautés fu entre autres fiere,
por çou l'avoie forment ciere.
En la tor entre mes puceles,
dont il i a .VII.XX, de beles,
a honor servir le faisoie.
Sor totes ciere le tenoie.
En li avoie tele amor
k'en voloie faire m'oisçor.
Por çou qu'ele ert et bele et gente
avoie en li mise m'entente.)

Unlike Felix, the emir is completely unconcerned by her lineage: trusting his own assessment of her "face value"—seven times her weight in gold— he places the illegitimate daughter of a Christian slave above the daughter of the greatest ruler of Latin Christendom.[63] Unlike a petty backwater king who requires a daughter-in-law of high lineage to reinforce the dignity of his own, the emir of Babylon *confers* status on all the people and objects around him.[64] In retrospect, Felix's failure to recognize Blancheflor's worth exposes him as an outsider to the "closely knit international court culture" of the tributary Mediterranean.[65]

The emir's palace is also, however, the site of a horrific ritual combining the "evil custom" typical of romance with the Oriental despotism of the *Thousand and One Nights*.[66]

The emir's custom is to keep a wife for one whole year and no longer. Then he sends for his kings and dukes, whom he has behead her. He doesn't want any cleric or knight to have the woman he has had. (1965–71)

(Li amirals tel costume a
que une feme o lui tenra
un an plenier et noient plus,
puis mande ses rois et ses dus;
dont liu fera le cief trencier.
Ne veut que clerc ne chevalier
ait la feme qu'il a eüe.)

For all its extravagance, the emir's Bluebeard-like rapacity is oddly tempered: surrounded by one hundred forty nubile maids, the emir weds and beds only one at a time—an astonishing example of serial polygamy. Ostensibly an example of oriental violence and excess, the emir's evil custom in fact offers a perverse "solution" to one of the problems confronting the twelfth-century nobility: how to manage its feudal politics of lineage in the face of the church's increasing insistence on the indissolubility of marriage. Before the Gregorian reforms, nobles made and unmade marriages with relative ease. By the mid-twelfth century, however, such serial polygamists were targets of censure or even excommunication. In the grim logic behind the emir's nightmarish practice, wives one can no longer repudiate are dispatched by more radical means. Furthermore, by preventing any other man from possessing one of his cast-off wives, he avoids the dilemma faced by Louis VII of France, who divorced Eleanor of Aquitaine only to see her wed his vassal and chief rival, the future Henry II of England.[67] Instead, murder offers him a perverse resolution to the genealogical impasse posed by new ecclesiastical restrictions on marriage.[68]

The second half of the emir's annual custom consists of a remarkable ceremony that combines the Fatimid caliph's ritual review of his treasures with the dynamics of a Byzantine brideshow.[69] Each year, the one hundred forty girls in the emir's harem process through the beautiful gardens surrounding the Tower of Maidens. Through a kind of "natural" selection, the one on whom a magical tree sheds its flowers and leaves is designated the emir's new bride. Nature's will, it turns out, is in complete harmony with his own: "if there's a girl with him whom he loves best and is the most beautiful, he wills the flower to fall on her, by enchantment" (2089–92) (se il a o soi pucele / que il miex aime et soit plus bele, / sor li fait par encantement / la flor caïr a son talent). This year, the emir makes clear, his choice will fall on Blancheflor—the prerogative of a privileged collector.

* * *

A treasury and harem, the Tower of Maidens is also a protected inner sanctum, a liminal site where distinctions break down and fundamental categories of identity are called into question. Within its confines, the illegitimate captive mingles on equal footing with the daughter of Latin Christendom's most exalted ruler—their bond expressed in the same language of reciprocal love and togetherness earlier used to describe the bond between Floire and Blancheflor:

She was Blancheflor's companion; she was the king of Germany's daughter. The two *loved each other* very much; *together* they attended the emir. She was the most beautiful of all the girls in the tower—after Blancheflor. (2357–62, emphasis added)

> (Ele ert a Blanceflor compaigne;
> fille estoit au roi d'Alemaigne.
> Elle les .II. molt *s'entramoient,*
> *ensanle* a l'amirail aloient.
> La plus bele estoit de la tour
> de toutes, aprés Blanceflor.)

Previously rejected by Felix as "a poor creature of low station" (1078) (povre cose de bas endroit), Blancheflor now surpasses the German princess in beauty and equals her in gentility.

Symbolic center of the emir's realm, the Tower of Maidens is guarded by a "doorkeeper" (2197) (uissier)—a liminal figure mediating between the external world of mercantile exchange and the interior world of transgressive desires.[70] To gain entry to the tower, Floire engages this porter in a game of chess. The choice is overdetermined: besides being a stylized form of combat,[71] chess—and chess pieces—belong to the shared culture of objects circulating around the medieval Mediterranean.[72] In the Latin Christian world, moreover, chess frequently evokes contexts of cross-cultural contact—like the chess players depicted on the Islamic-style *muqarnas* ceiling of the Norman king Roger II of Sicily's Palatine Chapel in Palermo, or the two crusaders shown playing chess in their tent in a thirteenth-century manuscript illumination of William of Tyre's *Historia rerum in partibus transmarinis gestarum* while a battle between Christians and Saracens rages above their heads.[73] In *Floire*, chess provides a forum for intense negotiation. At first, the doorkeeper accuses our protagonist of being "a spy or a traitor" (2199) (espie u traïtour); to deflect his suspicion, Floire first claims to be an architect studying the structure in order to build one like it in his own land, then accepts his invitation to a game of chess.

As they play, the porter covetously eyes Floire's niello goblet and offers to buy it. This is the opportunity Floire has been looking for: "I'll *give* it to you for love," he says, "for it will be *repaid*, if ever you see me in need" (2234–36, emphasis added) (par amor le vos *donrai*, / por çou qu'il m'ert *gerredonés* / se mon besoing ja mais veés). Speaking the language of gift (*don*) and countergift (*guerredon*), Floire seeks to bind his interlocutor in a system of reciprocal obligation.[74] The gatekeeper responds with a spontaneous offer of feudal obedience:

He falls at his feet, offering his homage; Floire accepts it, doing the smart thing. The porter pledges that, for love, he will serve him as his lord; he could be sure of that: never would his pledge be violated. (2243–48)

> (As piés li ciet, offre s'oumage;
> Flores le prent, si fait que sage.
> Cil fiance que par amor[75]
> le servira comme signor,
> de çou soit il seürs et fis
> que j'a n'en iert fais contredis.)

When Floire calls in his *guerredon*, enlisting the new vassal's aid in reaching Blancheflor, the gatekeeper is understandably dismayed: "The porter heard him and was astounded; he felt himself grievously tricked: 'I've been duped,' he said, 'it's true! your treasure deceived me'" (2261–64) (Li portiers l'ot, molt s'esbahi, / forment se tint a escarni: / "Engigniés sui," dist il, "c'est voirs! / Deceü m'a li vostre avoirs"). Still, he cannot escape the inexorable logic of the gift: "But that's the way it is; I can't do anything about it. You've snared me, and I can't escape" (2267–68) (Mais ensi est k'el n'en puis faire, / lacié m'avés, n'en puis retraire).

The doorkeeper's capitulation triggers a wholesale collapse of difference, beginning with the distinction between the literal and the figurative. Capitalizing on the metaphorical possibilities of his name, Floire gains entry into the Tower of Maidens hidden in a basket of flowers, "camouflaged" by a bright red shirt that matches the color of the blossoms. When the basket is misdelivered to Gloris instead of Blancheflor, the German princess immediately falls in with the conceit: "Blancheflor, dear friend, do you want to see a beautiful flower—one that I think you'll love when you see it? There aren't any flowers like it in this land" (2375–79) (Bele compaigne Blanceflor, / volés vos veoir bele flor / et tele que molt amerés, / mon essient, quant le verrés? / Tel flor n'a nule en cest païs). Seeing the flowers, Blancheflor, who has just been despairing over her impending marriage to the emir, is suddenly transfigured with happiness—leaving Gloris knowingly to remark: "This *flower* is very powerful to cure such great pain so quickly" (2431–32, emphasis added) (Grant vertu a icele *flors*, / qui si tost taut si grans dolors).[76] Safe within the tower, Floire and Blancheflor enjoy a brief idyll, described with just enough poetic ambiguity to justify Floire's later protestation of the innocence of their tryst: "they had as much joy as they wished, happily taking their pleasure" (2285–86) (orent joie a lor talent, / si se deduisent l'ïement).

Two weeks later, however, Floire and Blancheflor are found sleeping together in circumstances that trigger a new round of confusion in the play of equivalences. A chamberlain sent to summon Blancheflor reports finding her and *Gloris* lying "mouth to mouth and face to face" (2599) (bouce a bouce et face a face). Why this mistake? "Because," the narrator explains, "Floire had no beard on his face and chin, nor any visible moustache: in the tower there was no maiden fairer of face" (2585–88) (K'a face n'a menton n'avoit / barbe, ne grenons n'i paroit: / en la tor n'avoit damoisele / qui de visage fust plus bele). When earlier observers mistook Floire and Blancheflor for siblings, their misprision blurred differences of rank and religion. Here, the confusion between Floire and Gloris blurs divisions of religion and gender. At first, the emir scoffs at his chamberlain's report—not because he finds the prospect of two girls sleeping together impossible but because he has just seen Gloris and knows it cannot have been she. Thus, he reasons, it must be "some man" (2606) (aucuns) in bed with his intended. But going to see for himself, he, too, is stymied by Floire's constitutive lack: "on his face, there was no indication he was a man, for he had neither beard nor moustache on his chin" (2638–40) (En son vis nul sanlant n'avoit / qu'il fut hom, car a son menton / n'avoit ne barbe ne grenon).

In other contexts, Floire's lack of facial hair might signify his extreme youth—the protagonists having just been described as "children" (2625)—or even his "westernness" in comparison to easterners (Muslim and Christian alike) for whom beards were "the glory of the face, the chief dignity of man."[77] In this primal scene, however, the confusion between Floire and Gloris produces a "touch of the queer" typical of the indeterminacy pervading this text.[78] By a complex syllogistic logic at this unstable nexus of religion, status, and gender, if Blancheflor is more beautiful than Gloris, then she is also more beautiful (and thus, within the aesthetic economy of the harem, more valuable) than Floire, the prince she had earlier been deemed unworthy to marry. The confusion is quickly and dramatically resolved, however, when the emir orders the sleeping lovers stripped. Facial hair, it turns out, is not Floire's only lack:

"Uncover the chests of the two girls," says he to the chamberlain. "First we'll see their breasts, then we'll wake them." The latter uncovered them: it became apparent that it was a man lying there. [The emir] is so upset he is speechless. (2647–53)

> ("Descoevre," fait il, "les poitrines,"
> au cambrelenc, "des .II. mescines;
> les mameles primes verrons
> et puis si les esvillerons."
> Cil les descoevre, s'aparut
> que cil est hom qui illuec jut.
> Tel duel en a ne pot mot dire.)

This "discovery" reduces the fearsome Bluebeard to a hapless cuckold. When King Marc comes across Tristan sleeping with Iseut, he finds them in isolation in the middle of the forest. The emir, in contrast, makes his humiliating discovery in a bedchamber at the very heart of his court and capital. His initial impulse to slay Floire "immediately" (2654) (eneslepas) conforms to French customary law, which authorized a husband who caught his wife in flagrante delicto to slay the adulterous lovers on the spot.[79] Just as quickly, however, the emir's curiosity gets the better of him; like the sultan in *The Thousand and One Nights*, he cannot resist the desire to hear the adventure not of Blancheflor but of Floire. This stay of execution leads to the most remarkable transformation of all, the "Franking" of the Saracen emir.

* * *

At the outset, the emir's ability to command the presence of "every king who held land from him" (1372–73) (cascuns rois / qui de l'amiral terre tiennent) at his annual bride-choosing ritual is a mark of his tributary power: "Kings and emperors come, along with dukes, counts, and almaçours, filling the king's palace with his people, of his faith" (2697–2700) (Vienent roi et empereour, / et duc, et conte, et aumaçor. / Tous emplist li palais le roi / de sa gent qui sont de sa loi). Collecting vassal-kings as he collects beautiful women, the emir of Babylon reigns supreme, his power uncontested. After Floire and Blancheflor are discovered *in flagrante delicto*, however, this assembly of tributary vassals is transformed into something resembling a feudal council of barons. The seneschal's plea that the lovers be tried *before* their execution curiously combines an insistence on "due process" with the assumption that the princes' verdict—like that of the bride-choosing—will automatically reflect the emir's will: "don't kill them until your people have judged them; then kill them *through judgment*" (2686–88, emphasis added) (nes ociés mie / tant que jugié l'aient vo gent, / ses ociés *par jugement*). What *jugement* might mean still remains to be determined. The emir bases his case on his rights of ownership, demonstrated in Blancheflor's enormous purchase price: "I bought a maiden; I paid a great amount of gold for her: seven times her weight" (2715–16, 2718) (une pucele . . . acatai./ . . . / Grant masse d'or por li donai: /. . . . VII. fois son pois). He asks his vassals to avenge his shame, *par jugement* (2748). But at this point the trial that began as a mere formality takes on a life of its own. One king rises to his feet and says that having heard the emir, they must now listen to Floire: "The way I see it, to accuse him without allowing him a response is not due process" (2757–58) (De l'encouper, si com j'entent, / sans respons n'est pas jugement). Another, however, disagrees:

There too was Lord Ylier, the strong and proud king of Nubia.[80] "Lord king," he says, "by the faith I owe you, I don't concede any part of this. If my lord seized him in the act, he would have every right to kill him; for if one catches *a thief* in the act, one owes him no appeal. As he openly commits his crime, he should die without trial." (2759–68, emphasis added)

> (De l'autre part est dans Yliers
> rois de Nubie fors et fiers:
> "Dans rois," fait il, "foi que vos doi,
> del tot en tot pas ne l'otroi.
> Se me sire el forfait le prist,
> grant droit eüst que l'ocesit,
> que s'on prent *larron* el forfait,
> vers lui ne doit avoir nul plait.
> Ses mesfais mostre apertement,
> morir l'estuet sans jugement.")

As in French customary law, this argument turns on Floire's having been apprehended in flagrante delicto—not as an adulterer but as a thief who has robbed the emir of his honor. Convinced by the king of Nubia's words, the vassal-kings render a unanimous verdict condemning both Floire and Blancheflor to death. In contrast to the judgment of Ganelon at the end of the *Chanson de Roland*, the trial by jury produces a capital sentence reflecting the ruler's desire.

As the lovers are led to the stake, however, the jurors begin to have second thoughts. Influenced, as it seems, by the protagonists' beauty (to which the text devotes eighty lines), "they would very willingly have overturned the verdict, had they dared" (2917–18) (Molt volentiers dont trestornaissent / le jugement se il osassent). At first, the emir remains implacable, unmoved by the lovers' efforts to plead for each other's lives, debating the fine points of intention, prior knowledge, and motive. But when, facing immediate death, Floire and Blancheflor each vies to be killed before the other, even the emir drops his sword in hesitation. As "pity" (2994, 2995, 3000, 3002, 3004) (pitié) contends with justice, a sympathetic duke steps in with a face-saving expedient: " 'Lords,' he says, '*we all ought to counsel our lord* in this suit in a way that would bring him honor . . . What would people say if he killed him? It's not very praiseworthy, in my opinion!' " (3010–12, 3019–20). ("Signor," fait il, "*bien deverions / tot consillier a no signor* / de cest plait qu'il fust a s'onor . . . / Et que dira on s'il l'ocit? / N'est pas grant los, si com je cuit!") Evoking the vassalic obligation to *consilium*, the duke retroactively recodes the emir's moment of hesistation as the deliberation of a just feudal lord. Let the emir discover the "trick" (3016, 3029) (engien) used to gain access to the tower, he advises, the better to prevent such intrusions in the future. With one voice, the vassal-kings endorse the wisdom of this plan.[81]

All of them said: "It's a good thing to do! Grant it them, noble king!" Thus all of them asked for mercy; and when the king heard them, *not wanting to contradict them all*, he pardoned [the lovers], doing the noble thing. All the barons thanked him and greatly praised him. (3073–80, emphasis added)

> (Tot escrient: "Boin est a faire!
> Otroie lor, roi deboinaire!"
> Ensi prient trestot merci;
> et quant li rois les a oï
> *nes vaut pas contredire tous,*
> pardone lor, si fait que prous.
> Tot li baron l'en mercïerent
> et de cel fait molt le loerent.)

Staying Floire's execution, the emir is transformed. Having opted for mercy over vengeance—for the counsel of his vassals over autocratic will—he now listens, entranced, to the tale of Floire's adventures, sharing a laugh over the ruse of the basket of flowers and spontaneously providing his own happy ending:

And the king acted honorably: with everyone watching, he took Floire's hand and then did *a very Frankish thing*: he took Blancheflor by the hand and then took Floire's hand again. Then he spoke *in a Frankish fashion*: "I give you back your friend," he said. (3109–15, emphasis added)

> (Et li rois a fait molt que prous,
> Flore a le main prist voiant tous
> et aprés a fait *grant francise,*
> par le main a Blanceflor prise
> et Flore par le main reprent.
> Aprés a parlé *frankement*:
> "Je vos rent, fit il, vostre amie.")

In standard translations, the words "franc[h]ise" and "frankement" are typically rendered as "nobility" (or "freedom") and "nobly," respectively.[82]

Returning the words to their etymological root, on the other hand, gives us the incongruous spectacle of the emir of Babylon conducting himself, literally, "like a Frank." Swept up in the spirit of the moment, he not only pardons Floire but knights him and gives him Blancheflor as his bride: "he has them taken to church and has [Floire] marry his sweetheart" (3124–25) (mener les fait a un mostier, / s'amie li fait espouser). In an exemplary act of generosity, the emir bestows a prized piece from his collection on a provincial petitioner.

The most dramatic transformation, however, is still to come. At Blancheflor's suggestion, the emir marries Gloris—announcing, moreover, that he will keep her for life:

The emir grants them that he will keep her his/her whole life. Gloris showed great joy; drawing close to Blancheflor, she kisses her sweetly 100 times. The emir takes her by the hand: he has her wear a golden crown and causes her to be honored as his wife. (3135–42)

> (li amirals lor otrie
> qu'il le tenra tote sa vie.
> Gloris molt grant joie en a fait,
> vers Blanceflor adont se trait,
> .c. fois le baise doucement.
> L'amirals par le main le prent,
> corone d'or li fait porter
> et comme s'oissor honerer.)

The abolition of iniquitous customs is a standard feature in the romances of Chrétien de Troyes, where the protagonist ends a baleful ritual (like the Joie de la Cort in *Erec et Enide* or Pesme Avanture in *Le Chevalier au Lion*) by defeating the knight or malevolent being upholding it. Here, in contrast, the emir *voluntarily* abandons his serial polygamy (though we are not told what happens to his previous wife) and contracts a new union in perfect accord with the reformist insistence on the indissolubility of marriage. Inspired by the perfect love between Floire and Blancheflor, the "Franking" of the pagan emir thus culminates in two cross-confessional marriages: the Saracen prince of "Naples" weds his Christian sweetheart, while the emir himself marries the German king's daughter Gloris.[83] At the very moment crusaders were setting their sights on Fatimid Egypt, *Floire et Blancheflor* attributes the "conquest" of Babylon not to Latin Christendom's military might but to the exceptional beauty of its women.

The "happy ending" triggered by the emir's generosity comes to fruition when word arrives of the death of Felix and his queen. Declining the emir's offer of a rich kingdom, gold crown, and high court honors if only he will remain,[84] Floire eagerly sets out for home, his grief over his parents' death vying with his delight over his marriage to Blancheflor. As in *Aucassin et Nicolette*, the disappearance of the older generation seems to announce a new youthful regime of love and cross-cultural tolerance. But then, inverting the epic conclusion of the conversion of the Saracen queen, *Floire*—in a surprising and unmotivated move—ends with the conversion of the Saracen *king*, as Floire suddenly decides to embrace Blancheflor's faith:

Floire had himself christened and afterward crowned king. For the sake of Blancheflor, his friend, he subsequently led a Christian life. He had with him three archbishops of the Christian faith. They blessed his crown and piously baptised him. (3301–8)

(Flores se fait crestïener
et aprés a roi coroner.
Por Blanceflor, la soie amie,
mena puis crestiiene vie.
.III. archevesques ot o soi
qui sont de crestiiene loi.
Sa corone li presignierent
et saintement le baptisierent.)

Together with the "Franking" of the emir of Babylon, Floire's transformation *par amur* redounds to the glory of Christianity and affirms the victory of feudal Europe. But where the symbolic power of Orable and Bramimonde's conversions lay in their singularity, Floire—in an early example of *cuius regio, eius religio*—insists on the conversion of all his people as well.[85] His barons, like good vassals, readily obey: "be sure that few delayed, on account of their lord, who asked it of them" (3319–20) (saciés que peu en demora, / por lor signor qui lor pria). The common people, however, are another matter, and Floire grants no quarter to those who resist: "If anyone refused baptism or didn't want to believe in God, Floire had him flayed, burned at the stake, or dismembered" (3323–26) (Qui le baptesme refusoit / ne en Diu croire ne voloit, / Flores les faisoit

escorcier, / adroir en fu u detrencier). This zero-tolerance policy has little
to do with either the easy *convivencia* formerly practiced at Felix's court
or the historical practices of the Spanish Reconquest.[86] Instead, it recalls
(or rather, by the logic of the prequel, anticipates) the closing scenes of
the *Chanson de Roland*, where Charlemagne's troops ravage the mosques
and synagogues of Saragossa, "hanging, burning or killing" all those refusing conversion (3660–70). Strikingly at odds with the rest of the text,
this conclusion functions as a radical palinode, as if retroactively compensating for *Floire et Blancheflor*'s audacious cultural politics. *Floire* seems to
return to the worldview that "pagans are wrong and Christians are right."

*   *   *

What are we to make of this stunning turnaround? Medieval culture,
as we are starting increasingly to recognize, is filled with artifacts susceptible of delivering different messages to different audiences.[87] Perhaps our
text is just such a polysemous object. For listeners fired by an ideology of
crusade and conquest, Floire's conversion provides a satisfying conclusion,
recuperating the text's otherwise disturbing destabilization of fundamental
categories of faith, class, and gender. As the father of Berthe aux Grands
Pieds, Floire transmits to Charlemagne a hereditary claim to rule a Chris-
tianized Spain—resignifying Charlemagne's battle for Saragossa as part of
a specifically dynastic reconquest.[88] Conversely, the story of Floire and
Blancheflor simultaneously attributes to Christendom and to Charlemagne
himself a complexity uncontainable within the bounds of "a medieval Europe of simple paternity and unambiguous truths and meanings."[89] Sold as
a slave and trafficked overseas, Blancheflor materializes modalities of encounter and exchange that gesture toward another kind of civilizational
history—one that replaces the linear history of *translatio* and the exclu-
sionary history of discrete national traditions with narratives of deviance
and transgression: of pilgrimages gone astray and plots that swerve unpre-
dictably from Santiago to Cairo, mapping cultural networks that confound
the simple binarism of Roland's preemptive pronouncement that "pagans
are wrong and Christians are right." By making visible this world of alternate flows and desires, *Floire et Blancheflor* reminds us that the dividing
line between what we are tempted to call "East" and "West" was in fact
"thoroughly permeable . . . even in situations of conflict," and that "cultural histories apparently utterly distinct, and traditionally kept entirely
separate, are ripe to be rewritten as shared East/West undertakings."[90]

4

Colonial Possessions

Wales and the Anglo-Norman Imaginary in the Lais *of Marie de France*

IN CHAPTER 3 THE IBERIAN SETTING OF *Floire et Blancheflor* served as the starting point for an alternate vision of *translatio*, displacing our focus from feudal Europe toward the mercantile Mediterranean. In this chapter, I read the Welsh setting of two *lais* of Marie de France as what Mary Louise Pratt calls a contact zone: an area of "the spatial and temporal copresence of subjects previously separated by geographic and historical disjunctures, whose trajectories now intersect" in ways that reveal "the interactive, improvisational dimensions of colonial encounters so easily ignored or suppressed by diffusionist accounts of conquest and domination."[1]

Though illicit love is central to medieval romance, these adulterous affairs rarely result in illegitimate children. Adulterous queens like Iseut and Guenevere remain barren because, in a society so strongly based in genealogical politics, the threat of illegitimacy was regarded as "too serious to be treated lightly in literature."[2] The *lais* of Marie de France, however, present two exceptions: "Yonec," the classic tale of a *mal-mariée* who finds solace with a lover who comes to her in the form of a bird; and "Milun," in which an unmarried maid takes a poor but valiant knight as her lover. Each affair results in the birth of a son who grows up to vindicate the secret love shared by his parents. Despite variations in plot and tone, these two *lais* dare to imagine what more traditional romance cannot: the genealogical consequences of *fin'amor*. In "Yonec" and "Milun," the birth of an illegitimate son is the point where courtly desire runs up against the limits of the feudal politics of lineage.[3]

Why these exceptions? The answer, I suggest, lies in the other thing the two *lais* have in common. Both are set in South Wales: "Yonec" in Caerwent and Caerleon, and "Milun" in "South Wales" (Suhtwales) as well as on the Continent.[4] Generally, this setting has been ignored or, at best, taken as adding a touch of "local color."[5] Yet in the twelfth century, South Wales was a "contact zone" where the shared culture of post-Carolingian Europe met the so-called Celtic fringe which, though Christian, remained outside the bounds of this nascent imagined community. When the Normans arrived in the wake of their conquest of England, they found a distinctive and, in their eyes, alien culture—pastoral, seminomadic, and highly decentralized, in contrast to the manorial and increasingly rationalized feudal system characteristic of eleventh-century Normandy. Clerics were particularly scandalized by indigenous marriage and inheritance practices, persistently condemning the Welsh for "taking a cavalier attitude towards the bonds of matrimony, choosing partners within the prohibited degrees, keeping mistresses, divorcing their wives, and treating legitimate and illegitimate children as equals."[6] Such customs had long been common in other parts of Latin Christendom as well. But as the reformist church began insisting on exogamy and the indissolubility of marriage, and as the feudal nobility began practicing primogeniture, Welsh traditions of endogamy, partible inheritance, and "trial marriage" came increasingly to exemplify Welsh deviance.

Recent criticism has suggested the relevance of postcolonial theory to the medieval Welsh context. Most such studies have centered on the work of Gerald of Wales (Giraldus Cambrensis), the twelfth-century author whose own lineage exemplified the hybridity of "Cambro-Norman" Wales.[7] But cross-cultural interactions are an abiding feature of Marie's *lais* as well, from the project of *translatio* thematized in the prologue to the bi- and trilingual titles given "Bisclavret" and "Laüstic."[8] In this chapter I read Marie's two Welsh *lais* as alternating visions of the colonial encounter. From the common plot of the illegitimate son who seeks out the biological father he has never known, "Yonec" and "Milun" present distinct visions of the relationship of the indigenous past to the Anglo-Norman present. In "Yonec," the *mal-mariée*'s dissent from the feudal politics of lineage is at once an erotic fantasy and an allegory of native resistance to colonial rule, figured as the romantic desire for a scion of the occluded civilization. In "Milun," traces of the conflict between colonizer and colonized are erased, giving way to a larger feudal world bound together by common chivalric practices. Customs associated with the feudal politics of lineage are represented as atavistic and, in the twenty years it takes the plot to unfold, displaced by the utopian vision of a new Cambro-Norman society based on conjugal love. As recent analyses have shown, colonial encounters are always messier than dominant ideologies imply. Beneath the surface of these two charming *lais*, Marie affords us a glimpse of the political and cultural complexity of post-conquest Wales.[9] We begin with a brief overview of that complexity.

* * *

The Norman colonization of Wales began soon after the conquest of 1066. In the river valleys of the southeast, progress was rapid: Norman knights quickly overwhelmed the lightly armed Welsh infantry. Like the Anglo-Saxons, however, they soon learned that Wales was easier to conquer than to hold. In the highlands, the mountainous terrain produced a fragmented and localized culture whose basic political unit was the kinship group (*tref*) and largest institutional structure the *commote*, ruled by a prince (*tywysog*) who held court (*llys*) in great timbered halls. Since anyone could become *tywysog* by overthrowing the incumbent, plotting and sedition were endemic. The same political fragmentation that made Wales so easy to conquer meant that (in contrast to Anglo-Saxon England) there were few institutions through which power could be exercised and maintained. Thus even the most crushing military victory could prove indecisive.[10] To compensate for the instability of the frontier, William the Conqueror created the Marcher earldoms of Chester, Shrewsbury, and Hereford, entrusted to loyal vassals given exceptional powers.[11] Still, colonization remained partial and uneven. Like the Anglo-Saxons before them, the Normans dominated the lowlands (well-suited to their manorial economies), building castles on the lands seasonally vacated by seminomadic indigenous pastoralists. Above six hundred feet, where Norman knights lost whatever advantages they otherwise enjoyed over Welsh archers and infantry, the highlands remained in native hands.[12]

At first, colonizers and colonized faced each other across a great cultural divide. In the late eleventh century, the Normans were in the vanguard of what historian Robert Bartlett has called "the making of Europe": the consolidation and diffusion of a set of institutions and practices, emerging in the heartland of the old Carolingian empire, that included a standardized Roman liturgy, the international religious orders, the minting of coins, court chanceries, the use of the Carolingian miniscule, universities, and chivalry—even the preference for universal Christian names (like John or Henry) over local ones (like Duncan or Pribislaw).[13] As these institutions and practices became increasingly normative, cultural differences and misunderstandings arose between groups like the Normans and those, like the Welsh, who were indisputably Christian but not yet (in Bartlett's sense) "European." To Norman knights accustomed to open-field skirmishes, the highlanders' reliance on infantry and guerrilla warfare was literally unchivalrous. Clerical marriages and inheritable ecclesiastical benefices were "calculated to give deep offence to anyone conversant with the norms and teaching of the post-Gregorian church."[14] As is often the case, markings of difference clustered around perceived sexual transgressions: Welsh practices of endogamy, concubinage, trial marriages, and the inheritance rights accorded to illegitimate children provided ready-made targets for Anglo-Norman nobles and churchmen.

At the same time, the conquest brought colonizer and colonized together in a shared process of accommodation and acculturation. At the highest social levels, their disparate systems were, in a sense, superimposed: Marcher lords began behaving like native princes (*twysogion*), while *twysogion* became royal vassals.[15] Henry I (ruled 1100–35) established feudal ties with native Welsh princes to curb the power of his father's border earls; "overlordship" became a flexible means of controlling geographically distant areas where "existing patterns of authority were fluid."[16] Meanwhile, communication was facilitated by professional interpreters (*cyfarwyddiadid* and latimers)—often high-ranking men granted fiefs in exchange for their service.[17] By the mid-twelfth century, the two systems had begun to merge: several generations of alliances and intermarriage had produced a hybrid Cambro-Norman elite, exemplified by the historian Gerald of Wales.[18]

When Henry I died, however, native princes capitalized on the succession wars between Mathilda and Stephen to revive the kingdoms of Gwynedd (north-northwest Wales), Powys (center-east), and Deheubarth (south). In Welsh political geography, these traditional kingdoms existed in name only; with no permanent institutional structures to support them, they "expanded, contracted, fragmented, and even disappeared, as military fortunes ebbed and flowed."[19] Any strong and charismatic *tywysog* might claim the title of king. In the tenth century the king of Deheubarth, Hywel Dda (d. 950), even succeeded in uniting all of Wales. Once the king died or was overthrown, however, his kingdom simply disappeared. The obverse was that when conditions were once again favorable—as they were during the political turmoil of the Norman wars of succession—such kingdoms could suddenly reappear, as if by magic.[20]

When Henry II became king in 1154, he assiduously set out to re-cover the royal prerogatives wielded by his grandfather, Henry I. Among these was control over Welsh marcher barons and native princes alike.[21] Early in his reign, Henry (sometimes identified as the "nobles reis" to whom Marie dedicated her *lais*) was faced with numerous native revolts, particularly by Rhys ap Gruffydd—the formidable "Lord Rhys" who be-came king of Deheubarth (South Wales) in 1155.[22] Lands Henry captured from the Welsh were returned to their hereditary Anglo-Norman lords. In 1171, however, Henry inaugurated a new policy, naming Rhys justiciar for South Wales as part of a new balance of power between the Marcher lords and the native princes of *pura Wallia*.[23] Through all these shifts, Caerleon (where the conclusion of "Yonec" is set) remained, as we shall see, a site of particular contest.

This political turmoil notwithstanding, the kaleidoscope of shifting power relations had produced "a distinctive Cambro-Norman society. . . . [n]either purely Welsh nor wholly Norman."[24] South Wales, where Anglo-Norman colonization was heaviest, emerged as a "social space of subaltern encounters" in which geopolitically distinct peoples "manufac-ture new relations, hybrid cultures, and multiple-voiced aesthetics."[25] The communities that grew around Anglo-Norman settlements were cultur-ally diverse, but faced a "chronic lack of manpower, the necessity of ac-commodating large numbers of native Welsh within the social order, the constant threat of encroachments by unconquered Welsh tribesmen, the desire not to stray too far from the mainstream of life of Anglo-Norman society, the desire to prevent royal and ecclesiastical domination, the goal of exploiting the frontier through further conquests."[26] Meanwhile, in the castles of the Welsh Marches, French, Welsh and English minstrels came together in a cultural mix exemplified in the trilingual prologue to "Laüstic." The result was the matter of Britain: Celtic (hi)stories "trans-lated" into Latin by Geoffrey of Monmouth, and then into Old French by Wace, Marie de France, and Chrétien de Troyes.[27]

In the opening scene of Chrétien de Troyes's *Conte du Graal*, Perce-val encounters five knights who perceive him through the standard tropes of the Norman imaginary. In their eyes, "gallois" is synonymous with rus-tic, and Perceval's ignorance of courtly forms is a natural consequence of his "ethnicity": "All Welshmen are, by nature, more irrational than ani-mals in the field" (243–44) (Galois sont tuit par nature / Plus fol que bestes an pasture). When Perceval later sets out for court, his mother persuades him to leave two of his three javelins behind, "because it looked too Welsh" (609) (Por ce que trop sanblast Galois).[28] Marie, in contrast, transforms such denunciations of Welsh difference into visions of the multiform ways the Celtic past haunts the Cambro-Norman present. In "Yonec" and "Milun," transgressive aspects of Welsh sexuality provide not simply variants on the plot of courtly love but meditations on the complexity of twelfth-century Cambro-Norman relations.

"Yonec"

In the guise of a conventional tale of courtly love, "Yonec" narrates a crisis in the feudal politics of lineage. As the story opens, the aged advocate of Caerwent takes a wife, explicitly "to have children who would be his heirs" (19–20) (pur enfanz aveir, / Ki aprés lui fuissent si heir). He chooses a young and beautiful girl of noble birth, but after their marriage he grows jealous and locks her in a tower, where she pines away under the guard of his old widowed sister:

He kept her like this *more than seven years.* They never had any children, nor did she ever leave that tower, neither for family nor for friends. (37–40, emphasis added)

> (Issi la tint *plus de set anz.*
> Unques entre eus n'eurent enfanz
> Ne fors de cele tur n'eissi,
> Ne pur parent ne pur ami.)

One day she suddenly starts dreaming of the way things used to be, when beautiful ladies took handsome lovers. Wishing that she, too, might enjoy such an adventure, she is startled when a magnificent hawk (*ostur*) flies in through the window, turns into a handsome knight, and pledges her his love. The two conduct a secret affair, with the bird-man, Muldumarec, appearing to the lady whenever she wishes. Soon, however, her new radiance triggers her husband's suspicions; he lays a trap, catching and wounding the bird-man. Dying, Muldumarec tells his sweetheart she is pregnant with their son, Yonec, who will some day avenge them. Then he flees. She follows, tracking him through a magical landscape to a great castle within a fabulous walled city. Inside, her dying lover gives her a ring

to erase her husband's memory and a sword to give their son when he is
grown. Returning to Caerwent, the lady bears a son—a handsome, brave,
strong, and generous youth whom the advocate rears as his own. When it
is time for Yonec to be knighted, all three journey to Caerleon for the
feast of Saint Aaron. In the castle's abbey, they are shown the magnificent
tomb of a former king of the land who, they are told, was killed in Caerwent "for the love of a lady" (522) (Pur l'amur d'une dame ocis). The lady
reveals that the king was Yonec's father, then falls dead in a swoon. Grab-
bing Muldumarec's sword, Yonec kills his stepfather—thus avenging his
mother's sorrow. In this version of a happily-ever-after ending, Yonec is
acclaimed king of the land.

That the advocate should marry "to have children" (19) (pur enfanz
aveir") is perfectly understandable. Nowhere was the feudal politics of lineage more important than in Wales where, during the twelfth century, several major earldoms established by William the Conqueror twice passed,
"through marriage or gift," to new lineages when ruling families failed in
the male line.[29] Such marriages—contracted for political advantage—took
little account of personal inclinations. (The disastrous ending of Marie de
France's "Equitan" serves as a cautionary tale to anyone foolish enough to
value elective affinities over genealogical expediency.[30]) From the late
eleventh century, such dynastic politics were threatened (admittedly more
in theory than in practice) by reformist churchmen's insistence that marriage could be contracted only with the consent of both partners.[31] In
"Yonec," the lady is clearly married in the old fashion, shared by the
Anglo-Norman and Celtic kin nobility alike.[32] Later, when she finally
breaks her silence, she rails first against those who had "given" her to the
old man in marriage: "A curse on my family, and on all the others who
gave me to this jealous man, who married me bodily!" (81–84) (Maleeit
seient *mi parent / E li autre communalment /* Ki a cest gelus me donerent
/ E de sun cors me marïerent!). Her powerlessness in her marriage is
pointedly contrasted to the agency she exercises in her secret affair with
Muldumarec, where she only has to think of him for him to appear. The
advocate, for his part, is caught between the feudal politics of lineage and
the church's increasing insistence on the indissolubility of marriage. Dynastic expediency might dictate that he repudiate his childless wife, but reformist churchmen would threaten him with excommunication if he did.

In "Yonec," however, the familiar courtly plot of the *mal-mariée* is
inflected by its Welsh setting. By the late twelfth century, the "heroic days

of conquest and colonization" had given way to a distinctive Marcher society governed by its own law and custom.[33] Nevertheless, certain Welsh
marriage and inheritance patterns persisted—among them the tradition of
trial marriage. The law code of Hywel Dda (assembled under Rhys ap
Gruffyd in the late twelfth century and recorded in the early thirteenth)
stipulated that marriages became fully official only after seven years.[34] This
is echoed in Gerald of Wales's report that the Welsh "will only marry a
woman after living with her for some time, thus making sure that she will
make a suitable wife, in disposition, moral qualities *and the ability to bear
children.*"[35] The impulse to judge a marriage's success in genealogical
terms was of course common among Latin Europe's ruling elite. But as
reformist churchmen began insisting ever more stringently on the indissolubility of marriage, it was easy for the Anglo-Norman clergy to
take trial marriages, along with other Welsh customs, as proof of their
deviance.[36]

After seven childless years, the advocate's marriage clearly counts as
a failure. In courtly terms, the couple's sterility confirms the unnaturalness of their May–December union. In the Welsh context, a man who
had married expressly to have children would surely, after seven years,
be expected to dismiss the wife who had failed to provide them. The
lady, in turn, might plausibly have taken her loveless and barren marriage to the old *gelos* to be a terrible but temporary misfortune. But as
the seven-year deadline comes and goes, the advocate's failure to repudiate her marks him as either remarkably compliant with reformist church
dictates or unusually uxorious, sacrificing genealogical expediency to a
possessiveness now overtly pathological. Little wonder if the lady, newly
deprived of all hope of liberation, chooses this moment to break her
silence:

"Alas," she says, "that I was ever born! My fate is very hard. I'm imprisoned in
this tower and I'll never get out of here except by dying. What is this jealous old
man afraid of that he keeps me so imprisoned? He's completely mad and out of
his senses! They always fear being betrayed!" (67–74)

("Lasse," fait ele, "mar fui nee!
Mut est dure ma destinee!
En ceste tur sui en prisun,
Ja n'en istrai par mort nun.
Cist vielz gelus, de quei se crient,

Qui en si grant prisun me tient?
Mut par est fous e esbaïz!
Il crient tuz jurs estre trahiz!")

Trapped in a loveless marriage, imprisoned by her jealous husband, abandoned by family and friends, the lady begins to dream compensatory
dreams of the way things used to be:

I've often heard that one could once *find* adventures in this land that brought relief to the unhappy. Knights might *find* young girls to their desire, noble and
lovely; and ladies *find* lovers so handsome, courtly, brave, and valiant that they
could not be blamed and no one else would see them. If that might be or ever
was, if that has ever happened to anyone, God, who has power over everything,
grant me my wish in this! (91–104, emphasis added)

(Mut ai sovent oï cunter
Que l'em suleit jadis *trover*
Aventures en cest païs
Ki rehaitouent les pensis.
Chevalier *trovoent* puceles
A lur talent, gentes e beles,
E dames *truvoent* amanz
Beaus e curteis, pruz e vaillanz,
Si que blasmees n'en esteient
Ne nul fors eles nes veeient.
Si ceo peot estrë e ceo fu,
Si unc a nul est avenu,
Deus, ki de tut ad poësté,
Il en face ma volenté!)

Like Marie de France herself, the lady has been listening to indigenous
tales of *aventure*; instead of *translating* them, however, she seeks to *relive*
them—her amorous aspirations linked to Marie's literary ones by the repetition of the verb *trover*. In her wistful evocation of the adventures "formerly found in this land," the desire for escape is fused with a nostalgia
for and sympathy with the indigenous past.

Welsh history provided spectacular examples of women exercising
sexual agency, like Nest—the daughter of Rhys ap Tewdwr (prince of Deheubarth) and maternal grandmother of Gerald of Wales. By her marriage
(c. 1100) to Gerald of Windsor, the Norman castellan of Pembroke, she

had three sons and a daughter (Gerald of Wales's mother, Angharad).[37] In the meantime, she also produced three illegitimate sons by three different fathers: Henry FitzHenry (by King Henry I of England), Robert FitzStephen (by Stephen, constable of Cardigan), and William FitzHai (by Hait, the sheriff of Pembroke).[38] The most dramatic episode in her sexual history, however, occurred in 1109, when she captured the attention of her second cousin, Owain of Powys. In a description reading less like history than romance, historian J. E. Lloyd recounts how Owain, having "heard much" of Nest's beauty,

resolved to pay a visit to the castle of Cenarth Bychan, where she was at the time in residence with her husband, and see with his own eyes the graces of form and feature which were the occasion of so much eloquence. He found them not a whit less marvellous than they were reported, and left the castle with the determination, in spite of all laws and regardless of risk, to become possessor of the fair one who had been not inaptly styled the "Helen of Wales." One dark night he and some fifteen companions stealthily worked their way into the stronghold by burrowing under the threshold of the gate; directly they were within the wall they rushed with wild cries upon the sleeping inmates and added to the alarm and confusion by setting fire to the buildings. By the advice of his wife, Gerald attempted no resistance, but made a hurried escape through a garderobe, thus the raiders found their task an easy one, and, having burnt and dismantled the castle, Owain carried off Nest and her children to Ceredigion. The story suggests that the heroine did not play an altogether unwilling part in the affair; at any rate, she did not disdain afterwards to use her influence over her lover to bring about the return of Gerald's children to their father's roof. None the less, the outrage was a challenge to the king, of which Henry [I] did not fail to take prompt notice.[39]

The political stakes here are unmistakable. Inflamed by secondhand accounts of his cousin's beauty, the native Welsh prince launches a raid that results in the burning and destruction of a Norman castle and the flight of its garrison. Nest's complicity—the suspicion that she may not have played "an altogether unwilling part in the affair"—registers Anglo-Norman anxiety over both the political and sexual promiscuity of the native noblewomen through whom the new hybrid Cambro-Norman society was being produced. Owain and Nest's kinship, making any sexual relationship between them incestuous, further confirms Welsh deviance.[40] No wonder the outrage they generate touches not just Gerald of Pembroke, but the king and the whole Anglo-Norman colonial order.

For Marie's heroine, "adventure" arrives in the shape not of an ardent cousin who burrows under a wall but of a great bird that flies in the

window, morphs into "a handsome and noble knight" (115) (Chevaliers
bels e genz), and boldly declares his love:

I have loved you for a long time and desired you in my heart. I've never loved any
woman except you and will never love another. But I couldn't come to you or
leave my palace if you hadn't requested it. Now I can be your lover! (127–34)

> (Jeo vus ai lungement amee
> E en mun quor mut desiree;
> Unkes femme fors vus n'amai
> Ne jamés autre n'amerai.
> Mes ne poeie a vus venir
> Ne fors de mun paleis eissir,
> Si vus ne n'eüssez requis.
> Or puis bien estre vostre amis!)

Like Owain, he has nursed his passion from afar. His ability to come to
her, however, is entirely dependent on *her* will—completely reversing her
powerlessness in her marriage to the advocate. Taken by the bird-man's
beauty, she nevertheless hesitates on one important count:

She answered the knight and said she would make him her sweetheart, if he believed in God (and if their love were thus possible), for he was very handsome.
Never in her life had she seen such a handsome knight nor would she ever see one
as handsome. (137–44)

> (Le chevalier ad respundu
> E dit qu'ele en ferat sun dru,
> S'en Deu creïst e issi fust
> Que lur amur estre peüst,
> Kar mut esteit de grant beauté:
> Unkes nul jur de sun eé
> Si bel chevalier n'esgarda
> Ne jamés si bel ne verra.)

Ostensibly, she wants to prove to herself that Muldumarec (who has after
all just flown in the window) is a man and not a demon come to seduce
her. She is a good Christian: this much we know from her distress that her
husband's jealousy had prevented her from attending mass: "I can't go to

church nor hear God's service" (75–76) (Jeo ne puis al mustier venir / Ne le servise Deu oïr). Now she needs to know the handsome knight is a believer before she will grant him her love.

Within the colonial allegory, however, the lady's question may be read as an expression of skepticism concerning Welsh Christianity. As we have seen, Anglo-Norman churchmen coming to Wales in the wake of the conquest found much in the native church to "cause amazement and prompt condemnation." Religious life, like political life, was highly decentralized: each district had a mother church (*clas*) consisting of an abbot and a group of canons, many of whom married and transmitted their offices to their children. Bishoprics (essentially federations of daughter churches linked by their common cult of a local saint) were fluid, with no hierarchy or metropolitan structure. With no standardized usages and no diocesan structure, practices varied from "the excessive asceticism of the holy hermits to the secularism and corruption of monks scarcely distinguishable from the tribesmen about them."[41] For Norman churchmen, such idiosyncracies might be explained "in terms of isolation and archaism; at worst they had to be condemned as the deviations of a local church which had ignored the norms and categories of the church universal and surrendered itself entirely to the ethos and practices of a secular, aristocratic, and heroic society."[42] In response, they "Normanized" the Welsh church by literally reterritorializing it: the land was divided into parishes grouped into dioceses administered by Norman bishops subordinate to the archbishop of Canterbury. In South Wales, churches devoted to local saints were displaced by Benedictine abbeys dedicated to universal saints whose increasing popularity exemplified the "europeanization of Europe" and were frequently located "in the shadow of the new Norman castles" dominating the lowlands.[43] The ecclesiastical colonization of Wales, in other words, was as visible as and even more systematic than the political.

In this light, Muldumarec's declaration of faith reads not simply as assurance that he is no demon, but as a vindication of Welsh Christianity:

"Lady," he says, "you've spoken well. Not for anything would I wish for there to be any accusations, doubts or suspicions about me. I believe in the Creator who brought us out of the sorrow that our father Adam got us into by biting into the bitter apple; He is and will be and has always been life and light to sinners. If you don't believe me, ask for your chaplain . . . I will take your form and will receive the Lord's body; I will spell out my belief to you: nevermore will you doubt it!" (145–64)

("Dame," dit il, "vus dites bien.
Ne vodreie pur nule rien
Que de mei i ait acheisun,
Mescreauncë u suspesçun.
Jeo crei mut bien el Creatur,
Ki nus geta de la tristur
U Adam nus mist, nostre pere,
Par le mors de la pumme amere;
Il est e ert e fu tuz jurs
Vie e lumiere as pecheürs.
Si vus de ceo ne me creez,
Vostre chapelain demandez . . .
La semblance de vus prendrai,
Le cors Damedeu recevrai,
Ma creance vus dirai tute:
Ja mar de ceo serez en dute!")

In asserting that he is a good Christian, Muldumarec speaks not only for himself but for all his people, affirming the orthodoxy of an occluded indigenous culture sometimes suspected of being less than fully Christian. By offering to take communion in her place, he both assuages her fear and interpellates God as a witness and complacent supporter of their adulterous love; in assuming her own form, he embodies the possibility of transgressing the binary oppositions subjugating her to the possessive old *gelos*.[44]

In the adulterous tales of Tristan or Lancelot, the lady's illicit lover is a prominent member of her husband's court. In contrast, Muldumarec (like Lanval's fairy mistress) remains hidden, in accordance with the indigenous model of ladies who took lovers "no one else could see" (100) (nul fors eles nes veeient). But if he is invisible, *she* is not: her new radiance arouses her husband's suspicion, leading to his discovery of her secret affair. In Welsh tradition, a woman caught in adultery might hope for a happy resolution: "Goronwy ap Moriddig [author of a Welsh lawbook] used to say that a man who lies with another man's wife is not bound to pay anything while the woman approves the act; but if the deed becomes known, the woman should pay *sarhaed*, 'insult-price' to her husband, or else the husband may freely repudiate her and let her turn away from him."[45] The advocate, however, is not so complacent. Instead, he booby-traps his wife's window and snares the bird-man on his next visit. Though

mortally wounded, Muldumarec tells the lady not to grieve and, in a curious variation on the Annunciation,

He comforted her gently, said that sorrow would do no good, but that she was
pregnant with his child. She would have a son, brave and strong, who would comfort her; she would call him Yonec. He would avenge both of them and kill their
enemy. (325–32)

>   (Il la cunforte ducement
>   E dit que dols n'i vaut nïent:
>   De lui est enceinte d'enfant.
>   Un fiz avra, pruz e vaillant;
>   Icil la recunforterat.
>   Yönec numer le ferat.
>   Il vengerat e lui e li,
>   Il oscirat sun enemi.)

In asserting his paternity and instructing his mistress to name their son
Yonec, Muldumarec explicitly claims him for indigenous rather than
Anglo-Norman culture.[46] By cmerging European standards, the baby the
lady carries is feudal society's worst nightmare: an illegitimate child passed
off as her husband's son and heir—a scenario so explosive that, at we have
seen, romance writers typically refused to touch it.

In Wales, on the other hand, children born out of wedlock could be
legitimized for purposes of inheritance:

Welsh law differed fundamentally from the law of the Church and of England in that
it knew no sharp antinomy between legitimate and illegitimate children: what mat-
tered was a child's affiliation to his father. If the child's parents lived together, there
was a natural presumption in favour of paternity. If they did not, a formal procedure
of affiliation might be necessary: if successfully affiliated, a son born outside wedlock
in *llwyn a pherht*, "bush and brake," could inherit a share of his father's land.[47]

The contrast between Welsh and Anglo-Norman attitudes appears in a
colorful story Gerald of Wales tells about a Welsh princess named Nest
(granddaughter of Grufydd ap Llewelyn). Married to Bernard of Neufmarché, one of William's early Marcher barons,[48] Nest

fell in love with a certain knight, with whom she committed adultery. This
became known, and her son Mahel assaulted her lover one night when he was

returning from his mother. He gave him a severe beating, mutilated him and packed him off in great disgrace. The mother, disturbed by the remarkable uproar which ensued, and greatly grieved in her woman's heart, fled to Henry I, King of the English, and told him that her son Mahel was not Bernard's child, but the off-spring of another man with whom she had been in love and with whom she had had secret and illicit intercourse. This she maintained rather from malice than be-cause it was true, confirming by an oath which she swore in person before the whole court. As a result of this oath, which was really perjury, King Henry, who was swayed more by prejudice than by reason, gave Nest's eldest daughter, whom she accepted as Bernard's child, in marriage to a distinguished young knight of his own family, Milo FitzWalter, constable of Gloucester, adding the lands of Brec-knock as a marriage portion. Later on Milo was made Earl of Hereford by Matilda, Empress of Rome and daughter of Henry I.

In this astounding example of what Jeffrey Jerome Cohen calls the "de-ployment of Welshness," Nest admits not just to one lover but two, and falsely declares her *legitimate* son a bastard in order to disinherit him. Paradoxically, however, the main beneficiary is Henry I's kinsman, Milo FitzWalter: in the end, the perfidy and promiscuity of highborn Welsh ladies works to the advantage of the king.[49] Conversely, in "Yonec" our heroine returns home to bear her son, then lives "many days" (456) (meint di e meint jur) with her husband, creating the "natural presump-tion" that Yonec is his son, the heir he had specifically married to procure— not the illegitimate son of the ruler of a mysterious and occulted indigenous kingdom.

In his *Journey through Wales*, Gerald of Wales tells of a Swansea priest who as a young man had been taken by small people "through a dark un-derground tunnel and then into a most attractive country, where there were lovely rivers and meadows, and delightful woodlands and plains. It was rather dark, because the sun did not shine there. The days were all overcast."[50] When the heroine of "Yonec" jumps from her tower to pur-sue her wounded lover, the bloody trail leads her to just such an other-world:

She set out to track the blood that the knight was shedding on the road she was traveling. She wandered on this path and held to it until she came to a hill. There was an entrance in this hill that was wet with blood. She couldn't see anything ahead of her but she was convinced her lover had gone in. Hurriedly, she entered: she found no light within. She continued on the straight path until she exited the hill and came to a very beautiful field. She found the grass moist with blood, which distressed her a lot. She followed the track through the field. (342–59)

(A la trace del sanc s'est mise
Ki del chevalier degotot
Sur le chemin u ele alot.
Icel sentier errat e tint,
De si qu'a une hoge vint.
En cele hoge ot une entree,
De cel sanc fu tute arusee;
Ne pot nïent avant veeir.
Dunc quidot ele bien saveir
Que sis amis entrez i seit:
Dedenz se met a grant espleit.
El n'i trovat nule clarté.
Tant ad le dreit chemin erré
Que fors de la hoge est issue
E en un mut bel pré venue.
Del sanc trovat l'erbe moilliee,
Dunc s'est ele mut esmaiee.
La trace ensiut par mi le pré.)

On the other side she finds a walled city enclosing silver buildings, surrounded by marshes and a port harboring more than three hundred ships. Following the trail of blood to the inner chamber of the palace, the lady finds her dying lover. He gives her a ring to erase the advocate's memory and a sword that she is to pass on to their son when he is grown. Then he sends her home, back through the hill, to her own land.

Accessible only through the magical tunnel, Muldumarec's kingdom— like Gerald's magical realm—occupies nearly the same space as the prosaic world, as if in anamorphic alternation with it.[51] Later, Muldumarec's subjects relate that at his death, his kingdom had fallen into abeyance: "Since then we have had no lord, but have waited many days, just as he told and commanded us, for the son the lady bore him" (523–26) (Unques puis n'eümes seignur, / Ainz avum atendu meint jur / Un fiz qu'en la dame engendra, / Si cum il dist e cumanda). In feudal Europe, a kingdom thus held in abeyance would be a fantasy indeed: the death of a ruler without a legitimate heir was sure to produce a scramble for power among rival claimants. In Wales, on the other hand, such a disappearing kingdom evokes the transitory realms of the *twysogion*, ready to be revived by a new charismatic prince. Like Gwynedd or Deheubarth, Muldumarec's land disappears at his death, only to await a propitious moment to reemerge. Here the messianic overtones of the son's anticipated return merge with the geo-temporal "fluidity" of Wales's political geography.

In Marie's colonial tale, the Welsh king's illegitimate son becomes the perfect realization of Anglo-Norman chivalry. As Muldumarec had predicted, Yonec grows up to be "a brave and valiant knight" (426) (chevaliers pruz e vaillanz), an exemplar of courtly values: "In all the kingdom you couldn't find one so handsome, brave, or strong, so generous, so munificent" (462–64) (El regné ne pot hum trover / Si bel, si pruz ne si vaillant, / Si large ne si despendant).

The dénouement is set years later when the advocate, his wife, and son journey to Caerleon to celebrate the feast of Saint Aaron "according to the custom of the land" (474) (a la custume del païs). Strategically located at the crossing of the old Roman road and the Usk River, Caerleon was a significant site in both history and fiction. In the *Domesday* accounts of 1086, it marked the edge of the Norman frontier.[52] In the twelfth century, it was the center of the Anglo-Norman lordship of Caerleon-and-Usk, held by the earls of Pembroke.[53] During the wars following Henry I's death, the native prince Morgan ab Owain seized Usk castle and made Caerleon a Welsh lordship.[54] Though Henry II later reestablished control of the lowlands, upland Caerleon remained under native rule. Tensions remained acute.[55] In 1171, Henry took Caerleon castle from Morgan's brother, Iorwerth.[56] Two years later, during the Great Revolt against Henry II, Iorworth's son Hywel captured all Gwent Iscoed (Lower Gwent) except the castles.[57] Then in 1175, Henry II forced Richard Strongbow, the Norman earl of Lower Gwent, to restore Caerleon to Iorwerth ab Owain. The following year, Richard died without male heirs; his lands remained under royal control until 1189, when a newly crowned King Richard gave Strongbow's daughter Isabel in marriage to the loyal family retainer, William Marshal. Meanwhile, Caerleon remained independent but "moved increasingly in the orbit of the greater kingdoms."[58] In contemporary literature, on the other hand, Caerleon connotes not political turmoil but Arthurian grandeur—the site of King Arthur's plenary court in Geoffrey of Monmouth's seminal *Historia Regum Britanniae* (late 1130s), Wace's *Roman de Brut*, in Chrétien de Troyes's *Perceval.*[59]

Marie's account of Caerleon features two buildings characteristic of Anglo-Norman colonial settlements: a castle, the "visible expression and guarantee of conquest," and an abbey, "spiritual arm" of the military conquest.[60] "They came to a castle; in all the world there was none more beautiful! There was an abbey within with many monks" (481–84) (viendrent a un chastel; / En tut le mund nen ot plus bel! / Une abbeïe i ot dedenz / De mut religïuses genz). The importance of the ecclesiastical establishment is signaled by the pride the abbot takes in showing his visitors around: "He entreated them to stay, showing them his dormitory, chapter house, and refectory" (492–94) (Mut les prie de surjurner: / Si lur musterrat sun dortur, / Sun chapitre, sun refeitur).

Curiously, Saint Aaron, whose feast day they have come to celebrate, was not one of the international saints in whose favor so many Welsh churches had been disendowed but an indigenous saint, a local third-century Romano-Briton martyr.[61] This discrepancy reflects the fact that in the later twelfth century, a native Welsh church had begun to reemerge in Cistercian guise. In 1179, Hywel ab Iorwerth—the native ruler who challenged the Anglo-Norman earls of Pembroke for control of Caerleon—endowed Llantarnam abbey as a daughter house of Strata Florida, which was strongly identified with Welsh interests.[62] Such foundations served as venues for native assemblies and mausolea[63]—perhaps like the magnificent tomb the abbot shows the advocate and his family:

They found a large tomb covered with silk, a band of precious gold running from one side to the other. At the head, the feet, and at the sides were twenty lighted candles. The candle holders were pure gold, the censers which perfumed that tomb during the day to do it great honor were of amethyst. (500–508)

(Une tumbe troverent grant,
Coverte d'un palie roé,
D'un chier orfreis par mi bendé.
Al chief, as piez e as costez
Aveit vint cirges alumez;
D'or fin erent li chandelier,
D'ametiste li encensier
Dunt il encensouent le jur
Cele tumbe par grant honor.)

When the visitors inquire who is buried there, the locals respond with the tale of their king who died for love:

They began to cry and, as they cried, to tell how it was the best knight—the strongest and proudest, handsomest and best loved—ever born in this world. He had been king of this land; no king had ever been as courtly. He had been caught at Caerwent and killed for the love of a lady. (513–22)

(Cil comencierent a plurer
E en plurant a recunter
Que c'iert li mieudre chevaliers
E li plus forz e li plus fiers,
Li plus beaus e li plus amez
Ki jamés seit el siecle nez.
De ceste tere ot esté reis,
Unques ne fu nuls si curteis.
A Carwent fu entrepris,
Pur l'amur d'une dame ocis.)

Recognizing the story as her own, the lady turns to her son and, in quick succession, reveals that the king was his father, slain by the advocate, gives him Muldumarec's sword, then falls dead on his tomb.

Like the historical Nest, the lady here robs her husband of his son and heir by revealing his paternity and her infidelity. Acting on the Welsh imperative that a "slain man's kinsfolk" avenge his death in order to "remove the dishonour it had caused them," Yonec takes up Muldumarec's sword and beheads the man he had always considered his father in order to avenge a dead man he has never known.[64] "He took his stepfather's head off with the sword that had belonged to his father: thus he avenged him and his mother" (544–46) (Sun parastre ad le chief tolu; / De l'espeie ki fu sun pere / Ad dunc vengié lui e sa mere). In this highly condensed scene, the transfer of Muldumarec's sword to his son functions as a kind of posthumous *cynnwys*, affiliating Yonec to the father he had never known and legitimizing him for purposes of inheritance. Moreover, by slaying his stepfather in the abbey church, Yonec symbolically adduces ecclesiastical approval for his act—exemplifying the Welsh "assimilation of lay and ecclesiastical values" by which "the right of vengeance" could be "jealously upheld in the name of the saint."[65] Where Muldumarec had taken pains to prove he was a good Christian, his son openly vindicates native practices of inheritance and vengeance.

The advocate's concern with dynastic continuity thus ends, ironically, in the resurgence of Muldumarec's kingdom: endowed with his father's sword, Yonec is acclaimed king by his late father's subjects. In wistfully evoking the way things used to be, the lady unleashes the return of the (autochthonous) repressed, not only as erotic fantasy but as political revenge. In this version of the colonial allegory, both father and stepfather die violently. By slaying his stepfather, Yonec not only avenges his father's death and his mother's unhappiness but restores the old, occulted order: the advocate's murder is the "surplus"—the constitutive excess—that enables the reimposition of traditional rule.[66]

"Milun"

Like "Yonec," "Milun" takes place in South Wales and turns on an illegitimate birth. A baron's daughter falls in love, sight unseen, with a famous knight named Milun. Taking him as her lover, she bears a son, whom she sends to her sister in Northumbria. Married off to a local lord, she secretly corresponds with Milun over the next twenty years. When their son reaches adulthood, he receives his father's ring and a letter disclosing his parents' identity. Proud of his father's reputation, he makes his way to Brittany, where his chivalry wins him the epithet Peerless (Sanz Per). Milun, not suspecting this brilliant young man is his son, meets him at a tournament at Mont Saint Michel. As they are about to clash, Milun recognizes the young man's ring, which leads to an emotional reunion between father and son. Happy to hear that his parents still love each other, Sanz Per decides to bring them together by slaying the stepfather he has never met. At that moment, word arrives of the stepfather's death. Father, mother, and son enjoy a happy reunion, with Sanz Per presiding over the marriage of his parents.

"Born in South Wales" (9) (de Suhtwales nez), Milun seems to inhabit the hybrid Cambro-Norman society of the late eleventh and twelfth centuries. Unlike Yonec or Muldumarec, he (like Gerald of Wales) bears a name that marks him as culturally if not ethnically Norman.[67] A simple knight who makes his living by his sword, Milun becomes a star on the wide circuit of European chivalry. Making his way to Brittany, he builds a reputation not through the kind of adventures found in the *matière de Bretagne* but in tournaments that attract a mixed crowd of "Normans and Bretons, Flemings and Frenchmen" (386–87).[68] That Milun should go abroad to gain fame is ironic, since historically Wales was one of the places chivalric "youth" might realize their aspirations in fact rather than fiction.[69] On the politically unstable Cambro-Norman frontier, "the vassal's obligations of military service . . . were never in danger of becoming archaic." It was a land of opportunity for the disenfranchised: for younger sons of great families, as well as for poor but valiant knights who "had everything to gain and nothing to lose by pursuing their careers in Wales, for there they would have military adventure in abundance and possibly a territorial fortune as a reward."[70] Still, by the last quarter of the twelfth century, "the age of rapid Anglo-Norman advance in Wales had drawn to a close"[71]—a constriction that propelled members of the new mixed-blood nobility to seek new frontiers, as in the Cambro-Norman conquest of Ireland.

Milun, however, chooses to make his way in the world of international chivalry. His skill, we are told, is famous as far away as Ireland, Norway, Gothland, Logres, and Scotland (15–17), earning him the esteem of the powerful: "Because of his prowess he was much loved and honored by many princes" (19–20) (Par sa pruësce iert mut amez / E de muz princes honurez). It also earns him the heart of a young girl,[72] who falls in love with him through hearsay:

In his country there was a baron—I don't know his name. He had a beautiful daughter who was a very courtly maid. She had heard Milun spoken of and began to love him very much. (21–26)

> (En sa cuntree ot un barun,
> Mes jeo ne sai numer sun nun;
> Il aveit une fille bele
> E mut curteise dameisele.
> Ele ot oï Milun nomer,
> Mut le cumençat a amer.)

Concealing the girl's (and her father's) identity under a protestation of ignorance, Marie intimates the social impossibility of an affair between a baron's daughter and a landless knight.[73] Nevertheless, the liaison is conducted with exemplary courtesy: the girl sends Milun a message offering him her love; he happily acquiesces and, sending her his ring in return, promises to come to her whenever she wishes. Before long, Milun is a frequent visitor to her courtly enclosure.

The sunny tale of love turns dark, however, when the girl finds herself pregnant:

She sent for Milun and made her lament, and told him what had happened: she had lost her honor and her worth, when she'd gotten mixed up in such a situation. She would be put to the sword or sold abroad. *Such was the custom of the old ones* as they held at that time. (56–64, emphasis added)

> (Milun manda, si fist sa pleinte,
> Dist li cument est avenu:

S'onur e sun bien ad perdu,
Quant de tel fet s'est entremise;
De li ert faite granz justise:
A gleive serat turmentee
U vendue en autre cuntree.
Ceo fu custume as ancïens,
Issi teneient en cel tens.)

In the general prologue to Marie's *Lais*, "the custom of the old ones" (9) (custume as ancïens) refers to classical authors' penchant for speaking obscurely, so that those coming after them might "gloss the letter" (15) (gloser la lettre) of their texts "and add the surplus of their understanding" (16) (E de lur sen le surplus mettre). Here, in contrast, "custume as ancïens" designates the atavistic punishment meted out to unwed mothers. Where in "Yonec" the olden days evoked ladies with handsome and courteous lovers, in "Milun" they signify instead the intolerance of a staunchly patriarchal society.

Despite the menace hanging over her, the girl energetically takes charge of her own fate. Where Fresne's mother anonymously disposes of her incriminating child, the lady summons Milun and details her plan:

"When the child is born," she says, "you will take it to my sister, who is married in Northumbria—a rich lady, worthy and wise. You will send word to her, in writing and orally, that this is her sister's child, on whose account she has endured many pains. Now take care that it is well brought up, whatever it is—daughter or son." (67–76)

("Quant li enfes," fait ele, "ert nez,
A ma serur le porterez
Ki en Norhumbre est marïee,
Riche dame, pruz e senee,
Si li manderez par escrit
E par paroles e par dit
Que ceo est l'enfant sa serur,
S'en ad suffert meinte dolur.
Ore gart k'il seit bien nuriz,
Queil ke ço seit, u fille u fiz.")

In an interesting variation on Welsh practices, the illegitimate child is "affiliated" in advance not with its father but with its mother through a secret complicity among sisters that circumvents the strictures of the feudal politics of lineage. Where Yonec's identity is conserved in a ring and a *sword*, Milun's unborn child is dispatched to his mistress's sister along with a ring and a *letter*: "I will send her a letter; in it will be written the name of [the baby's] father / and his mother's adventure" (78–80) (un brief li enveierai; / Escriz i ert li nuns sun pere / E l'aventure de sa mere).[74] Milun, the child's biological father, becomes the messenger who conveys the newborn to its maternal aunt and delivers these tokens of its identity. His inability to decide the fate of his own son (in contrast, for example, to Muldumarec) underscores the power gap separating a baron's daughter from a simple knight, however exalted his reputation. After discharging his mission, Milun goes abroad to earn his way as a knight-for-hire: "he went outside his land, seeking wages for his valor" (121–22) (eissi fors de sa tere / En soudees pur sun pris quere).

Meanwhile, his mistress is betrothed to "a very powerful man from the region" (125) (un mut riche humme del païs). In the brief delay before her wedding, missing Milun and fearful that her illicit pregnancy will be discovered, she falls prey to a kind of desperation the heroine of "Yonec" experiences only after seven years:

"Alas," says she, "what shall I do? I am to have a husband? How can I take him? I'm no longer a virgin. I'll be a servant all my life. I didn't know it would be like this, but thought I would have my friend. [I thought] we would conceal this affair between us, that I would never hear it told anywhere. It would be better for me to die than to live! But I am not free, but have many guards, old and young, around me: my chamberlains, who always hate good love and delight in sorrow. So I will be made to suffer. Alas! that I can't die instead!" (133–48)

> ("Lasse," fet ele, "que ferai?
> Avrai seignur? Cum le prendrai?
> Ja ne sui jeo mie pucele;
> A tuz jurs mes serai ancele.
> Jeo ne soi pas que fust issi,
> Ainz quidoue aveir mun ami;
> Entre nus celisum l'afaire,
> Ja ne l'oïsse aillurs retraire.
> Mieuz me vendreit murir que vivre!
> Mes jeo ne sui mie delivre,
> Ainz ai asez sur mei gardeins
> Vieuz e jeofnes, mes chamberleins,

Ki tuz jurz heent bone amur
E se delitent en tristur.
Or m'estuvrat issi suffrir,
Lasse! quant jeo ne puis murir!")

Her distress is a useful reminder that the Welsh tolerance of illegitimate children did not mean that their attitude to marriage "was in any way cavalier." It was "the solemn duty of the girl's kinsfolk to guard her virginity until she was given in marriage; it would be no small public shame for them, as well as for her, if they were found to have failed in their duty."[75] In the end, however, her worries are groundless: on the appointed day, she is married, and no one notices anything amiss.

The *lai*'s best-known feature is the twenty-year exchange of letters the protagonists maintain by hiding their correspondence in the feathers of a white messenger-swan. Feeling "very sad and pensive" (152) (mut . . . dolenz e mut pensis) without his beloved, Milun soon devises a way to contact her: "He wrote his letter and sealed it. He had a swan he loved very much. He tied the letter to its neck and hid it in its plumage" (161–64) (Ses lettres fist, sis seela. / Un cisne aveit k'il mut ama: / Le brief li ad al col lïé / E dedenz la plume muscié). He then commends the swan to a messenger, with instructions to deliver it to his lady.

"Milun" is the third of three consecutive *lais* in which birds play central narrative functions. After "Yonec," in which Muldumarec takes the form of a goshawk (*ostur*), comes "Laüstic," in which a nightingale singing outside a lady's window provides a pre-text for her secretly to meet with her lover. In "Milun," the swan serves as the *medium* of the lovers' ongoing communication, the near homophony of the words "cygne" (swan) and "signe" (sign) highlighting the *lai*'s fascination with the materiality of the word.[76] If the message Milun had delivered to his lady's sister "in writing and in speech" (71–72) (par escrit / E par paroles e par dit) was characterized by its built-in redundancy, the letters he sends her trigger a metonymic fetishization of writing itself, as the girl lavishes on the parchment all the affection she is unable to show her absent lover:

Under [the swan's] plumage she felt the letter. Her blood stirred: she knew well it came from her lover. . . . She [and her maid] disengaged the letter, and she broke the seal. At the top she found "Milun." Recognizing her lover's name, she kissed it a hundred times, weeping, before she could speak any further! (218–30)

(Desuz la plume sent le brief;
Li sancs li remut e fremi:
Bien sot qu'il vint de sun ami . . .
Le brief aveient deslïé,
Ele en ad le seel brusié.
Al primier chief trovat "Milun";
De sun ami cunut le nun:
Cent feiz le baisë en plurant,
Ainz qu'ele püïst dire avant!)

In the twelfth century's two great adulterous romances, writing remains marginal: Béroul's Tristan and Iseut communicate through hushed tones, secret signs, and ambiguous language, while Chrétien's *Chevalier de la Charrete* shows writing to be blatantly deceptive, always already susceptible of forgery.[77] In "Milun," on the other hand, literacy is no longer the monopoly of clerics. The energy and imagination Tristan and Iseut expend arranging clandestine trysts our heroine devotes to finding ways of writing to Milun: "she tried so hard that, by art and strategem, she obtained ink and parchment" (253–54) (Tant quist par art e par engin / Ke ele ot enke e parchemin).[78] Through the medium of writing, the protagonists maintain an extraordinary twenty-year affair, translating the volatility of courtly passion into a sustained, long-term devotion—a prosaic variation of the lyric theme of *amor de lonh*. In Marie's calculus, true love seems to flourish in inverse proportion to physical proximity, with "Chaitivel" at one end of the scale and "Milun" at the other. Though it is Milun's prowess that first catches his sweetheart's attention, it is his faithful correspondence that nurtures and retains her affection.

The ending of "Milun" closely parallels that of "Yonec" but completely rewrites it. Like Yonec, the couple's illegitimate child grows up to be a brave and valiant knight. When he comes of age, his aunt gives him his mother's ring and letter, telling him his father was the best knight in the land. Wishing to prove himself, the young man heads to Brittany, where his prowess and largesse earn him the name "Sanz Per"—peerless, but also a homophone for "sanz pere," fatherless. Meanwhile, Milun sets out to defeat the newcomer, never suspecting he is his son. When the two come face-to-face in a tournament at Mont Saint Michel, Sanz Per knocks his father from his saddle. At that moment, Milun recognizes his assailant's ring: " 'Friend,' he says, 'listen to me! By God Almighty, tell me, what is your father's name? What is your name? Who is your mother?' "

(433–36) ("Amis," fet il, "a mei entent! / Pur amur Deu omnipotent, / Di mei cument ad nun tis pere! / Cum as tu nun? Ki est ta mere?"). Despite the superiority of his maternal lineage, Sanz Per seeks to identify himself with the father he has never known:

I'll tell you as much as I know about my father. I think he was born in Wales and his name is Milun. He loved the daughter of a rich and powerful man, and secretly engendered me in her. (445–50)

> (Jo vus dirai
> De mun pere tant cum j'en sai.
> Jeo quid k'il est de Gales nez
> E si est Milun apelez.
> Fillë a un riche humme ama,
> Celeement m'i engendra.)

Overjoyed, Milun reveals his identity and recounts how he and the boy's mother have continued to love each other and exchange messages despite her marriage. For Sanz Per, the solution is simple: "By my faith, fair father, I'm going to bring you and my mother together! I will kill her husband and have you marry her" (497–500) (Par fei, bels pere, / Assemblerai vus e ma mere! / Sun seignur qu'ele ad ocirai / E espuser la vus ferai). Fate, however, spares Sanz Per from this displaced patricide: landing in South Wales, father and son receive the news that the lady's husband has died; in an inversion of the conclusion of "Yonec," "the father-lover remains alive and the husband dies conveniently instead of being killed by a vengeful stepson."[79]

In "Milun," the happily-ever-after consists not in the return of an occluded past but in the opening of a new, utopian future. After meeting his mother, who is delighted to find him so "pruz e gentiz" (524), Sanz Per in effect legitimates himself by presiding over the marriage of his parents: "*They never asked their kin: without anyone else's counsel,* their son brought the two of them together: he gave his mother to his father" (525–28, emphasis added) (*Unc ne demanderent parent: / Sanz cunseil de tute autre gent* / Lur fiz amdeus les assembla, / La mere a sun pere dona).[80] In contrast to the lady's first marriage, in which "her father gave her a lord" (124) (Sis peres li duna barun), this union is consistent with the reformed model of marriage, whose sole requirement is the mutual consent of the partners—except there is no priest to sanctify the proceedings. It is a remarkable inversion of the feudal politics of lineage.

Falling outside all recognizable models of medieval marriage, this match legitimizes both Sanz Per (now no longer fatherless) and Milun as well, uniting him with the woman previously beyond his reach. In a sense, the belatedness of this marriage mocks the chivalric ideal: the valiant knight fulfills the *joven*'s dream—but twenty years late and through the intervention of his own illegitimate son. At the same time, this resolution signals the emergence of a new Cambro-Norman meritocracy in which the kinship group (*tref*) no longer plays the dominant role. Simultaneously the progeny and progenitor of this plot, Sanz Per parlays his illegitimacy into a utopian family—and chivalric—romance.

In "Milun," Marie ironically takes pains to conserve a tale thematizing the erasure of the past. As elsewhere, she emphasizes her own work of transcription: "Of their love and fortune the ancients made a *lai*, and I, *who have put it down in writing*, take great pleasure in retelling it" (531–34, emphasis added) (De lur amur e de lur bien / Firent un lai li auncïen, / E jeo, *ki l'ai mis en escrit*, / Al recunter mut me delit). Two things, however, set this epilogue apart from that of "Yonec."[81] First, given the protagonists' twenty-year correspondence, Marie's claim to have transcribed a traditional *lai* overwrites her tale's most distinctive feature, its thematization of writing. Second is the pleasure Marie derived from her task. Elsewhere, Marie likes to highlight her fidelity to her source: "I have told you the truth [la verité] about the *lai* I've recounted here" ("Chievrefoil," 117–18).[82] Here, her emphasis on her own pleasure—"I took great pleasure in retelling [it]" (534) (Al recunter mut me delit)—forms a striking contrast to the "surplus of their *intellect*" (16, emphasis added) (de lur *sen* le surplus) invested by those still engaged in translating texts from the Latin.

*　*　*

For Marie, the project of glossing the letter of her predecessors is both a creative intellectual act and a moral imperative. In "Yonec" and "Milun" it is also a political commentary on the uses of the past—a matter of particular importance in the borderlands and in transitional cultures. The two *lais* offer radically different representations of the relations between an indigenous past and a colonial present. In "Yonec," the past is a repository of nostalgia and desire that promises escape from the harsh demands of the feudal politics of lineage. Figuratively buried in the person of Muldumarec, it is resurrected in his son, Yonec, who violently slays his curmudgeonly stepfather to restore the old order to power. In "Milun," the past is represented as a merciless patriarchal regime that sells wayward daughters into bondage. Both for noblewomen and for outstanding knights, hope lies not in the atavistic past but in an idealized future exemplified by Sanz Per. In contrast to the violence that in "Yonec" is at once revenge and ritual sacrifice, this transition comes as a peaceful withering away of the old. In place of the conflictual model of colonizer versus colonized, "Milun" proposes a new Cambro-Norman society that functions as a chivalric meritocracy. Spun out over the years, the protagonists' transgressive love results in a new social order transcending the divisions between the native and the colonial past, between high lineages and landless knights. Under the sign of chivalry, Sanz Per—no longer haunted by the political and familial violence "formerly found" in the land ("Yonec," 92) (que l'em suleit jadis trover)—becomes the champion of a bright and peaceful future.

PART III

CRISIS AND CHANGE IN THE THIRTEENTH CENTURY

In the twelfth century, Old French verse articulated the feudal nobility's emerging self-consciousness in tension with the hegemony of Latin church culture. As we have seen in Parts I and II, the vernacular genres of the *chanson de geste* and courtly romance served as vehicles to explore (among other things) the complexities of cultural contact and the contradictions of feudal society. The vitality of these genres was linked to that of the historical conjuncture in which they appeared. But it was not to last. Already in 1180, the political balance among the princes who patronized the first wave of vernacular literary texts was beginning to shift. Before that date, "the king and his princes ruled together"; from that point forward, Philip Augustus of France set out to establish the monarch's authority as different in kind from that of his great vassals. Henry I of Champagne (d. 1181), Henry II of England (d. 1189), and Philip of Alsace, count of Flanders (d. 1191), "represented the Indian summer of *auctoritas*"—the personal ascendancy resulting from a reputation for leadership, the authority of utterance or appearance—as a cohesive force.[1] Not coincidentally, these three princes played central roles in the late twelfth-century florescence of vernacular literature. Count Henry's wife Marie and Philip of Alsace were the patrons named in Chrétien de Troyes's *Chevalier de la Charrete (Lancelot)* and *Le Conte du Graal (Perceval)*, respectively, while Henry II is thought to be the "noble king" to whom Marie de France dedicated her *Lais*. The transitional generation of princes who succeeded them—Henry II and Thibaut III of Champagne, Baldwin IX of Flanders—lacked the political and cultural authority of their elders and, in any case, soon had their energy and attention drawn to the eastern Mediterranean, where (in the wake of Saladin's reconquest of Jerusalem in 1187) Latin Christians tried to reestablish their power in the Holy Land through the unsuccessful ventures of the Third and eventually the Fourth Crusades.

As we noted in the introduction, however, the opening decades of the thirteenth century brought a remarkable cluster of changes that reordered the geopolitical map of both Latin Europe and the eastern Mediterranean. The Fourth Crusaders' conquest of the Byzantine Empire and the establishment of the "Latin Empire" of Constantinople (1204) made the Franks a true colonial force in the east and contributed substantially to the rise of the Venetian commercial empire. However, the young generation of feudal princes who might have stabilized their power at home was instead drawn to Constantinople or to the remnants of the crusader kingdom of Jerusalem—often dying prematurely and leaving their patrimonies to minors and heiresses whose weakness benefited the expansionist ambitions of the French king.

In 1204—the same year as the crusader sack of Constantinople—King John of England lost possession of the duchy of Normandy. Two years before, he had seized and married Isabelle, the twelve-year-old heiress of the county of Angoulême, who was betrothed to Hugh of Lusignan, count of La Marche—John's vassal in Poitou. Irate, Hugh took his grievance to Philip Augustus, *John*'s overlord for his continental possessions. When John failed to answer the French king's summons, Philip declared his fiefs forfeit and in 1204 (taking advantage of John's own succession dispute with his nephew Arthur of Brittany) captured Normandy, depriving the English king of his patrimony. John's efforts to recover these possessions—and the huge military expenditures entailed—contributed to the baronial revolts (culminating in Magna Carta in 1215) that would trouble the rest of his reign. One longer-term political effect was the concentration of the dynasty's focus on England; a corollary cultural effect was the consolidation of a distinctive insular literature in both Anglo-Norman and Middle English, different from the development of Old French literature on the continent.[2]

Meanwhile, the reordering of the rest of Latin Europe and beyond continued. The combined victory of the kings of Castile, Aragon, and Navarre over the Almohads at the battle of Las Navas de Tolosa (1212) marked a new phase in the Spanish Reconquest, both in the extent of the territory won for "Christendom" and in the cooperation, rather than the factional rivalry, of these three Christian kings of Iberia.

These territorial expansions on the Iberian peninsula were accompanied, however, by an inward turn against Christendom's internal others. The Albigensian Crusade, launched in 1209 in response to the assassination of a papal legate the previous year, targeted the Cathar heretics of Occitania but soon mutated into a struggle against the traditional regional nobility (previously divided by their allegiance to either the count of Toulouse or the king of Aragon)—part of the emerging impulse toward centralization visible both in the expansionist tendencies of French king Philip Augustus (who triumphed at the battle of Bouvines in 1214) and in the will toward regulation cultivated by Pope Innocent III at the Fourth Lateran Council (1215), which addressed the status of Jews and lepers as well as heretics.

Not accidentally, this series of sociopolitical perturbations was accompanied by a reorganization of vernacular poetics, as if the sudden loss of old forms and values demanded a renovation of existing literary genres. In 1202, for example,

> an obscure court writer, Nicolas de Senlis, found himself the recipient of a strange request, which led him to translate into French a Latin text then known as the *Chronicle of Turpin* and falsely attributed to the famous archbishop, the killer of Saracens in the *Chanson de Roland*. The request for the translation itself was unremarkable at the time: the end of the twelfth and the beginning of the thirteenth century was a period characterized by the feudal lords' attempts to consolidate the political and ideological foundations of their power, so translations of texts that justified the power of individuals or their families were in growing demand. This was what the lord of Senlis, Baudouin V, Count of Flanders, had in mind. What was unusual is the request by his sister Yolande, Countess of Saint Pol, that the translation be in prose, or, in the very words of the translator, *en romans sans rime*: "in the vernacular, unrhymed."[3]

This was a turn, as Jeffrey Kittay and Wlad Godzich emphasize, of surpassing strangeness. Within a few years, moreover, Nicolas de Senlis's translation was followed by a spate of others. As Gabrielle Spiegel notes, what is striking about this new vernacular historiography is "the extreme chronological and geographical concentration of the texts and their known patrons."

Virtually every identifiable patron of an early prose history belonged to a small group of Franco-Flemish lords circulating in the orbit of the count of Flanders in the opening decades of the thirteenth century. Hugh and Yolande of Saint-Pol, Renaud of Boulogne, Robert VII of Béthune, Michel of Harnes, William of Cayeux, and Roger IV, castellan of Lille, shared far more than their common practice of commissioning historical works in Old French prose. They were members of a tightly knit circle of Franco-Flemish aristocrats who lived in close proximity to one another, often intermarried, and, in the crucial years of the early thirteenth century, were caught up in an era of political turmoil unmatched in Flemish medieval history. Only toward midcentury, when the monarchy had imposed its authority and was firmly in control of the realm, did the patronage of vernacular historiography shift to the royal court.[4]

The shift in vernacular culture, however, extended far beyond the emergence of prose. The early thirteenth century brought a number of experimentations in literary form: the alternation of verse and prose in the *chantefable Aucassin et Nicolette* and of narrative and lyric verse in *Le Roman de la Rose ou de Guillaume de Dole*; the emergence of the dream allegory in *Le Roman de la Rose* of Guillaume de Lorris; and the great prose romance cycles of the mid-thirteenth century. Like the appearance of prose historiography, datable with remarkable precision, they reflect divergent responses to the growing suspicion about the "truth value" of verse and to the new ideological demands posed by the threats to prevailing forms of aristocratic power. Part III of *Medieval Boundaries* examines three texts from the early thirteenth century: *La Conquête de Constantinople*, Robert de Clari's vernacular chronicle of the Fourth Crusade; *La Fille du comte de Pontieu*, the first attested French "prose romance" set in the same Franco-Flemish milieu that produced the vernacular prose *Pseudo-Turpins*; and *La Chanson de la Croisade Albigeoise*, narrating the second stage of the Albigensian Crusade around the pivotal years 1213–16, whose protagonists include many of the same feudal nobles encountered in the Fourth Crusade and at the battle of Bouvines.

5

Brave New Worlds

Robert de Clari's La Conquête de Constantinople

THE DIVERSION OF THE FOURTH CRUSADE and the Western sack of Constantinople in 1204 inaugurated a Latin "empire" that, like the crusader states themselves, constituted an early example of European colonialism. Of the two vernacular accounts of this expedition, Robert de Clari's *La Conquête de Constantinople* has long suffered by comparison with the more celebrated chronicle of Geoffroy de Villehardouin, one of the crusade's organizers.[1] Impugned for its historical inaccuracies and stylistic poverty, it at best attracts notice for Robert's fondness for colorful detail, condescendingly praised as revealing the perspective of the common man.[2] Alexandre Micha's assessment is typical: Clari, he writes, "shows a pronounced taste for the anecdote, for little events which may have no political import, but constitute an album of personal memories. . . . He recounts as one speaks, according (it seems) to notes taken at the time of the event and unrevised. . . . But because he puts something of himself in his work, it belongs not only to history but to literature."[3]

This chapter seeks to overturn the binary that privileges "history" as essential while marginalizing "literature" as ornamental. The elements of Robert's text that commentators find most "literary"—most naive, exotic, and maladroit—are, I will argue, sites of intense historical work. Clari's narrative hesitancies reflect not an uncertain command of events but the failure of available mental structures adequately to account for the unprecedented turns the Fourth Crusade had taken. In a society built on received cultural models, the sack of Constantinople and the wonders encountered there eluded conventional structures of understanding. It is the singularity of this experience that must have moved both Villehardouin and Clari to compose their chronicles—in itself an extraordinary gesture that bespeaks the importance literacy had assumed among the feudal nobility and the credibility Old French had attained as a written language. Yet unlike the generation of "romancers" who had begun composing in Old French a half century before, Villehardouin and Clari were knights, not clerics "translating" preexisting Latin sources. The obvious model for narrating their adventure was the *chanson de geste*, the traditional genre of cultural contact. Previous chroniclers poured vernacular accounts of historical campaigns into the epic mold, in the *Chansons des croisades*. By the early thirteenth century, however, a new model was available: vernacular prose, recently invented in Francophone Flanders.

In her study of the emergence of Old French prose, Gabrielle Spiegel omits *La Conquête de Constantinople* and other crusading chronicles from consideration, despite the fact that they "emanate from the same northern French region" and "discuss the crusading activities of the same group of northern and Flemish lords among whom the patronage of vernacular historiography was so marked," simply because they address "deeds performed in distant lands and of an almost exclusively military character" rather than the "rapid and far-reaching social changes taking place in France" in the opening years of the thirteenth century. But Clari's *Conquête*, I would argue, registers these changes and their consequences as vividly as those texts "more closely focused on France,"[4] casting his experience in the narrative and conceptual molds available to a thirteenth-century knight. The trouble is that these models—previously so flexible and resilient—are themselves destabilized by the tale Robert has to tell. Between the lines of "digressions" long characterized as either charming or embarrassing, we read the fissures in the feudal mentality giving way under the pressure of lived experiences.[5] As the crusade leaders, victims of their own "innumeracy," fall prey to the calculations of the merchant princes of Venice; as Frankish soldiers gape in wonder at the Christian city they have conquered; as feudal loyalties clash with class interests in the division of the spoils, Clari's text struggles to preserve but ultimately abandons traditional notions of lineage, Christian piety, and feudal honor.

*   *   *

From the beginning, the Fourth Crusade was pervaded by an air of belatedness. Jerusalem had been lost to Saladin in 1187, and the Third Crusade had failed to recapture it. The generation of princes who had transformed twelfth-century politics and letters had died: Count Henry of

Champagne in 1181; Henry II of England in 1189; Count Philip of Flanders at the siege of Acre in 1191; Richard the Lionheart, hero of the Third Crusade, in a campaign against a rebellious vassal in 1199. John Lackland and his nephew Arthur of Brittany were struggling over Richard's inheritance, while Philip of Swabia and Otto of Brunswick were contesting the German imperial title. So the leadership of the new crusade fell to the generation that had recently come of age: Thibaut III of Champagne and his cousin Louis of Blois (who, according to Villehardouin, took the cross at a tournament held at Ecry-sur-Aisne) as well as his brother-in-law, Baldwin IX of Flanders.[6] Count Thibaut died before the campaign got underway; meanwhile, an embassy including Geoffroy de Villehardouin had negotiated the fateful contract with the Venetians, which contributed to the diversion of the crusade and the sack of the great Christian city of Constantinople.

The opening of the *Conquête de Constantinople* rehearses the conventional structures of twelfth-century society even as it hints at the disruptions to come. After situating "the history of those who conquered Constantinople" (1.1–2) (li estoires de chiaus qui conquisent Coustantinoble) in the time of Pope Innocent III, Philip Augustus of France, and Emperor Philip of Swabia, Robert's enumeration of those who took the cross at the instigation of the charismatic preacher Fulk of Neuilly is an exercise in social classification.[7] First come the great feudal princes: Thibaut, count of Champagne; Baldwin, count of Flanders and his brother Henry; Louis, count of Blois; Hugh, count of Saint Pol; Simon, count of Montfort, and his brother Gui (1.16–20).[8] Next come the bishops: Nevelon of Soissons; Garnier of Troyes; the bishop of Halberstadt in Germany; Jean de Noyon, bishop-elect of Acre; the abbot of Loos; and "other abbots and so many other clerics we can't possibly name them all for you" (1.29–30). Then Robert returns to the secular nobility, also beyond number: "we couldn't name all the barons who were there, but we can name some of them for you" (1.30–33); pride of place goes to Pierre of Amiens (Robert's overlord, we only later learn[9]), followed by a long list of nobles grouped (as in the catalogue of Charlemagne's troops in the *Chanson de Roland*) by regional affiliations. He begins with those he knows best, the men of Flanders, before moving on to those of Burgundy, Champagne, Ile-de-France, and the Chartrain and ending with "so many other knights from France, Flanders, Champagne, Burgundy, and elsewhere that we can't name them all for you" (1.65–68). The opening section of his catalogue is typical—his will to accuracy and completeness vying with the limitations of space and memory:

my lord Enguerrand of Bove, one of four brothers (one was named Robert, one Hugh, and another brother a cleric); Baldwin of Beauvoir, Matthew of Warlincourt, the advocate of Bethune, and his brother Conon; Eustace of Canteleux, Anseau of Cayeux, Renier of Trit, Wales of Frise, Giard of Manchecourt, Nicholas of Mailly, Baldwin Cavarom, Hugh of Beauvais, and many other high-ranking knights—Flemish and from other lands—all of whom I can't name for you; my lord Jacques d'Avesnes was there; from Burgundy, there were Eudes of Champlitte and his brother William, who had a lot of people in the army; and there were many other Burgundians, all of whom I can't name for you. (1.34–48)

(mesires Engerrans de Bove, lui quart de freres: li uns en eut a non Robers, li autres Hues, et uns clers leur freres; Bauduins de Biauveoir, Mahiex de Wauslaincourt, li avoés de Betune et Quenes ses freres, Wistasses de Canteleu, Ansiax de Caieu, Reniers de Trit, Wales de Friuses, Girars de Manchicort et Nicholes de Malli, Bauduins Cavarom, Hues de Biauvais, et mold d'autres chevaliers haus hommes, qui Flamenc estoient et d'autres païs, que nous ne vous savons mie tous nommer; et si y fu mesires Jakes d'Avesnes. Et si y fu de Bourgougne Oedes de Chanlite et Willames ses freres, qui molt eurent de gent en l'ost; et si en y eut d'autres assés de Borgoune que nous ne vous savons mie tous nommer)

These barons, Robert sums up, were "the most powerful men" (li plus rike homme), those who "bore standards" (1.69–70) (si portoient baniere).[10] But for the reversal placing the great princes before the clerics, Robert's classification to this point vividly conveys the hierarchical ordering of feudal society.[11]

Here, however, an interesting disruption occurs: Robert flashes forward from the time of his narration (the beginning of the expedition in 1202) to the time of his writing, in order *prospectively* to record "those— rich and poor—who did most deeds of prowess and of arms" (1.72–73) (chiax qui plus y fisent de proesches et d'armes, de riques et de povres):

Pierre de Bracheux (who was, of all the poor and the great, the one who showed the most prowess), his brother Hugh, André of Dureboise, my lord Pierre of Amiens (the brave and the fair), Mathieu of Montmorency, Mathieu of Warlincourt, Baudouin of Beauvoir, Henry, brother of the count of Flanders, and Jacques of Avesnes: these were the great men who fought the most. (1.74–82)

Except for André of Dureboise, all those mentioned have already appeared in the text. Here, however, they are named not in order of rank or regional affiliation but by the level of valor they will *subsequently* display in the events yet to come. First place goes to a relatively modest-ranking noble, Pierre de Bracheux. Robert's beloved overlord, Pierre of Amiens, comes fourth—the earlier description ("fair, brave, and valiant") that at the time seemed so wholly formulaic assuming new meaning, given amid this list of those who distinguished themselves for their valor. In an astounding example of the way the lived experience of the crusade would reshuffle the conventional categories of medieval society, the only great prince to be mentioned—Henry of Hainault, a future emperor of Constantinople—comes in eighth, sandwiched between the two mid-level lords, Baudouin of Beauvoir and Jacques of Avesnes. Then, in an even more radical departure, Robert lists sixteen "poor" knights among those responsible for "the most feats of arms and prowess" (1.91–92). Here, pride of place goes to "the cleric Aleaume de Clari, in Amienois" (1.87–88), who (though Robert does not explicitly say so) is his own brother—and the only name to receive a supplementary annotation: "[he] was very brave there, performing bold acts and acts of prowess" (1.88–89) (molt y fu preus et molt y fist de hardement et de proesches). Emerging from the anonymity of history, these exemplary *bellatores* stake a place alongside the *rike homme* who were their overlords by dint of their prowess and courage. Nor does Robert forget to include the campaign's unsung heroes, "many other good people, cavalry and infantry—so many thousands we do not know how many" (1.92–94) (molt d'autre boine gent a cheval et a pié, tant de milliers que nous n'en savons le nombre).

For historians, it is precisely Robert's inadequate control over such "facts" that renders his chronicle inferior to Villehardouin's. One can point to his poor arithmetic in recounting the distribution of the 100,000 marks the crusaders receive for restoring Alexios IV to the Byzantine throne: the Venetians, Robert notes, took half; of the remaining 50,000, 36,000 went to pay the Franks' outstanding debt to the Venetians and the remaining "20,000" to reimburse those who had advanced money for the passage (56.10–15). His mistake is adduced as an illustration of his simplicity and hence the unreliability of his manuscript. But this failure, I argue, was not Robert's alone. The Fourth Crusade's diversion to Constantinople resulted from the vast debt the Franks incurred. While historians have focused on the question of the Venetians' responsibility—was it accident or conspiracy?—a look at the cultural "innumeracy" of feudal Europe explains the Franks' inadequacy in negotiating the practices and technologies of commercial life in the medieval Mediterranean.[12]

If epic was the vernacular genre most appropriate for the narration of crusading, its tone of exaggeration was at odds with the "numeracy" required for arranging transport with the Venetians. Of English chronicler Ralph of Coggeshall's claim that Fulk of Neuilly gave the cross to 200,000 people, historian John Godfrey comments, "Writers of the time were fond of vast, round numbers, often quite incredible, and Ralph was using the words 'ducenta millia' as meaning 'a very large number.' "[13] In Old French literature as well, numbers count not for statistical accuracy but for symbolic effect. Our first glimpse of Charlemagne in the *Chanson de Roland* shows him surrounded by "15,000 from the sweet land of France" (109); the rearguard of his retreating army, like the vanguard, contains 20,000 men (802)—scarcely a match for the 100,000 Saracens about to attack them. The same exaggeration characterizes the purportedly more "sophisticated" genre of romance: Chrétien de Troyes's *Erec et Enide* concludes with a celebratory feast featuring five hundred tables seating one hundred knights each, with a thousand knights passing the bread, a thousand the wine, and a thousand the food (6918–19, 6928–29). Wealth and expenditures were likewise not calculated to the nearest sou but rendered in impressionistic turns. In the *Roland*, as we have seen, Marsile promises Charlemagne a magnificent tribute including seven hundred camels, a thousand molted hawks, and four hundred mules laden with gold and silver if only he will lift his siege. In Marie de France's description of the fairy mistress's tent in the *lai* of "Lanval," the inexpressibility topos is recast as a kind of topos of unaffordability: "Neither Queen Semiramis, however much more wealth, or power, or knowledge she had, nor the emperor Octavian could have paid for one of the flaps. There was a golden eagle on top of it, whose value I could not tell, nor could I judge the value of the cords or the poles that held up the sides of the tent; there is no king on earth who could buy it, no matter what wealth he offered" (80–92).

In negotiating with the Venetians, lords like Geoffroy de Villehardouin—undoubtedly nourished on such rousing examples of epic and romance—were called on to produce estimates largely foreign to their conception of the world. True, certain feudal princes like Henry of Champagne and Philip of Flanders had broken new ground in the use of administrative bureaucracies.[14] But in money management skills the Italians remained far ahead of the French.[15] In Robert's account, emissaries were sent to Venice to contract for the transport of "4000 knights with their baggage and 100,000 footmen" (6.7–8). The Franks must have congratulated themselves on bargaining the total down from "100,000 marks" to 87,000, with 25,000 payable in advance (6.35–40). Yet for all the crusade leaders' best efforts, only 1,000 knights and 50,000–60,000 footmen (that is, 25 and 60 percent, respectively, of the number contracted) turned up at Venice the following year (11.23–26).[16] Despite repeatedly passing the plate, with many contributing more than their allotted share, the Franks fell short by 36,000 marks—a sum they then promised to pay out of future booty. The fleet finally sailed under this cloud of indebtedness, the crusaders' "innumeracy" having made them vulnerable to the machinations of Venetian commercial politics.

* * *

La Conquête de Constantinople contains two long historical digressions that seem to exemplify Robert's inability to hold a straight narrative line. The first (sections 18–28) narrates the complex and turbulent course of late twelfth-century Byzantine politics; the second (sections 33–38) focuses on Conrad of Montferrat, elder brother of crusade leader Boniface "the marquis." These digressions appear at a crucial point in the narration: as the crusading army winters in the Adriatic port of Zara—the Christian city they have just captured at Venetian instigation—its leaders "realize" their supplies are insufficient for the planned Egyptian campaign. As they ponder their financial dilemma, the doge of Venice cannily evokes the fabulous wealth of the Byzantine Empire. Meanwhile, Boniface of Montferrat supplies a ready justification for attacking Constantinople: to restore Alexios, son of the deposed emperor Isaac II Angelos, to the Byzantine throne. In this context, the logic behind Robert's apparently cumbersome flashbacks becomes perfectly clear: the first supplies the historical background of Alexios's claim, while the second explains Boniface's hostility toward Constantinople. Their explanatory power derives from the principles of legitimacy they invoke, constitutive of the world that crusaders like Robert de Clari inhabited: hereditary succession, family loyalty, and the inviolability of the feudal bond. At the same time, the historical gaps and silences in the text gesture toward the fragility of the very ideals that, in good faith or bad, will be called on to justify the string of events leading to the crusader sack of Constantinople.

The first digression casts the long reign of Emperor Manuel Comnenos (1143–80) as the golden age of French-Byzantine relations. Extolled as "the richest and most generous of all the Christians who ever lived" (18.6–7), Manuel, Robert tells us, "loved the French very much and had great faith in them" (18.10–11)—so much so that, on their advice, he sends messengers to King Philip requesting the hand of his sister for his own son Alexios.[17] So splendid are the ambassadors that "the king of France and his people marveled (se merveillierent) at the envoys' great nobility" (19.10–12)—an indication of the impression Byzantine wealth and splendor made even on the most powerful monarchs of the Latin West. Not surprisingly, Philip is happy to dispatch his sister at the request of "as noble and as rich a man as the emperor" (19.16–17).

Though the nine-year-old Agnes was duly delivered to Constantinople and married to the ten-year-old Alexios, Emperor Manuel's death later the same year (1180) unleashed two decades of political chaos. In 1183 young Alexios II was deposed and murdered by his cousin Andronicos I. Blinding his political opponents, Andronicos also "took all the beautiful women he found and lay with them by force, and married the empress, who was the king of France's sister, and committed acts of such great disloyalty that no traitor or murderer has ever done as many as he" (21.25–29) (prenoit toutes les beles femmes que il trovoit, si gesoit a eles a forche; et prist l'empeerris a femme, qui estoit suers le roi de Franche, et fist tant de si grans desloiautés, que onques nus traïtres ne nus mourdrissierres tant n'en fist comme il fist). Shortly thereafter, the usurper is himself overthrown by Isaac II Angelos, who emerges as the hero of Robert's account: saved from political persecution by a miracle that invests his accession with an aura of divine judgment, he is acclaimed emperor by the people of Constantinople. Soon, however, Isaac is overthrown by his own brother, who takes the throne as Alexios III. In this palace coup, Isaac is blinded and thrown in prison, but his son—another Alexios—flees to the West, seeking allies against his usurping uncle. Now, as son of the deposed emperor, he is welcomed in the crusader camp as the "rightful heir" (droit oir) of the Byzantine Empire.

Promising them a huge reward if they will help him recover his throne, Alexios furnishes the crusade leaders just the pretext they need for diverting the expedition to Constantinople. Central to their decision, at least in Robert's rendition, is Alexios's status as *droit oir* of the Byzantine Empire. In the twelfth and thirteenth centuries, genealogy was becoming the dominant discourse in which to legitimize political claims.[18] This had not always been the case: under Charlemagne and his successors, honors conferred for the lifetime of an individual on his death reverted to the king, who might then bestow them on another lineage entirely.[19] Gradually, however, fiefs came to be seen as hereditary, with genealogical succession

TABLE 5.1.   House of Comnenos

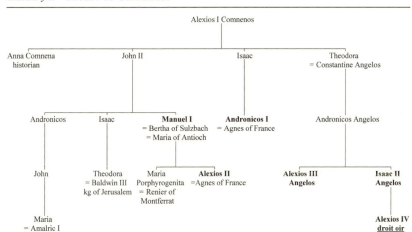

the principle regulating the transmission of power.[20] When the crusaders—already discomfited by their conquest of the Christian city of Zara—query their bishops as to the propriety of a Byzantine campaign,

> the bishops answered by saying it was in no way a sin, but a great act of charity; for since they had *the rightful heir who had been disinherited*, they could very well help him recover his rights and avenge himself on his enemies. Then they made the young man swear on relics that he would keep the promises he had previously made them. (39.10–16, emphasis added)

> (li vesque respondirent et disent que che n'esoit mie pechiés, ains estoit grans aumosnes, car puis qu'il avoient *le droit oir qui deserités estoit*, bien li pooient aidier a sen droit conquerre et de ses enemis vengier. Adont si fisent le vaslet jurer seur sains que il leur tenroit ches convenenches qu'il leur avoit dit par devant.)

The bishops' willingness to authorize an expedition against the Christian city of Constantinople is hardly a surprise: as early as the Second Crusade (1147–48), the bishop of Langres had expressed the hostile opinion that the Byzantine Empire was Christian in name only.[21] And, in Robert's account, they underwrite their authorization by appealing to the genealogical principles that would have resonated so strongly with the crusaders.

At the same time, naming Alexios the *droit oir* effaces the violent discontinuities of recent Byzantine history, particularly the contradictions surrounding the accession of his father, Isaac II. Though Isaac was a great-grandson of Alexios I Comnenos, the story Robert tells legitimates his accession to the imperial throne not by dynastic right but by a curious combination of divine and popular support, embodied in his miraculous escape from Andronicos and subsequent acclamation by the populace. Furthermore, the appeal to the feudal politics of lineage, meant to solidify Alexios's position, in fact undermines it, since any claim based on dynastic rectitude as the Franks understood it would in fact have favored Alexios III (the villain of this piece), Isaac's elder brother.

The rivalry between a *droit oir* and a usurping uncle, moreover, is sure to have sounded familiar to some in the crusader camp. At Richard the Lionheart's death in 1199, the English succession had been disputed by his brother John and their nephew Arthur, posthumous son of their late brother Geoffrey, count of Brittany (see Table 5.2). While the English barons recognized John as king of England, the French king Philip Augustus supported the teenaged Prince Arthur's claims to Normandy, Anjou, and Aquitaine. The "resolution" of this dispute exactly coincided with the timing of the Fourth Crusade: John captured Arthur in 1202 and is presumed to have had him killed in captivity in 1204.[22] As vassals of the king of France, many of the crusade leaders would have been called upon to support Arthur as *droit oir*; at the same time, Philip's strategic intervention in the dynastic disputes of his Angevin vassals would surely have discomfited the Franco-Flemish nobility, which was staunchly committed to resisting the French king's expansionist policies.

The feudal politics of lineage likewise underlie Robert's second digression on Conrad of Montferrat, ostensibly designed to explain his younger brother Boniface's animosity toward Alexios III: "no one put more effort into [arguing for] the necessity of going to Constantinople than the marquis of Montferrat, because he wanted vengeance for a misdeed that the emperor of Constantinople . . . had done him. Now we'll leave our history and tell you about the misdeed on account of which the marquis hated the emperor of Constantinople" (33.20–26). The story of Conrad's Byzantine adventures is relatively brief. Stopping in Constantinople on his way to the Holy Land, Conrad defends the emperor against an enemy assault, only to learn shortly afterward that the emperor is plotting against his life. That night he leaves the city for the crusader port of Tyre. The rest of the digression describes Conrad's adventures in the Holy Land: his maritime defense of Tyre against Saladin's blockade; his marriage (1190) to Queen Isabelle of Jerusalem; and his murder by Assassins, followers of the legendary Old Man of the Mountain, barely two weeks after being recognized as king of Jerusalem. Robert concludes: "Now we have recounted the misdeed on account of which the marquis of Montferrat hated the emperor of Constantinople, and why he put greater effort and greater insistence on going to Constantinople than anyone else; and now we will return to our previous subject" (39.1–5).[23] Just how this digression accounts for Boniface's anti-Byzantine sentiment remains somewhat puzzling. True, the emperor's treachery is depicted as completely unmotivated. Perhaps we are meant to understand that, by precipitating the marquis's departure for the Holy Land, Alexios was directly responsible for Conrad's death.

What the digression does clearly illustrate is the chaos besetting the crusader kingdom in the late twelfth century. In his characteristically straightforward manner, Robert's account of this history reveals the increasing fragility of feudal ideals in the face of lived feudal crises. In the crusader states of Outremer, genealogical continuity proved spectacularly difficult to maintain. Accidents of birth and the high mortality rate in a region constantly at war repeatedly brought the accession of women and minors. This ongoing concern reached dramatic levels with the accession (1174) of Baldwin IV, a known leper expected to die without direct heirs. Faced with this dynastic quandary, the lords of Outremer arranged for the king's sister Sibylle to marry William Longsword, elder brother of Conrad and Boniface of Montferrat; after his death the following year, she was married to Guy of Lusignan, younger son of a noble Poitevin family. Within a decade, however, Guy's political and military incompetence led to his disastrous defeat at the battle of Hattin (1187), resulting in Saladin's capture of Jerusalem. When Sibylle died in 1190, the barons of Outremer moved to replace the ineffectual Guy.[24] At the very moment when the French king Philip Augustus was facing excommunication for repudiating his wife, Ingeborg of Denmark,[25] Sibylle's younger sister, Isabelle, was forced to separate from her husband, Humphrey of Toron, and to marry Conrad of Montferrat, who had proven his mettle in breaking Saladin's blockade of Tyre. But Conrad, as we have seen, was assassinated within two weeks of securing the title of king. Isabelle once again quickly remarried, this time to Count Henry II of Champagne—nephew of both Richard the Lionheart and Philip Augustus, and the elder brother of Count Thibaut, who helped promulgate the Fourth Crusade in 1202 (see Table 5.2).[26]

TABLE 5.2.   Kings of Jerusalem and the Rulers of the Latin West

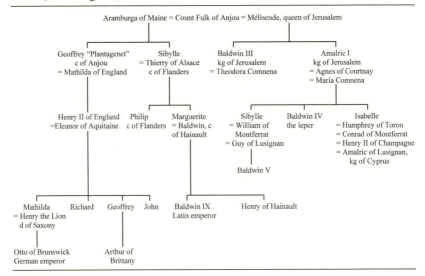

Amid this desperate dance designed to procure a suitable leader for the kingdom of Jerusalem, Robert casts the political rivalry between Guy of Lusignan and Count Raymond of Tripoli as a kind of male bride-choosing contest:

And the dead king had two married sisters: the elder one, to whom the kingdom had fallen, had [as her husband] my lord Guy of Lusignan in Poitou, and the younger one had my lord Humphrey of Toron. One day, all the high barons of the land—the count of Tripoli, the Templars and the Hospitallers—assembled in Jerusalem, at the Temple; among themselves they said they would separate my lord Guy and his wife, because the kingdom had fallen to his wife, and that they would give her another baron who was more competent to be king than my lord Guy. And they did it: they separated them, and when they had separated them, they couldn't ever agree to whom they would marry her, until the point where they put all bets on the queen, who had been my lord Guy's wife. So they gave her the crown for her to give to whomever she wanted to be king. So that one day all the barons and the Templars and Hospitallers assembled, along with the count of Tripoli (who was the best knight in the kingdom and who though the lady would give him the crown), and my lord Guy (who had had the queen to wife). When they had all assembled and the lady held the crown, she looked up and down. Then she saw him who had been her lord; she stepped forward, and put [the crown] on his head. Thus my lord Guy became king. When the count of Tripoli saw this, he was very sad and left for his country, Tripoli, with ill will. (33.101–28)

(Si avoit li rois qui mors fu deus sereurs mariees: si avoit uns chevaliers, mesire Guis de Luisegnun en Poitau, l'ainsnee a cui li roiames estoit eskeus, et mesires Hainfrois de Touron avoit le mainsnee. Si s'asanlerent un jor tout li haut baron de le tere et li cuens de Tripe et li Temples et li Hospitax en Jherusalem, au Temple, et disent entr'aus qu'il departesisent monseigneur Guion de se femme, pour chou que li roiames estoit eskeus a se femme, et qu'il li donnaissent autre baron qui fust plus soufisans a estre rois que mesire Guis n'estoit, et il si fisent. Il les departirent, et quant on les eut departis, si ne se peurent onques acorder a qui il le mariaissent, tant qu'il se misent seur le roine du tout, qui avoit esté femme monseigneur Guion. Se li ballierent le corone, et ele le donnast a cui que ele vausist qui rois fust. Tant qu'il se rasanlerent un autre jor tout li baron et li Temples et li Hospitaus, et se y fu li cuens de Tripe, qui estoit li mieudres chevaliers du roiame, qui cuidoit que le dame li donnast le corone, et si i fu mesires Guis, qui avoit eu le roine a femme. Quant il se furent tout assanlé, et le dame tint le corone, si esgarda amont et aval; si i voit ele chelui qui avoit esté ses barons, si va ele avant, se li met ele u chief. Ensi si fu mesires Guis rois. Quant li cuens de Tripe vit chou, si en fu si dolens qu'il s'en ala en sen païs, a Tripe, par mautalent.)

In this extraordinary scene,[27] the precariousness of the feudal politics of lineage becomes apparent. As the elder of Baldwin's two sisters, Sibylle is queen by hereditary right; given responsibility for choosing the king of Jerusalem, however, she ignores the collective will of her barons and selects precisely the ex-husband they had deemed unworthy of the position—alienating the "best knight in the kingdom" in the process. Robert leaves no doubt as to Guy's incompetence: taken prisoner by Saladin, he barters the city of Ascalon for his freedom. At Tyre, however, Conrad of Montferrat denies him and his men entrance to the city:

And those within answered that they would not enter, until the marquis came to the walls and told him he would not enter. "Ba! what's this?" said the king, "am I not lord and king of [Tyre]?" "In the name of God," said the marquis, "you are neither lord nor king, and neither will you enter, for you have dishonored everything and have lost all the land, and what's more the shortages within are so great that if you and your people came in, the city would be completely lost from hunger. And I would rather," said the marquis, "that you be lost—you and your people who have hardly any great deeds [to your credit]—rather than we who are inside the city." (34.28–39)

(Et chil de dedens respondirent qu'il n'i enterroient, tant que li marchis vint as murs, si dist qu'il n'i enterroit: "Ba! comment?" fist le rois, "de ne sui jou sires et rois de laiens?" "En non Dieu," fist li marchis, "ne sires ne rois ne n'estes vous, ne vous n'i enterrés, car vous avés tot houni et le terre toute perdue, et d'autre part le kiertés est si grands chaiens, que si vous et vo gent i entriés, que le vile seroit

tote perdue de fain. Et jou ai plus kier," fist li marchis, "que vous soiés perdus, et
vous et vo gent de qui il n'est waires grans esplois, que nous qui chaiens sommes ne
le vile.")

Though Robert boldly shows Conrad challenging the authority of the
crowned king of Jerusalem, it is beyond the limits of his political imagination
to represent even such a king being deposed. His report that both "King
Guy" and his wife died soon afterward (38.1–2) is historically inaccurate:
though Sibylle died in 1190, Guy held the kingship until 1192, relinquish-
ing it in exchange for Cyprus. By advancing the date of Guy's death,
Robert avoids the messiness of a disputed succession, which saw the widower of one queen-regnant contesting the claims of her sister and would-
be successor.[28] Nevertheless, his breathless account of the following two
years reveals the cynicism and raw pragmatism of the dynastic politics of
Outremer:

So the kingdom fell to the wife of my lord Humphrey of Toron, who was the
queen's sister. And they went and took my lord Humphrey's wife away from him,
and gave her to the marquis. Thus the marquis became king, then had a daughter
by her, and then the marquis was killed by Assassins, then they took the queen
and gave her to Count Henry of Champagne. And then they besieged Acre and
took it. (38.2–10)

(Si escaÿ li roiaumes a la femme monseigneur Hainfroi du Toron, qui estoit suers
le roine. Si va on, si taut on a monseigneur Hainfroi se femme, si le donna on au
marchis. Ensi si fu li marchis rois, puis en eut il une fille,[29] et puis fu li marchis
ochis de Haussassis, puis si prist on le roine, si le donna on au conte Henri de
Champangne. Et puis aprés si assist on Acre et si le prist on.)

Seemingly in a hurry now to end his excursus and return to his main tale,
Robert dispatches the one military gain of the Third Crusade, the siege
and capture of Acre, in a single line—having to his satisfaction accounted
for Boniface of Montferrat's animosity toward the great Christian city of
Constantinople.

*   *   *

Constantinople occupied an unstable position in the twelfth-century
Western imaginary. As long as the Greeks and the Latins had relatively little contact, their theological, cultural, and political differences could be
subsumed in an idealized vision of Christendom. During the First Crusade

and its aftermath, however, westerners grew increasingly suspicious of the Greeks and resentful of what they perceived of as their unreliability or even open treachery. For the armed pilgrims who had come to liberate the Holy Land from infidel Muslims, the Byzantine Greeks and other eastern Christians—nominally their coreligionists but so markedly different in culture—came to constitute a kind of third term troubling the reassuring binary opposition between (Latin) Christianity and Islam. This sense of antagonism pervades Odo of Deuil's *De Profectione Ludovici VII in Orientem*, which attributes the failure of the Second Crusade to Byzantine duplicity. Twelfth-century vernacular literature cast the Greeks in an equally ambivalent light: Chrétien de Troyes's *Cligès* ascribes to the Eastern Empire a history of fraternal rivalry and disputed succession, while the parodic *Pèlerinage de Charlemagne* represents Constantinople as a site of artifice, wealth, and complacency.[30] The knights of the Fourth Crusade thus arrived in Constantinople imbued with a century-long history of suspicion, resentment, and betrayal. In Robert de Clari's *Conquête*, Constantinople becomes the stage for the Franks' encounters with the sultan of Konia, the pilgrim king of Nubia, and the nomadic Cumans—anecdotes typically cited as illustrations of Robert's naïveté and his fascination for colorful but historically irrelevant detail, "ordinarily the stuff of romancers rather than historians."[31] Far from being merely ornamental, however, these passages show the crusaders' fundamental conceptual categories pushed to their limit. In Constantinople, the Franks confront strange and exotic characters who disrupt the forms, distinctions, and values of feudal-Christian society.

The crusaders first approach Constantinople with a solemn pageantry giving little hint of the conceptual crises to come. The Latin fleet assembles off the coast with banners flying; it "was the most beautiful thing in the world to look at," eliciting the admiration of the crowd that gathers on the city walls to observe the spectacle "with wonder" (40.14–15, 17). The Franks reciprocate their stupefaction, "once again marvel[in]g sorely" (40.21) (s'en remerveillierent molt durement) at the city's great size. For the assault itself, the crusaders array themselves in battalions under the command of the great princes: the count of Flanders, the count of Saint Pol, Henry of Hainault, the marquis of Montferrat, and Louis of Blois, concluding with contingents of Champenois and Burgundians (45.2–17). This formation, like the catalogue at the beginning of Robert's text, *performs* the crusaders' political organization. A strange charivari-like episode appended to the end of the scene, however, hints at some of the disorder to come:

Then they took all the boys that kept the horses and all the cooks who could bear arms and they had them all armed with quilts and saddle cloths and copper pots and maces and pestles, and they were so ugly and hideous that the common foot soldiers of the emperor, who were outside the walls, were seized with great fear and terror when they saw them. (45.18–25)

(Et aprés prist on tous les garchons qui les chevax gardoient, et tous les cuisiniers qui armes peurent porter; si les fist on trestous armer et de keutes pointes et de peniax et de pos de coivre et de piletes et de pestiax, si k'il estoient si lait et si hideus que le menue gent a pié l'empereeur, qui estoient par dehors les murs, en eurent grant peur et grant hisde, quant il les virent.)

While not yet thematizing the class-consciousness that will emerge after the second assault on Constantinople, this passage reveals a heterogeneity generally concealed beneath the conventional motifs of epic and historical discourse. Astutely deploying incongruity and spectacle to their advantage, the Franks install their *droit oir* as Emperor Alexios IV and set about discovering the wonders of the Byzantine capital.

The first marvel the crusaders encounter in Constantinople is the visit of the deposed ruler of Konia, capital of the Seljuk sultanate of Rum. The son and designated successor of Sultan Kilij Arslan II, Kaykhusraw had been deposed by his brother Sulaymanshah in 1197. Seeking support at the Byzantine court,[32] he casts his request in terms calculated to appeal to the Franks:

"Surely, lords," he said, "you have done a deed of great nobility and prowess to have conquered so great a place as Constantinople, which is the head of the world, and to have put the rightful heir of Constantinople back on this throne and crowned him emperor. . . . Lords," said the sultan, "there is something I want to ask of you. I have a brother, *younger than myself*, who has taken from me by treason the land and lordship of Konia, of which I was lord and of which *I am the rightful heir*."[33] (52.38–48, emphasis added)

("Chertes, seigneur," fist-il, "vous avés fait molt grant barnage et molt grant proeche, qui si grant cose comme Constantinoble est, qui est li kiés du monde, avés conquis, et avés remis le droit oir de Coustantinoble en sen siege et coroné l'avés a empereeur. . . . Seigneur," fist li soudans, "je vous vaurroie proier d'une cose que je vous dirai. Jou ai un mien frere *mainsné de mi*, qui m'a soustraite me tere et me seignorie du Coine par traïson, dont g'estoie sires et dont *je sui drois oirs*.")

In naming himself the "rightful heir" of Konia, the deposed sultan conspicuously appeals to the very principle the crusaders had used to justify their expedition against Constantinople. In emphasizing that the usurper is his *younger* brother (un mien frere mainsne de mi), he underscores the violation of the feudal practice of primogeniture. Having flattered the Franks by praising their *grant barnage* and *molt grant proeche*, he now—like Alexios—offers them a rich reward if they will restore him to his throne.

Kaykhusraw, however, is in a position to offer the crusaders something Alexios could not: "If you wish to help me conquer my land and lordship, I will give you very plentifully of my wealth, *and will have myself baptized along with all my vassals*—if I can regain my lordship, and if you wish to help me" (52.49–53, emphasis added) (Se vous me voliés aidier a conquerre me tere et me seignourie, je vous dourroie molt grant plenté de men avoir, et *si me feroie crestiener et tous chiax qui a mi se tenroient*, se je ravoie me seignourie, et se vous me voliés aidier). Yet offered the prospect of converting a Seljuk prince into a Christian ally, the crusade leaders immediately refuse. Perhaps they are swayed by the example of epic—like the *Chanson de Roland*, in which Marsile's promise of conversion turns out to be a ploy to convince Charlemagne to lift his siege, or the *Prise d'Orange*, in which it is not the Saracen king but his wife who is the conventional subject of conversion. In the event, the Franks reject the sultan's offer on purely pragmatic grounds: "because they still had their reward to collect from the emperor, and because it would be dangerous to leave Constantinople, with things as they were, they dared not leave it. When the sultan heard this, he was very angry and left" (52.60–65) (car il avoient encore leur couvenanches a avoir de l'empereeur, et que che seroit uns perix de laier si grant cose comme Coustantinoble est en tel point comme ele estoit; si ne l'osseroient laissier. Quant li soudans oï chou, si en fu tous courchiés, si s'en rala). Revealing just how distant this expedition remains from the thirteenth-century interest in mission, the Franks—unmoved by appeals to dynastic legitimacy or by the sultan's promise of conversion—are already looking beyond the linked feudal and spiritual values underlying the crusades to the wealth and advantage to be reaped from their control of the city the sultan has described as the "head of the world."

This episode of the Seljuk prince who speaks like a Frank finds its obverse in the crusaders' encounter with a French princess who behaves as an utter stranger.

After the barons had taken Alexios to the palace, they asked if the sister of the king of France, who was called the French empress, were still alive. And they were told yes, and that she was married; that a high-ranking man of the city named Branas had married her, and that she was living in a palace nearby. (53.1–6)

(Aprés quant li baron eurent mené Alexe u palais, si demanderent de le sereur le roi de Franche, que on apeloit l'empeerris de Franche, se ele vivoit encore, et on dist ouil et que ele estoit mariee, que uns haus hons de le chité, li Vernas avoit a non, l'avoit espousee; si manoit en un palais pres d'iluec.)

The French empress was Agnes, the daughter Louis VII of France had dispatched to the Byzantine court in 1179. Upon her arrival, the nine-year-old princess had been greeted with lavish court ceremonials appropriate to her standing as future empress.[34] Among the gifts she may have received was a "small and intimate book" written in a large, clear script in simple vernacular Greek, featuring a "detailed miniature cycle" representing the incorporation into the Byzantine court of a foreign imperial bride.[35] The text opens in the middle of the speech of an unnamed Western king poignantly lamenting his daughter's departure:

> the one who is inseparable, indissoluble from me,
> she who is my eyes and soul, breath, heart,
> sustenance, comfort, release from pain,
> alleviation of my grief, increase of my life,
> and sustenance of my breath—how shall I let her go?
> How would I be able to see the loss of my daughter?
> How would I be able to endure such bitterness?
> [and] how shall I tolerate such an unendurable grief?
> It is very difficult to accomplish and I shall not attempt it.
> But then, I turned my mind to the greatness, O Monarch, of your
>   empire,
> to the fear of your power, to the glory of your deeds
> and the splendor of your throne,
> I did not wish at all to disregard your letter.
> And lo and behold I send you [as] bride my much-beloved daughter,
> inseparable from me, O powerful ruler,
> hoping that another second father she may discover,
> the great *autokrator* and father-in-law in you. (8r-v)

The letter, presumably cast in the voice of Louis VII of France, portrays Agnes as the king's most precious possession, whom he can bear to part with only because of the overriding magnificence of the emperor—and the empire—to which she is summoned.[36]

If Agnes did come to regard Manuel Comnenos as a "second father," she was soon to be doubly orphaned: both Louis VII and Manuel died in 1180, shortly after her marriage to the new boy-emperor, Alexios II. Politics degenerated in the cross fire between factions clustered around two members of the imperial family: Alexios's mother, the Regent Maria of Antioch, and his half-sister, Maria Porphyrogenita—married that same year to Renier of Montferrat (yet another brother of Conrad and Boniface).[37] In 1183, as we have seen, Alexios was deposed and executed by his cousin Andronicos I, who seized the throne and forcibly married the young dowager-empress in a match memorably described by the Byzantine chronicler Niketas Choniates: "he who stank of the dark ages was not ashamed to lie unlawfully with his nephew's red-cheeked and tender spouse who had not yet completed her eleventh year, the overripe suitor embracing the unripe maiden, the dotard the damsel with pointed breasts, the shriveled and languid old man the rosy-fingered girl dripping with the dew of love."[38] Two years later, Andronicos himself was dead, paraded through the streets of Constantinople tied backward on the back of a camel and torn apart by the mob amid the urban disorder that brought Isaac II Angelos, father of the crusaders' *droit oir*, to power.[39] Agnes, it seems, disappeared from public view.

If Robert's account is accurate, the crusaders' total ignorance of the fate of the sister of the king of France indicates how thoroughly the political chaos of the late twelfth century had disrupted the Franco-Byzantine relations her marriage had been meant to assure. But any gratification the crusaders might experience at learning she is still alive quickly turns to consternation: in going to pay their respects to the French king's sister, they find not an ally and a countrywoman but an aggrieved foreigner annoyed at their presence and angry at their intervention in imperial politics:

So the barons went there to see her, and greeted her, and pledged her service; but she was very cold to them and very angry with them for having come and crowned Alexios. And she was unwilling to talk with them but spoke through an interpreter: the interpreter said that she didn't know any French at all. (53.7–13)

TABLE 5.3.   Fourth Crusaders and the Eastern Mediterranean

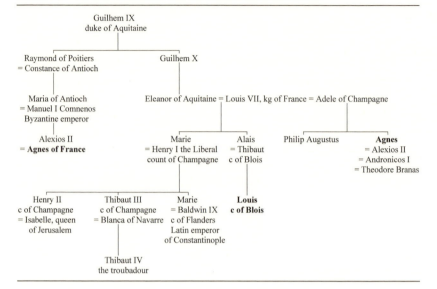

(La si l'alerent veir li baron, et si le saluerent, et molt li pramissent a faire lui servige, et ele leur fist molt mauvais sanlant et molt estoit corchie de chou qu'il estoient la alé et de chou qu'il avoient chelui Alexe coroné; ne ne voloit parler a aus, ains i faisoit parler un latimier, et disoit li latimiers qu'ele ne savoit nient de Franchois.)

Parading her alienation and claiming ignorance of her own mother tongue, Agnes embodies the complete breakdown of a dynastic politics meant to consolidate a Capetian-Comnenan alliance and, ideally, to produce a line of half-French emperors (like the half-Greek, half-Arthurian protagonist of Chrétien de Troyes's *Cligès*). This embarrassing reception is redeemed, just barely, by the crusade leader Louis of Blois by virtue of their family connection: "Count Louis, who was her cousin, made himself known (s'acointa) to her" (53.13–14). His appeal must have worked, for after the foundation of the Latin Empire, Agnes's husband, Theodore Branas, was the only high-ranking Byzantine to support the Franks.[40]

If the sultan of Konia and the "empress of France" blur the edges of some fundamental feudal categories, two subsequent encounters present immeasurably stranger and more radical others: the pilgrim-king of Nubia and the nomadic Cumans. These are the parts of Robert's narrative taken to exemplify his fascination with the exotic, a taste for the wondrous typifying medieval travel literature. Yet rather than reaffirming the "self," as spectacles of alterity often do, these instances unsettle the crusaders' identity by defamiliarizing two of its constitutive elements: Christianity and chivalry.

The first episode occurs when the Frankish leaders, seeking diversion, visit the palace of the Byzantine emperor. The spectacle they find there profoundly challenges their understanding:

And while the barons were there in the palace, a king came there whose skin was all black, and who had a cross in the middle of his forehead made with a hot iron. This king was staying in a very rich abbey in the city, in which the former emperor Alexios had commanded he should be lodged and [treated as] lord and young master, as long as he wished to stay. When the emperor saw him coming, he rose to meet him with great ceremony. Then the emperor asked the barons: "Now do you know who this man is?" "Not at all, sire," said the barons. "In faith," said the emperor, "this is the king of Nubia, who has come on pilgrimage to this city." And through an interpreter they spoke to him and asked him where his land was; in his language he answered the interpreter that his land was a good hundred days' journey beyond Jerusalem, and that he had come from there to Jerusalem on pilgrimage. And he said that when he left his land he had fully sixty countrymen with him; when he reached Jerusalem only ten were alive; and when he came from Jerusalem to Constantinople, only two of them were alive. And he said that he wanted to go on pilgrimage to Rome and from Rome to St. James, and then come back to Jerusalem, if he should live so long, and then die there. And he said that everyone in his land was Christian, and that when a child was born and baptized they made a cross in the middle of his forehead with a hot iron, just like he had. And the barons gazed at this king with very great wonder. (54.3–32)

(Si comme li baron estoient laiens u palais, si vint illueques uns rois qui toute avoit le char noire, et avoit une crois en mi le front qui lui avoit esté faite d'un caut fer. Chis rois si sejornoit en une molt rike abeïe en le chité, ou Alexes, qui avoit esté empereres, avoit kemandé que il fust et en fust sires et demisiaus, tant comme il i vausist sejorner. Quant li empereres le vit venir, si se leva encontre lui et s'en fist molt grant feste. Si demanda li empereres as barons: "Savés vous ore," fist il, "qui chist hons est?—Sire, nennil," fisent li baron. "Par foi!" dist li empereres, "ch'est li rois de Nubie, qui est venus en pelerinage en cheste vile." Et fist on parler latimiers a lui, et fist on lui demander ou se tere estoit, tant qu'il respondi as latimiers, en sen langage, que se tere estoit encore cent journees dela Jherusalem, et de la estoit il venus en Jherusalem en pelerinage; et si dist que, quant il mut de sen païs, qu'il mut bien soixante hommes de se tere avec lui; et quant il vint en Jherusalem n'en i eut il de vis que dis, et quant il vint de Jherusalem en Coustantinoble, n'en avoit il que deus vis. Et si dist qu'il voloit aler en pelerinage a Rome et de Rome a Saint Jake et puis revenir s'ent ariere en Jherusalem, s'il pooit tant vivre, et puis illueques morir. Et si dist que tot chil de se tere estoient crestien, et quant li enfes estoit nes

et on le baptisoit, que on li faisoit une crois en mi le front d'un caut fer ausi comme
il avoit. Si esgarderent li baron chu roi a molt grant merveille.)

At first, the king's black skin seems to signify his utter alterity.[41] In twelfth-
century vernacular literature, depictions of blackness appear (as we have
seen in the *Chanson de Roland*) in exotic figures influenced by the learned
tradition of the "marvels" of antiquity or occasionally in figures like the
hideous ploughman of *Aucassin et Nicolette*, with his "big head blacker
than coal" (24.14–15), marking the unbridgeable divide between nobles
and rustic *vilains*. In contrast, the description of the Nubian king unfolds
to reveal an uncanny similarity-in-difference. The brand on his forehead
identifies him as a fellow Christian; yet unlike the crusaders, who bear the
sign of their faith stitched on their clothes, the Nubian king has it inscribed on his body.[42] He is a pilgrim like themselves; but his journey, from
Nubia to Santiago de Compostela and back again, spans the entire Christian world—a remarkable feat of endurance that reduces the Franks' own
trials to petty inconveniences and the pageantry of their expedition to
noisy bluster.[43] Faced with such distortions of their fundamental cultural
categories, the Frankish barons are reduced to silence and wonder. As
Latin Christians belonging to a church whose language and rituals had
been largely standardized since the time of Charlemagne, they are unpre-
pared for the multiplicity of Christian sects proliferating in the eastern
Mediterranean—let alone for the black pilgrim-king whose every trait
simultaneously inverts and redoubles their own.

Another *molt grant merveille* arises in Robert's account of the Cumans,
warriors in the service of Constantinople's sometimes ally, sometimes adversary, John the Vlach. Like the Huns before them, the Cumans (Kipchak)
were a tribal confederation probably composed of nomadic peoples of
mixed language and ethnicity. Between the eleventh and the early thirteenth
centuries, they dominated the Eurasian steppe from the Danube to western
Siberia. They began raiding the borders of the Byzantine Empire in 1078 but
by the end of the century could be found fighting for the Byzantines as well
as against them. In the twelfth century they affected Bulgarian, Georgian,
and Rus' politics, and in the thirteenth century played an important role in
the formation of the Hungarian state.[44] For Robert, however, they are simply nomads whose primitive ways elicit a kind of ethnographic interest:

Now Cumania is a land bordering on Vlachia, and I will tell you what kind of people the Cumans are. They are a savage people, who neither plow nor sow, and

have neither huts nor houses, but felt tents—dwellings in which they take shelter; they live on milk, cheese, and flesh. In the summer, there are so many flies and gnats that they hardly dare come out of their tents until winter. (65.10–18)

(Or est Commaine une tere qui marchist a Blakie; si vous dirai quel gent chil Commain sont. Che sont une gent sauvage qui ne erent ne ne semment, ne n'ont borde ne maison, ains ont unes tentes de feutre, uns habitacles ou il se muchent, et se vivent de lait et de formage et de char. Si y a en esté tant de mouskes et de mouskerons que il n'osent issir hors de leur tentes waire preu devant en l'iver.)

Living on meat and milk without agriculture or fixed settlements, the Cumans at first glance seem infinitely more primitive than the serfs and peasants of the medieval West. Once on horseback, however, they prove to be unrivaled warriors:

In winter they come out of their tents and their country when they want to make a raid. . . . Each one has a good ten or twelve horses, so well trained that they follow them wherever they want to take them, and they mount them one after another . . . and they do not stop going, night or day. And they ride so hard that they cover in one day and one night fully six days' journey, or seven or eight. And while riding out they take nothing until turning for home; but when they are returning, then they collect prey and take captives and whatever they can. Nor do they go armed, except that they wear a garment of sheepskin and carry bows and arrows. They do not worship anything except the first animal encountered in the morning, and the one who encounters it worships it all that day whatever animal it may be. Now John the Vlach had these Cumans in his service and he used to come every year to raid the emperor's lands, even up to Constantinople, and the emperor was not strong enough to defend himself against him. (65.18–41)

(En yver si issent hors de leur tentes et de leur païs, quant il voellent faire leur chevauchie. . . . Cascuns d'aus a bien dis chevax ou douze; si les ont si duis qu'il les sivent partout la ou il les voellent mener, si montent puis seur l'un et puis seur l'autre . . . ne ne cessent d'esrer et par nuit et par jour. Si vont si durement que il vont bien en une nuit et en un jor sis journees ou set ou uit d'esrure. Ne ja tant comme il vont, riens ne carkeront ne ne prenderont devant au repairier; mais quant il repairent, dont si acuellent proies, si prennent hommes, si prenent chou qu'il puent ataindre; ne ja n'iront autrement armé fors qu'il ont unes vesteures de piax de mouton et portent ars et saietes avec aus; ne ne croient autrement fors en le premiere beste qu'il encontrent le matinee, et chis qu'il l'encontre, si i croit toute jour quele beste che soit. Ichés Commains avoit Jehans li Blakis en s'aiwe et venoit cascun an preer le tere l'empereur dusk'a meesme de Coustantinoble, ne n'avoit li emperes tant de pooir qu'il s'en peust deffendre.)

The Franks must have found the Cumans' nomadism wildly disconcerting. *Chevalerie*, after all, was literally a culture of horses: to a western knight, his warhorse (*destrier*) signified both military superiority and social prestige.[45] Yet for all the tactical advantages the mounted warrior enjoyed, the crusades had dealt the Franks a humiliating lesson on the limits of feudal warfare. On the First Crusade, as their horses died from heat and famine on the long march through Anatolia, some of Latin Christendom's greatest knights had been reduced to riding pack animals and even oxen.[46] Now, in the Cumans, they encounter strangers whose primitive ways are coupled with a horse-manship surpassing their own, whose "ten or twelve horses" each bespeaks an intimidating excess of *cheval-erie*.[47] Any anxiety felt by the Franks would have been especially acute in the early thirteenth century, as the primacy of chivalry itself was threatened by the expanding use of mercenary troops, combined with an increasing indebtedness caused by the escalating cost of arms and luxury commodities.[48] Indeed, for many knights, the Fourth Crusade surely represented an opportunity to reassert the strategic and symbolic importance of feudal warfare. Instead, it now brought them face-to-face with the Cumans who—making war in winter rather than spring, fighting with bows and arrows rather than lance and sword, conducting lightning raids rather than armed sieges—scramble the signifiers of chivalry as radically as the Nubian king had those of Christianity.

This sense of disorientation is reversed later in the text in a curious episode following the Franks' second conquest of Constantinople. Pierre de Bracheux (one of the crusaders who in Robert's eyes distinguished themselves by their valor) rides out to meet John the Vlach, who has been harrying the newly installed "Latin" regime. This time, it is the Franks who puzzle the Vlachs and the Cumans, impressing them with their prowess:

"Lord, *we marvel greatly at your fine chivalry*, we also marvel greatly that you have come questing in this country, that you have come here, to so distant a country, to conquer land. Don't you," they said, "have lands in your own country to support you?" My lord Pierre answered: "Well!" said he. "Haven't you heard how Troy the great was destroyed and by what trick?" "Well, yes!" said the Vlachs and the Cumans. "Well," said Pierre, "Troy belonged to our ancestors: those who escaped came and settled there where we are from; and because it belonged to our ancestors, we have come here to conquer land." With that, he took his leave and returned [to the camp). (106.23–38)

("Sire, *nous nous merveillons molt de vo boine chevalerie*, et si nous merveillons mout que vous estes quis en chest païs, qui de si loingtaines teres estes, qui chi estes venu pour conquerre tere. De n'avés vous," fisent-il, "teres en vos païs dont

vous vous puissiés warir?" Et mesires Pierres respondi: "Ba!" fist il, "de n'avés vous
oï comment Troies le grant fu destruite ne par quel tor?" "Ba ouil!" fisent li Blak et
li Commain, "nous l'avons bien oï dire, mout a que che ne fu." "Ba!" fist mesires
Pierres, "Troies fu a nos anchiseurs, et chil qui en escaperent si s'en vinrent manoir
la dont nous sommes venu; et pour che que fu a nos anchisieurs, sommes nous chi
venu conquerre tere." A tant si prist congié, si s'en revint ariere.)

The nomads' bafflement at the crusaders' conquest of Constantinople
provides a perfect opening for the Franks. In Pierre's masterful reversal,
the topos of *translatio imperii* serves (as in Chrétien de Troyes's *Cligès*)
to legitimize the Franks' conquest of Constantinople by a kind of right of
return. The Cumans, whose extraordinary horsemanship had earlier so intimidated the crusaders, are comfortingly reinscribed as simple nomads,
ignorant of the master narratives of history and duly awed by the Franks'
own *boine chevalerie*.

*   *   *

Ultimately, however, the political, social, and epistemological chaos
unleashed by the Fourth Crusade is too great to be contained by a simple reaffirmation of the Franks' *boine chevalerie*. Soon after their conquest of Constantinople, the Franks become disillusioned with their
droit oir, now installed as Alexios IV. In response to their repeated re-
quests for the payment owed them, the puppet emperor treats his former
benefactors with imperial disdain: "he answered . . . that he would not
pay them a thing—that he had paid them too much and wasn't afraid of
them at all; instead, he ordered them to go away and vacate his lands: let
them be sure that, if they did not leave his lands soon, he would harrass
them" (59.6–11). Enraged, Enrico Dandolo, the blind and ancient doge
of Venice, convokes the anointed emperor and rebukes him like a recalcitrant boy, excoriating him (in Robert's vivid rendition) in the second-
person familiar:

"Alexios, what do you think you are doing?" said the doge. "Take heed: we pulled
you out of great misery and have made you lord and crowned you emperor," said
the doge. "Aren't you going to keep your agreement with us? aren't you going to
do something more about it?" "No," said the emperor, "I won't do anything
more than I've done!" "No?" said the doge. "Wicked boy, we pulled you out of
shit," said the doge, "and will return you to shit. I challenge you: be warned that
I will seek to do you all the harm in my power from this moment forward."
(59.22–31)

("Alexe, que cuides tu faire?" fist li dux, "preng warde que nous t'avons geté de grant caitivité, si t'avons fait seigneur et coroné a empereur; ne nous tenras tu mie" fist li dux, "nos convenenches, ne si n'en feras plus?" "Naie," fist li empereres, "je n'en ferai plus que fait en ai!" "Non?" dist li dux, "garchons malvais; nous t'avons," fist li dux, "geté de le merde et en le merde te remeterons; et je te desfi et bien saches tu que je te pourcacherai mal a men pooir de ches pas en avant.")

Dispensing with any show of reverence to the emperor, Dandolo reveals the crude economic motive lurking just beneath the crusaders' intervention in the Byzantine succession. A dispute over one hundred unpaid marks is sufficient to turn the *droit oir* of Constantinople into a *garchon malvais* whom the Franks prepare to cast off the moment he proves insufficiently pliant. By the same token, the crusaders who two years before had set out enveloped in religious and chivalric idealism have themselves been transformed into a greedy and contentious mercenary band.

Nor are the Franks the only ones unhappy with their puppet emperor. In Constantinople itself, resistance to the crusaders was crystallizing around Alexios Ducas "Murzuphlus," son-in-law of the deposed emperor Alexios III.[49] At this juncture, with the crusaders' own legitimacy on the line, the *droit oir* turned *garchon malvais* is reinvested with an imperial dignity (being twice referred to as "the emperor") while Ducas's opposition to Alexios IV—in contrast to the crusaders' own—is coded as faithlessness and base treason. "Meanwhile, the Greeks (those who were *traitors* toward *the emperor*) and Murzuphlus (whom *the emperor* had freed from prison) came together one day and plotted a great *treason*. They wanted to make another emperor of him—someone who would deliver them from the Franks, for they didn't like Alexios at all" (61, 13–19, emphasis added). Ducas's perfidy toward the emperor who had liberated him from prison [geté de prison] verbally parallels the emperor's own betrayal of the crusaders, who had rescued him from shit [geté de le merde]. In his ensuing account of Alexios's assassination, Robert portrays his death as a clear case of murder:

then at night, [Murzuphlus] entered the chamber where *his lord the emperor, who had freed him from prison*, was sleeping and had a cord tied around his neck and had him strangled, along with his father Isaac. When this was done, he returned to those who were going to make him emperor and told them of it, and they went and crowned him emperor. When Murzuphlus was emperor, the news spread through the city: "What is this? In faith, *Murzuphlus is emperor! He has murdered his lord!*" (62.2–11, emphasis added) (si s'en entra [Morchofles] par nuit en le cambre ou *ses sires li empereres, qui le geta de prison*, se dormoit, si li fist lachier une corde u col, si le fist estranler et sen pere Kyrsaac ausi. Quant il eut chou fait, si vint ariere a chiaus qui le devoient faire empereur, si leur dist; et chil alerent, si le coronerent et s'en fisent empereur. Quant Morchofles fu empereres, si s'en ala le nouvele par le chité: "K'est, que n'est, par foi! *Morchofles est empereres, s'a sen seigneur mordri!*")

Here the repetition, formulaic phrasing, limited vocabulary, and paratactic style—in short, all the traits typifying the inelegance of early vernacular prose—vividly hammer home the heinousness of Ducas's deed. In showing him sneaking up on his sleeping victim by night, Robert adduces the elements of secrecy and treachery distinguishing murder from legitimate homicide.[50]

*   *   *

Political assassinations were far from unknown in Latin Europe: famous examples include Charles the Good, the count of Flanders murdered in 1128 by disgruntled *ministeriales*; Conrad of Montferrat, who was literally "Assassinated," as we have seen, just after being recognized as king of Jerusalem (1192); and, in the cause célèbre of the twelfth century, Saint Thomas Becket (1170).[51] Each of these deaths had had substantial political consequences. Here, the crusaders' mixed reaction to Alexios's murder reflects their ambivalence toward the boy alternately cast as *droit oir* and *garchon malvais*: "Some cursed anyone who cared that Alexios was dead, since he hadn't respected his agreement with the pilgrims. Others said it weighed on them that he had been killed in this way" (62.14–18). Ultimately, however, Alexios's death serves the crusaders well: relieved of all obligation toward the emperor they themselves had created, they are now free to cast themselves as his avengers. Mobilizing their sense of feudal outrage toward the regicide, they respond with contempt to Murzuphlus's demand that they leave Constantinople:

When the barons heard what Murzuphlus had ordered, they replied: "Who?" they said, "*He who treacherously murdered his lord by night* has sent this word to us?" And they sent back word to him that they now defied him and he should beware, that they would not abandon the siege until they had avenged the one he had murdered and had retaken Constantinople and gotten back in full the things Alexios had promised them. (62.24–33, emphasis added)

(Quant li baron oïrent chou que Morchofles leur avoit mandé, si respondirent: "Qui?" fisent il, "*chis qui sen seigneur a mordri par nuit en traïson* si nous a mandé

chou?" Si li manderent ariere que ore le desfioient il et qu'il se gardast d'aus, et
que il n'en partiroient du siege, s'aroient chelui vengié que il avoit mordri et si
raroient pris autre fois Coustantinoble et si raroient tout pleinement les convenenches que Alexes leur avoit en convent.)

Condemning Murzuphlus (who had meanwhile assumed the imperial
throne as Alexios V) as a murderer and usurper, the Franks now launch a
second assault on Constantinople—no longer on behalf of an ousted pre-
tender but against a corrupt political order of faithless lords and treacherous vassals. Casting themselves as both the aggrieved victims of Alexios
IV's broken promises and the avengers of his scandalous murder, the crusaders who had once set out to recapture the Holy Land now decide to
seize the rich Byzantine Empire for themselves.

* * *

For all their overdetermined indignation at Alexios's murder, the
Franks' discomfiture at their second conquest of Constantinople emerges
in the discursive or generic shifts its narration occasions. As we have seen,
their initial attack on the city was choreographed with a pageantry easily
assimilatable to the discourse of epic. This second assault is described with
an eye to underscoring the righteousness of the crusaders' cause. Count
Henry of Hainault (Baldwin IX's brother and successor as Latin emperor)
captures an icon of the Virgin and a Byzantine imperial banner, presaging
both a spiritual and a political triumph. As the battle hangs in the balance,
the city's defenders taunt the crusaders, even mooning them: "the
Greeks . . . lowered their breeches and showed [the Franks] their asses"
(72.21–22). The Latin bishops gather the Franks together to rally their
sagging morale: "[They] proclaimed that the battle was righteous [droi-
turiere] and that they were right to attack them, for formerly, those of the
city had been obedient to the law of Rome, but now they disobey it, saying that the law of Rome was worthless, and that all those who believed in
it were dogs. And the bishops said that therefore they should be attacked,
and that this was no sin [pechiés], but rather a great act of charity [grans
aumosnes]" (72.8–16). Drawing on a long history of the Franks' suspicion
toward the Byzantine Empire, this condemnation shatters any illusion of
a united Christendom.[52] Going one step further, the bishops then equate
Ducas's assassination of Alexios with the betrayal of Christ, casting their
erstwhile Greek allies as the enemies of God: "Then the bishops preached

throughout the army . . . showing the pilgrims that the battle was righteous [droituriere], for [the Greeks] were traitors and murderers, and they had been disloyal when they murdered their rightful lord [leur seigneur droiturier]: they were worse than Jews. And the bishops said that, in the name of God and the pope, they would assail all those who attacked them; . . . and let them not be afraid of attacking the Greeks, for they were enemies of God [enemi Damedieu]" (73.3–16). Once again interpellated as (armed) pilgrims with right on their side, the knights of the Fourth Crusade who had set out two years before to take Jerusalem from the Turks now set their sights on Constantinople and their Greek coreligionists.

Where Geoffroy de Villehardouin consistently "subordinates individual accomplishments to broad political and military objectives,"[53] Robert, at this crucial moment of the siege, shifts his gaze away from the crusader army toward specific individuals to whom he is linked by ties of kinship, feudal loyalty, and regional pride. Accordingly, the first exploits he celebrates are those of his brother and his overlord: "Now there was a clerk, Aleaume of Clari by name, who was so brave [preus] in every need that he led every assault in which he took part. At the tower of Galata this clerk showed more prowess [plus de proeches] himself, man for man, than anyone else in the army, except Lord Pierre of Bracheux" (75.15–20). For the first time, Robert writes *himself* into the text, the better to highlight his brother's heroic abandon:

When Aleaume the clerk saw that no one dared enter, he came forward and said he would enter. There was a knight there, a brother of his named Robert de Clari, who stopped him and said he would by no means enter. Saying he would, the clerk got down on his hands and knees. When his brother saw this, he seized him by the foot and began to pull him, so that it was in spite of his brother, willing or not, that the clerk got in. (76.1–9)

(Quant Aliaumes li cers vit que nus n'i osoit entrer, si sali avant et dist qu'il i enterroit. Si avoit illuec un chevalier, un sien frere, Robers de Clari avoit a non, qui li desfendi et qui dist qu'il n'i enterroit mie; et li clers dist que si feroit, si se met ens a piés et a mains; et quant ses freres vit chou, si le prent par le pié, si commenche a sakier a lui, et tant que maugré sen frere, vausist ou ne dengnast, que li cler i entra.)

Once inside, Aleaume is assaulted by the Greek defenders; but when he draws his knife and charges, they scatter "like animals" (76.14) before him. Meanwhile, Pierre of Amiens follows him through the breach, urging his men on against Ducas: "Now, lords, now do well! Now we'll have

battle: here's the emperor coming. Take care that no one be so bold as to
retreat, but concentrate on doing well!" (77.6–9) (Or, seigneur, or du
bien faire! Nous arons ja le bataille; veschi l'empereur ou il vient. Wardés
qu'il n'i ait si hardi qui refust arriere, mais or pensés du bien faire!"). As
the Byzantine defenders retreat, Pierre's men open the gate to the main
body of Franks, precipitating the sack of the great city of Constantinople.

Just over a century after the First Crusaders gazed upon Constantinople in wonder, their descendants fell upon the Byzantine capital in a
sack "unparalleled in history," targeting not only the city's wealth but (as
in the devastation wrought by the drunken Franks in the *Pèlerinage de
Charlemagne*) seeking its symbolic destruction, including the sexual humiliation of its women. Paraphrasing the Byzantine chronicler Niketas
Choniates, the crusade historian Steven Runciman gives a vivid account
of the three-day spree. Frenchmen and Flemings, he writes,

were filled with a lust for destruction. They rushed in a howling mob down the
streets and through the houses, snatching up everything that glittered and destroying whatever they could not carry, pausing only to murder or to rape, or to
break open the wine-cellars for their refreshment. Neither monasteries nor
churches nor libraries were spared. In St Sophia itself drunken soldiers could be
seen tearing down the silken hangings and pulling the great silver iconostasis
to pieces, while sacred books and icons were trampled under foot. While they drank
merrily from the altar-vessels a prostitute set herself on the Patriarch's throne and
began to sing a ribald French song. Nuns were ravished in their convents. Palaces
and hovels alike were entered and wrecked. Wounded women and children lay dying in the streets. For three days the ghastly scenes of pillage and bloodshed continued, till the huge and beautiful city was a shambles. Even the Saracens would
have been more merciful, cried the historian Nicetas, and with truth.[54]

Like Villehardouin, Robert gives little hint of this orgy of desecration and
destruction. Framed in tight close-up on the heroic actions of his brother,
Aleaume de Clari, and his overlord, Pierre of Amiens, his narrative casts
the Franks' victory, quite simply, as the vindication of Latin rectitude over
Greek perfidy: "because of [the Greeks'] treason and disloyalty and the
murder that Murzuphlus had done, [God] willed that the city should be
taken and all the people of the city dishonored" (74.54–57).

* * *

If the experience of crusade could *produce* the common identity
"Frank," it could also serve to undo it. During the siege itself, for example,

the crusaders had come face-to-face with the Byzantine emperor's English and Danish mercenaries—starkly disrupting the carefully constructed binary between "Latins" and "Greeks." Infinitely more devastating is the bitter disillusionment occasioned by the victors' division of the spoils after the sack of the city. Robert's sense of betrayal is palpable:

Then the high men, the rich men, came together and agreed among themselves to take the best houses of the city, without the common people or the poor knights of the army knowing anything about it. And from that time on *they began to betray the common people* and to bear bad faith and bad company, which they later paid for very dearly, as we shall tell you. So they ordered all the best houses and the riches of the city seized, and they had taken all of them before the poor knights and the common people of the army realized it. And when the poor people realized it, they went and took what they could get, each as best he could. They found a lot and a lot was left, for the city was very large and populous. (80.11–26)

(Adont si s'asanlerent li haut homme, li rike homme, et prisent consel entr'aus, que le menue gent n'en seurent mot ne li povre chevalier de l'ost, que il prenderoient les meilleurs ostex de le vile; et tresdont *commenchierent il a traïr le menue gent*, et a porter leur male foi et male compaingnie, que il compererent puis molt kier, si comme nous vous dirons aprés. Si envoierent saisir tous les melleurs ostex et les plus rikes de le vile, si qu'il les eurent tous saisis anchois que li povre chevalier ne le menue gent de l'ost s'apercheussent. Et quant le povre gent s'aperchurent, si alerent dont qui miex miex, si prisent chou qu'il atainsent; assés en i trovérent et assés en prisent et assés en i remest, car le chités estoit molt grans et molt pueplee.)

As the great barons seize what they can for themselves, with utter contempt for the common knight and soldier, the fictional unity of Latin Christendom is again shattered—this time along class rather than regional lines.

Eventually, this betrayal is partially redeemed by a more general distribution of a share of the city's immense wealth "to each knight, to each mounted sergeant, and to all the common people of the army; to the women and children; to everyone" (98.6–8). Once again, Robert's brother is at the center of the action. Denied his portion of the spoils on the grounds that he is a cleric, Aleaume protests that "he had a horse and hauberk like a knight, and had fought as much and more as any knight there" (98.14–17)—arguing for a *functional* definition of knighthood that privileges "acts" over "identities."[55] His claim is supported by the count of Saint Pol, who confirms that Aleaume had shown more valor than three hundred knights. Thus, writes Robert with visible satisfaction, "the cleric proved [desraisna] that clerics as well as knights should have their share" (98.23–24)—undoing the ideological distinction between *oratores* and *bellatores* in the process.

As the crusaders establish their control over Constantinople, Robert—an "innocent sightseer, the typical tourist, open-eyed and widemouthed"—indulges in a pilgrim's tour of the wonders of the imperial city.[56] Ample space is devoted to the city's magnificent palaces—models for the one that so overwhelms the fictional Franks in the *Pèlerinage de Charlemagne*. Pride of place, however, goes to the invaluable relics constituting the Byzantines' spiritual wealth: fragments of the True Cross, the tip of the Holy Lance, Christ's blood and tunic, the crown of thorns, the Virgin's robe, and the head of Saint John the Baptist.[57]

The treachery of the *rike homme*, however, is not forgotten. For Robert, their inequity toward the army's common knights is an unredeemable violation of feudal ideals: they will not escape retribution. The following year, at the battle of Adrianople, they suffer a devastating defeat at the hands of the Cumans—the same horsemen Robert had earlier described with such wonder:

When those in the army saw these Cumans clothed in their sheepskins, they had no fear of them and took them no more seriously than a troop of children. And these Cumans and these people came very fast, rushing at the Franks and killing many of them and defeating them all in this battle. Thus the emperor was lost: it was never known what became of him, Count Louis [of Blois], and many other high men, and so many others that we don't know how many, but at least three hundred knights were lost there. (112.16–26)

Geoffroy de Villehardouin explains the disaster at Adrianople as the result of a tactical blunder: during the siege of the city, John the Vlach "sent his Comans charging right up to [the Franks'] camp. A call to arms was raised; our men rushed out in disorder and pursued the Comans for a full league or more. This was a foolish action on our part, for when they wished to turn back the Comans let fly a veritable storm of arrows at them, and wounded many of their horses" (120–21). For Robert, on the other hand, the Franks are undone by their arrogance: their defeat at the hands of the nomadic archers they had haughtily disdained was just retribution for the great princes' betrayal of their feudal subordinates: "Thus truly did God take vengeance on them for their pride and for the bad faith they had shown the poor people of the army, and for the terrible sins they had committed in the city after they had taken it" (112.31–35) (Ensi faitement se venja Damedieus d'aus pour leur orguel et pour le male foi qu'il avoient portee a le povre gent de l'ost, et les oribles pekiés qu'il avoient fais en le chité, aprés chou qu'i l'eurent prise). Returning to the nascent class-consciousness elicited in the earlier scene of the division of the spoils, Robert announces the rupture of the reciprocal, hierarchical bonds constitutive of feudal society, throwing the fundamental categories of the medieval social imaginary into confusion.

In the aftermath of Adrianople, the election of a new emperor to replace the missing Baldwin IX reveals new fissures in the western alliance. In exchange for recognizing the accession of Baldwin's brother Henry of Hainault, the doge of Venice demands a precious icon, "an image of Our Lady, painted on a panel . . . the first image of Our Lady ever made or depicted" (114.4–5, 8–9). Nothing better sums up the commodification of values responsible for the deviation of the Fourth Crusade than this open exchange of a religious treasure for political power.

The crusaders' awkward transition from western-feudal to eastern-imperial models of rule is illustrated in Robert's account of the new emperor's two marriages. Soon after his accession, Henry marries the daughter of Boniface of Montferrat—a typical Latin alliance meant to heal the internecine quarrels that had arisen following the crusaders' conquest of the city.[58] The empress, however, dies shortly thereafter, leaving Henry a widower in the market for a second wife. Meanwhile, Henry,

who was a very good emperor, took counsel with his barons about what he could do about these Vlachs and Cumans, who were making war on the empire of Constantinople and who had slain his brother, the Emperor Baldwin; and the barons advised him to send a message to Boris, who was king of Vlachia, and order him to give him his daughter to be his wife. (116.23–30)

(qui molt fu boins empereres, se conseilla a ses barons que il porroit faire de ches Blaks et de ches Commains, qui si faitement werioient l'empire de Coustantinoble et qui l'empereeur Bauduin sen frere li avoient mort; tant que li baron li loerent qu'il envoiast a chelui Burus, qui estoit rois de Blakie, et que il li mandast qu'il li donnast sa fille a femme.)

The emperor bristles, protesting that he would never wed a woman "of such lowly birth" (116.31) (de si bas parage).[59] Here two key elements of medieval Western society threaten to come into conflict: the feudal politics of lineage, and the respect the overlord—even an emperor—owes the good advice (*consilium*) of his vassals. Undeterred by Henry's horror at the prospect of marrying a barbarian princess, the barons impress upon him the importance of the Vlach alliance:

And the barons say: "Lord, yes you will! we strongly advise you to make peace with them, for they are the strongest, most feared people in the empire or on earth." And the barons went on so long that the emperor sent two high-ranking knights there, beautifully turned out. And the messengers went very fearfully into that savage land, and when they got there, people wanted to slay them. (116.31–39)

(Et li baron disent: "Sire, si ferés! nous vous loons bien que vous vous acordés a aus, car che sont le plus fort gent et le plus doutee de l'empire ne de le tere." Et tant parlerent li baron que li empereres i envoia deus chevaliers haus hommes, et si les fist atourner molt belement, et s'en alerent li message molt doutanment en chele sauvage tere, et quant il vinrent la, si les vaut on destruire.")

Where the *Chanson de Roland* opens with the pagan king's peace of-fering of four hundred mules and fifty carts loaded with treasure, Robert's *Conquête* concludes with the delivery of Emperor Henry's barbarian bride:

Then King Boris outfitted his daughter very richly and *very nobly*, and many peo-ple with her; then he sent her to the emperor, giving him sixty pack animals loaded with riches: gold, silver, silk cloths, and rich jewels. Every single pack ani-mal was covered with a piece of red samite, so long it trailed a good seven or eight feet behind. They never went through mud nor bad roads, for none of the pieces of samite were damaged, all for daintiness and *nobility*. (117.1–10, emphasis added)

(Adonques si fist atorner Burus li rois se fille molt rikement et *molt noblement*, et assés gent avec lui; si l'envoia a l'empereeur, et li fist baillier soisante sommiers tous carkiés d'avoir et d'or et d'argent et de dras de soie et de rikes joiaus; ne n'i avoit sommier qui ne fust couvers d'un vermel samit, qui estoit lons qu'il trainoit bien set piés ou uit a cascun par derriere, ne ja tant n'alaissent par boe ne par laides voies que ja en fust nus des samis escorchiés, tout par cointise et *par nobleche*.)

The magnificence of the by now formulaic tribute of gold, silver, silk, and jewels effaces previous objections to the bride's "lowly birth," effectively transforming the barbarian princess into a Byzantine empress—her nobil-ity inherent in her dress and baggage train, if not of her person.

The penultimate section of the *Conquête* skips quickly to Emperor Henry's death in 1216—cause for "great harm and very great pity" (119.5–6) (grans damages et mout grans pitiés). In his concluding section, Robert inserts himself into the narrative for only the second time, evok-ing his eyewitness status both to guarantee the truth of his account and

to excuse the incapacity of human memory to retain all the extraordinary
events of the crusade:

Now you have heard the truth: how Constantinople was conquered, how Baldwin,
count of Flanders became emperor, and my lord Henry his brother after him. He
who was there and saw and heard it attests to it: the knight Robert de Clari, [who]
had the truth of how it was conquered set down in writing. And though he may
not have recounted the conquest as beautifully as many a good teller would have,
still he has at all times told the very truth, and there are so many true things that he
can't remember them all. (120.1–11)

(Ore avés oï le verité, confaitement Coustantinoble fu conquise, et confaitement li
cuens de Flandres Bauduins en fu empereres, et mesires Henris ses freres aprés,
que chis qui i fu et qui le vit et qui l'oï le tesmongne, Robers de Clari, li chevaliers,
et a fait metre en escrit le verité, si comme ele fu conquise; et ja soit chou que il ne
l'ait si belement contee le conqueste, comme maint boin diteeur l'eussent contee,
si en a il toutes eures le droite verité contee, et assés de verités en a teutes qu'il ne
peut mie toutes ramembrer.)

By explicitly identifying himself as a knight and contrasting his impoverished rendition not with the more learned account of a cleric but with the
better-crafted one of a *boin diteeur*, Robert shows that vernacular prose
historiography—like vernacular literature—must first of all be understood
in relation to "the life of the French aristocracy, as it attempted to deal
with the consequences of rapid and far-reaching social changes taking
place in France."[60] But unlike the mid-twelfth-century translations whose
authority was guaranteed *avant la lettre* by their connection to hegemonic
Latin culture, Robert's first-person account is an experiment that moves
the French feudal nobility, long the *sujet de l'énoncé* of epic and romance,
to the unaccustomed position of *sujet de l'énonciation*.

*   *   *

For the Franks, the "Latin Empire" proved less valuable than they
could ever have imagined, lasting only fifty-seven years before being retaken by Michael VIII Palaeologus in 1261.[61] By attracting western adventurers who might otherwise have sought their fortunes in the Holy Land,
its existence arguably hastened the fall of crusader Acre in 1291. The greatest beneficiaries of 1204 were indisputably the Venetians, who profited
handsomely from the elimination of Byzantine competition in the eastern Mediterranean. The same discrepancy between Venetian mercantile

superiority and French military-feudal force that underlay the diversion of the Fourth Crusade better equipped the Italians to profit from this sudden shift in geopolitical power. Awarded a strategically chosen three-eighths of the spoils, they established an overseas empire that underwrote their preeminence in the late medieval Mediterranean.[62]

What motivated great barons like Baldwin IX to undertake an adventure that ultimately proved so detrimental to their own interests? Beyond the religious fervor that had moved crusaders from all ranks of society for over a century, the Franco-Flemish nobility had a long history in the affairs of Outremer. Baldwin's journey to the East was part of a well-established family tradition, what Robert Bartlett calls the "aristocratic diaspora" of the high Middle Ages.[63] At the turn of the thirteenth century, the great vassals of France may have felt they had little to fear from Philip Augustus, locked in struggle with the kings of England and under a ban of excommunication (as we saw above) for having repudiated his second wife, Ingeborg. In assuming leadership of the Fourth Crusade, Baldwin stood to gain moral authority over his king.[64] What he failed to foresee was the havoc his adventures would wreak on the political stability of Flanders. By remaining in the East as emperor of Constantinople, he "spared [himself and his sovereign] a good deal of worry over an uncertain [feudal] loyalty."[65] His capture and presumed death at the battle of Adrianople, however, left the rule of Flanders to his infant daughter Jeanne. Philip Augustus was quick to assert his feudal prerogatives at the accession of a minor. The deaths of the count and countess "left their western lands prey to external aggression and internal disorder. The unhappy people, deprived of their count, who had maintained order and given them relative security, while holding French ambitions in check, were ruled first by a minor under incompetent and possibly treacherous guardianship, and then in succession by two unstable and self-willed women."[66] Ironically, the crusaders' conquest of Constantinople and Baldwin IX's election as Latin emperor—combined with military reversals and genealogical accident—left Flanders vulnerable to the expansionist policies of the French king.[67] The very principles through which the great lords of northern France legitimized their conquest contributed to their undoing.

In *Orientalism*, Edward Said demonstrates how closely nineteenth-century colonialism was linked to discourses constituting "the Orient" as the object of Western knowledge and analysis.[68] Robert de Clari's text shows that in the early thirteenth century, something like the opposite occurred. The Franks' experience in the eastern Mediterranean *disrupted* the mental categories that organized their world. The deviation of the Fourth Crusade both resulted from and made glaringly obvious the inadequacy of discourses of legitimation that had driven Latin Christendom's military expeditions to the eastern Mediterranean for over a century. Out of the confusion produced by the Franks' conquest of Constantinople—their elation at the marvels now in their possession but also the epistemological dilemma of having sacked the greatest city in Christendom—emerged two extraordinary eyewitness accounts of the Fourth Crusade. Villehardouin's narrative—motivated by the need to explain, to justify the unthinkable—draws on a new discourse of facticity and pragmatism, "authorized" by his privileged vantage point as leader and eyewitness. Robert's, on the other hand, struggles to pour new experiences into old conceptual molds. The result is an uneven and extravagant but far more revealing chronicle of an important turning point in world history and the history of European mentalities.

6

The Romance of MiscegeNation

Negotiating Identities in La Fille du comte de Pontieu

IN THIS CHAPTER, WE TURN TO *La Fille du comte de Pontieu*, a curious thirteenth-century prose romance that radically unsettles the medieval Europe "of simple paternity and unambiguous truths and meanings" underlying so much literary historiography.[1] Sometimes called the first French "nouvelle," it tells a strange tale of rape, attempted murder, apostasy, and reconversion.[2] Like *La Conquête de Constantinople*, it emanates from the region where vernacular prose first emerged. Like *Floire et Blancheflor*, it takes the Santiago pilgrimage trail as a plot device to transport its heroine deep into medieval Iberia, imagined as a space of hybridity where military confrontation gives way to mercantile exchange. Moreover, it casts Saracen Spain as a utopian space where the scandals besetting feudal society may be resolved in an outlandish play of conversion and miscegeNation.[3] Shifting our attention from roots to routes, *La Fille* articulates a medieval vision of difference that irreversibly unsettles the reassuring binarism of Roland's battlefield declaration, "Pagans are wrong and Christians are right." In this ideological remapping, religion is less a fixed identity than a strategic position: exiled for her infractions against the feudal politics of lineage, the count of Pontieu's daughter remakes herself as a Saracen queen before being reintegrated into Christian society.

The text opens with a journey into Spain born out of genealogical crisis. The count of Pontieu has married his nameless daughter to a "poor landless youth" (20) (povres bacelers) called Thibaut de Domart. Five years later, the couple is happy but childless: "it didn't please God to give them an heir, which greatly troubled everyone" (35–36) (ne plut a Diu qu'il eusent nul oir, dont molt pesa a cascun). One night, Thibaut (perhaps inspired by the miracle of a childless Frenchwoman who has a son just after her husband's pilgrimage to Santiago) conceives the idea of appealing to "my lord Saint James" (39–40) (monsengneur saint Jake).[4] He plans to go alone but, by means of a rash boon, his wife elicits his permission to accompany him. On the road they are ambushed by common brigands (in contrast to the marauding pagans of *Floire et Blancheflor*) who tie up Thibaut and rape his wife. Once they have gone, the lady, instead of freeing her husband, mysteriously and without explanation tries, unsuccessfully, to kill him. Back in Pontieu, when the count learns what has happened, he seals his daughter in a barrel and casts her into the sea. Fortuitously, she is rescued by a shipload of merchants who, noting her beauty, give her to the sultan of Almería as a present. Alone in a foreign land, the count's daughter converts to the sultan's faith, marries him, and (with a fertility absent in her first marriage) bears him a son and daughter in quick succession. One day, the count, his son, and Thibaut are taken captive in Almería. Visiting them in prison in her guise as sultana, the lady reveals her identity only upon hearing them repent of the wrong they have done her. Then she engineers the prisoners' escape; together with her Saracen-born son, they all set off by sea, making landfall in Brindisi. From there they journey to Rome, where the pope receives the lady back into the Christian faith, baptizes her son, and reconfirms her marriage to Thibaut. The formerly sterile couple now produces two sons—the eventual heirs to the counties of Pontieu and Saint Pol, which Thibaut inherits from a maternal uncle. Meanwhile, the daughter left behind in Almería grows into a great beauty known as "la belle Captive." Married to a valiant Turk called Malakin of Baudas, she gives birth to a daughter destined to become the mother of "Saladin the courtly."

Place-names like Ponthieu, Saint Pol, and Domart situate *La Fille du comte de Pontieu* in the same milieu that produced the first examples of vernacular prose.[5] Ponthieu, a "small, but strategically significant" county on the north-eastern border of Normandy, was ruled by a line of counts conspicuously aligned with the kings of France in their rivalry with the Norman kings of England.[6] In 1194, Count William of Ponthieu married the French king Philip Augustus's sister Alice; in the early thirteenth century, when our text was composed, the historical *fille du comte de Ponthieu* (see Table 6.1) was their daughter, Marie (born c. 1198).[7] Saint Pol (the countship inherited by Thibaut de Domart at the end of our tale) likewise played an important role in the politics of northeastern France but in the opposite camp. Count Hugh IV (whose wife, Yolande, commissioned the first of the *Pseudo-Turpin* translations in 1202) was part of the Franco-Flemish coalition that rebelled against Philip Augustus in 1182 and 1197 (revolts led by Flemish counts Philip of Alsace and Baldwin IX,

TABLE 6.1.   The Counts of Ponthieu

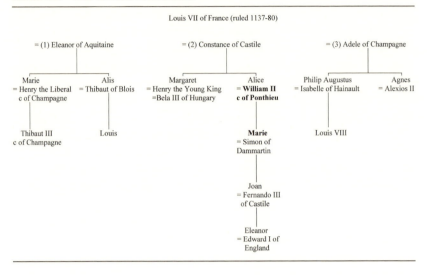

respectively). In 1198 Hugh made peace with the French king, pledging homage and swearing to "serve him against all others, except his immediate overlord, the count of Boulogne."[8] As we saw in Chapter 5, Hugh was a veteran of the Fourth Crusade, playing a small but honorable role in Robert de Clari's account of the conquest of Constantinople; he died in the East and was succeeded by his son-in-law Gaucher of Châtillon, a cousin of the French king, destined to cut an honorable figure in *La Chanson de la Croisade Albigeoise*.[9] In 1214, both the count of Ponthieu (the French king's brother-in-law) and the count of Saint Pol (his cousin) fought on the French side at Bouvines, the decisive battle that destroyed the remnants of the once powerful anti-French coalition.[10]

*   *   *

La Fille du comte de Pontieu depicts a Latin Christendom in disarray. Besides the genealogical crisis threatening the lineage of Thibaut de Domart, one of the major pilgrimage routes of the medieval West is shown plagued by lawlessness: en route to Santiago, Thibaut and his wife are set upon by eight men, "armed like thieves, on big horses, each with a lance in his hand" (110–11). Ignoring his greeting, they turn and attack; though unarmed—he is, after all, on pilgrimage—he wrests a sword from one of his assailants and kills three of them before being subdued and shackled.[11]

In medieval French literature, sexual violence against women usually takes highly conventional forms, euphemized in the knight's "seduction" of the peasant shepherdess (in the lyric *pastourelle*) or sublimated as ritualized abduction.[12] Here, rape functions as a brutal act of retribution: enraged at the deaths of their companions, four of the five surviving assailants demand Thibaut's wife for their own. The fifth, however, has something different in mind: " 'Lords, we have little to gain by keeping her. Rather, let us take her into the forest and *do what we will with her*, then put her back on the road and let her go.' This is what they did" (140–43, emphasis added) ("Sengeur, en li retenir n'arons nous mie grant preu, mais menon le en ceste forest et *faisons de li nos volentés*, puis le remetons a voie et le lasons aler.' Ensi le fisent).

Given the prominence this text in particular accords genealogical concerns, this violation of the count's daughter is an assault on feudal society itself, exposing the fragility of the very public order nobles were supposed to protect.[13] The enormity of the rape and its consequences are quickly forgotten, however, with a sudden and astonishing turn in the lady's behavior:

And my lord Thibaut saw her and said: "Lady, for God's sake, untie me, for these brambles are hurting me." The lady saw the sword of one of the slain brigands lying there; picking it up, she approached my lord Thibaut, saying: "Lord, I will deliver you." Then she tried to run him through. He saw the blow coming and braced himself, and struggled so strongly that he got his hands and back on top. And she struck him in such a way that she wounded him on the arms and cut the straps. Feeling his hands freed, he drew them in, broke the bonds, jumped to his feet, and said: "Lady, so please God, you will not kill me today!" And she said, "Surely, lord, that pains me." And he took the sword from her, put his hand on her shoulder, and led her back to the road they had come on. (145–59)

(Et mesire Tiebaus le vit et dist li: "Dame, pour Diu, desliés me, car ces ronses me grievent molt." La dame vit une espee gesir ki fu a un des larons qui ocis fu, si le prist et vint vers monsegneur Tiebaut, si dist: "Sire, je vous deliverai." Elle le cuida ferir parmi le cors, et il vit le cop venir, si le duta, et si durement tresali que les mains et li dos li furent deseure. Et elle le fiert si q'elle le bleça es bras et copa les coroies. Et il senti les mains laskier, et saca a lui, et rompi les loiens, et sali sus en piés, et dist: "Dame, se Diu plaist, vous ne me ocirés huimais!" Et elle li dist: "Certes, sire, ce poise moi." Il li toli l'espee et li mist le main sur l'espaule et l'en remena le voie qu'il estoient venu.)

Like Guenevere's coldness to Lancelot after he risks life and limb to save her, the lady's shocking behavior introduces an element of opacity that helps drive the story forward.[14] Without a word of reproach, Thibaut takes his wife to a nearby abbey and journeys to Santiago without her, collecting her once again on his way home. Astonishingly, they return to Pontieu and resume their former life, "except that he didn't lie in her bed" (180).

Thibaut's refusal to sleep with his wife underscores the paradoxicality of his predicament. They had set out for Santiago, after all, to pray for a child; but now any child the lady might bear, miraculous or otherwise, would be tainted by the suspicion of illegitimacy. Not until the count asks him to relate "some adventure you've seen or heard of" (187–88) (aucune aventure que vous avés veue u oï dire) does Thibaut slowly and reluctantly recount, in the third person, what had befallen "a knight and a lady" (194–95) he declines more specifically to name. When the count hears that the anonymous "knight" has returned home with his wife, he is incredulous:

"Thibaut, that knight was of another mind than I, for, by the faith I owe you, I would have hanged her from the branch of a tree by the braids or a briar stem or the leather strap itself." "Lord," says my lord Thibaut, "then the matter would never have been as believable as it will be when the lady herself bears witness to it." (199–205)

("Tiebaut, autre sens eut li chevalier ke jou n'eusse, que, par le foi que jo doi vous, que je l'euse la pendue a le brance d'un arbre par les treces, d'une ronse u de la coroie meisme." "Sire," fait mesire Tiebaus, "se ne fust mie la cose si bien creue comme elle sera quant la dame meismes le temongnera.")

As it dawns on him that the "lady" in question is his own daughter, the count completely ignores the scandal of her rape, honing in instead on her attack on her husband:

Tremendously angry, he summoned the lady and asked if what my lord Thibaut had said were true. And she asked, "What?" "That you tried to kill him." "Lord," she said, "yes." "Why did you want to do that?" "Lord," she said, "for such a reason that I'm still sorry I didn't do it." (210–16)

(A le grant ire qu'il avoit, il apiela la dame et li demanda se voirs estoit que messire Tiebaus avoit dit, et elle demanda: "Coi?" "Q'ensi le vausistes occire." "Sire," fait elle, "oïl." "Pour que le vausistes vous faire?" "Sire," fait elle, "pour çou q'encore me poise ke jo ne le fis.")

Her value in the politics of lineage already doubly compromised by her childlessness and her rape, the lady compounds her liability through her unexplained violence: her refusal to account for or repent of her action confirms her rupture with the feudal patriarchal order. Overriding the appeals of both his son and son-in-law, the count orders his daughter sealed in a barrel and thrown into the sea.

Cast out of French feudal society, the lady is transported into the mercantile world of the Mediterranean. Though regular maritime traffic between Flanders and the Mediterranean still lay a half century in the future,[15] the lady is fished out of the water by "a merchant ship coming from Flanders, heading for Saracen lands for profit" (237–38) (une nes marceande devers Flandres qui s'en aloit en tere de Sarrasins pour gaangnier)—surely evoking the Italians who had been trading with the Islamic world since before the millennium. Significantly, the merchants who rescue the lady identify themselves by neither "nationality" nor religion, but profession:

The ship continued on until it reached Almería. When they had docked, galleys came to meet them and asked them who they were; they said: "*We are merchants.*" They had warrants from the authorities allowing them to go everywhere in safety. They took the lady ashore . . . and asked one another what they should do with her. One of them said they should sell her; another said, "If you took my advice, we would make a present of her to the sultan of Almería, which would improve our business." (254–64, emphasis added)

(Tant corut la nef ke ele vint devant Aumarie, et quant il eurent havene pris, galies vinrent encontre aus qui leur demanderent ques gens erent, et disent: "*Marceant somes.*" Il avoient leur conduis des haus homes qu'il pooient aler en totes parties sauvement. Il misent la dame sor terre . . . et demanda li uns a l'autre qu'il en feroient, et li uns dist qu'i le venderoient, et li autres dist: "Se j'en fuise creus, nos en ferons present au soudant d'Aumarie, s'en amendera nos afaires.")

Moving in a pragmatic world of commerce and negotiated concessions, these merchants are experienced enough to appreciate the importance of earning the good will of the local sultan and savvy enough to know how to obtain it.

Situated on the southeastern coast of Spain, Almería (al-Mariyya) began as an arsenal and naval base founded by Caliph ʿAbd al-Raḥmān III in 955.[16] Providing sea links to the Maghreb, Alexandria, Syria, and Latin Europe, it soon became the premier port of Muslim Iberia, praised by geographers as the "Gateway to the East, the Key to Profit, the City in the

Land of Silver, on the Sand of Gold and on the Emerald Shore."[17] Under its *ṭāʾifa* kings (c. 1031–86), it developed a rich literary court. Under the Almoravids (1086–1147), it became famous for its manufacture of silk: rich brocades in distinctive reddish browns, dark greens or blues, yellows, and ivory, adorned with pearl-bordered rondels enclosing stylized human and animal figures drawn from ancient Near Eastern repertoires and decorated with Arabic inscriptions.[18] Its production of silk, as well as other commodities like ironwork and glass, made it so prosperous that, according to the Muslim geographer al-Idrīsī, in all of al-Andalus "there were no people richer or more commercial than its inhabitants, nor merchants with more expertise in all types of merchandise."[19]

In the first half of the twelfth century, Almería became a regular Genoese port of call—part of a western Mediterranean circuit comprising al-Andalus and the northwest African coast, counterbalancing Venetian hegemony in the east. By 1143 the route was so well traveled that a standard tithe was established in Genoa for each ship returning from Almería.[20] In dealing with the Muslim rulers of the western Mediterranean, the Genoese opportunistically combined military aggression with a politics of accommodation. In 1137 they negotiated a treaty that (like the *conduis* enjoyed by our fictional merchants) secured them trading rights throughout Almoravid lands—the first in a series of agreements renewed at regular intervals well into the following century. Ten years later, they joined in Alfonso VII of Castile's siege and capture of the city, sharing in the immense booty, which included large numbers of women and children subsequently sold on the slave markets of Marseille and Genoa.[21] When the Muslims (this time the Almohads) retook Almería in 1157, the Genoese simply reverted to business as usual, renegotiating treaties guaranteeing them access to Andalusian and North African markets. At the same time, Genoese merchants began frequenting the trade fairs of Champagne—surely one of the ways *soies d'Aumarie* made their way into noble households across Latin Europe, becoming a byword for luxury in vernacular French epic and romance.[22] By the last quarter of the century, Chrétien de Troyes's titular protagonist Cligès, accustomed to the wealth and splendor of both the Arthurian and Byzantine courts, takes Almería silks as the standard by which to measure his love: "were he duke of Almería, Morocco, or Tudela, he wouldn't have taken a *cenele* in exchange for his present bliss" (S'or fust Cligés dus d'Aumarie, / Ou de Marroc ou de Tudele, / Ne prisast il une cenele / Avers la joie que il a).[23]

The gift the anonymous merchants give the sultan evokes the least savory aspect of cross-cultural exchange. Slavery, as the historian Olivia Remie Constable notes, was "a very real part of both Christian and Muslim life in the medieval Mediterranean world," an important part of "the commercial side of interfaith relations."[24] Through the twelfth century, the slave trade ran predominantly from north to south: pagans from northern and eastern Europe were transported through Christian lands to the Islamic world. In al-Andalus, female slaves in particular were prized as domestic servants, musicians, dancers, and concubines.[25] The Genoese capture of Almería in 1147 marked a reversal in the flow of trade: by the early thirteenth century, Christian victories in the "reconquest" of Iberia meant ever greater numbers of Muslim slaves exported to Latin Europe–a lucrative trade in which the Genoese played a prominent role.[26]

For the count of Pontieu's daughter, disowned by her father and expelled from her home, enslavement brings an astounding upturn in fortune. Seeing her beauty, the young sultan of Almería

began to desire and love her, and (through a translator) asked her to tell him to what lineage she belonged. She didn't want to say anything about it. From what he saw in her, he was convinced she was a noblewoman; he asked whether she were Christian and told her that, if she would abandon her faith, he would marry her. (272–78)

(le commença a couvoitier et a amer, et li fist reqere par latiniers q'ele li desist de quel linage ele estoit. Ele nule verité n'en vaut dire. Il pensa bien a çou que il veoit en li qe ele estoit haute feme, et le fist reqere se ele estoit crestienne, et ke, se ele voloit sa loi laisier, k'il le prenderoit.)

In medieval Iberia, Muslim rulers commonly took Christian wives and concubines, without obliging them to convert.[27] Our text, on the other hand, rationalizes the sultan's willingness to marry a Christian slave of undefined lineage by ascribing it to the impetuosity of youth: he is *jovenes hom* (265–66), more ruled by desire than by reason.[28] The lady, in contrast, comes from a world in which marriage is a homosocial contract between men. Unmoored from all family connections and knowing what it means to be raped, she quickly weighs her choices: "She understood that it was better to act *for love* than *to be forced*, and notified him that she agreed" (278–79, emphasis added) (Ele vit bien que mix li valoit faire *par amours* que *par force*, si li manda qu'ele le feroit).

The lady's acceptance of the sultan's suit *par amours* represents a complex reversal of the motif of the Saracen queen, in which the pagan woman's conversion to Christianity symbolically completes the Frankish conquest of her land. In Chapter 2, I suggested that this motif was particularly attractive for representing the Franks' contact with advanced Mediterranean cultures that, having little to gain from conversion, could be seduced only in the imagination, in the figure of the bold princess ready to exchange a royal Saracen husband for a brave Christian count. Conversely, when the count of Pontieu's daughter freely chooses to abandon her faith out of strategic self-interest, she turns the tables on the feudal patriarchy that had discarded her.[29] Declining to reveal the lineage she is now rejecting, she reinvents herself *ab nihilo* as a Saracen queen.

In the conventional language of epic, as we have seen, the Saracen queen is indistinguishable from any beautiful woman of high station. This absence of explicitly racializing markers has sometimes been construed as an ethnocentric erasure of religious and cultural difference.[30] History, however, suggests an alternate interpretation: in al-Andalus, with its palimpsest of Phoenician, Greek, Roman, Visigothic, Arabic, Berber, Jewish, and black African populations, physical appearance was a notoriously unreliable sign of religion. The great caliph ʿAbd al-Raḥmān III, for example, had red hair, light skin, and blue eyes, and is reported to have dyed his hair black "to make himself look more like an Arab."[31] In 1215, just three years after a joint Castilian-Aragonese victory at the battle of Las Navas de Tolosa brought vast stretches of al-Andalus under Christian rule, the Fourth Lateran Council mandated that Jews and Saracens living in Christian lands wear distinctive dress, lest "*through error* Christians have relations with the women of Jews or Saracens, and Jews and Saracens with Christian women."[32] In Iberia, such cases of mistaken religious identity occur well into the fourteenth century, bespeaking "a general inability to distinguish Muslims from Christians solely by means of appearance."[33] The impulse to correlate religious faith with somatic features, it turns out, says more about modern presuppositions than about lived medieval realities.

La Fille pushes such questions of identity and cultural difference to their limit. In a world in which nobles "defined themselves by their families" and religion "meant membership [in] a community much more than adherence to a set of principles or beliefs," the lady's willing embrace of the sultan and his faith is a self-cancelling act.[34] Expelled from her home, she now abandons the last vestige of her former identity. Or does she? The representation of her apostasy remains suggestively vague. To become Muslim requires only the enunciation of the profession of the faith; whether the poet's audience knew this or not, the absence of any overt ritual marking the lady's conversion is striking: "once she had renounced her faith he married her, and his great love for her increased" (280–81) (Il l'espousa quant ele fu renoïe et criut en molt grant amour envers li).[35] When the pagan queen Bramimonde converts at the end of *La Chanson de Roland*, she is baptized in the waters of Aix and given the Christian name Juliane. The count's daughter, never having had a proper name in the first place, has none to relinquish, nor is she given a new one. Instead, her successful assimilation is marked by her immediate fecundity, inseparable from her quick mastery of the Saracen tongue:

she had been with him only a short time when she conceived and had a son. She spent time with the people and spoke and understood Saracen. And a short time later she had a daughter. Thus she was with the sultan some two and a half years, and understood Saracen and spoke it very well. (281–86)

(et petit fu avec lui quant elle conçut et eut un fil. Elle fu de le conpengnie a la gent et parla et entendi sarrasinois. Et petit demoura aprés qe ele eut une fille. Ensi fu bien deus ans et demi avoec le soudant, et entendi sarrasinois et parla molt bien.)

Since lineage was the language in which the feudal nobility articulated its legitimacy, negotiated its alliances, and staked its political claims, the two children the lady bears in such quick succession (in contrast to her five barren years with Thibaut) eloquently confirm the "felicity" of her new marriage.[36] In the twelfth and thirteenth centuries, the link between genealogical continuity and political stability can hardly be overstated: the lack of a direct heir or the accession of women or minors commonly occasioned unrest and confusion.[37] Having failed to provide Thibaut de Domart with an heir, the count's daughter now secures the sultan's lineage and confirms her place as his queen. Like the Christian knights serving the Muslim kings of al-Andalus, she demonstrates the porousness of the confessional divide even as she figures Christendom's loss as pagandom's gain.

   Casting linguistic fluency as a privileged sign of assimilation, however, opens a space for radical indeterminacy. The explicit marking of linguistic difference is rare in twelfth-century French literature: in the *Roland*, Christians and Saracens literally speak the same language, requiring no go-betweens to proffer treaties, plot conspiracies, or harangue each other in battle.[38] In this light, *La Fille*'s insistence on the lady's quick mastery of *sarrasinois* seems calculated to underscore her cultural assimilation.[39]

Yet unlike conversion, bilingualism does not demand that one relinquish the old in order to acquire the new. The confusion this can entail surfaces in a remarkable story in a *ḥisba* manual from early twelfth-century Iberia detailing the scams unscrupulous merchants might perpetrate on unsuspecting clients.[40] In Olivia Remie Constable's paraphrase,

> a buyer from out of town arrived in Cordoba and purchased a Christian slave girl whom, he was assured, had been recently acquired from the frontier regions. This was demonstrated by the fact that she only spoke a northern language. Because she had been recently imported, he paid an exorbitant price, after which he bought beautiful clothes for her and prepared to take her home. However, at this point she revealed—in fluent Arabic—that she was actually a free Muslim woman, and threatened to take him before a judge unless he did as she instructed. "If you fear [losing] your money," she counseled, "take me to Almeria, where you can increase what you originally paid [because] Almeria is a terminus for ships and a center for merchants and travelers." The implication, here, was that foreign merchants would pay a higher price to buy a slave for export to other regions of the Islamic world. When the duped buyer tried to complain to the original seller, the latter claimed to have left the business. Finding himself trapped, the man heeded his slave's advice, allowed her to keep her new finery, took her to Almeria, and sold her at a profit—presumably handing over a certain amount of this money to her.[41]

Besides calling attention to Almería's importance as a center of the slave trade, this episode undermines the either/or binary underpinning conversion. Rather, bilingualism introduces the more unsettling logic of the both/and: the lady's "northern language" marks her as Christian *at the same time that* her "fluent Arabic" identifies her as Muslim. This ambivalence reminds us that in medieval Iberia, language—like physical appearance—was an unreliable predictor of religious affiliation. Four centuries of *convivencia* had produced a multilingual society in which Latin, Hebrew, vernacular Romance, and Berber coexisted, with Arabic as a *shared* medium of culture. Exemplary here is the complaint of a ninth-century bishop of Cordoba that while few Christians could write passable Latin, many were fluent in Arabic, composing poetry "with greater art than the Arabs themselves."[42] Even more astonishing is the way this example inverts the power hierarchy dividing masters and slaves.[43] Originally marked as the silent object of exchange, the bilingual woman turns the tables on her owner, threatening him with judicial punishment (since Muslims were prohibited from enslaving fellow Muslims) not in order to gain her freedom but to orchestrate and profit from her own subsequent resale. "Can the subaltern speak?"[44] The answer is a resounding "yes"—and in two languages to boot: the bilingual woman disrupts binary difference.

* * *

Meanwhile, the count of Pontieu comes sorely to regret the "sin" (293) (pecié) he has committed against his daughter. Her expulsion has in fact brought feudal politics to a standstill: "my lord Thibaut didn't dare remarry, and the count's son, seeing his friend's pain, didn't want to become a knight, [even though] he was well of an age when he could have" (289–92) (mesire Tiebaus ne s'osoit remarier, et li fix le conte, por le doleur qu'il veoit que si ami avoient, ne voloit chevaliers devenir, et s'estoit bien d'aage q'estre le peust). To expiate his sin, the count takes the cross. When his son and Thibaut decide to accompany him, he momentarily balks: "why did you take the cross? Now the land will remain empty" (300–301) (por coi estes vous criosiés? Or remanra la tere vuide)—a fleeting allusion, perhaps, to the power vacuum crusading had created in northeastern France. Nevertheless, all three leave for the East, less as crusaders than as penitential pilgrims: "They very piously made their pilgrimage to all the places they knew God should be worshipped. And when the count had done that, he still wanted to do something more, so he and his companions pledged one year's service to the Temple" (305–10) (Fisent leur pelerinage molt saintement en tous les lieus u il seurent c'on devoit Diu servir. Et quant li quens eut çou fait, il pensa q'encore voloit il plus faire, si s'adona au service dou Tenple un an, il et sa conpagnie).[45] On their way home from the port of Acre, however, the pilgrims are swept up in a great storm that carries them clear across the Mediterranean: the first land they see is "Saracen land, called Almería" (324–25) (tere de Sarrasins et si l'apeloit on le tere d'Aumarie). Deciding that anything is preferable to drowning, the count asks that he and his party be put ashore.

Consigned to prison, the count is about to be delivered to the sultan's archers for target practice when the lady intervenes. Trading on her command of her native tongue, she asks permission to see him: "Lord, I speak French, and would speak with this poor man, if it pleased you" (350–51) (Sire, je sai françois, si parleroie a cest povre home, se vos plaisoit). Concealing her identity, the sultana appears to the captives for

all intents and purposes as a Saracen queen—her bilingualism the only visible link between her past and her present:

I am Saracen and know [magical] arts; and I tell you that you have never been
closer to a shameful death than you are now, if you don't tell me the truth; I will
know if what you are saying is true: what became of your daughter, who was married to this knight? (426–31)

(Je sui Sarrasine et sai d'art, si vos di que vous ne fustes onques pres de si hon-
teuse mort que vous estes ore, se vous voir ne me dites, et jou sarai bien se vous
dirés voir. Vo fille, que cil chevaliers ot espousee, que devint ele?)

Her declaration "Je sui Sarrasine" is part of a carefully crafted performance that plays on stereotypes of the foreign sorceress in order to elicit
the confession she desires. As the count, still not recognizing her, describes how his daughter had tried to kill her husband, their exchange reveals the gendered gap in their perception of the events on the Santiago
trail. "Ah!" sighs the sultana, "I know why she wanted to kill him . . . for
the great shame he had seen her suffer" (462–65). ("A! . . . bien sai por
quoi ele le vaut ocirre . . . Por le grant honte qu'il avoit veu que ele avoit
soufferte"). When the count protests that "he never would have treated
her any worse on account of it" (469–70) (ja por ce peiur sanllant ne l'en
eusse fait), she drily replies, "Lord, that's not what she thought" (470–71)
(Sire . . . che ne cuidoit ele mie adont). Her dynastic value already compromised by "her delay in producing an heir" (436) (l'atargement d'oir
qu'ele ne pot avoir), the lady had reacted in desperate revolt against her
devaluation in the feudal politics of lineage.
     In refashioning herself as sultana of Almería, the count's daughter
revalorizes her worth in feudal Christian society. Her repeated assertion
"Je sui Sarrasine" helps erase the triple scandal of her sterility, her rape,
and her attack on her husband. As a proud Saracen queen, she—like
Bramimonde or Orable—becomes a prize whose defection would
openly signify Latin Christendom's superiority over Islam, her previous
history subsumed in generic convention. Unlike those queens, however,
she is seduced neither by Christian love nor by the promise of a warrior's devotion but by the heartfelt contrition her father, husband, and
brother express over the "cruel venjanche" (475) they had exacted from
her. If you learned the lady were still alive, the sultana asks, what would
you say? One after another, they exclaim that nothing would make them
happier:

"Lady," said the count, "I would hardly be as happy to released from this prison and have twice the land I ever had!" "Lady," said my lord Thibaut, "I would hardly be as happy to have the most beautiful lady in the world and to have the kingdom of France along with her!" "Certainly, lady," said the young man, "no one could give me or promise me anything that would make me as happy!" (478–86)

("Dame," fait li quens, "je ne seroie mie si liés d'estre delivrés de ceste prison et d'avoir autant de terre en crutures que jou oi onques!" "Dame," fait mesire Tiebaus, "et je ne seroie mie si liés d'avoir le plus bele dame du mont et d'avoir le roiaume de France avoec lui!" "Chertes, dame," fait li joules, "n'on ne me porroit douner ne prametre de quoi je fusse si liés!")

The lady immediately breaks down in tears and reveals her identity by rehearsing their family relations: "you are my father and I am your daughter; and you are my lord, and you are my brother" (491–93) (vous estes mon pere, et . . . je sui vostre fille, et vous estes mes barons, et vous estes mes freres). Yet she tempers their joy by enjoining them to secrecy:

When they heard this . . . and went to bow before her, she stopped them and said: "I am Saracen, and ask you not to show any joy over anything you've heard, but simply go on as before and leave everything to me." (493–98)

(Quant il oïrent chou . . . et si firent sanllant d'umelier vers li, et ele leur desfendi et dist: "Je sui Sarrasine, et si vous pri que de cose que vous aiés oïe nul plus biau sanllant n'en faites, mais sinplement vous maintenés et moi laisiés couvenir.")

On the one hand, her assertion "Je sui Sarrasine" simply recapitulates her opening words to the prisoners. Yet in light of their intervening conversation her pronouncement cannot help but assume new meaning. This time, the line between performance and mimicry seems too close to call. Her words at once warn the prisoners not to betray her, promise that she will use her power to their advantage, and remind them that her present identity is no disguise: whatever else she is or has been, she is, having renounced her faith to marry the sultan, a genuine Saracen queen.[46]

The prisoners' escape turns on two episodes highlighting the multivalence of interconfessional relations. First, the sultana asks her husband to spare the prisoners on account of the entertainment they can provide: the eldest knows how to play chess and can teach them. As in *Floire et Blancheflor*, the game of chess (*eschiés*) serves as a medium of cross-cultural contact and negotiation—with the added twist that it is here represented as a game a Christian might teach a Saracen, reversing the historical lines of diffusion that brought chess to Latin Europe through the Muslim Mediterranean.[47] Second, the lady makes the astonishing proposition that her old husband should serve her new one: "My lord the sultan must go on campaign, and [as] I know you well, I ask you to go with him; if you were ever a gallant man, show it now!" (500–503) (Li soudans me sire en doit aler en une chevaucie, et je vous connois bien, si querrai que vous irés avoec li, et se vous onquest fustes predoume, moustrés le ore!) Before Thibaut can respond, she takes the proposition to her husband:

"Lord, one of my prisoners heard about your war and told me that he would willingly go with you, if he had leave." "Lady," he said, "I wouldn't dare, lest he played me false." "Lord," she said, "trust him, for I will hold the [other] two, and if he betrays you, I'll hang them by the throat." "Lady," he said, "I will give him a horse, arms, and whatever he needs." (504–12)

("Sire, li uns de mes prisons a oï parler de vostre guerre et m'a dit qu'il iroit volentiers avoec vous, s'il en avoit laiseur." "Dame," fait il, "je n'oseroie, qu'il ne me fesist fauseté." "Sire," fait ele, "seurement le faites, car jou retenrai les deus, et se cil vous mesfaisoit, je penderoie ces par les gueles." "Dame," fait il, "et jou li livrerai ceval et armes et ce qu'il le convenra.")

Trusting his wife's loyalty and judgment, the sultan takes Thibaut into battle, where he takes so many prisoners the sultan considers making him a vassal: "were he willing to accept great lands, I would certainly grant them" (525–26) (s'il voloit grant terre prendre, chertes jou li douroie). Though recently returned from a penitential crusade in the Holy Land, Thibaut—like the many mercenaries we considered in Chapter 1—willingly accepts service with his Saracen captor and benefactor.[48]

In his memoirs, Usāmah ibn Munqidh, the twelfth-century lord of Shayzar (Caesaria) in northern Syria, tells the story of a captive Christian his father had sent as a gift to a friend:

The maid suited Shihāb-al-Dīn, and he was pleased with her. He took her to himself and she bore him a boy, whom he called Badrān. . . . On his father's death, Badrān became the governor of the town and its people, his mother being the real power. She entered into conspiracy with a band of men and let herself down from the castle by a rope. The band took her to Sarūj, which belonged at that time to the Franks. There she married a Frankish shoemaker, while her son was the lord of the Castle of Jaᶜbar.

For Usāmah, the fact that the nameless ex-captive would abandon a position of honor and power to marry a shoemaker illustrates Frankish intransigence: "The Franks (may Allah's curse be upon them!) are an accursed race, the members of which do not assimilate except with their own kin."[49] The course our heroine now adopts helps confirm this perception: beloved by the sultan and the mother of his heir, she nevertheless trades on her influence to engineer an escape. Telling her husband she is pregnant and needs a change of air, she arranges a sea voyage, taking the three prisoners along for "company" and "protection." Unlike Usāmah's lady, she brings her Saracen son along, fully aware of the enormity of her act: "I've taken much from the sultan in taking from him myself and his son" (j'ai molt tolu au soudant quant jou li ai tolu mon cors et son fil), she later says, dispatching the ship in which she and the prisoners have escaped back to Almería: "I don't wish to take anything else from him" (562–64) (ne plus de sez cozes jou ne li bé a tolir).

Despite her flight, however, the sultana's assertion "Je sui Sarrasine" is no mere act; even as they put ashore at Brindisi, she remains wary of her Christian kin.[50] Reminding them that she can still return to Almería if she wishes, she demands assurances for the safety of her Saracen son: " 'Lords,' she said, 'consider my son: what will we do with him?' 'Lady, may he be welcomed with great profit and honor!' " (559–62) ("Seigneurs," fait ele, "ves chi mon fil, qu'en ferons nous?" "Dame, a grant bien et a grant houneur soit il venus!"). Only then does she definitively decide to return to Christendom. Provisioned "by merchants and Templars" (571) (par marceans et par Templiers), the travelers proceed to Rome, where the pope hears their confession and then

baptised the child with the name William. Then he restored the lady to true Christianity, and confirmed her and her husband in true marriage, and imposed penance on each for their misdeeds. (577–81)

(bautisa l'enfant et ot nom de Guilliame. Aprés, il remist la dame en droite crestienté, et conferma et li et son seigneur en droit mariage, et douna chascun penitance de ses mesfais.)

Though the lady is restored to her family, rank, and religion, this "happy ending" is far from a return to the *status quo ante*. Cast out of a *feudal* society that treated marriages as homosocial political contracts, she now returns to a Latin *Christendom* in which secular practices have come under ecclesiastical control. The pope's "confirmation" of the lady's (first) marriage, we should note, gestures toward complications in contemporary canon law: since Innocent III (1198–1216) had ruled that

"infidel marriages were indissoluble under the same conditions that ap-
plied to Christian marriages, that is, the parties must have consented
freely, and they must have ratified their consent by sexual intercourse,"
her marriage to the sultan is arguably more binding than her previous
marriage to Thibaut (for which the text had failed to register her personal
consent).[51]

*   *   *

Where epics like the *Prise d'Orange* unabashedly cast the conversion
of the Saracen queen as pagandom's loss and Christendom's gain, *La Fille
du comte de Pontieu* (like *Floire et Blancheflor*) trades on the overtly symmetrical but much more problematic move of the conversion of the Saracen prince. Given its emphasis on the feudal politics of lineage, the birth
of two sons to the reunited couple would seem to signal the story's
"happy ending."[52]

By God's will, my lord Thibaut had two sons by his wife. The count's son died
and was greatly mourned, and the count of Saint Pol was still alive. Now Lord
Thibaut's children were in expectation of [inheriting] two countships, to which
they succeeded in the end. (598–603)

(Mesires Tiebaus eut par le volonté de Dieu deus fiex de sa fame. Li fiex au conte
morut, dont grans deus fu fais, et li quens de Saint Pol vivait. Or furent li enfant
monsegneur Tiebaut en atente des deus contés ou il parvinrent en le fin.)

Previously compromised by the failure to produce an heir, Thibaut's marriage to the daughter of the count of Pontieu is now doubly assured: the
descendants of the noble but relatively humble Thibaut de Domart will
inherit both Pontieu and Saint Pol. He thus realizes the fondest dream of
chivalric youth—acquiring a great feudal honor—not through his own
skill-at-arms but by consenting to take back the wife who had previously
tried to kill him.

In the zero-sum game of the feudal politics of lineage, however,
Thibaut's gain is his stepson's loss. Taken from his homeland and baptized a Christian, William is the count of Pontieu's first-born grandson
and, by the logic of primogeniture, should succeed to his grandfather's
honor. Yet he is passed over in favor of his younger half-brother of "pure"
Christian lineage, receiving as a sort of consolation prize a small Norman
barony from a match engineered by his grandfather:[53]

The count of Pontieu attended a great feast, where there was a nobleman from Normandy called my lord Raoul de Préaux. This Raoul had a very beautiful daughter. The count of Pontieu talked so much that he brought about his grandson William's marriage to his daughter, for this Raoul had no other heir. William married her and became lord of Préaux. (591–98)

(A une haute feste li quens de Pontieu fu, si ot un haut home de Normendie c'on apeloit monsegneur Raoul de Praiax. Chis Raous avoit une molt bele fille. Li quens de Pontieu parla tant qu'il fist le mariage de Guilliame sen neveu et de sa fille, car chis Raous n'avoit plus d'oirs. Guilliame l'espousa et fu sires de Praiax.)

This exchange recasting a potential William of Pontieu as William of Préaux is striking since William, as we have seen, was the name of the count of Ponthieu who married the French king's sister Alice. The historical William of Préaux, on the other hand, was a Norman vassal whose knowledge of Arabic helped save Richard the Lionheart from capture in a curious incident from the Third Crusade. Hawking outside Jaffa in 1191, the king was ambushed by a party of Turks. In the melee, "one of the king's companions named William des Préaux shouted out loudly in the Saracen language that he was the *melech!*—which means king. The Turks believed William, seized him immediately and led him away as a prisoner to their army," sparing Richard from capture.[54] In this vertiginous play between history and fiction, *La Fille du comte de Pontieu* imputes a Saracen past to a crusader remembered for his strategic use of Arabic and his stint as a prisoner of war. Between the vassal who passes himself off as a king and ends up a captive and the Saracen prince who trades the splendor of Almería for the obscurity of a small Norman honor, the name William of Préaux figures a mutability challenging the fundamental categories of feudal society.

If William's fate reinscribes Christian-Saracen difference even as it purports to efface it, his younger sister's underscores the abiding trauma of gender. When the sultan learns of his wife's flight, "he loved the daughter left behind less; nevertheless, she grew to be very beautiful" (586–88) (la fille qui demoree estoit, mainz l'ama; neporquant ele crut et devint molt bele). Known as "the Fair Captive" (608) (la Bele Cetive), she wins the heart of a vassal named Malakin of Baudas (609).[55] In the tale's tantalizing epilogue, she is married off and becomes the maternal grandmother of "Saladin the courtly" (621) (courtois Salehadin).[56] This fictional genealogy, as critics point out, may have been meant to attenuate the humiliation of the crusaders' loss of Jerusalem in 1187 by suggesting that the Saracen leader who defeated them was, after all, part-Christian.[57]

However, *La Fille* also allows us to read the crusaders' setbacks in the eastern Mediterranean as the sultan of Almería's revenge on Latin Christendom for the loss of his wife and heir or, again, as the vindication of the underloved Bele Cetive: the price exacted from feudal Europe for its homosocial exclusion of women at home and abroad.

This indeterminacy lurking just below the surface of our tale's happy ending evokes a barely concealed history of crisis: the lineages of the counts of Pontieu and Saint Pol, the sultan of Almería, and the lord of Préaux all fail in the direct male line. Haunted by a series of dynastic disasters—sterility, rape, the death of one son and the apostasy of another—*La Fille du comte de Pontieu* hints at the sequence of genealogical misfortunes that rendered the Franco-Flemish nobility so vulnerable to the predations of French king Philip Augustus just after the turn of the thirteenth century.[58] *La Fille du comte de Pontieu* resolves these internal crises by expelling the problematic woman into "pagan" Spain. As sultana of Almería, she can activate the plot of the Saracen queen whose conversion reinvigorates feudal society and reconfirms its values through her willingness to leave "difference" behind.

In his article "La Compromission," Alexandre Leupin argues that the parodic *Pèlerinage de Charlemagne* corroded epic discourse from within, toppling Charlemagne's phallogocentric regime even as the blustery Franks toppled the pillars of the Byzantine king's magnificent palace. *La Fille du comte de Pontieu* does something similar to the paradigm of the Saracen princess: inhabiting it from within, pushing it to excess, stripping it of its ideological power. The lines of fracture appear not around the sultana but her son, whose displacement from the Pontieu succession points to a lingering trace of the *difference* his conversion was meant to efface. If the epic of the Saracen queen affirms the assimilationist power of the feudal Christian order, the romance of the Saracen prince leaves as its ideological residue the hapless Guillaume de Préaux, whose historical destiny it is to be mistaken for the crusader king Richard. In this confused historical palimpsest, *La Fille du comte de Pontieu* imagines an outlandish expedient for restoring genealogical rectitude—one that undermines the feudal politics of lineage even as it saves it.

*   *   *

La Fille du comte de Pontieu is an intensely genealogical drama, turning on broken lines of succession and cross-cultural miscegeNation.

TABLE 6.2.   Three Princesses

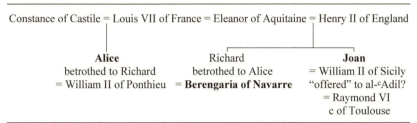

Constance of Castile = Louis VII of France = Eleanor of Aquitaine = Henry II of England

Alice	Richard	**Joan**
betrothed to Richard	betrothed to Alice	= William II of Sicily
= William II of Ponthieu	= **Berengaria of Navarre**	"offered" to al-ʿAdil?
		= Raymond VI
		c of Toulouse

These thematics reflect, I think, the importance of the roles women played in the political landscape of the late twelfth and early thirteenth centuries—their limited access to formal power notwithstanding. To conclude, I turn to the stories of three historical princesses: Berengaria of Navarre, Joan of England, and Alice of France—the wife, sister, and cast-off fiancée, respectively, of Richard the Lionheart, king of England (see Table 6.2). Exemplifying the vicissitudes of the feudal politics of lineage, their lives—which intersected with intensity during the winter of 1190–91—bear uncanny connections to the tale of *La Fille du comte de Pontieu*.

Berengaria was the daughter of Sancho VI of Navarre, whose Iberian kingdom straddled the Pyrenees at the point where the four French pilgrimage routes to Santiago de Compostela converged to form the *camino francés*.[59] Sancho III the Great of Navarre had first united the kingdoms of Christian Iberia around the turn of the millennium: later kings of León-Castile and Aragon as well as Navarre were his descendants. In the second half of the twelfth century, Sancho VI built a network of dynastic alliances across western Europe: his sister, Margaret, married the Norman king William I of Sicily and was the mother of William II (see Table 6.3). In 1191, Berengaria married Richard in a political match designed to secure the southern approach to Aquitaine during the king's absence on crusade. Despite its political advantages, however, the marriage was a dynastic failure: when Richard died in 1199, Berengaria was still childless; in an agreement with French king Philip Augustus, she ceded her dower lands in Normandy for the city of Le Mans, where she died in 1230.[60]

Joan's life is somewhat more colorful. The youngest of Richard's three sisters, she was betrothed at the age of eleven to King William II of Sicily (Berengaria's first cousin) and dispatched with great pomp to a land striking for its wealth and cultural hybridity.[61] When William's grandfather,

TABLE 6.3.   The House of Navarre

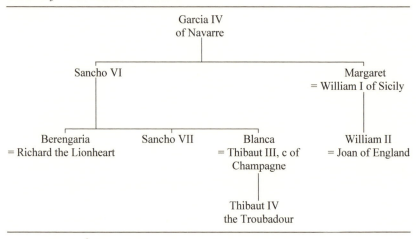

the upstart count Roger II, assumed the title of king in 1130, he had adopted an iconography not from the Capetian or Ottonian north but from the ceremonial courts of Constantinople and Cairo, building on the Mediterranean legacy of his Greek- and Arabic-speaking subjects.[62] On arriving in Palermo, Joan was lodged in La Zisa (one of the Islamic-style palaces dotting the outskirts of the city), and crowned in the Norman kings' Palatine Chapel, in which Byzantine-influenced wall mosaics were combined with a painted, Fatimid-style *muqarnas* ceiling.[63] Though by the late twelfth century the influx of foreigners from the north had begun to attenuate Sicily's distinctive character, it still remained clearly outside shared "European" norms. Ibn Jubayr, the Iberian traveler who visited Palermo in 1183, approvingly compared William II to a Muslim king, noting that he "reads and writes Arabic, favors Muslim physicians and astrologers, and populates his court with ministers and chamberlains, eunuch pages, handmaidens and concubines, who practice Islam as a more or less open secret." He further noted that in Palermo itself, Christian women "follow the fashion of Muslim women, are fluent of speech, wrap their cloaks about them, and are veiled. . . . they parade to their churches . . . bearing all the adornments of Muslim women, including jewellery, henna on the fingers, and perfumes."[64]

    In her twenty-two years as queen of this Mediterranean kingdom, Joan (like her sister-in-law Berengaria) produced no children to inherit

her husband's throne—a failure of lineage with important dynastic consequences. When William II died in 1189, he was succeeded by his aunt
Constance, wife of the future Hohenstaufen emperor Henry VI. Thus by
an accident of genealogical fate, southern Italy came under imperial
rule—a realignment of the geopolitical map with significant consequences
in the thirteenth century and beyond.[65]

Joan, meanwhile, was given other roles to play in the Angevin politics of lineage. Accompanying her brother Richard on the Third Crusade,
she became a pawn in a fantastic plot set in the Holy Land. Having recovered the port of Acre but unable to retake Jerusalem, Richard made a
startling proposition: that Joan should marry Saladin's brother al-ʿĀdil.
According to the Muslim chronicler Bahāʾad-Dīn, "She would live in
Jerusalem, and her brother was to give her the whole of Palestine that was
in his hands: Acre, Jaffa, Ascalon, and the rest, while the Sultan was to
give al-ʿĀdil all the parts of Palestine belonging to him and make him their
king, in addition to the lands and fees he already held." Saladin, the chronicler continues, "immediately approved the terms, knowing quite well that
the King of England would never agree to them and they were only a trick
and a practical joke on his part." In fact, after lengthy negotiations,
Richard sent word that

The Christian people disapprove of my giving my sister in marriage without con-
sulting the Pope, the head and leader of Christianity. I have therefore sent a messenger who will be back in three months. If he authorizes the wedding, so much
the better. If not, I will give you the hand of one of my nieces, for whom I shall
not need paper consent.[66]

Joan, for her part, "was horrified when she heard the suggestion. Nothing, she said, would induce her to marry a Moslem. So Richard asked al-
ʿĀdil whether he would consider becoming a Christian. Al-ʿĀdil politely
refused the honour, but invited Richard to a sumptuous banquet."[67] In
the meanwhile, Bahāʾad-Dīn concludes, "the hostilities continued and
took their inevitable course."[68]

However contrived, the al-ʿĀdil episode raises two interesting points.
The first is the imaginative power exerted by the feudal politics of lineage.
While Richard may never have seriously meant to offer his sister to Saladin's brother, it is telling that his diplomatic feint was poured into the
language of dynastic alliance.[69] The second is the way Saladin is construed
as the site of the reconciliation of cultural difference; in the later Middle

Ages, he was destined to become an exemplar of courtliness and is even represented as having been Eleanor of Aquitaine's lover.[70] Meanwhile, Joan herself was destined for other dynastic ends: in 1196 Richard married her to Count Raymond VI of Toulouse, a match that helped resolve succession disputes dating back to the time of Eleanor of Aquitaine's grandfather, Duke Guilhem IX.[71] The following year Joan gave birth to a son, Raimondet, destined (see Chapter 7) to play a heroic role in the *Chanson de la Croisade Albigeoise.*[72]

The last of our trio of princesses is Alice of France—mother, as we have seen, of the historical *fille du comte de Pontieu*. Daughter of Louis VII and his second wife, Constance of Castile, she had been betrothed to Richard in 1169 and brought up at the Angevin court. When Richard's elder brother Henry the Young King died in 1183 leaving Alice's sister Margaret a widow, their half-brother Philip—now king of France—began to press for Richard's marriage to Alice in order to reconfirm the French-Angevin alliance. Richard steadfastly refused (occasioning rumors that Alice had been his father's mistress). The betrothal was not formally broken, however, until 1190, when Richard—stopping in Sicily to pick up his sister, the widowed Queen Joan, en route to the Third Crusade—negotiated Alice's return to Philip along with a payment of 10,000 marks; Richard's new fiancée, Berengaria of Navarre, arrived by sea shortly thereafter.[73] Despite the treaty, Alice was returned to her brother only in 1195; he immediately married her to Count William II of Ponthieu, whose lands formed a strategic buffer between Normandy and Flanders. Their daughter Marie (born c. 1198) was betrothed at the age of ten to Simon of Dammartin. In 1214, Simon fought on the losing side at Bouvines and, exiled from France, took refuge in England, leaving Marie behind. When Count William died in 1221, Philip Augustus confiscated Ponthieu and gave it to his cousin, Robert of Dreux.[74] In 1225 (after Philip's death), Marie secured succession rights for her children. She became a famous patron of letters and at her death (c. 1251) was succeeded as countess of Ponthieu by her daughter Joan, queen of Castile.[75] The count of Ponthieu's daughter, it turns out, was destined to be the great-grandmother not of Saladin but of Edward II of England.

*   *   *

The postcolonial text, Samia Mehrez writes, challenges "both its own indigenous, conventional models as well as the dominant structures and institutions of the colonizer in a newly forged language." It does this by "exploding and confounding different symbolic worlds and separate systems of signification in order to create a mutual interdependence and intersignification."[76] Earlier I suggested that the bilingualism of the daughter of the count of Pontieu served just such a purpose, undermining the either/or binarism that so frequently structures representations of cultural contact. If the *Chanson de Roland* works to *produce* cultural difference, *La Fille du comte de Pontieu* openly contests the notion of "a medieval Europe of simple paternity and unambiguous truths and meanings."[77] Like *Floire et Blancheflor*, it conscripts cultural contact to a project of miscegeNation that attributes a hybrid ancestry to both Charlemagne and Saladin—two of the most important figures of the Christian and Muslim Middle Ages, respectively.

What does Saladin's hybrid ancestry mean? One critic reads the "confident, beneficial attribution, both of a Christian bloodline to no less than a Saladin, and of a Saracen bloodline to the Picard descendants of Raoul de Préaux" as indicative of "a powerful sense of the positive potential of interethnic exchange and cultural diversity" that contrasts with the "primitive epic idealization of a pure family, a pure class, or a pure race."[78] But the representation of miscegeNation in *La Fille du comte de Pontieu*, I would argue, is visibly less "confident" or "beneficial" than in *Floire et Blancheflor*; rather, it is a means of simultaneously suggesting and finessing the failures—military, genealogical, and epistemological—of the early thirteenth century Franco-Flemish nobility. It is perhaps no accident that at the very moment ideologues were highlighting French king Philip Augustus's connections to Charlemagne, *La Fille* cast Saladin—the Muslim leader who, within living memory, had conquered the crusader capital of Jerusalem—as the descendant of Philip's own niece, daughter of the historical count of Ponthieu.[79] Composed amid the same sense of political and epistemological crisis that produced *La Conquête de Constantinople*, *La Fille du comte de Pontieu* remixes motifs and genres in a provisional and unstable balance.

7

Uncivil Wars

Imagining Community in La Chanson de la Croisade Albigeoise

IN HIS 1882 ESSAY "QU'EST-CE QU'UNE NATION," Ernest Renan singled out the Albigensian Crusade, along with the sixteenth-century Wars of Religion, as historical traumas all Frenchmen had in common: "Tout citoyen français *doit avoir oublié* la Saint-Barthélemy, les massacres du Midi au XIIIe siècle."[1] The notion that the cohesion of a nation is grounded in its past is of course central to the Romantic nationalisms of the mid- to late nineteenth century. Yet Renan's formulation, as Benedict Anderson points out, is somewhat peculiar: "in the ominous tone of revenue-codes and military conscription laws," he was instructing his readers already to have forgotten what his own words "assumed that they naturally remembered!" This paradox, he continues, is exacerbated by a language that "blurs unnamed victims and assassins behind the pure Frenchness of 'Midi'." The effect is to figure the Albigensian Crusades as "reassuringly fratricidal wars between—who else?—*fellow Frenchmen*." Thus, Anderson concludes,

we become aware of a systematic historiographical campaign, deployed by the state mainly through the state's school system, to "remind" every young French-woman and Frenchman of a series of antique slaughters which are now inscribed as "family history." Having to 'have already forgotten' tragedies of which one needs unceasingly to be "reminded" turns out to be a characteristic device in the later construction of national genealogies.[2]

The 1880s, as we saw in Chapter 1, were also the decade in which the study of medieval literature was institutionalized in France: at the same time that French high school students were being encouraged to cultivate the *Chanson de Roland* as a *lieu de mémoire*—a living example of "how great France already was and how she was loved more than eight centuries ago"—they were also being interpellated as national citizens by the common experience of having *forgotten* the Albigensian Crusades.[3]

What was this event that all Frenchmen must have forgotten? In summer 1209, an army of 20,000 marched south from Lyon in the campaign today known as the Albigensian Crusade. Its immediate cause was the assassination of papal legate Peter of Castelnau, ambushed (January 1208) outside Beaucaire just after excommunicating Count Raymond VI of Toulouse for his unseemly tolerance toward Cathar heretics. Outraged, Pope Innocent III called on French king Philip Augustus to punish this act of violence.[4] Embroiled in his own war against King John of England and opposed to the pope's military intervention, Philip declined the request but reluctantly allowed his vassals, the duke of Burgundy and the count of Nevers, to lead the campaign in his stead. Thus in summer 1209, an army of French and German knights and clerics, armed with plenary indulgences like those granted crusaders fighting in the Holy Land or in Spain, launched "one of the most savage of all medieval wars," whose ultimate consequences "went far beyond its aims."[5] Its purpose was to eliminate the dualist heresy that had taken root across Occitania during the twelfth century, and its target were the nobles who, though not heretics themselves, were deemed to have been lax in eradicating Catharism from their domains.

The history of the Albigensian Crusade comes down to us in three main sources: the Latin chronicles of Pierre of Les Vaux-de-Cernay and William of Puylaurens,[6] and an extraordinary vernacular poem called the *Chanson de la Croisade Albigeoise*. Composed in Occitan in the form of a *chanson de geste*, this curious hybrid text is the work of two different authors: Guilhem de Tudela (in Navarre), a cleric and crusade supporter who narrates events from the start of the war to the eve of the battle of Muret in 1213; and an Anonymous Continuator whose sympathies lay neither with the crusaders nor with the heretics but with what he depicts as an emerging Occitanian resistance.[7] In this chapter I focus on this Anonymous Continuation (covering the period from Muret through Prince Louis's siege of Toulouse in 1219), examining how it transforms the tale of Christianity's struggle against heresy into the story of an emerging regional consciousness. Countering the clerical vision of a corrupt and recalcitrant secular nobility, criminally lax in its refusal to persecute heretics and Jews, the Anonymous constructs the image of a society under siege—a society defined by its devotion to the twinned courtly virtues of *pretz* and *paratge*, whose martyr is the dashing King Pedro II of Aragon, and whose hero is the young Raimondet (the future Count Raymond VII of Toulouse). Structured around a respect for traditional values of honor, vassalage, and *lignage*, this society is represented as harmoniously integrating people up and down the feudal hierarchy, replacing the battle between Christians and heretics with a new kind of imagined community.

*   *   *

If, as Renan suggests, the southern massacres of the thirteenth century helped produce France as a nation, it is no surprise that recovering the political imaginaries that preceded them requires a concerted effort not of *re*construction but of *de*construction. Such work of demystification—aimed at nothing less than undoing the teleology of the French nation—is more easily said than done for, as the historian Fredric Cheyette has observed, the Albigensian Crusade "casts a long shadow backward" over twelfth-century history. "The conquerors—nobles, clergy, and above all kings—not only reshaped the culture and rituals of power, they rewrote history to defend and justify what they had done. Their rewriting, in large part unrecognized for what it is, has endured to the present day." Today, the awkwardness even of naming this land between the Rhone and the Pyrenees without resorting to the politically anachronistic term "southern France" (Cheyette opts for "Occitania") bespeaks the difficulty of disengaging our study of medieval history and literature from the paradigm of the French nation.[8]

In twelfth-century Occitania, on the other hand, "France was an alien country, far away."[9] In his famous riddle poem, "Farai un vers de dreit nïen," Guilhem (William) IX of Aquitaine declares himself untroubled by the fact that he has never seen his lady love, "For there was never a Norman or a Frenchman in my house" (29–30) (C'anc non ac Norman ni Franses / Dins mon ostau).[10] However obscure or nonsensical his logic, his implication is clear: French and Normans from north of the Loire belong to a different cultural sphere from Guilhem and his fellow Occitanians. In the later twelfth century, it is true, the shared experience of the Second Crusade and a series of strategic dynastic marriages helped bring the elites of the "north" and "south" closer together.[11] (Exemplary here is Richard the Lionheart, the king of England so affectively attached to the duchy of Aquitaine, who composed lyric in both Occitan and Old French.[12]) Still, the political landscape of Occitania and Provence was dominated by the rivalry between the counts of Toulouse and the count-kings of Barcelona-Aragon; even the Genoese and the Pisans were a more immediate presence than the king of France, Count Raymond's sovereign and nominal overlord.[13]

All this changed with Pope Innocent's call; throughout Occitania, nobles—heretics and good Christians alike—were about to find out what it meant to have Normans, Frenchmen and other foreigners "in their house." The initial phases of the campaign brought the crusaders a complete and devastating victory. At their approach, Count Raymond rushed to join them in order to protect his own lands from invasion. The crusading army then targeted the count's young nephew, Raymond Roger Trencavel, viscount of Béziers and Carcassonne—also accused of excess toleration of Cathars in his lands. Like his uncle, Raymond Roger tried to submit, but the crusade leaders rejected his plea and marched on Béziers. When the good Christians of the city refused to surrender their Cathar neighbors to the besieging army, the crusaders decided to make an example of them. In an act that set the tone for the war to come, papal legate Arnaud-Amaury, abbot of Cîteaux, ordered a general massacre, allegedly uttering the infamous words, "Kill them all; God will recognize his own."[14] Raymond Roger, captured during the siege of Carcassonne, died in captivity, raising the question of what would become of the Trencavel lands. Great feudal lords like the duke of Burgundy and the counts of Nevers and Saint Pol wanted nothing to do with this principality far from their own lands and "conquered by the sword."[15] So Simon de Montfort, a minor baron from the Ile-de-France who had fought bravely in the course of the crusade, was named the new viscount of Carcassonne and Béziers.[16]

The complication was that the Trencavals were vassals of King Pedro II of Aragon: Carcassonne and Béziers (which bisected the lands of count of Toulouse) constituted a crucial piece of his vast "feudal empire" running from Cerdagne and Besalú to Provence.[17] The suspicious circumstances surrounding Raymond Roger's death (he had died in captivity after having been seized in violation of the crusaders' own safe conduct) put his overlord in a difficult position. Eventually, Pedro accepted Simon's fealty for the Trencavel lands, even betrothing his son, the future Jaime I, to the latter's daughter Amicia.[18] Under Simon, however, the war begun as "an attack on heretics" was becoming "an attempt . . . to carve out a vast barony that would stretch from the Garonne to the Rhone."[19] In 1212, Simon dispossessed the counts of Foix, Comminges, and Béarn, three more of the Aragonese king's vassals. At first Pedro tried negotiating with papal legate Arnaud-Amaury and other crusading bishops for his vassals' reinstatement. However, when "it became clear that they had no intention of allowing any of the southern princes to remain in possession of their dominions," the king broke with the crusade, defied Simon de Montfort, and returned to Spain to raise an army in defense of his Occitanian vassals.[20]

In the *Chanson de la Croisade Albigeoise*, events to this point are narrated by Guilhem de Tudela. Reflecting the crusader viewpoint, he condemns Catharism as "the mad belief" (1.9) (la fola crezensa), "the heresy" (2.4) (la eretgia) and the "great folly" (2.12) (gran folia), and the heretics themselves as "the wrong-believing people" (3.15) (la mescrezuda jant) and "the felonious heretics" (107.6) (los felos eretges). Guilhem's crusader sympathies produce, however, some odd identifications, as in his description of the combatants at the siege of Minerva: "*Our* French and Champenois, those from Maine, Angevins, and Bretons from Brittany, Lorrainers, Frisians, and those from Germany" (49.7–9, emphasis added) (li *nostri* Frances e cels de vas Campanha, / Mancel e Angevi, e Breton de Bretanha, / Loarenc e Friso e celh de Alamanha). To write "*our* French" in *Occitan* is a paradox worthy of that poet of nonsense, Guilhem IX.[21] This list, moreover, strategically groups together men from Ile-de-France (like Simon de Montfort) and Champagne with subjects of the recently dismembered Angevin empire (Philip Augustus having seized King John's continental possessions in 1204) and the German empire, whom the French would confront at the battle of Bouvines in 1214.

At the same time, this list strongly resembles the catalogue of Charlemagne's troops in the *Chanson de Roland*: Bavarians, Alemanni, Normans, Bretons, Poitevins and Auvergnats, Flemings, Lorrainers and Burgundians (laisses 218–25)—itself an echo, as we saw in Chapter 1, of the unified Christendom Fulcher of Chartres constructed out of the distinctive ethnicities participating in the First Crusade. A few laisses later, Guilhem de Tudela describes the crusading army besieging the city of Termes as composed of "Germans, Bavarians, Saxons and Frisians, Mançois, Angevins, Normans and Bretons, Lombards, *Provençaux and Gascons*. The lord archbishop of Bordeaux, Amanieu d'Albret and men from Longon were there" (56:22–26, emphasis added) (Alaman e Bavier e Saine e Frison, / Mancel e Angevi e Norman e Breton, / Logombart e Lombart, *Proensal e Gascon*. / Lo senher arsevesques qu'es de Bordel i fon, / N'Amaneus de Lebret e cels de vas Lengon). This time, the allied force of French and German imperial troops is expanded to include men from northern Italy as well as Occitanians and Provençaux themselves: an important assertion of Latin Christian unity to describe a "crusade" directed largely against feudal leaders whose orthodoxy is never seriously in question.[22]

These echoes of the *Roland* are not surprising; composed in imitation of the *Chanson d'Antioche*, the *Chanson de la Croisade Albigeoise* was meant generically to align the Albigensian wars with crusades in the Middle East and the Iberian peninsula.[23] As the crusaders take Montferrand, Baudouin of Toulouse (Count Raymond's younger brother) is called "brave and valiant" (pros e valhant), the equal of "Oliver or Roland" in battle (72:9–10). The battle for Castelnaudary is explicitly cast in epic terms:

Now listen how the battle is joined in such a manner as has never been heard since the time of Roland or of Charlemagne, who defeated Aigolant and won Galiana, daughter of King Braimant, in spite of Galafre, the courtly emir from the land of Spain. (93:31–36)

(Ara aujatz batalha·s mesclar d'aital semblant
C'anc non auzitz tan fera des lo temps de Rotlant,
Ni del temps Karlemaine, que venquet Aigolant,
Que comquis Galiana, la filha al rei Braimant,
En despieg de Galafre, lo cortes almirant
De la terra d'Espanha.)

Other evocations of epic are more subtle, as where Simon de Montfort is left "brooding" (36.3) (fortment pensis) at the defection of his troops at the end of the first season of campaigning:

For few of his friends want to remain with him; most of them want to head back toward Paris: the mountains are wild and the passes narrow, and they don't wish to be killed in the country. However, nine or ten (I'm not sure) of the most daring and most powerful barons did stay. (36.4–9)

(Car paucs volo remandre ab lui de sos amis;
Tuit li plusor s'en volo retornar vas Paris:
Las montanhas so feras e·ls passatges esquis
E no volon pas estre ins el païs aucis.
Pero si n'i remazo, no sai o nou o dis,
De los plus autz barons e dels poestadis.)

The poet's evocation of the *montanhas* and *passatges* to be braved recalls
Charlemagne's mournful contemplation of the landscape in the *Chanson
de Roland*: "See the defiles and the narrow passes: decide for me who
will be in the rearguard" (741–42) (Vëez les porz e les destreiz passages:
/ Kar me jugez ki ert en rereguarde). Simon, then, is at once Charles,
burdened by the pensiveness of command, and Roland, remaining in enemy lands with a small but valiant contingent of warriors while the main
army sets out for home. As in the *Roland*, most of the crusaders are ea-
ger to leave—not after "seven full years" (*Roland*, 2), but a mere forty
days: "All those who were there were doing *their forty days' service*, so
that when some came, others left" (56.27–28, emphasis added) (Lai fan *la
carantena* tuit aicel que i son, / Que cant la uni venon e li autre s'en
vont).

The war that had begun as a crusade takes a palpable turn toward
colonization at the Council of Pamiers (1212), where the victorious crusaders decide to impose their own northern customs on the territories
they have vanquished:

At the Parlement of Pamiers, there are many clerics, great bishops and worthy
lords. Know that they imposed *usages and customs*—practices—on this great,
wide land. They had charters and sealed letters drawn up, then they returned to
their lands. (127.1–6)

> (Al parlament de Pamias a mots clerc ajustetz
> E i ac mant ric ivesque e mant baro de pretz.
> *Uzatge e costuma*, co om fai, so sabetz,
> Meseron els païs, que son e grans e letz;
> D'aiso fan faire cartas e breus ensageletz,
> E puissas si s'en son en lor païs tornetz.)

In this period, a great lord holding a multiplicity of lordships typically
governed each according to its own local traditions. Thus the blanket
imposition of the *us et costume* of Paris represented a radical reordering
of Occitanian society—an outrage that helped turn the crusade into a
war of Occitanian resistance.[24] The great turning point of the campaign
came with Pedro II of Aragon's decision to take the field against Simon
de Montfort at Muret. At this moment Guilhem de Tudela's narrative breaks off—or, rather, is seamlessly taken up by the Anonymous
Continuation.[25]

Muret (1213)

The defection of the Aragonese king was especially momentous since, unlike Raymond of Toulouse, perennially suspect for insufficient rigor toward heretics, Pedro was one of Latin Christendom's most brilliant champions. In 1212, he had helped inflict a crushing defeat on the Almohads at the battle of Las Navas de Tolosa, hailed as a turning point of the Spanish Reconquest.[26] In the Albigensian Crusade, however, he found his role as defender of Christendom increasingly at odds with his Occitanian interests. His defection reveals how radically the war, as prosecuted by Simon and the increasingly intransigent southern bishops, violated contemporary perceptions of due feudal process. Pedro ruled the "Crown of Aragon," a feudal confederacy uniting the kingdom of Aragon and the county of Barcelona, forged by Pedro's father and grandfather from an overlapping network of dynastic and feudal alliances (see Table 7.1). In the *Liber feudorum maior*, a cartulary compiled under his father, Alfonso II (1162–96), comital power is defined not territorially but through relationships between lineages. Most of the cartulary's miniatures depict the ritual of homage: "an individual, kneeling, places his or her hands between the hands of a second individual, usually seated."[27]

In the twelfth century, the count-kings' ambitions in Occitania brought them into conflict with the counts of Toulouse.[28] By the turn of

TABLE 7.1.   The Houses of Aragon and Toulouse

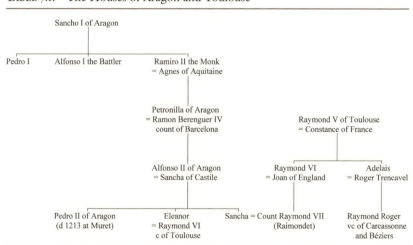

the thirteenth century, however, Pedro and Raymond VI resolved this
long rivalry with the double marriage of the king's sisters Eleanor to
Count Raymond (betrothed 1200, married 1204) and Sancha to his son,
the future Raymond VII (betrothed 1205, married 1211).[29] In the *Chanson
de la Croisade Albigeoise*, Pedro explains his decision to oppose the crusade to his entourage (*mainea*) by underscoring values of kinship and the
proper conduct of war:

King Pedro of Aragon rode out with his household; he summoned all the men of
his kingdom and gathered a great and noble company. He announced and explained to them that he intended to go to Toulouse to oppose the crusade, because it was *wasting and destroying* the whole country. Furthermore, the count of
Toulouse had appealed for mercy, that his lands not be burned or laid waste, for
he had done no harm or wrong to any living soul. "And as *he is my brother-in-law*,
having married my sister, and as I have married my other sister to his son, I will go
and help them against these accursed people who are trying to *disinherit* them."
(131.6–18, emphasis added)

> (Lo reis Peir' d'Aragon s'en vait am sa mainea
> E a tota sa gent de sa terra mandea,
> Si que n'a gran companha e bela ajustea.
> A totz a la paraula diita e devizea
> Qu'el vol ir a Tolosa contrastar la crozea,
> Que *gastan e destruzo* tota la encontrea;
> E lo coms de Tolosa a lor merce clamea
> Que no sia sa terra arsa ni malmenea,
> Que no a tort ni colpa a neguna gent nea.
> "E car *es mos cunhatz* e a ma sor espozea,
> E eu ai a so filh l'autra sor maridea.
> Irai lor ajudar d'esta gent malaurea
> Que·ls vo *dezeretar*.")

For Pedro, the "crusade" against heretics has become a force of destruction. (The verb *gastan* resonates with the *terre gaste* of Chrétien de
Troyes's *Perceval*: the devastation befalling a land whose ruler is dead or
incapacitated.) But it is the injustice done to the count of Toulouse that
the king takes as decisive. Raymond, he protests, has been wronged, and
as his brother-in-law, it is his duty to defend him: "*The clergy and the
French* want to *disinherit* the count, my brother-in-law, and evict him
from the land; no one can attribute any *blame or guilt* to him; they just

want to displace him" (132.1–4) (*Li clergue e·ls Frances* volon *dezeretar* / Lo comte mon cunhat e de terra gitar. / *Ses tort e senes colpa*, que om no·ls pot comtar, / Mas sol car a lor platz, le volon decasar).

As Jonathan Sumption observes, kinship ties alone would never have persuaded a "shrewd and ambitious politician" like Pedro to take on the crusaders; he was acting out of feudal self-interest to protect the Pyrenean vassals on whom his own power depended.[30] Yet as we have repeatedly seen, respect for kinship was a common medieval value: when the king of Aragon evokes the wrong done to his brother-in-law, he appeals to the value system mobilized by Latins, Greeks, and Saracens alike in Robert de Clari's *Conquête de Constantinople*. Lineage was the language in which the medieval nobility expressed its identity: even Guilhem de Tudela refers to Count Raymond as "Lady Constance's son" (107.1) (lo filhs dama Constansa), simultaneously recognizing his royal blood (Constance was the sister of Louis VII of France) and his kinship to French king Philip Augustus, his first cousin.[31]

While Pedro underscores the obligations imposed by kinship, Count Raymond is busy building common cause with his longtime rivals, the burghers of Toulouse. In Toulouse, the power vacuum created by the count's frequent absences had proven a perfect milieu for the emergence of an Italian-style urban council of the type that had begun appearing in Occitania in the 1130s. By mid-century, justice in both *cité* and *bourg* was adminstered by a unified council. In the 1180s, as Raymond V tried to reclaim certain comital prerogatives, count and council were almost constantly at war. By 1190, twenty-four elected officials, called *capitouls*, were largely in control of the city.[32] Now, in the midst of the Albigensian Crusade, Raymond VI appeals to the council and townsfolk for aid in retaking the city of Pujol:

"Lords," said the count, "here's why I've sent for you: I've spied on my enemies, who want to destroy us and harrass us so that we can't reap this year's harvest. And look how close they are: this side of Lantar." "Lord," said the people, "let's go besiege them: you have many companions, and God is on your side. We're all armed, and will be able to cut them to pieces. And the valiant count of Foix (God save him!) and the count of Comminges can accompany you—with the Catalans, who have come to help you." (132.26–39)

("Senhors," so ditz lo coms, "per so·us ei faits mandar:
Mos enemics ei faitz aisi prop espïar,
Que nos cujan destruire, e·ns volo destrigar

Que no puscam ongan d'esta part estivar;
E ve·ls vos aisi prob, que son de sa Lantar."
"Senhor," so ditz lo pobles, "anem los enserrar;
Que pro avetz companhos, si Dieus vos vol aidar,
Que nos em tuit garnit, que·ls sabrem pecïar.
E lo pros coms de Foiss, que Dieus salve e gar!
E aicel de Cumenge vos podo afolcar,
E ab los Catalas, que·us son vengut aidar.
E pos em tuit garnit pessem de l'espleitar
Ans que n'aien saubuda ni s'en puscan tornar
Li vilan taverner.")

Here, Raymond's interests and those of his subjects converge. The count
represents the crusaders as *his* enemies (*mos* enemics) but emphasizes the
common danger they pose: *nos* cujan destruire. Rising up with one voice,
the people (lo pobles) of Toulouse signal their acceptance of the common
enterprise through the use of a first-person plural (anem) conjoining the
people with the count and his companions. In the account of the battle
proper, the crusaders are recoded as "French *mercenaries*" (133.1, emphasis
added) (Frances *soldadier*), while the southern coalition unites allies of disparate social levels:

The noble count of Toulouse . . . together with the count of Foix (the brave Roger
Bernard), and the count of Comminges, who came nobly prepared; with them
were the Catalans, whom the king had left with them, and the people of Toulouse,
who came, prompt and lively: knights, burghers, and commoners. (133.2–7)

(E·l rics coms de Tolosa . . .
E ab lui·l coms de Foiss, e·l pros Rotgiers Bernatz,
E lo coms de Cumenge, que i venc gent asesmatz;
Ab lor li Catala, que·l reis lor ac laissatz,
E·l pobles de Tholosa, que i venc tost e viatz,
Li caver e·l borzes e la cuminaltatz.)

One of the *capitouls* now steps forward explicitly to pledge the city's
support:

First a wise lawyer spoke, a member of the Capitol and an eloquent man: "My
lord, great count and marquis, listen, please: and you too, all you others gathered

here. We have brought up the catapaults and siege weapons to fight hard against the enemy, for I trust in God we shall defeat them quickly, as *we are in the right and they are in the wrong*. They are destroying our inheritance before our very eyes." (133.8–16, emphasis added)

> (Primeirament parlet us legista senatz,
> Qui era de Capitol e es gent emparlatz:
> "Senher, rics coms marques, si vos platz, escoutatz,
> Vos e trastuit li autre c'aisi etz ajustatz.
> Nos avem las peireiras e los engens cargatz,
> Par tal que·ls enemics durament combatatz;
> Qu'en Dieu ai esperansa que tost sian sobratz,
> *Que nos avem gran dreit ed els an los pecatz*
> Car nos vezem destruire las nostras eretatz.")

In the "nos"/"nostras" of the final line, the consuls align their own plight with that of their count: both find their heritage threatened at the hands of Simon de Montfort.

The battle of Muret proved a catastrophic defeat for this emerging southern alliance. The *Chanson*'s account opens with an anticipatory lament, regretting in advance the loss of *paratge*, that elusive value soon to emerge as the "dominant ethos" of the Anonymous Continuation:[33] "The whole world was devalued by it, be sure of it: for *Paratge* was destroyed and driven out, and all Christendom disgraced and debased. Now listen, my lords, and hear what happened" (137.1–4) (Totz lo mons ne valg mens, de ver o sapiatz, / Car *Paratges* ne fo destruitz e decassatz / E totz Crestianesmes aonitz e abassatz. / Aras aujatz, senhors, co fo, e escoutatz). The battle of Muret was lost in a welter of strategic mistakes and miscalculations. Years later, Pedro's son Jaime I of Aragon (who was five years old at the time) attributed his father's defeat to his fatigue from having "lain with a lady" the night before and from the disarray among his allies: "those on the king's side knew neither how to place order in the lines nor how to move in formation, and each noble fought for himself, and broke with the rules of arms. And because of their disorder and the sin that was in them, and because they had not shown mercy to those who were inside, the battle had to be lost."[34] The *Chanson* shows Pedro, swallowed up in the tide of battle, belatedly trying to identify himself to his attackers: "And he shouted, 'I am the king!' but no one heard him"

(140.11) (E el escrida: "Eu so·l reis!" mas no i es entendutz). Seeing him
fall, his troops disperse in a panic. Pedro's faithful vassal Dalmas de Creixell
articulates the enormity of their loss: "God help us! great evil is heaped
upon us, for the good king of Aragon is dead and confounded, and so
many other lords lie dead and defeated" (140.24–26) (Dieus ajuda! grans
mals nos es cregutz, / Que·l bos reis d'Arago es mortz e recrezutz, / E
tant baro dels autres que so mortz e vencutz). For his part, Count Raymond—his brother-in-law dead and his army in disarray—advises the
burghers of Toulouse to submit to Simon, then slips away into exile. The
episode, which had opened with a sense of foreboding, now closes on a
note of loss and valediction: "Great was the damage and the sorrow and
the loss when the king of Aragon was left dead and bleeding, along with
many other lords, on whose account all Christendom and all peoples were
greatly abased" (141.1–4) (Mot fo grans lo dampnatges e·l dols e·l perde-
mentz / Can lo reis d'Arago remas mort e sagnens, / E mot d'autres
baros, don fo grans l'aunimens / A tot crestianesme et a trastotas gens).
By attributing the loss to "all Christendom," the poet pointedly vindicates the religious as well as the feudal rectitude of the losers at Muret,
whose destruction turns the world of *paratge* on its head.

Lateran IV

Pedro's death marks the entrance onto the historical stage of Raymond VI's
son, Raimondet. The poem compresses the two years following the coalition's crushing defeat at Muret into a single laisse, juxtaposing Prince
Louis's triumphant return to "Fransa" with the exile of Raymond VI, "who
departed *faiditz*, wandering, afflicted, by land and by sea" (142.9–10)
(que·s n'es anatz faiditz / Per terra e per mar a trop estat marriz).[35] A few
lines later, the dispossessed count is shown making his way to Rome for the
Fourth Lateran Council (1215)—one of the watershed events dividing the
twelfth-century culture of fidelity from the thirteenth-century culture of
taxonomy and regulation. There, amid "Cardinals, bishops, abbots, priors,
counts, and viscounts from many lands" (143.5–6), Raymond appears accompanied by his sixteen-year-old son Raimondet, poised to assume his
place as the new hero of the Occitanian resistance.

Descended from the kings of France and England and from Count
Alfons of Toulouse[36]—the "best lineage there is or ever was" (143.15) (milhor linage que sia ni anc fos)—Raimondet commands everyone's attention,

the exaltedness of his birth (see Table 7.2) magnifying the injustice done him by rapacious churchmen:

The Pope looked at the child and his manner, and recognizes his lineage; he heard the injustices of the Church and the clergy, who oppose him: his heart is so pained by Pity and Ire that he sighs and sheds tears from both eyes. But the count gains nothing from right, faith, or reason. (143.20–25)

> (L'Apostolis regarda l'efant e sas faisos,
> E conosc lo linatge e saub las falhizos
> De Glieza e de clercia, que son contrarios:
> De pietat e d'ira n'a·l cor tant doloiros
> Qu'en sospira e·n plora de sos olhs ambedos.
> Mas lai no val als comtes dreitz ni fes ni razons.)

In feudal society, as we saw in Chapter 5, lineage was the dominant discourse of right, needing only military might to legitimize the most implausible of claims. Here, in contrast, Innocent III acknowledges that Count Raymond—a good Christian—has been wrongly disinherited; but what can he do? Acting "out of fear of the clergy, which frightens him" (143.33) (per paor de clercia de qu'el es temoros), this most powerful of medieval popes pleads his own helplessness. Shrugging off a key value of the old feudal order, he confirms Simon de Montfort in possession of Raymond's lands even as he acknowledges the validity of the latter's complaint.

The outrage provoked by the dispossession of the counts of Toulouse explodes in a dramatic address by Roger Bernard, count of Foix. Significantly, he focuses his tirade on the injustices done not to the father but to the son, underscoring the youth and innocence of the now disinherited Raimondet:

I have come to your court for true justice: I, the mighty count, my lord, and his son too, who is a fair child, good, intelligent and *very young*. And since the law does not accuse him nor reason reproach him, since he has harmed or wronged no living thing, I am astonished: how, for what reason, could any honest man stand for him to lose his *inheritance*? (144.16–23)

> (Soi vengutz en ta cort per jutjar leialment,
> Eu e·l rics coms mos senher, e sos filhs ichament,
> Qu'es bel e bos e savis e *de petit jovent*,
> Ez anc no fe ni dig engan ni falhiment.

E pos dreh no l'encuza ni razos no·l reprent,
Si non a tort ni colpa a nulha re vivent,
Be·m fas grans meravilhas per que ni per cal sent
Pot nulhs prosom suffrir son *dezeretament*.)

In practice, of course, youth was a political liability—whether in the form of overanxious *jovens* (like Henry the Young King), everready to rebel against their elders, or minor heirs (like Pedro of Aragon's five-year old son Jaime), whose accession weakened the power of territorial lordships.[37] Amid the perturbations of the Albigensian Crusade, however, youth and lack of experience are recoded as a political asset, a key argument in favor of dynastic continuity. This theme, eloquently sounded by the count of Foix, is reprised and developed by Raymond of Roquefeuille, speaking on behalf of the underage heir of *his* overlord, the late Raymond Roger Trencavel:

Lord Pope! have mercy and pity on *an orphan child, an exiled youth*, son of the honored viscount, killed by the crusaders and Simon de Montfort, when he was handed over to them. *Paratges was lowered* by this act, by third or by half, when he was wrongly and sinfully martyred. No cardinal or abbot of your court believes more strongly in Christianity than he. As they have killed the father and disinherited the son, Lord, return his land to him; salvage your dignity! If you don't choose to return it to him, may it please God that his sin be on your soul. (146.32–43, emphasis added)

(Senher dreitz apostolis, merce e pietat
aias d'*un effan orfe, jovenet ichilat*,
filh del onrat vescomte, que an mort li crozat
E·n Simos de Montfort, cant hom l'i ac lhivrat.
Ladoncs *baichec Paratges* lo tertz o la mitat,
e cant el pren martiri a tort e a pecat;
e no as en ta cort cardenal ni abat
agues milhor crezensa a la crestiandat.
E por an mort lo paire e·l filh dezeretat,
Senher, ret li la terra, garda ta dignitat!
E si no la·lh vols rendre, Dieus t'en do aital grad
que sus la tua arma aias lo sieu pecat!)

Eight years old to Raimondet's nineteen, his father a victim of Simon de Montfort's double-dealing, the Trencavel heir calls forth a defense even more pointed and poignant than that surrounding the young count of

Toulouse. Where the crusaders had questioned the religious orthodoxy of the boy's hapless father, Raymond of Roquefeuille dares to question the good faith of Pope Innocent himself.

The Lateran Council proceeds to dismantle the Occitanian culture of fidelity. Speaking for the crusaders, Fulk of Marseille argues that to deprive Simon of lands conquered "by the cross and with shining sword" (148.10) (per crotz . . . e ab glazis luzens) would be to disinherit him of his right. At first, Innocent agrees to grant Simon the lands of the heretics but not of Raymond VI: "*Without right or reason*, how could I commit *so great a wrong? wrongly* disinherit the count, who is a true Catholic, take away his land, and transfer *his rights* to it [to Simon]?" (147.12–14, emphasis added) (*Ses dreg e ses razo* cum farei tant *gran tort* / Que·l coms, qu·es vers catholics, dezerete *a tort*, / Ni que·lh tolha sa terra, ni que *son dreit* trasport?). The terms *tort* and *dreit* simultaneously evoke the legalism of the papal court and the religious-feudal-moral ethos of Roland's battlefield exhoration, "Paien unt tort e crestiens unt dreit" (1015). When the bishops argue that Simon has purged the land of heresy, Innocent drily notes that this feat is compromised by his having "destroyed Catholics and heretics alike" (149.16) (destrui los catolics engal dels eretges). Raymond, he reiterates, is a good Catholic (148.73); furthermore, even "if the count were condemned—which he is not—*why should his son lose his land and inheritance?*" (149.40–41, emphasis added) (si·l coms dampnatz era, aiso qu'el pas non es, / sos filhs perque perdra la terra ni l'eres?). Taking up where the count of Foix left off, the pope himself eloquently defends Raimondet:

When the crusaders first came to the Biterrois to destroy the land and took Béziers, the child was so young and ignorant he didn't know bad from good, but would have wanted a little bird or bow or snare more than a duchy or marquisate. He is blameless: who among you would claim that he should lose lands, rents and revenues? Then there's his lineage—the most exalted there is. Since he has a courtly spirit, since there's no written or other evidence against him, who would dare say that he should be lost and live his life on others' riches? Shall not God, reason and mercy stand by such a one who ought to be giving rather than taking anything from anyone? For a man who depends for his life on another's wealth is better dead or never born at all. (149.48–65)

(. . . cant las crotz primeiras vengon en Bederres,
Per destruire la terra, e que Bezers fo pres,
L'efans era tant joves e tant nescia res
Que el pas no sabia ques era mals ni bes;

Mais volgra un auzelo o un arc o un bres
Que no feira la terra d'un duc o du'un marques.
E cal de vos l'encuza, si el pecaire non es,
Qu'el deia perdre terra ni la renda ni·l ces?
E de la sua part es lo sieu parentes,
De la plus auta sanc que sia ni que es,
E car en lui s'es mes us esperitz cortes,
Que no·l dampna ni·l jutja escriptura ni res,
Cals bocha jutjaria que aquest se pergues
Ni que prengua sa vida ab los autruis conres?
E no valdra Dieus ni razo ni merces
De lui que dar devria que d'autra re preses?
Car cel que l'autrui serca per pendre·ls autruis bes
Mais li valdria mortz o que ja no nasques.)

Even as he vindicates Raymond's orthodoxy and Raimondet's innocence, however, a resigned Innocent bends to the pressure of his radical clerics. Speaking less from principle than from pragmatism, he leaves Raymond's lands in Simon's possession: "Let Simon hold the land . . . since I cannot take it from him; let him keep it well, if he can, lest someone take it back from him" (150.1–3).

Speaking for Raimondet's uncle, King John of England, the archbishop of York steps in to protect the young count's maternal heritage. Calling the papal court itself to witness, he argues that even were he (wrongly) to be deprived of his father's lands, he should, *per dreit e per razo*, retain those of his mother. "For I have seen the deed in which the notary has written that the dowry is authorized by the court of Rome, and this court has final authority in matrimonial affairs" (150.13–15) (Car eu ei vist lo prolec or escrios lo notaire / Que Roma e la cortz autrejec lo doaire; / E pos de matrimoni est caps e governaire). Underscoring, like others before him, Raimondet's noble lineage, he sums up: "Is he to go about the dangerous world like a thief? Then indeed, *Paratge* would be dead and Mercy worthless" (150.19–20) (Ira doncs per lo mon perilhatz co mal laire? Doncs er lo mortz *Paratges* e Merces no val gaire). Deftly evoking the papal court's own jurisdictional claims, the archbishop drives home the legal distinction between patrimony and dower lands, even as he appeals to the same couplet of values, *dreit* and *razo*, raised by Innocent himself.[38]

TABLE 7.2. The Lineage of Raimondet

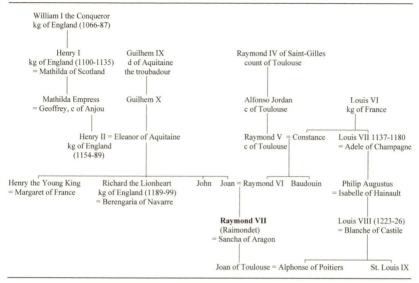

William I the Conqueror
kg of England (1066-87)

Henry I
kg of England (1100-1135)
= Mathilda of Scotland

Guilhem IX
d of Aquitaine
the troubadour

Raymond IV of Saint-Gilles
count of Toulouse

Mathilda Empress
= Geoffrey, c of Anjou

Guilhem X

Alfonso Jordan
c of Toulouse

Louis VI
kg of France

Henry II = Eleanor of Aquitaine
kg of England
(1154-89)

Raymond V = Constance
c of Toulouse

Louis VII 1137-1180
= Adele of Champagne

Henry the Young King
= Margaret of France

Richard the Lionheart
kg of England (1189-99)
= Berengaria of Navarre

John   Joan = Raymond VI   Baudouin

Philip Augustus
= Isabelle of Hainault

Raymond VII
(Raimondet)
= Sancha of Aragon

Louis VIII (1223-26)
= Blanche of Castile

Joan of Toulouse = Alphonse of Poitiers   St. Louis IX

Once again pleading his powerlessness faced with the consensus of his prelates, Innocent splits the difference: Raimondet retains the Venaissin and the marquisate of Provence; as for "Toulouse and Agen and Beaucaire" (150.26), they are his to recover—God willing. As he tells Count Raymond in the following laisse: "If I have disinherited you, God can restore you" (151.44) (S'ieu t'ai dezeretat, Dieus te pot eretar). In his refusal to pronounce definitively either for Simon or Raymond, Innocent inaugurates a new phase in the crusade that casts the battle for the south as a *judicium Dei* whose protagonist is the young count Raimondet.

Paratge

Introduced onto the stage of history at Lateran IV, Raimondet now makes his father's battle his own. Arriving in Provence to launch a campaign of reconquest, the young count is met by his father's loyal vassal Gui de Cavaillon.[39] Since Gui, like other Occitanian nobles of the day, was himself a troubadour (a master of the dialogic genres like the *tenso* and *partimen*), it is not surprising to find their meeing set in a landscape directly drawn from troubadour lyric:

With great joy they took lodging; in the morning dew, when sweet dawn was breaking and the birds were beginning to sing and leaves and flower buds were unfolding, the lords rode through the grass side by side, talking about arms and equipment. (154.1–5)

> (Ab gran joi' albergueron; e·l mati ab lo ros,
> Cant l'alba dousa brolha e·l cans dels auzelos,
> E s'espandig la folha e la flors dels botos,[40]
> Li baro cavalguero doi e doi per l'erbos.
> E pessan de las armas e de la garnizos.)

Such invocations of singing birds and blooming branches frequently serve to introduce the lyric *canso*, the genre of the poet's intense longing for his lady. Spring, however, was the season of war as well as love;[41] Gui's exhortation to Raimondet soon assumes the form of a *sirventes* (a political poem addressed to a prince rather than a powerful lady), interpellating him as the last hope of *paratge*.[42]

But Gui de Cavaillon, riding a bay horse, said to the Young Count: "This is the season when *Paratge* demands that you be bad and good; for the count de Montfort (who is destroying your barons), the Church of Rome and the preachers are turning *Paratge* to dishonor and shame. Thus is *Paratge* debased; if you don't raise it up, it will vanish forever. If you do not restore *Pretz* and *Paratge*, then the death of *Paratge* and the whole world are on you. You are the true hope of all *Paratge*: may you be valorous, or all *Paratge* dies." (154.6–17)

> (Mos Guis de Cavalho desobr' un caval ros
> A dig al *comte jove*: "Oimais es la sazos
> Que a grans obs *Paratges* que siatz mals e bos,
> Car lo coms de Montfort que destrui los baros
> E la Gleiza de Roma e la prezicacios
> Fa estar tot *Paratge* aunit e vergonhos,
> Qu'en aisi es *Paratges* tornatz de sus en jos;
> Que si per vos no·s leva per totz tems es rescos.
> E si *Pretz e Paratges* no·s restaura per vos,
> Doncs es lo mortz *Paratges* e totz lo mons en vos.
> E pus de tot *Paratge* etz vera sospeisos,
> O totz *Paratge* moria o vos que sitz pros.")

Evoked seven times in Gui's eleven-line speech, *paratge* concentrates the values of the Occitanian "culture of fidelity" threatened by Simon de Montfort and his clerical allies. Originally meaning "equality of condition or nobility" (of the co-heirs holding a fief in common), in troubadour verse it frequently signified high lineage: in her "A chantar m'er de so q'ieu no volria," the countess of Dia invokes her own "pretz e . . . paratges" to demand her lover's continued love. Critics and satirists like Marcabru and Guiraut de Bornelh cast *paratge* as a lost ideal, compromised by the poor behavior of the "malvatz rics."[43] The Albigensian Crusade, however, "radically changed the targets of these attacks" from the Occitanian nobility to the French and the Catholic clergy—"a patriotic reaction" to the "dramatic events" of 1209 and after.[44] In the *Chanson de la Croisade Albigeoise*, *paratge* assumes the added connotation of "the right of a nobleman to own his inherited lands"—that is, the right not to be disinherited by the likes of a Simon de Montfort.[45]

In casting Raimondet as the hero of *paratge*, Gui underscores the link between *paratge* and youth. Structurally, the dilemma of youth was their lack of function: knighted and brought up in a culture of military prowess but denied the power and responsibility of lordship during the lifetime of fathers or older brothers. In the twelfth century, the paragon of youth was Raimondet's maternal uncle, Henry the Young King (*rei jove*). Remembered today for his repeated rebellions against his father, Henry II of England (in 1173–74 and again in 1183), to his contemporaries Henry represented "the new chivalric culture of his time."[46] In one of his best-known *sirventes*, "Bel m'es quan vei," Henry's companion Bertran de Born sings the praises of that exuberant combination of prowess, joy, generosity, and extravagance over the crankiness and stinginess of age:

I like it when I see power changing hands, and when the old leave their houses to the young . . . then I like it, because the world is renewed better than by flowers and birdsongs. And whoever can change his lady or his lord, old for young, really ought to. (1.1–2, 5–8[47])

(Belh m'es quan vey camjar lo senhoratge,
e·l viel laixan als joves lurs maizos . . .
ladoncs m'es belh, qu'el segle renovelh
mielh qe per flor ni per chantar d'auzelh.
E qui dona ni senhor pot camjar,
vielh per jove, ben deu renovelar.)

The third strophe directly links youth and *paratge*, which thus appears as a rhyme word with "senhoratge" (1), "linhatge" (3), "coratge" (19), and "gatge" (33): "Young is the lady who knows how to honor *paratge*" (3.17) (Jov'es dona que sap honrar paratge).[48] For Bertran as for the Young King, *paratge* was part of an exciting (if dangerous) game pitting rebellious youth against their stern and punitive fathers.

The Albigensian Crusade, however, had inverted the political valences of youth and age.[49] The charismatic son of an ineffectual father, Raimondet demonstrated a prowess and leadership that, far from threatening his father's authority (as in the case of the Young King and Henry II), in fact rekindled hopes of restoring the *paratge* lost through the elder Raymond's political and military weakness. For the *faiditz* whom the crusade had dispossessed of their lands, exchanging an old lord for a young one was not a generational whim but a political necessity. (It is surely no coincidence that in a *tenso* with Pons de Montlaur, Gui prefers the young girl to the mature lady on the grounds that the former can improve as her love grows.[50]) In the person of the Young Count, "youth" and *paratge* assume their full political valence:

"Gui," said the Young Count, "my heart rejoices over what you've said; I'll answer briefly: if Jesus Christ keeps me and and my companions and restores Toulouse to me (as I hope), never will *Paratge* be dishonored or bereft, for there's no one in this world powerful enough to destroy me, except the Church. And my right and justification are so great that if I have enemies, evil or prideful—if anyone is a leopard toward me, I'll be a lion toward him!" (154.18–27)

> ("Gui," so ditz *lo coms joves*, "mot n'ai lo cor joios
> D'aiso qu'en avetz dig, eu farei breu respos:
> Si Jhesu Crist me salva lo cors e·ls companhos,
> E que·m reda Tholoza, don ieu soi desiros,
> *Jamais non er Paratges aonitz ni sofrachos;*
> Que non es en est mon nulhs om tan poderos
> Que mi pogues destruire, si la Glieza no fos.
> E es tant grans mos dreitz e la mia razos
> Que s'ieu ai enemics ni mals ni orgulhos,
> Si degus m'es laupart, eu li seré leos!")

Together with Gui's original speech, Raimondet's response forms a *tenso*—a poetic dialogue between two troubadours.[51] Having set the mood, the two talk "of both arms and love" (154.28) (de las armas e d'amours e dels dos)—the very stuff of courtly lyric—until they reach Avignon. There, *vielh* and *jove* alike pour into the streets with cries of "Tholosa!" "La joia!" and "Jhesu Crist glorios." After one line showing Raimondet going to church to pray (countering any lingering doubts about his religious orthodoxy) comes an expansive account of the celebratory banquet, featuring copious food and drink, "jongleurs, vielles, dances, and songs" (154.46) (jotglars e las viulas e dansas e cansos), and the loyalty oaths the people of Avignon proffer to the young count, their "Senher dreitz, amoros" (154.49). The joylessness and anticourtly spirit Bertran de Born had attributed to cranky ladies and stingy lords are in turn reascribed to the Catholic clergy and their grim champion, Simon de Montfort.

Beaucaire

It is in his birth city of Beaucaire that Raimondet comes into his own. Raymond VI, after receiving a stirring welcome from the people of Marseille and Avignon, leaves for Spain to seek new alliances. Commending his son to his few trusted counselors, the old count emphasizes their joint fortune: "if he wins land, you will gain great honor, but if he loses it, you all will suffer" (155.11–12) (si el cobra terra gran honor i auretz, / Pero, si la perdia, tuit vos i dampnaratez). This makes Beaucaire a proving ground for the yet untried Raimondet. Aided by local inhabitants, Raimondet mounts a spirited attack, quickly taking Beaucaire's outer perimeter. Preparing their assault on the innermost fortification, the southerners fervently call on God to restore *paratge* (157.24, 158.1). They then begin building a wall to protect themselves from a crusader attack from without. Their worksite becomes the stage for the first of several performances of a new and unusual kind of unity:

Never has any worksite seen such noble masons, for knights and ladies are carrying rubble, and young men and maids (are bringing) wood and stone, each one singing a ballad, verse, or *canso*. They did so much work in so little time that there was no reason ever to fear the French or Burgundians. (158.28–33)

(anc en nulha obra no vis tan ric masso:
que cavaer e donas aportan lo reblo

E donzels e donzelas lo pertrait e·l cairo,
que cascus ditz balada o verset o canso.
E fero tanta d'obra en petit de sazo
Que mais no·ls cal temer Frances ni Bergonho.)

A far cry from the epic battalions described in Guilhem de Tudela's part
of the poem, this army of noble and courtly masons presents an astonishing display of regional solidarity across class and gender lines. Provisions
(animals, poultry, grain, wine) pour in from the countryside in such abundance that "it looked like the promised land" (158.48) (ladoncs resemblet
terra de promissio). As Simon and his men draw up their battalions *outside* the perimeter, "those inside comported themselves like nobles (a
guiza be baro), shouting: 'Toulouse! Beaucaire! Avignon! Vallabrègues!
Redessan! Malaucène! Caromb!" (158:64–65). In a kind of regional *prise
de conscience*, opposition to Simon's army is made synonymous with a collection of local civic identities. Taking refuge in nearby Bellegarde, the
crusaders are thrown on the defensive, "for Marseille does not love them,
nor Montpellier; and Avignon and Beaucaire were first to attack them"
(159:6–7) (Que no·ls ama Maselha ni no·ls vols Montpesliers, / E Avinhos
e Belcaire los a comes primers).

   Meanwhile, trying to rally the spirits of the beleaguered crusaders
besieged in the inner keep of Beaucaire, Rainier of Chauderon exhorts
them in the name of the epic hero Guillaume d'Orange: "Lords, think of
short-nosed William, who suffered such troubles at the siege of Orange.
Whether in death or in life, let us all be knights: may neither Montfort
nor France ever have anything for which to reproach us" (159.49–52)
(Senhors, remembre vos Guilhelmet al cort nes, / Co al seti d'Aurenca
suffri tans desturbiers: / O de mort o de vida siam tug cavalers, / Que ja
Montfort ni Fransa no n'aion reproers). This scene corroborates the suggestion at the end of Chapter 2 that the legend of Guillaume's conquest
of the Saracen "Spain" provided a discourse ready-made to justify the
northern French invasion of the southern Rhone valley. Of course, actuat-
ing this narrative demands a willful conflation of Saracens and Occitanians—
a vision consistent with Guilhem de Tudela's epic representation of the
events of 1209 and their aftermath.[52] In contrast, the Anonymous Continuation replaces the epic discourse of heretics-cum-Saracens with the
Occitanian values of *pretz* and *paratges*. Here, the incongruity of this mo-
mentary return to northern French *epic* in a poem now permeated with the

ethos of troubadour *lyric* only serves to underscore the foreignness of these northern invaders.

The confrontation between "Montfort and Beaucaire" (159.74) is in fact a judgment of God: "God will recognize who is in the right, for He helps and exalts the most *legitimate heirs*" (159.75–76, emphasis added) (Dieus sab be conoicher cals es pus dreiturers / Per qu'el ajut e valha als plus *dreitz eretiers*).[53] Here divine judgment is articulated in the Occitanian discourse of fidelity, heavily infused with the lyrical commonplaces of troubadour verse:

In this whole war, it's obvious that God will restore the land to those who faithfully love him. For pride and right, loyalty and deceit have reached their peak. Battle is imminent. For a new flower is everywhere spreading, bringing back *Pretz and Paratge*. For *the brave young count*, able and ready, wants to oppose the disinheritors and destroyers, in order to raise the cross [of Toulouse] and diminish the lion [of the Montforts]. (160.1–9, emphasis added)

> (De tota aquesta guerra es parvens e semblans
> Que Dieus renda la terra als seus fizels amans;
> Car orgulhs e dreitura, l'ialtatz e engans
> Son vengut a la soma, car aprosma·l demans,
> Car una flors novela s'espandis per totz pans
> Per que *Pretz e Paratges* tornara en estans.
> Car *le valens coms joves*, qu'es adreitz e prezans,
> Demanda e contrasta los dezerestz e·l dans,
> Per que la crotz s'enansa e·l leos es mermans.)

The degree of "spin" involved in this vision may be gauged from an equally rousing but less idealized view of the siege in the *sirventes* "A tornar m'er" attributed to Tomier and Palaizi, two lords (*domini*) from the city of Tarascon (facing Beaucaire from the east bank of the Rhone). Composed (apparently) in the midst of the battle, their poem aims at enlisting the support both of local sympathizers and of the Catalans and Aragonese (strophes V and VI), faulted for failing to avenge the death of their "good king" (VI.44) (bon rei) Pedro II.[54]

And since we've come into the light, let he who can be valorous step forward. Let us defend our plains and marshes and not let ourselves be defeated through carelessness. Let us take the French without their arms: we know what they want: but

God and Right have changed their fate, despite those who would have sought
peace. (IV.25–32)

> (E puois oimais em vengut a la lus,
> traga·s enan sel que sabra veler!
> E devedem los plans e la palus
> e no·[n]s laissem sobrar per noncaler!
> Qu'ar li Frances tornon totz desarmaz:
> podem saber quals es lor volontatz.
> Mas Dieus e Dreitz lor a camjat lor sort,
> malgrat de cels que viseran l'art.)

In the *Chanson de la Croisade Albigeoise*, on the other hand, the restless
energy of youth that made Young Henry's campaigns against his father so
destabilizing and subversive is mobilized in opposition to Simon de
Montfort and the French. In rallying the natives of Beaucaire and the surrounding lands under the banner of the cross—emblem of the counts of
Toulouse—Raimondet turns the symbol of the crusades against the crusaders themselves.

If Raimondet's show of *paratge* bolsters the Occitanians, it correspondingly disheartens the crusaders. When Simon de Montfort com-
plains, "I am being disinherited by a fifteen year old boy" (160.18) (aisi·m
dezereta us tozetz de quinze ans), a member of his inner circle, Alain de
Roucy, is compelled to disagree: the count may be young (joves) but he is
no child; he is by nature good, fair, and strong—as one would expect,
since "he comes from the very best lineage: Lord Richard [the Lionheart]
was his uncle and Bertrand [count of Toulouse] his kinsman" (160.38–39)
(E es ben de lhinatge que·s milhor'e s'enans, / Qu'en Richartz fo sos oncles e sos parens Bertrans). More alarmingly for Simon, when the bishop
of Nîmes alludes to the "martyrdom" of one of their dead comrades,
Foucaud de Berzy erupts in scorn:

For God's sake, Lord Bishop, by such logic, good is debased and evil is doubled.
It's amazing the way *you clerics* give pardon where there's no repentance . . . For
I'll not believe, if it's not better proven, that any man who has died unshriven can
be worthy [of salvation]. (162.37–40, 43–44, emphasis added)

> (Per Dieu, senher·n avesques, de tal razo jutjatz
> Per que lo bes amerma e lo mals es doblatz;

E es grans meravilha de *vos autres letraz*
Com senes penedensa solvetz ni perdonatz . . .
Car ieu pas no creiria, si mielhs non o proatz,
Que nulhs hom sia dignes, si no mor cofessatz.)

Ironically, Foucaud's dissent marks him as simultaneously more *and* less Catholic than the bishop: in insisting on the necessity of proper confession, he vindicates clerical mediation in the administration of sacraments (in contrast, for example, to *Raoul de Cambrai*, in which feudal nobles hear the battlefield confessions of their dying comrades). Yet his dismissal of the bishop's reassurances concerning the dead man's salvation explicitly challenges the validity of Innocent III's 1208 plenary indulgence, stipulating the automatic salvation of those who died in the course of the war. Exposing the growing gap between official ideology and practical understanding, Foucaud's skepticism shows the inability of Simon's own men to reconcile their actions with the sanctity of crusade.

As the situation of those in Beaucaire's inner keep becomes increasingly desperate, Simon's advisors become restive. When Simon boasts of how he will use the wealth of Toulouse to subdue Provence and retake Beaucaire, Hugues de Lacy tempers his enthusiasm: "It's hard to take a castle from its natural lord; for they love the young count with a pure, heartfelt love and want him more than Christ. If ever they were traitors, [now] they wish to be loyal" (169:8–11) (Greu pot hom castel toldre a senhor natural, / Car ilh lo comte jove per fina amor coral / Aman mais trop e·l volon que Crist l'esperital. / E si anc trachor foron, volon estre leial). Moreover, where in most cases the besiegers have only to starve out the besieged, at Beaucaire the tables are completely turned:

Never have I seen such an unusual siege: those within have joy, repose, and shade, good bread, clear water, good beds and lodging, and Genestet wine on tap, while we are out here with nothing but dust, sweat, heat, cloudy watered wine, and hard bread without salt. (169.20–26)

(Car anc mai no vi seti tant fort descominal:
Car cel de dius an joia e sojorn e umbral
E bon pa e clara aiga e bos leitz e ostal
E·l vi de Genestet que lor ve per canal;
E nos estam sa forta e·l perilh terrenal,
E non avem mas polvera e la suzor e·l cal
E vin torbat ab aiga e pan dur senes sal.)

When the defenders stave off a great assault, Simon is "out of his mind" (170.9) with rage and disappointment at this sign that God has turned against him. Yet he hesitates to lift the siege lest he seem "recreant" (170.15) (recrezens). By this point even his own brother Gui calls his behavior into question: "As long as you got all the goods and silver, you didn't care if people died" (170.20–21) (Ab sol que sia vostre tot l'avers e l'argens, / Vos sol non avetz cura de la mort de la gens). Motivated by greed, Simon has acted with scandalous disregard for the values that knights like Alain de Roucy and Gui de Montfort share with the southern defenders of *paratge*. Forced to lift his siege in order to save the lives of his men in the inner keep, Simon must cede the castle of Beaucaire to Raimondet, "for he is valiant, wise, just, and courtly, from the best lineage and with rich relations among the nobility of France and the good English king" (171.7–9) (Car es valens e savis e adreitz e cortes / E del milhor linatge e del ric parentes / Del barnatge de Fransa e del bo rei Engles). In the person of Raimondet, *paratge* makes its return, vindicated after seven years of slaughter and humiliation.

Toulouse (1216)

Raimondet's victory at Beaucaire sets the stage for his father's triumph in Toulouse.[55] Stinging from his loss at Beaucaire, Simon rides against Toulouse, determined to wring enough money from its leaders to finance a new campaign. Though his brother Gui and others again counsel prudence, Simon's high-handed ways quickly unite the townspeople against him.[56] As their houses and coffers are broken into, "knights, burghers, sergeants and militia members" (172.66) (Cavaler e borzes e sirvent e geudo) come running, armed with a motley assortment of axes, scythes, bows, and blades. Against the heated protests of Gui and Alain de Roucy, Simon launches a demolition campaign to raze the city itself:

There you'd see pavements and towers knocked down, walls, rooms, and battlements. They demolished roofs and workshops, parapets and colorfully decorated chambers, doors, vaults, and high pillars. (178.47–51)

(Ladoncs viratz abatre los solers e las tors
E los murs e las salas e los dentelhs majors.

E detrencan li ome e.ls tetz e·ls obradors
E·ls ambans e las cambras complidas de colors
E·ls portal e las voutas e los pilars ausors.)

Having destroyed *paratge* (180.4), Simon rides off, leaving the Toulousains in their misery and humiliation. But not for long: returning from
Spain, Count Raymond convenes his counselors and receives their ringing
endorsement. First the count of Comminges weighs in: "Lord, hear me: if
you take Toulouse and hold it, *Paratge* will be restored to brilliance; you
will have illuminated yourself and us as well; for if you recover your heritage, we will all have enough land" (181.23–27) (Senher, mi escoutatz: /
Si vos cobratz Toloza, per so que la tengatz, / totz *Paratges*·s restaura e
reman coloratz, / e vos e totz nos autres avetz enluminatz; / que pro au-
rem tuit terra, si vos etz eretatz). Roger Bernard of Foix quickly adds:
"Lord count, I can tell you this: if you recover Toulouse, you'll hold the
key to your entire heritage, and *Pretz* and *Paratge* can be restored. If only
you'd go there, we will defend it" (181.29–32) (Senher coms, be.us posc
diire, si Toloza cobratz, / de tot vostre heretatge tinetz las claus e·l datz /
e totz *Pretz e Paratges* pot esser restauratz; / que be la defendriam si vos
sol i anatz). Reentering Toulouse under cover of a propitiously timed mist,
the count is joyously greeted by "the people: great and small, lords and
ladies, wives and husbands" (182.67–68) (lo pobles, lo maier e·l petitz /
e·ls baros e las donas, las molers e·l maritz)—a remarkable cross-section of the
community who hail Raymond as "nostre senher," responsible for reviv-
ing, restoring, and curing *pretz e paratges* (182.75–77).

Where Simon attacked *paratge* by razing the city's buildings and
palaces, the Toulousains celebrate its return by reconstructing their forti-
fications. As the count and his subjects prepare for the inevitable counter-
attack, the mundane work of rebuilding the city's walls is transformed
into a communal effort superseding all social distinctions: as at Beaucaire,
everyone pitches in, working and singing in utopian harmony:

Never in any town have I seen such noble laborers, for the counts were hard at
work, along with all the knights, the burghers and their wives, brave merchants,
men, women and courteous money-changers, boys and girls, servants, messengers: everyone had a pick, a shovel or a garden fork. Every one of them joined
eagerly in the work. And at night they all kept watch together; lights and candle-
sticks were placed along the streets, drums and tabors sounded and bugles
played. In heartfelt joy, women and girls sang and danced to merry tunes.
(183.67–78)

(E anc e nulha vila no vis tan ric obrer,
Que lai obran li comte e tuit li cavaler
E borzes e borzezas e valent marcadier
E·lh home e las femnas e·l cortes monedier
E li tos e las tozas e·l sirvent e·l troter;
Qui porta pica o pala o palagrilh leugier.
Cascus a la fazenda a lor cor viacer.
E la noit a la gaita son tuit cominaler;
Estan per la carreiras li lum e·l candeler;
E las tambors e·ls tempes e grailes fan temper;
Las tozas e las femnas per lo *joi* vertader
Fan baladas e dansas ab sonet d'alegrier.)

As daytime work brigades seamlessly give way to nocturnal revels, we witness the emergence of an imagined community blurring lines of class and gender in a civic-courtly version of the leveling of difference that had made Catharism seem so threatening to orthodox powers.

Even as solidarity builds among the defenders, Simon's inner circle suffers an erosion of morale. Quarrels erupt between those favoring Simon's hard line and those who increasingly decry the loss of courtesy and honor. Gui de Montfort calls his brother "evil and tyrannical" (185.38) (mals e tirans), suggesting that the crusaders had forfeited their moral credibility in their earlier refusal to negotiate with the Toulousains: "You can swear by the saints, but I'll never believe that God hasn't turned away from us on account of our deceptions" (185.44–5) (Qu'ieu pas no creiria, neis qui.m juraval·ls sants, / Que Dieus viratz no·s sia per los nostres engans). Alain de Roucy, the voice of crusader rectitude, calls Simon "overbearing" (outracujatz) and "excessive" (190.26, 30) (desmezuratz). This breakdown in crusader unity metaphorically haunts Foucaud de Berzy's address to the troops:

"My lords, I am neither Breton, English, nor German. So listen carefully to my vernacular. Each of us must grieve and sigh, for we have lost honor and glory; we have disgraced the whole of France, parents and children; she has suffered no more appalling shame since Roland died." (185.17–22)

("Senhors, ieu no soi Bretz, Engles ni Alamans,
Per qu'ieu·s dic per entendre que aujatz mo romans.
Cascus de nos deu esser planhens e sospirans

Car nos avem perdudas las honors e·ls bobans;
E tota Fransa aunida e·ls parens e·ls efans,
Que no pres major onta pois que moric Rotlans.")

The foregrounding of linguistic difference highlights "ethnic" divisions within the crusading army, while the glory won by Roland is negated by the shame Simon has brought on France. Many crusaders, like the count of Soissons, increasingly feel like strangers in a strange land: "We are new penitents from a foreign land. We'll gladly serve the Church for the full forty days, to the very end; then we'll go back by the way we came" (201.36–39) (Nos em d'estranha terra novel penedenser / E servirem la Glieiza de grat e volentier / Tota la caranten, tro.l termini derrier; / E poish tornar nos n'em par aquel eish sender). Their eagerness to leave just as soon as they fulfill the letter of their obligation contrasts with the devotion shown by Dalmas de Creixell—the late king of Aragon's loyal vassal, determined to see the siege out to its end: "I came from my land to avenge my lord. I will stay in the town without going elsewhere until the siege is lifted or they are defeated" (191.69–71) (Eu vengui de ma terra per venjar mo senhor / E estarai en la vila que non irai alhor / Tro qu'en levetz lo seti o qu'en cobretz milhor).[57]

Even as Simon's closest advisors voice their discontent, Count Raymond's allies convene to express their unanimous support. The longest and most symbolically resonant endorsement comes from Raymond's faithful vassal, Count Roger Bernard of Foix, addressing the barons of Toulouse:

You should be very glad, for all your ancestors were good and loyal toward God and [their] lord. You have honored yourselves and them for you have recently spread a flower that lights the darkness and makes brightness appear; you have brought all *Pretz* and *Paratge* into the light; they had been wandering throughout the world, aimless, causing you good men to shed many tears. (191.48–55)

(Gran gaug devetz aver car tuit vostre ancessor
Foron bo e leial vas Dieu e vas senhor,
E vos avetz ondratz vos meteises e lor
Car avetz espandida novelament tal flor
Per que l'escurs s'alumpna e pareis la claror;
Que tot *Pretz e Paratge* avetz trait a lugor,
Que·s n'anava pel segle, e no sabia or,
E car vos etz proome en avetz fait mant plor.)

Addressing this assembly of a beleaguered feudal nobility and the urban patriciate, Roger Bernard uses the language of troubadour verse, evoking the springtime *incipits* of countless *cansos* and *sirventes*. Once the crusaders attack, however, the poem returns to the new discourse of local solidarity to record yet another performance of urban plenitude:

Then they blew horns and clarions, ran to the ropes and primed the trebuchets. Members of the Capitol, carrying staves, distributed food, fair gifts and presents; and the people brought picks, shovels and tools. Nothing was left behind: not a wedge, hammer, bucket, cooking pot, tub, or stake. They began working on the doors and hatches. Knights and burghers handled the stones, together with ladies and young men, little girls, boys, and maidens, the great and the lowly, all singing ballads and songs and verses. Outside, the mangonels were repeatedly firing at them, archers and slingers loosed bolts and stones knocking bowls and pitchers off their heads, smashing handles and head-pads and piercing their legs, hands, and fingers. But so firm and strong was their courage, not one of them took fright. (203.96–1114)

> (Ladoncs sonan li graile e li corn a sonetz
> E corro a las cordas e tendo·ls trabuquetz.
> E·ls baros de Capitol portant los bastonetz
> E lhiuran las viandas e·ls bels dos e·ls larguetz;
> E lo pobles aporta pics, palas e espleitz;
> E no i remas nulh antz, ni cunhs mi marteletz
> Ni semal ni caudeira ni cuba ni paletz.
> E comensan las obras e·ls portals e·ls guisquetz;
> Cavalers e borzes recebro·ls caironetz
> E donas e donzelos e tozas e tozetz
> E donzelas puizelas, li gran e·ls menoretz,
> Que cantan las baladas e cansos e vercetz.
> Mas li peirer de fora lor gietan mantas vetz,
> E li arc e las frondas, peiras e caireletz,
> Que dels caps lor abato orzols e grazalatz
> E lor rompon las manjas e los cabessaletz
> E passan per las cambas e pels mas e pels detz;
> Mas tant an los coratges e bos e fortaletz
> C'us no s'en espaventa.)[58]

Toulousains of both sexes and all ages and classes come together wielding picks, shovels, and kitchenware in an incongruous spectacle as contrary as one could imagine to the fierce, formalized battle scenes of the *Chanson de Roland*.

The siege of Toulouse is brought to an abrupt end by Simon's death. First, his brother Gui is wounded in the groin—the conventional wound of symbolic disempowerment.[59] Shortly after, Simon is struck in the face by a stone from a mangonel operated by women:

> As Sir Gui was speaking and beginning to shout, inside the town there was a mangonel—built by a carpenter and dragged with its platform from Saint Sernin—being operated by ladies, girls, and women. Now a stone arrived just where it was needed and struck the count on his steel helmet, shattering his eyes, brain, back teeth, forehead and jaw. And the count fell down dead, bleeding and black. (205.121–29)

> (Mentre·n Guis se razona e deve clamaders,
> Ac dins una peireira, que fe us carpenters,
> Qu'es de Sent Cerni traita la peireira e·l soler
> E tiravan la donas e tozas e molhers.
> E venc tot dreit la peira lai on era mestiers
> E feric si lo comte sobre e'elm, qu'es d'acers,
> Que·ls olhs e las cervelas e·ls caichals estremiers
> E·l front e las maichelas li partic a cartiers;
> E·l coms cazec en terra mortz e sagnens e niers.)

Where the dashing Pedro of Aragon had died on horseback, heroically if futilely identifying himself as king, Simon de Montfort—conqueror of Occitania—falls ignominiously, "killed by a stone, like a criminal" (205.139) (*mortz ab una peira, cum si fos aversers*). For the elated Toulousains, such a death was just reward for the man who had "destroyed, killed and banished *Paratge*" (180.4) (*destruit Paratge e mort e decassat*): "Rejoice! God is merciful: now *Paratge* shines forth, and will henceforth be victorious. And the count, who was evil and murderous, is dead, unshriven, because he was a man of blood" (205.149–52) (*La joya! car es Deus merceners, / E ar Paratges alumpna es er oimais sobrers. / E·l coms, qu'era malignes e homicidiers, / Es mortz ses penedensa, car era glaziers*). As in the earlier scene with Foucaud de Berzy, the conviction that Simon has died unshriven (*ses penedensa*) undermines the identification of the Albigensian campaign with a crusade. Moreover, according to the Anonymous Continuator, the same doubt prevails even in the crusader camp: when Fulk of Marseille, bishop of Toulouse, calls for Simon to be buried in the tomb of

Saint Paul, "for he is a saint and a martyr" (206.37) (Car el es sans e martirs), the count of Soissons vigorously dissents: "Don't call him holy: no
one lies more than any man who calls him a saint, for he died without
confession" (206.44–45) (No l'apeletz santisme, que anc melhs no mentic
/ Nulhs hom que sant l'apela, car descofes moric).

   Left leaderless by Simon's death, the crusaders resort to genealogical
protocol to replace him: "since the count is dead, let us make a count of
his son, Lord Amaury; let us give him the land conquered by his father"
(206.24–25, 27) (pos lo coms es mortz, . . . fassam ades comte de so filh
n'Amaldric, . . . e donem li la terra que·l paire comqueric). At the same
time, they call on the French king to send aid in the form of *his* son Louis
(206.31) (lo sieu filh Lozoïc).[60] But the passing of the torch to the
younger generation, which had served the Occitanian resistance so well in
the case of Raimondet, was less inspired for the crusaders. Amaury was
eighteen years old; "he had Simon's courage and resourcefulness, but
none of his personal charisma and, more significantly perhaps, none of his
fanatical self-righteousness."[61] For the next six years, Amaury led a war of
attrition against Raimondet in the face of weak military and financial support from his allies in the north. Finally, in 1224, he himself abandoned
Occitania, leaving Raymond VII as count of Toulouse in all but name.[62]

   Momentum shifted again, decisively, in 1226, when Louis VIII (who
succeeded his father, Philip Augustus, in 1223) launched a new campaign.
The troops accompanying him were less a crusading army than "a royal
army in the service of the church"; many of the count's allies, war weary,
hastened to make peace with the king. In 1228, facing the threat of a new
crusade, Raymond VII himself surrendered—the terms of his capitulation
formalized in the treaty of Meaux (or Paris) the following year. Besides
his territorial losses (Nîmes, Beaucaire, and Saint Gilles), the count was
forced to humiliate himself in front of Notre Dame, to pay huge indemni-
ties (part of which went for the foundation of the University of Toulouse),
and to demolish the walls of Toulouse and thirty other towns. The "most
important of all the crown's acquisitions in 1229," however, was Raimondet's nine-year-old daughter, Joan, betrothed to Alphonse of Poitiers,
nine-year-old younger brother of the boy-king, Louis IX.[63] Such dynastic alliances were, of course, business as usual among the medieval nobility, but the terms of this particular union were extraordinary: though in
1229 Joan was Raymond VII's only child, the treaty expressly excluded
any sons he might subsequently have from inheriting title to Toulouse
and stipulated that should Joan die childless, Toulouse would pass to

Alphonse and his heirs and then to the French crown—laying the ground for the absorption, in 1271, of the rich county of Toulouse into the kingdom of France.

*   *   *

Nothing could seem further from the bloody drama of the Albigensian Crusades than the curious *chantefable, Aucassin et Nicolette*—its two charming protagonists, wrapped in their devotion to one another, floating obliviously through a world by turns brutal and fantastic. In Chapter 2, I analyzed its plot as a variant of the motif of the Saracen queen: when Nicolette is revealed to be the daughter of the pagan king of Carthage, the familyless waif with nothing to recommend her is suddenly transformed into a Saracen princess whose defection from home, family, and religion carries immense ideological weight. Were we tempted to compare *Aucassin* with any other text, the obvious choice would be *Floire et Blancheflor*, that *other* tale of two young lovers linked by their mutual resemblance but separated by religion and class. Yet unlikely as it seems, there is much to link *Aucassin* to all three texts we have considered in Part III. Dialectal traits and its use of prose place it in the same northeastern regions that produced *La Conquête de Constantinople* and *La Fille du comte de Pontieu*,[64] while the disdain Aucassin holds for the core values of feudal society— however comically expressed—resonates with the disappointments and ideological dislocations so vividly registered in those two texts, a reflection of the sociocultural realignments of the early thirteenth century.

At the same time, its setting, Beaucaire, clearly alludes to lands devasted by the Albigensian Crusade. Aucassin's father, Count Garin, is embroiled in an endless war against Count "Bougar" of Valence—an onomastic reference to Catharism's "Bulgarian" links.[65] Like so many medieval texts, *Aucassin et Nicolette* is impossible to date with precision; placing it in the aftermath of the siege of Beaucaire, however, renders some interesting results. One could, for example, easily place Garin's exhortation to Aucassin in the mouth of Count Raymond VI: "Son, take up arms, mount your horse, defend your land, help your vassals, and go to battle" (8.14–16) (Fix, car pren les armes et monte u ceval et defen te tere et aiues tes homes et va a l'estor). Aucassin's predilection for hell over heaven—for "fair clerks, fair knights who've died in tournaments and noble wars, . . . beautiful courtly ladies" (6.33–35) (li bel clerc, et li bel cevalier qui sont mort as tornois et as rices gueres, . . . les beles dames cortoises) over "those old priests and lame or one-armed wretches who squat in front of altars and in old crypts all day and night" (6.26–28) (ci viel prestre et cil viel clop et cil manke qui tote jor et tote nuit cropent devant ces autex et en ces viés creutes)—is clearly a vote for the culture of *paratge* over the dry and disciplinary world of Simon de Montfort and Fulk of Marseille. Even the upside-down world of Torelore, where the king lies in childbed and the queen wages war as a food fight, seems to reflect the sudden and impossible inversions that hit Occitania with the advent of the Albigensian Crusade.

A tangible link between the Franco-Flemish world of *Aucassin* and the Occitania of *La Croisade Albigeoise* is provided by the crusaders themselves—figures like the count of Saint Pol, one of the first patrons of vernacular prose, who fought alongside Philip Augustus at the battle of Bouvines and whose title is given to a fictional character in *La Fille du comte de Pontieu*. Pictured in the *Chanson de la Croisade Albigeoise* as answering the call of pope and king but reluctant to countenance the overthrow of a culture whose values so closely resembled their own, such nobles are shown fulfilling their forty-days' crusading vows and then turning for home—or staying, but voicing increasing dissent from Simon de Montfort's stringent rule.

In 1174, Beaucaire had been the setting of a great festival held to celebrate the reconciliation (negotiated by Henry II of England) between Alfonso II of Aragon (Pedro's father) and Raymond V of Toulouse. Described (no doubt hyperbolically) by the monastic chronicler Geoffrey de Vigeois, it typified the extravagance of court festivals held during the "Golden Age" of the 1170s and 1180s. (In 1172, for example, a seventeen-year-old Young King Henry held a whimsical Christmas banquet with 110 guests, all named Guillaume.) Unlike most of these celebrations, however, the Beaucaire gathering featured no military games, emphasizing instead feasting and largesse; its "apparent lack of deliberate organization" marked it, in comparison to other festivals, as isolated and "somewhat archaic."[66]

By the 1220s, this world must have seemed lost forever. Thanks to the policies of Innocent III and the actions, some principled and some not, of warriors like Simon de Montfort and clerics like Arnaud-Amaury and Fulk of Marseille, Occitania was well on its way to becoming "southern France."[67] In literary-historical terms, the Albigensian Crusade is significant for disrupting the rich court life in which troubadour poetry had flourished: in a kind of poetic diaspora, troubadours and jongleurs fled the ravages of Occitania for the Iberian and northern Italian courts where the first *chansonniers* were compiled. Oppositional voices continued to be heard in the lyrics of those poets, today little read, who railed against the French destruction of their homeland. By far the most sustained and, in many ways, most moving resistance to the events of the early thirteenth century, however, remains the Anonymous Continuation of the *Chanson de la Croisade Albigeoise*, vividly reanimating that uncivil war that, in the late nineteenth century, all Frenchmen were called upon to have forgotten.

Conclusion

My aim in *Medieval Boundaries* has been to understand the inaugural texts of the medieval French literary tradition not as formulaic instantiations of predetermined generic rules or ideological programs but as active, even aggressive, reformulations of both literary form and political vision. The long twelfth century was a period of rapid transformation in Latin Europe's relations both to its external others (legible in the contrast between the conquest of Jerusalem in 1099 and the conquest of Constantinople in 1204, or between the conquest of Saragossa in 1118 and the victory of Las Navas de Tolosa in 1212) and to "others" in one way or another on the margins of European society (in the conquest and assimilation of Anglo-Norman Wales, in the canons of Lateran IV, and in the Albigensian Crusade). In recontextualizing well-known and beloved works like the *Chanson de Roland* and the *Lais* of Marie de France in the political complications of their age, I hope to have shown that neither the nationalizing taxonomies of late nineteenth-century official culture nor the conventional orientalizing tropes deployed by an unreflective strain of late twentieth-century postcolonial medievalism can do justice to the complex and often astoundingly bold cultural work being done by texts we too often dismiss as charmingly simple or conventionally formulaic.

Without wishing to occult the histories of both external and internal violence that have gone into the long genealogy of modern "Western" society, *Medieval Boundaries* has sought to elucidate, against the grain of much recent criticism, alternate histories of peaceful contact and accommodation, of "business as usual" conducted beneath more strident assertions of conquest and crusade. In the introduction I pointed to the Eleanor vase as an object that succinctly materializes the kinds of intercultural complexities that underpin the texts that we reductively consign to the category of "medieval French literature." Let us conclude, then, with another object, the Cluny olifant, that—like Floire's Trojan goblet—troubles the civilizational histories that our study of the Middle Ages is so often meant to confirm.

An olifant, of course, plays a crucial role in the outcome of the *Chanson de Roland*: Roland's decision *not* to sound his olifant at the approach of Marsile's troops marks his determination to transform a culture of *parias* into a culture of war. Like most of the other seventy-five or so olifants still in existence, the one found today in Paris's Musée de Cluny was produced sometime in the eleventh or early twelfth century, probably in southern Italy, "in a style whose closest parallels are with the 11th-century art of Fatimid Egypt."[1] It belonged, in other words, to the "shared culture of objects" that prevailed around the shores of the Mediterranean between the tenth and twelfth centuries, in which both portable objets d'art and the motifs adorning them readily crossed religious as well as political frontiers.[2] The Cluny horn is unusual, however, in that the Fatimid-style arabesque and vegetal motifs in the horn's decorative borders are juxtaposed with vertical panels in its middle section; done in a "rough" and "awkward" style, these panels depict scenes and figures from Christian history: an Ascension, together with framed busts of six apostles and the four evangelists. In other words, at some point in its history, the Cluny olifant's nonreligious, princely design was literally inscribed with Christian meaning, reappropriating this rich courtly object for the culture of Latin Christendom. The fineness of the Fatimid motifs versus the "roughness" of the Christian overlay remind us that in the twelfth century the Muslim world—or, more broadly, the multicultural and multiconfessional Mediterranean—enjoyed a visible advantage in prestige and sophistication over the emerging culture of Latin "Europe." In that century, places like Spain and Norman Sicily, so often marginalized in modern histories of the medieval West, were in fact privileged points of access to this shared culture of objects. *Medieval Boundaries* has tried to show that, extricated from their showcases in the exhibition hall of western civilization, texts like *Floire et Blancheflor* and *La Prise d'Orange*—like the Eleanor vase and the Cluny olifant—suggest the extent to which cultures are produced not by the policing of borders but by transgressional flows.

Notes

Introduction

1. A good starting point for this literature is Cohen, ed., *The Postcolonial Middle Ages*. See also Ingham, *Sovereign Fantasies*, and Heng, *Empire of Magic*.

2. Bouchard, *Strong of Body*, 26.

3. On this battle, see Duby, *Le dimanche de Bouvines*.

4. On Lateran IV's place in the regulation of Jews, heretics, and lepers, see Moore, *The Formation of a Persecuting Society*.

5. R. R. Davies, "Henry I and Wales," 137.

6. Heng, *Empire of Magic*, 70.

7. David Abulafia, "Seven Types of Ambiguity, c. 1100–c. 1500," in Abulafia and Berend, 33.

8. Franco Moretti, *Atlas of the European Novel 1800–1900* (London: Verso, 1998), 1, 7–8.

9. On the tyranny that "l'absolutisation des frontières contemporaines" has exerted over the historiography of the Middle Ages in France, see Guerreau, *L'avenir d'un passé incertain*, 80–90.

10. Besides the texts cited in note 1, see Kathy Lavezzo, ed., *Imagining a Medieval English Nation* (Minneapolis: University of Minnesota Press, 2004).

11. Several of the following points are developed in greater detail in Kinoshita, "Discrepant Medievalisms."

12. Haidu, *The Subject of Violence*, 6.

13. This "emergent written culture in the vernacular," they point out, retains "very close ties to the oral culture inasmuch as most members of this culture are preliterate" (Kittay and Godzich, *The Emergence of Prose*, 15). Of course, texts in medieval Latin could be highly playful and disruptive as well.

14. Compare David Wallace's critique of the uneven temporalities ascribed to the fourteenth century—the "invisible but magical boundary" separating Chaucer's England from the city-states of the Italian peninsula that "inevitably, if not explicitly, evokes the imaginary medieval/Renaissance divide" (*Chaucerian Polity*, 9).

15. María Rosa Menocal challenges the usual valence of this moment of historical transition by emphasizing the pleasures of the unruly, polyglot world *foreclosed* by the events of 1492. She, too, however, notes the difference between the fourteenth and fifteenth centuries—" 'medieval' in some of the worst senses of the stereotype"—and the age that preceded them. See *Shards of Love*, 39–40.

16. Ania Loomba, " 'Local-manufacture made-in-India Othello fellows': Issues of Race, Hybridity and Location in Post-Colonial Shakespeares," in *Post-Colonial Shakespeares*, ed. Ania Loomba and Martin Orkin (London: Routledge, 1998), 144.

17. Inspired by Said's insight that the delineation of Orientalism as a field of study is revealing, "since no one is likely to imagine a field symmetrical to it called Occidentalism," we may experiment with reversing these scholarly projects: "Christianity and the East: The Making of an Image," or "Eastern Views of Christianity in the Middle Ages" (Said, *Orientalism*, 50). For an analysis of Daniel's project and his influence on Said, see Tolan, *Saracens*, xvi–xvii.

18. These visual metaphors evoke the scientific detachment mobilized in the eighteenth- and nineteenth-century projects such as the *Description de l'Égypte*. See Said, *Orientalism*, 86–87. For the power of the deployment of the gaze at the height of the age of European colonialism, see Timothy Mitchell, "Egypt at the Exhibition," in *Colonising Egypt* (Berkeley: University of California Press, 1991).

19. Tolan, *Saracens*, xvi.

20. My account of the Eleanor vase and the identification of Mitadolus as ʿImād al-Dawla (the *laqab* or regnal name of ʿAbd al-Malik ibn Hūd) come from Beech, "The Eleanor of Aquitaine Vase." We will meet Alfonso I of Aragon and the Banū Hūd kings of Saragossa again in Chapter 1.

21. Pico Iyer, *Video Night in Kathmandu and Other Reports from the Not-So-Far East* (New York: Vintage Books, 1989), and Néstor García Canclini, *Hybrid Cultures: Strategies for Entering and Leaving Modernity*, trans. Christopher L. Chiappari and Silvia L. López (Minneapolis: University of Minnesota Press, 1995).

22. See Baraz, *Medieval Cruelty*.

23. Nirenberg, *Communities of Violence*, 7–8, 19, 32. Nirenberg seeks to displace the binary opposition of "tolerance" and "intolerance," emphasizing instead their "fundamental interdependence."

24. Burnett, *The Introduction of Arabic Learning into England*, 31–32. See Chapter 3, p. 00.

25. Joan was subsequently married to Raymond VI of Toulouse and became the mother of Raimondet, hero of the Occitanian resistance in the *Chanson de la Croisade Albigeoise*. See Chapters 6 and 7.

26. Bartlett, *The Making of Europe*. Some of the best work in postcolonial medievalism has focused on the othering of the Welsh and the Irish (anticipating the internal colonialisms and Orientalizing representations of the sixteenth through the early twentieth centuries). In addition to the works cited in note 1, see M. Warren, *History on the Edge*.

27. A word is in order about my use, throughout this work, of the term "feudal." Citing the ambiguity and fraught history of the concept of feudalism, some historians find it advisable to avoid it and its derivatives altogether. See Reynolds, *Fiefs and Vassals*, 3–14, and Bouchard, *Strong of Body*, 35–38. Yet the term retains currency in studies of French aristocratic culture, in works such as Georges Duby's *Les trois ordres ou l'imaginaire du féodalisme* (Paris: Gallimard, 1978); Jean-Pierre Poly and Eric Bournazel's *La mutation féodale: Xᵉ-XIIᵉ siècle* (Paris: Presses Universitaires de France, 1980, 1991), in English as *The Feudal Transformation: 900–1200*, trans. Caroline Higgitt (New York: Holmes and Meier,1991);

and Evergates, *Feudal Society in Medieval France*. I use the term to refer to the culture of the great territorial princes who, "in the absence of a direct royal presence, . . . shaped the character and institutions of the French provinces" (Evergates, "Aristocratic Women," xviii), particularly in the second half of the twelfth century. It revolves around a complex of values—the Occitanian permutation of which Fredric Cheyette (in *Ermengard of Narbonne*) calls a "culture of fidelity"—largely displaced by the epistemic changes of the thirteenth century (and available for nostalgic revival in the fourteenth). We will return to Cheyette's work extensively in Chapter 7.

Chapter 1. *"Pagans Are Wrong and Christians Are Right"*

1. "[L]a *Chanson de Roland* joue pour les études médiévales en tant que discipline, en tant qu'institution, un rôle fondateur . . . . Etre médiéviste c'est, au plus vrai, prendre position sur la C. R." (Cerquiglini, "Roland à Roncevaux," 40).

2. *La Chanson de Roland*, ed. Short, hereafter cited parenthetically by line numbers, with my translations.

3. See Kinoshita, "Pagans Are Wrong and Christians Are Right," 79–81.

4. Samuel Huntington, *The Clash of Civilizations and the Remaking of World Order* (New York: Simon and Schuster, 1996).

5. The story is prominently told in the introduction to the modern translations by Short (8–9), Goldin (3–4), and Burgess (9–10).

6. ʿAbd al-Raḥmān I belonged to the Umayyad dynasty of caliphs of Damascus, which was overthrown by the rival ʿAbbasid line in 750. Taking refuge in Muslim Iberia, he established in 756 a kind of Umayyad court-in-exile. His centralized rule was contested by various rebels, who often used expressions of loyalty to the ʿAbbasids to enhance their claims to autonomy from Cordoba.

7. The first quotation is from Sénac, *Les Carolingiens et al-Andalus*, 4 (my translation), the second from Goldin, *Song of Roland*, 4. Sénac adds: "The Carolingians' scant knowledge of the Muslim world rendered their comprehension of these oppositions more tenuous still; beyond a doubt, the difficulties Charlemagne met with in Spain were largely the result of this situation." Andalusian society was divided, for example, between those who claimed descent (real or fictive) from the original Arab invaders, and indigenous Christian converts and their descendants (called *muwalladūn*).

8. "Real life demands of us a thousand compromises a day, but the *Song of Roland*, like the *Iliad*, is a poem of absolutes. . . . This is an ethic of brutal pride, of high pulses and cut arteries, of *démesure*" (Vance, *Reading the Song of Roland*, 1). For Bakhtin, epic refers to an inaccessible past: "In its style, tone and manner of expression, epic discourse is infinitely far removed from discourse of a contemporary about a contemporary addressed to contemporaries" (*The Dialogic Imagination*, 13–14). See also Auerbach, "Roland against Ganelon."

9. The *mulūk al-ṭāwaʾif* (party kings) emerged during the *fitna* (disorder) of 1008–31 out of the political ruins of the caliphate of Cordoba. Originally numbering about thirty, by the Almoravid invasion of 1086 only about nine remained,

including Almería, Granada, Majorca, Saragossa, Seville, and Toledo. Kennedy, *Muslim Spain and Portugal*, chap. 6.

10. MacKay, *Spain in the Middle Ages*, 17.

11. "At barbarus, saniori vsus consilio, immensam pecuniam auri et argenti pretiosarumque vestium conglomerat, atque accepta formidinis fide, ad regis presentiam humiliter properans, excellentiam illius obnoxius postulat, vt acceptis muneribus fines suos vastare desistat. Ad hoc et se et regnum suum sue potestati comissum dicit. *Porro Fernandus rex barbarum, quamuis ficta loqutum intelligebat et ipse longe animo gereret, tamen pro tempore* accepta pecunia Cartaginensem prouinciam expugnare desinens, multa honustus preda in Campos Gotorum se recepit." *Historia Silense*, ed. Dom Justo Perez de Urbel and Atilano González Ruiz-Zorrilla (Madrid: Consejo Superior de Investigaciones Científicas, 1959), 197, cited in Barton and Fletcher, *The World of the Cid*, 54–55. (The underlined passage is a quotation from Sallust's *Bellum Iugurthinum*.) Despite its name, the *Historia Silense* (a "composite historical miscellany") was probably composed not at Santo Domingo de Silos (in Castile) but at San Isidoro de León, c. 1109–18.

12. Werckmeister, "Cluny III and Santiago," 105. This was part of Fernando's effort to bring León-Castile into closer alignment with the "European" mainstream. See Chapter 3, pp. 79.

13. MacKay, *Spain in the Middle Ages*, 17–18.

14. Later that same year, Sancho II was assassinated, and Alfonso (suspected, along with his sister Urraca, of complicity in the murder) became king of a united León-Castile.

15. O'Callaghan, *History of Medieval Spain*, 198, 200, 205.

16. Ibid., 205.

17. Barton and Fletcher, *World of El Cid*, 91. After the Cid's death in 1099 (the same year as the First Crusaders' conquest of Jerusalem), Valencia quickly reverted to Muslim rule. See also Fletcher, *The Quest for the Cid*, 125–42.

18. Consider Reverter, the viscount of Barcelona (d. 1144), who led the Almoravids' North African wars against the Almohads (Kennedy, *Muslim Spain and Portugal*, 184). Christian mercenaries are found in Muslim service even after the great Christian victory at the Las Navas de Tolosa in 1212 (Barton, "Christian Mercenaries," 26, 29). Conversely, in the fourteenth century, Alfonso III of Aragon named the Granadan noble Mahomet Abenadalill his vassal for life and commander in chief of all Muslims in his army. Mahomet remained in Alfonso's service even after his eventual return to Granada. The king's letter of transit stipulated he was to be "treated with 'love and honor' and given 'counsel and aid' " throughout Alfonso's realms (Catlos, "A Muslim Mercenary").

19. On Gelasius II's proclamation at the Council of Toulouse (1117), see Reilly, *The Medieval Spains*, 110, and Lomax, *Reconquest*, 84.

20. After the Muslim conquests of c. 711, Saraqusta (the old Roman colony of Caesar Augusta) had become the "furthest march" of Muslim Iberia. On this frontier centralized power was weak, so regional governors exercised considerable autonomy, sometimes reaching open revolt. Similarities between various border regions of medieval Europe are examined and theorized in Abulafia and Berend, *Medieval Frontiers*.

21. On al-Muqtadir's poetic gatherings, see Robinson, "Seeing Paradise." Al-Muʿtamin's treatise was known to Maimonides in the twelfth century and circulated as far as Central Asia in the fourteenth. Ahmed Djebbar, "Al-Muʿtaman [*sic*] ibn Hûd, roi de Saragosse et mathématicien," in *Les Andalousies*, 200–202. Al-Muqtadir had paid *parias* to Fernando I of Castile in return for protection from Ramiro I of Aragon. O'Callaghan, *History of Medieval Spain*, 196.

22. Robinson, "Arts of the Taifa Kingdoms," 56–57. Its name derives from al-Muqtadir's full name, Abū Jaʿfar Ahmad ibn Sulaymān. See Barrucand and Bednorz, *Moorish Architecture*, 116–21.

23. Guichard, *Al-Andalus 711–1492*, 121–22. Alfonso named his first cousin, First Crusade veteran Gaston de Béarn, as governor. Other Occitanians in Alfonso's service included Gaston's brother, Centule of Bigorre, Bernard Ató of Carcassonne, and Alphonse Jourdain of Toulouse. Lacarra, "La Conquista de Zaragoza," 65–96.

24. Lacarra, *Alfonso el Batallador*, 67–72. Muslims were given one year to vacate the city center.

25. Nor was this accommodationism limited to secular rulers. In thirteenth-century Valencia, for example, Templars and Hospitallers allowed recently conquered Muslims to "retain their main mosque and to practice their religion freely" (Forey, "The Military Orders," 5). On the surrender treaty, see Lacarra, "La Conquista de Zaragoza." On Muslim communities in Christian Aragon, see Catlos, *The Victors and the Vanquished*.

26. O'Callaghan, *History of Medieval Spain*, 197. Menocal sees the conquest of Barbastro as a key event through which Arabic lyric influenced the emergence of the troubadour tradition. See her *Ornament of the World*, 18–29; and idem, *The Arabic Role in Medieval Literary History*.

In 1085, Alfonso VI of León-Castile similarly promised the vanquished Muslims of Toledo that they could keep their lives, property, and religion (including the great mosque) in exchange for the taxes they had been accustomed to paying their own kings. Subsequently, Alfonso's queen, Constance of Burgundy (niece of Abbot Hugh of Cluny), and Bernard de Sédirac, the newly appointed Cluniac archbishop, seized the great mosque and rededicated it as a cathedral. "Alfonso was furious, but accepted the change at the request of the Muslims, who feared to stir hatred against themselves." Lomax, *Reconquest*, 65–66.

27. Ebles had fought for Alfonso's father, Sancho I, in 1073. Guenée, "Généalogies."

28. Bertrand of Laon was made count of Carrión de los Condes in 1117 and died with Alfonso the Battler at the battle of Fraga in 1134 (Guenée, "Généalogies," 456). Rotrou II of Perche, a close ally of the kings of England, came south with many Norman knights; appointed governor of Tudela after its conquest in 1123, he remained in Aragon until at least the early 1130s. Contemporary Spanish sources mention many *francos* with Norman toponymics (Thompson, *Power and Border Lordship*, 71–78). On the Occitanians in Alfonso's service, see note 23, above.

29. Also fighting with Alfonso was Guilhem IX of Aquitaine, the troubadour-duke whose compositions have sometimes been credited to his firsthand familiarity

with Andalusian lyric traditions: this may have been the occasion on which ʿImād al-Dawla gave him the rock crystal vase mentioned in the introduction. Beech, "The Eleanor of Aquitaine Vase." See above, pp. 00.

30. Such cross-confessional accommodationism appears in the late twelfth-century epic *Raoul de Cambrai* when a pagan king battling his Saracen overlord turns to his Frankish prisoner, Bernier of Vermandois, for help. Addressing him as "Christian, brother" (6733) (Crestiie[n]s, frere) he promises him his freedom, life-long friendship, and twenty pack animals laden with "silk cloth, pure gold, and silver deniers" (6744) in exchange for his aid. See Kinoshita, "Fraternizing with the Enemy." *Raoul* dates to the late twelfth century.

31. In which case, perhaps we can read the "vaulted chamber, painted and inscribed with many colors" (2593–94) (cambre voltice; / Plusurs culurs i ad peinz e escrites) in which the wounded Marsile receives Baligant's ambassadors as a distant reflection of the octagonal dome and brilliantly colored geometrical designs of the Aljafería's exquisite mosque and *mihrab* (prayer niche), echoing elements in the Dome of the Rock in Jerusalem and the Great Mosque of Cordoba. On the dating of the Oxford manuscript of the *Roland* to c. 1130–50, see Samaran, "Sur la date approximative du *Roland* d'Oxford"; for an alternate date of c. 1165–80, see Short, "The Oxford Manuscript of the *Chanson de Roland*."

32. "Eschec" from the Germanic *schâch* ("booty"). "Treüd," used elsewhere, is from the Latin *tributum*. Greimas, *Dictionnaire de l'ancien français*.

33. Vance, "Roland and Charlemagne," 60. A key part of his exhortation to his men is that "bad songs" not be sung about them: "Male cançun de nus chantét ne seit!" (1014).

34. Bédier transcribes "Sezilie" rather than "Sebilie" and leaves it untranslated, though Langlois lists it as a variant of "Sezille," Sicily (*Table des noms propres*, 616).

35. Lacarra, "La Conquista de Zaragoza," 69–70. See also *Song of Roland*, trans. Burgess, 8.

36. Unlike Charlemagne, however, Marsile conducts his council from a recumbent position: "Sur un perrun de marbre bloi se culched" (12). On the cultural resonances of chess, see Chapter 3, p. 96.

37. Compare the Frank in *La Prise d'Orange* who has acquired a knowledge of "turquois et Aufriquant, bedoïn et basclois" (328) by virtue of having spent three years as a prisoner of war.

38. This is Auerbach's point in "Roland against Ganelon": logical connections are made not by the poet but by the hearers, based on their shared worldview.

39. As Comfort writes, with a telling choice of metaphor, "As the likelihood is ever present that a Saracen may change his faith, it is important that he shall not be painted in advance in too black colors. The evidence would hardly show that the Christians thought of the Saracens as ethically or culturally inferior to themselves" ("Literary Role of Saracens," 633). Balaguer, as noted above, was one of Alfonso the Battler's conquests.

40. Jonin, "Le climat de croisade," 285.

41. Previous attempts at conversion were directed at the preliterate pagans on the northern and eastern frontiers of Christian Europe. However, for anecdotal accounts of conversions in the Iberian peninsula, see Kedar, *Crusade and Mission*, chap. 1. On literary representations of conversion, see Daniel, *Heroes and Saracens*, chap. 9.

42. Fulcher of Chartres's chronicle of the First Crusade (XIII, 4–5), cited in *The First Crusade*, ed, Peters, 48–49.

43. See Nicol, "The Crusades and the Unity of Christendom." The Fourth Crusaders' conquest of Constantinople is the subject of Chapter 5.

44. "It came to have a quasi-ethnic nuance, as in the phrase *gens latina*, 'the Latin people.' . . . [and] helped lend a kind of conceptual cohesion to groups of very varied national origin and language." Bartlett, *The Making of Europe*, 19.

45. Bartlett, *The Making of Europe*, 101–5. As we shall see in Chapter 4, regions like Wales and Ireland that were clearly Christian but outside this post-Carolingian core were subject to "Frankish" conquest and colonization.

46. See Duggan, *Concordance of the Chanson de Roland*.

47. These descriptions of the battalions contrast the individual presentation of the twelve peers, each with his personal entourage, before the rearguard's battle at Roncevaux. The current list is reprised near the end of the text in the groups of "judges" Charlemagne convokes for the trial of Ganelon (3700–3702).

48. Armenians are paired with "Moors" in one battalion (3227), Hungarians with the Huns in another (3254).

49. Compare Peter Haidu's provocative argument that Roland and the twelve peers must die "in order to perform the subjection of the warrior class . . . to a monarchy that does not yet exist, which awaits in the wings until the scene is set for its entrance." In this reading, "Saracens, enemies on the actorial level, are adjuvants on actantial level, helping to decimate the feudal class, the anti-subject," destined to be replaced by new men like Rabel and Guineman, apt subjects of a new kind of national state (*The Subject of Violence*, 149–51, 175, 189–91).

50. For a challenge to the theory of *démesure*, see R. Cook, *The Sense of the Song of Roland*, 148–59.

51. Hillenbrand, "The Ornament of the World," 115.

52. "'Be quiet, Oliver!' Count Roland responds; 'He is my stepfather; I don't want you saying a word about him'" (1026–27) ("Tais, Oliver!" li quens Rollant respunt, / "Mis parrastre est; ne voeill que mot en suns").

53. For more on the tributary culture of objects, see Chapter 3.

54. Duggan bases his conclusion on the Baligant episode's belatedness on the attenuated density of its formulaic language (*Formulaic Style and Poetic Craft*, chap. 3). On mercantile traffic between Muslim Spain and medieval "Babylon" (Cairo), see Chapter 3.

55. See Friedman, *The Monstrous Races*. It is no accident, I think, that this nod to the "monstrous races" occurs precisely in the part of the text closest to literate rather than oral traditions. On the use and abuse of selective quotation in recent readings of the *Roland*, see Kinoshita, "Political Uses and Responses to the Poem."

56. The two articles were Gaston Paris, "Etudes sur les romans de la table ronde," *Romania* 10 (1881): 465–96; and idem, "Etudes sur les romans de la table ronde: Lancelot du Lac," *Romania* 12 (1883): 459–534. See Hult, "Gaston Paris and the Invention of Courtly Love," 200–206, and Bloch, "Mieux vaut jamais que tard."

57. This phrase is John Benton's, in "The *Song of Roland* and the Enculturation of the Warrior Class."

58. Gaunt, *Gender and Genre*, 38. On the marginalization of women in the critical tradition on the *Roland*, see Kay, *Chansons de geste*, 25–26, and Burns et al., "*Une Bele Disjointure*," esp. 232–37.

59. Her examples are: *Aiol, Anseïs de Cartage, Aspremont, Boeve de Haumtone, Daurel et Beton, Elie de Saint Gille, Fierabras, Floovant, Folque de Candie, Guibert d'Andrenas, Mainet, La Prise de Cordres et de Sebille, La Prise d'Orange, Les Saisnes,* and *Le Siège de Barbastre*.

60. On the semantic complexities of *amer* in Old French epic, see Jones, *The Ethos of the Song of Roland*, 36–45. "Although derived from Latin *amare*, this verb does not always imply personal affection or emotional attachment . . . ; in many cases *amer* means 'to keep peace with' or 'to make peace with,' or 'to form an alliance with'" (36).

61. On pagan conversions, see Chapter 2, p. 261n. 85.

62. The poem in question is *La Prise d'Orange*, the subject of Chapter 2. On the figure of the Saracen princess, see Comfort, "Literary Role of Saracens," 658.

63. Bédier's edition of the *Chanson de Roland* has "plus de .XX. mil humes," keeping the two in perfect parallel.

64. Comfort, "Literary Role," 643–44.

65. Kay, *Chansons de geste*, 46.

66. Jenny Sharpe, *Allegories of Empire: The Figure of Woman in the Colonial Text* (Minneapolis: University of Minnesota Press, 1993), 8.

67. Bédier gives the reading "pendre."

68. Rather, it recalls the conquest of Jerusalem in 1099, where the slaughter was so indiscriminate that, according to chronicler Fulcher of Chartres, crusaders entering the Temple of Solomon "waded in blood up to their ankles." *The First Crusade,* ed. Peters, 209.

69. See Stranges, "The Significance of Bramimonde's Conversion," 190–96.

70. Bédier gives the reading "mes marches" (my borders).

71. See, for example, R. Cook, *The Sense of the Song of Roland*, 111.

72. Haidu notes, "Aude takes the position that no exchange is possible for Roland: it is an anomalous position in the codes of her society." His analysis, however, places Aude exclusively in relationship to Roland, not to Bramimonde (*The Subject of Violence,* 131–32).

73. In the rhymed versions of the Roland legend, collectively known as *Roncevaux,* the episode of Aude is expanded to upward of eight hundred lines, much of it devoted to Aude's sensational prophetic dreams. See Duggan, "L'épisode d'Aude."

74. Bramimonde is "the sole individualized Saracen survivor, and by her baptism, arranged at Charles' behest, she embodies the primary theme of the *chanson:*

the Christians are right, the pagans are wrong." Harrison, "Aude and Bramimonde," 675.

75. For later *chansons de geste*, more concerned with internal traitors than external enemies, holy war loses its ideological urgency, and Saracens are portrayed as wealthy, leisured, and refined: their "availability for conversion marks the possibility of romance values being assimilated to the Frankish world, just as the desirability—and desire—of the Saracen princesses allow for the peaceful appropriation of those values." Kay, *Chansons de geste*, 179–80.

76. See Comfort, "Character Types," 362, 421–22.

77. On various meanings of franc/franche, see Chapter 3, pp. 101–2.

78. In the Middle Ages the successful theft of a relic provided its own justification: if a saint allowed his or her relic to be "translated" from one institution to another, it was because the saint preferred the new one. Patrick Geary likens the theft of relics to the ritual kidnaping of brides (*Furta Sacra*, 133).

79. These sites figure in the twelfth-century *Pilgrim's Guide to Santiago de Compostela*, discussed in Chapter 3. On *lieux de mémoire*, see Pierre Nora, ed., *Les lieux de mémoire*, 7 vols. (Paris: Gallimard, 1984–92).

80. Haidu, *The Subject of Violence*, 214n. 4. Haidu's reading, as we have seen, emphasizes the poem's production of the monarchical state in which citizen-vassals like Rabel, Guineman, and Thierry supersede a quarrelsome nobility whose propensity for private warfare risks interfering with their feudal allegiance to the emperor.

81. On multiculturalism in contemporary France, see Alec G. Hargreaves and Mark McKinney, eds., *Post-Colonial Cultures in France* (London: Routledge, 1997).

Chapter 2. The Politics of Courtly Love

1. *La Prise d'Orange*, trans. Lachet and Tusseau, 12.

2. Menocal, "Signs of the Times," 497–98. For the critical literature on the motif of the Saracen princess, see p. 246n. 62. On the recent emergence, in the field of international relations, of a "neomedievalism" calculated explicitly to bracket issues of race and multiculturalism, see Lisa Lampert, "Race, Periodicity, and the (Neo-) Middle Ages," *Modern Language Quarterly* 65:3 (2004): 391–421.

3. See Kay, *Chansons de geste*, and above, Chapter 1, p. 35.

4. Menocal, "Signs of the Times"; de Weever, *Sheba's Daughters*. On "race" in medieval Iberia, see Chapter 6, p. 184.

5. Barbara Harlow, introduction to Malek Alloula, *The Colonial Harem*, trans. Myrna Godzich and Wlad Godzich (Minneapolis: University of Minnesota Press, 1986), xiv–xv.

6. Winifred Woodhull, *Transfigurations of the Maghreb: Feminism, Decolonization, and Literatures* (Minneapolis: University of Minnesota Press, 1993), 16.

7. That is, Guillaume seems to be awaiting the seasonal raids known as *ghazawat*. See Chapter 3, pp. 81–82.

8. All quotations are from Régnier's edition of the AB manuscript tradition, with my translations.

9. Laisse 7 devotes ten lines to the city and six to the queen, laisse 9 eleven to the city and ten to the queen, and laisse 10 seven to the city and eight to the queen.

10. *The Poetry of Cercamon and Jaufre Rudel*, ed. and trans. Wolf and Rosenstein, 146–50. In thirteenth-century *razos*, Jaufre's love is identified as the countess of Tripoli (Hodierna of Jerusalem, wife of Raymond II of Tripoli), on whose account he took the cross and traveled to the east. See *The Vidas of the Troubadours*, trans. Egan, entries 60, 61–62. The hero's overwhelming passion for a woman he has never seen also echoes the line of that other celebrated Guillaume—troubadour Guilhem IX of Aquitaine—who, in his nonsense poem, "Farai un vers de dreit nïen," sings dispassionately of his beloved: "I never saw her and I love her very much" (31) (anc non la vit ez am la fort). *The Poetry of William VII*, ed. and trans. Bond, poem 4.

11. *Pitre et quanele* are used in subsequent mentions as shorthand for this more developed list (249–50, 412–13). In *Le Pèlerinage de Charlemagne*, exotic products—"Ginger, cinnamon and pepper [coste, canele e peivre), other good spices, and many good herbs that I can't describe"—are on offer in the marketplace of the church of Sainte Marie la Latine, founded by the westerners (211–12).

12. On crusading as an armed pilgrimage, see Riley-Smith, *The First Crusade and the Idea of Crusading.* Compare Phillip E. Bennett's suggestion that in *La Prise* (as in Chrétien de Troyes's *Chevalier au Lion*), the conflation of woman and place instantiates a kind of succession motif in which the knight acquires territory through the seduction of the female landholder. Bennett, "The Storming of the Other World, the Enamoured Muslim Princess and the Evolution of the Legend of Guillaume d'Orange," in *Guillaume d'Orange and the Chanson de Geste: Essays Presented to Duncan Mcmillan in Celebration of His Seventieth Birthday by His Friends and Colleagues of the Société Rencesvals*, ed. Wolfgang von Emden and Philip E. Bennett (Reading: Société Rencesvals, 1974), 1–14.

13. *La Prise d'Orange*, ed. Régnier, 36.

14. This is the opening of Raymond Queneau's phantasmagoric novel, *Les Fleurs bleues*: history is "plutôt floue. Des restes du passé traînaient encore çà et là, en vrac." Queneau's protagonist, the duke of Auge, first looks around him in the year 1264: "Les Huns préparaient des stèques tartares, le Gaulois fumait une gitane, les Romains dessinaient des grecques, les Sarrasins fauchaient de l'avoine, les Francs cherchaient des sols et les Alains regardaient cinq Ossètes. Les Normands buvaient du calva . . . 'Tant d'histoire,' dit le duc d'Auge au duc d'Auge, 'tant d'histoire pour quelques calembours, pour quelques anachronismes. Je trouve cela misérable. On n'en sortira donc jamais?'" (Queneau, *Les Fleurs bleues* [Paris: Gallimard, 1965], 13–14).

15. On Tiebaut as a French name, see Lachet, *La Prise d'Orange*, 37. He also cites Henri Grégoire's thesis that the name derives from "Teutobochus," the Teutonic king whose name was engraved on the triumphal arch of Orange (37n. 67). On Aragon, see Chapter 1, pp. 21–22, and Catlos, *The Victors and the Vanquished*.

16. The interest was not necessarily mutual. The early thirteenth-century *Chronique nîmoise*, for example, follows the political fortunes of the pope and the emperor, the Genoese and the Pisans, and the princes of Aquitaine, Barcelona, and Toulouse (noting, inter alia, the conquests of Mallorca, Almería and Tortosa) but makes little mention of France. Philippe Martel, "L'époque médiévale," in *Histoire de Nîmes* (Aix-en-Provence: Edisud, 1982), 122.

17. On the crucial role played by marriage and female inheritance in the shifting alliances and political realignments in twelfth-century Occitania and Provence, see Cheyette, *Ermengard of Narbonne*, 25–33.

18. A treaty contracted in 1125 and renewed periodically thereafter set the Durance River as the boundary between the territories of the count of Toulouse, to the north, and those of the count of Barcelona, to the south. Between 1131 and 1162, Ramon Berenguer IV was closely involved in the politics of Provence, intervening in support of his brother, Count Berenguer Ramon I, and his nephew, Count Ramon Berenguer III.

19. Cheyette, *Ermengard of Narbonne*, 254, 259–60. The count's wife, Queen Petronilla of Aragon, was Eleanor of Aquitaine's first cousin. This marriage, contracted in 1137, was the origin of the feudal confederation known as the "Crown of Aragon." The marriage between Richard and Berengaria of Barcelona-Aragon never took place; instead, Richard later married another Berengaria, sister of Sancho VII of Navarre. See Chapter 6, p. 195.

20. *Raimbaut d'Orange*, Pattison, 7–13. Guillaume was the favored name of the lords of Montpellier; sometimes it was given to more than one son in the same generation, "in case the eldest should not survive" (Cheyette, *Ermengard of Narbonne*, 352). Raimbaut, on the other hand, was a prominent name in the lineage of Orange.

21. This reflects the old medieval practice of inventing new names by combining syllables from the names of different relatives—as in the case of the eighth-century couple Theoderic and Aldana, whose children were called Theodino and Albana. Bouchard, *Strong of Body*, 71.

22. *Raimbaut d'Orange*, ed. Pattison, 11. At the death of Tiburge, her sons, Guillaume and Raimbaut, in accordance with southern French practices, each inherited a part of Orange.

23. Tiburge was married to Bertrand des Baux (whose given name recalls/ anticipates that of one of Guillaume d'Orange's fictional nephews) and Tiburgette to Adhémar de Murviel, who in 1181, for motives unknown, murdered Alfonso of Aragon's younger brother Peire, recently invested as count of Provence under the name Ramon Berenguer IV. On the inheritance, see *Raimbaut d'Orange*, ed. Pattison, 25; on the assassination, see Cheyette, *Ermengard of Narbonne*, 275–77.

24. To the extent that Gloriete may be seen as a gyneceum, it alludes less to the Orientalist motif of the harem than to the courtly motif of the *mal-mariée*.

25. The inclusion of "basclois" in this list of languages reveals how foreign the Basques remained to "Latin" Europeans.

26. On the anxiety aroused in the early modern period of westerners "turning Turk," see Daniel Vitkus, *Turning Turk: English Theatre and the Multicultural Mediterranean, 1570–1630* (New York: Palgrave Macmillan, 2003).

27. Bartlett, *The Making of Europe*, 197.

28. See also ll. 258–59 and 281–82. On conversion patterns, see Chapter 1, note 41.

29. On the ideological compatibility of feudalism and courtly love, see Duby, "On Courtly Love," in *Love and Marriage*; on their shared language, see Bouchard, *Strong of Body*, 133–34. On the polyvalence of the verb *aimer*, see Chapter 1, note 59.

30. Hitti, "The Impact of the Crusades on Moslem Lands," 46–47. That Outremer constitutes one of the poem's subtexts is suggested in Guibert's opening speech comparing the fortress of Orange to any found from there to the river Jordan, and whose inhabitants he describes as Turks.

31. A. C. Krey, *The First Crusade: The Accounts of Eye-Witnesses and Participants* (Princeton, N.J.: Princeton University Press, 1921), 280–81 (emphasis added). Cited in *The First Crusade*, ed. Peters, 220. On the crusader states as an "apartheid" culture, see Prawer, "The Roots of Medieval Colonialism." This view, however, has recently been called into question.

In medieval Iberia, cross-confessional unions were more common, particularly among ruling elites. For a moment at the turn of the twelfth century, the heir of Alfonso VI of León-Castile (whom we met in Chapter 1) was Sancho, his son by a Muslim princess named Zaida (O'Callaghan, *A History of Medieval Spain*, 213). For Christian wives of the Muslim rulers of Cordoba, see Ruggles, "Mothers of a Hybrid Dynasty."

32. F. M. Warren, "The Enamoured Moslem Princess," 356–57. For other *chansons de geste* featuring this motif, see Chapter 1, p. 246n. 59.

33. See Knudson, "La princesse sarrasine dans *La Prise d'Orange*," and Lachet, *La Prise d'Orange*, chap. 3.

34. An interesting variation of this motif occurs in the twelfth-century Byzantine poem *Digenis Akritas*. See Kinoshita, "Politics of Courtly Love," 274n. 20.

35. As Roland Greene writes in another context, love is "a complex signifier whose linked meanings have been severely reduced, and sometimes lost altogether, since the seventeenth century." Greene, *Unrequited Conquests: Love and Empire in the Colonial Americas* (Chicago: University of Chicago Press, 1999), 5.

36. See Chapter 4 for a discussion of Marie de France's "Yonec."

37. On Almería in the French imaginary, see Chapter 6, pp. 181–82.

38. Lachet bases this suggestion on manuscript tradition C, a "romanesque" reworking of AB: less formulaic, rhymed instead of assonanced, and with an attenuated strophic structure. Lachet, *La Prise d'Orange*, chap. 4.

39. MacInnes, "Gloriette," 31. On the influence this image may have exerted on later medieval England, see Jeremy A. Ashbee, "'The Chamber called *Gloriette*': Living at Leisure in Thirteenth- and Fourteenth-Century Castles," *Journal of the British Archaeological Association* 157 (2004): 17–40.

40. On underground passages, see Merceron, "Par desoz terre."

41. Compare ll. 688–91.

42. This is repeated a few lines later: "I would rather die inside this tower than in sweet France among my relatives" (1428–29) (Mielz vueill morir en ceste tor ceanz / Qu'en douce France ne entor mes parenz). Contrast the previous

reluctance of the hapless Guïebert to accompany Guillaume to Orange in the first place; understandably, he would prefer to be in Chartres, Blois, or Paris, "in the king's land" (330–31) (en la terre le roi).

43. According to Lachet, the knowledge of herbs that allowed Guillaume to disguise himself in the first place is a trait typically associated with Saracen *women*—part of the poet's parodic transfer of qualities of the traditional Saracen princess onto the male protagonist (Lachet, *La Prise d'Orange*, 127–29). The trope of the resemblance between male and female lovers of different confessions recurs in *Aucassin et Nicolette* (see pp. 65–66 below) and in *Floire et Blancheflor* (see Chapter 3).

44. Compare the earlier line: "Guillaume sees her, and all his blood stirred" (668) (Voit la Guillelmes, tot li mua le sanc).

45. Compare "Equitan" in Kinoshita, "Royal Pursuits."

46. The passages devoted to Orable are remarkable for their brevity and restraint. In his initial description, Guibert rapidly mentions her well-formed figure, slender neck, light skin, and lively eyes (256–57, 278–80); when Guillaume finally sets eyes on her, he (or the narrator) takes note of her rich clothing, brilliant complexion, and fine form (660–67, 683–88). But neither here nor later, at the baptismal font when Orable is stripped naked for her "rebirth" as a Christian, does the narrator linger over particular physical attractions, as in Erec's famous blazon-like inspection of Enide.

47. On anticipatory grants and prospective conquests as "a futures market among the medieval aristocracy," see Bartlett, *The Making of Europe*, 90–92.

48. Though when Guillaume first tries to send Guïelin as messenger back to Nîmes, he affirms he would rather die in Gloriete than "in sweet France or at Aix-la-Chapelle" (1418–20).

49. In England, the succession of Henry I's daughter Mathilda (1135) set off a fifteen-year civil war. On the continent, Eleanor of Aquitaine's 1152 divorce from Louis VII of France and remarriage to the future Henry II of England radically transformed the politics of at least the next half century.

50. See Gravdal, *Ravishing Maidens.*

51. Leupin, "La compromission," 223. I take the notion of "misfire" from the speech act theory of J. L. Austin in *How to Do Things with Words.*

52. For more on *Aucassin*, see Chapter 7, pp. 233–34.

53. For Vance, the *Pèlerinage de Charlemagne* stages the encounter between Latin West and Byzantine East as the confrontation between two incommensurate epistemologies, represented by the relic and the icon. He links this poem to the failure of the Second Crusade and Louis VII's divorce from Eleanor of Aquitaine. Vance, "Semiotics and Power," 174n.

54. As we saw in Chapter 1, Constantinople is one of the conquests Roland attributes to his sword, Durendal (2329). For literary representations of the Greeks in Old French, see Kinoshita, "The Poetics of *Translatio*," and Chapter 5. In the twelfth century, the name Hugh would have evoked not the emperors of Constantinople but the Capetians, through their eponymous founder, Hugh Capet.

55. This line was at some point crossed out in the original manuscript (now lost); Paul Aebischer took this as license to omit it from his edition, arguing that

Oliver spent a chaste night with the princess and that it is Hugh whose behavior is "plus qu'étrange." *Le Voyage de Charlemagne*, ed. Aebischer, 90–91.

56. Compare Chrétien de Troyes's *Cligès*, whose half-Arthurian protagonist sexually humiliates the Greek emperor, his uncle Alis, by spiriting away the latter's wife, Fénice.

57. Described in the *Pèlerinage* as "Filz le cunte Aimeri [de Narbonne]" (765), Bernard, the father of Guillaume's nephews Bertrand and Guïelin, is formulaically described in *La Prise d'Orange* as "the hoary" (1092; see also 1329 and 1575) (li chenuz et li blanc).

58. From the late eleventh century, the comital family of Narbonne, which previously favored common regional names like Raymond or Berenguer, began adopting the name of the epic hero, Aymeri. The first historical Count Aymeri was the son of *Bernard* Berenguer. See Cheyette, *Ermengard of Narbonne*, 15, 23.

59. Comfort considers Hugh's daughter to be for all intents and purposes a Saracen princess, only then to note how this episode falls short of the model: Oliver wins her love, "but no point is made of it. The poet absolutely fails to develop the romantic episode. The accomplishment of Oliver's *gab* . . . , though not without a certain graceful gallantry, redounds entirely to his own prodigious valor as a wooer. The two later passages . . . in which the girl is mentioned are strikingly underdeveloped." Comfort, "Character Types," 42.

60. The critique of Orientalism is Lisa Lowe's in *Critical Terrains: French and British Orientalisms* (Ithaca, N.Y.: Cornell University Press, 1991), 5–7.

61. See, for example, Spivak, "Can the Subaltern Speak?"

62. On *translatio*, see Geary, *Furta Sacra*.

Chapter 3. *"In the Beginning Was the Road"*

1. "Au commencement était la route" (Joseph Bédier, *Les légendes épiques: Recherches sur la formation des chansons de geste*, 3rd ed. [Paris: Champion, 1926], 3:367).

2. *Le Conte de Floire et Blancheflor*, ed. Leclanche, is based on a late thirteenth-century manuscript (BN fr. 375) that also contains Benoît de Sainte-Maure's *Roman de Troie*. This is termed the "aristocratic" version to distinguish it from the later, "popular" variant, attested in a single manuscript, BN 19152 (edited by Pelan in *Floire et Blancheflor*). Leclanche dates the text to c. 1150, speculating that the titular protagonists refer to Louis VII of France and Eleanor of Aquitaine (divorced in 1152) ("La date du conte de *Floire et Blancheflor*"). Earlier commentators (for example, Lot-Borodine, *Le Roman idyllique*, 9n. 2) place it after 1160.

3. Chrétien de Troyes, *Cligès*, in *Oeuvres complètes*, 30–44. See also Kinoshita, "The Poetics of *Translatio*," 331–36.

4. On Bernard of Chartres, see Curtius, *European Literature and the Latin Middle Ages*, 119; on *translatio*, see pp. 29, 384–85.

5. Compare Bakhtin on the "adventure novel of ordeal" (*Dialogic Imagination*, 86–110). In the early twentieth century, Lot-Borodine grouped *Floire* with

Aucassin et Nicolette, Galeran de Bretagne, L'Escoufle, and *Guillaume de Palerme* in a genre she dubbed the "roman idyllique." See *Le Roman idyllique,* chap. 1.

6. Translations exist in languages ranging from Spanish, Italian, and Greek to Old Norse and Middle English. On the complexities of this tradition, see Grieve, *Floire et Blancheflor and the European Romance.* For a bibliography of different theories of origin, see Burns, *Courtly Love Undressed,* 287n. 10.

7. See, for example, Kibler, "Archetypal Imagery in *Floire et Blancheflor,*" *Romance Quarterly* 35:1 (1988): 11. As recently as 1998, one critic dismissed the possibility that *Floire* could be "seriously interested in pagan culture or the problems of inter-cultural romance." Phillip McCaffrey, "Sexual Identity in *Floire et Blancheflor* and *Ami et Amile,*" in *Gender Transgressions: Crossing the Normative Barrier in Old French Literature,* ed. Karen J. Taylor (New York: Garland, 1998), 135. On the variety of modern interpretations, see Burns, *Courtly Love Undressed,* 286n. 2.

8. The geniza was a tower in medieval synagogues used to store discarded documents until they could be properly buried. In the late nineteenth century, a large cache of material was recovered from the geniza in Old Cairo. Dating largely from the eleventh and twelfth centuries, these texts formed the basis of Goitein's reconstruction of a world in which Jewish merchants based in Fatimid Cairo maintained trading networks stretching from Almería to the Malabar coast of India. See Goitein, *A Mediterranean Society,* and idem, "The Unity of the Mediterranean World in the 'Middle' Middle Ages," in *Studies in Islamic History and Institutions,* 296–307.

9. In Toledo, the Mozarabic liturgy survived into the thirteenth century (Gonzálvez, "The Persistence of the Mozarabic Liturgy").

10. Fernando I's donations to Cluny, as we saw in Chapter 1, were financed by the *parias* extracted from the *ṭā'ifa* kingdoms. Alfonso's conquest of Toledo (1085) and the resulting Almoravid invasion (1086) meant a sudden loss of *parias* money, entailing a substantial reduction in his donations to Cluny. To compensate, Abbot Hugh developed Cluny's hold over churches on the French part of the Santiago trail, thereby profiting from the ever-increasing volume of pilgrimage traffic. Meanwhile, acquiescing to pressure from Bishop Diego Gelmírez, Pope Calixtus II (brother of the king's son-in-law, Raymond of Burgundy) raised Santiago to an archbishopric (1120), giving Rome a counterweight to the restored archbishopric of Toledo, which remained strongly attached to the old Mozarabic rite (Serafín Moralejo, "On the Road: the Camino de Santiago," in *Art of Medieval Spain,* 175–80). In Santiago itself, Gelmírez faced opposition from his cathedral canons, who objected to his reforms (forbidding them, for example, from dressing like knights and keeping wives or mistresses), and from the townspeople, who resented the cost of his massive construction projects. See Abou-el-Haj, "Santiago in the Time of Diego Gelmírez," 165, and Karen Rose Mathews, "Reading Romanesque Sculpture: The Iconography and Reception of the South Portal Sculpture at Santiago de Compostela," *Gesta* 39:1 (2000): 9.

11. This *Pilgrim's Guide* was the fifth and final volume of the *Liber Sancti Jacobi,* also known as the *Codex Calixtinus* from an apocryphal preface attributed to Pope Calixtus II. The first four volumes comprised liturgical pieces in honor

of Saint James, a book of miracles, a "translation" recounting Saint James's evangelization of Spain, and the *Pseudo-Turpin Chronicle*. See introduction to *The Pilgrim's Guide*, ed. Stones and Krochalis.

12. A variant manuscript, BNF fr. 1447, mitigates the scandal by substituting "son mari" for "son ami." This less scandalous option is adopted in the modern French translation by Williams and Guillet-Rydell and the English translation by Hubert.

13. In several versions of *Floire*, Felix (or Fenis) is king not of Naples but of Almería, providing another link to *La Fille du comte de Pontieu*. Both romances, moreover, were interpolated into later prose compilations: *Floire* (in a Spanish prose translation) into a fourteenth-century manuscript of Alfonso X's *Primera Crónica General*, *La Fille du comte de Pontieu* into *Histoire d'outre-mer et du roi Saladin*. See Grieve, *Floire et Blancheflor and the European Romance*, 20–36.

14. On the use of "Yspania" to refer to *Muslim* Iberia, see Constable, "Genoa and Spain in the Twelfth and Thirteenth Centuries," 645.

15. From Ibn ʿIdhârî al-Marrâkushî, *Kitâb al-Bayân al-Mughrib*, ed. G. S. Clin et E. Lévi-Provençal, *Histoire de l'Espagne de la conquête au XIᵉ siècle* (Beirut: Dar Assakifa, 1948), 295–97, cited in Bresc et al., *La Méditerranée entre pays d'Islam et monde latin*, 21 (my translation from the French). Al-Manṣūr was *hājib* (chamberlain) of Caliph Hisham II. On the title *hājib*, see below.

16. According to legend, Fernando III of Castile recovered the bells when he conquered Cordoba in 1236. Fletcher, *Moorish Spain*, 75; O'Callaghan, *History of Medieval Spain*, 126–30.

17. Derived from the pre-Islamic practice of camel raids, *ghazawat* were "governed by elaborate protocol;" "very little blood was ordinarily shed" (*Encyclopaedia of Islam*, 2:1055). The Italian term *razzia* derives from *ghazawat*.

18. See introduction to *De Expugnatione Lyxbonensi: The Conquest of Lisbon*, ed. Charles Wendell David, Records of Civilization 24 (New York: Columbia University Press, 1936), 18–21.

19. *Entre pays d'Islam et monde latin*, 105–6, from *Historia Compostellana*, ed. E. Falque Ray (Turnhout: Brepols, 1980), 174–76 (my translation from the French).

20. *Entre pays d'Islam et monde latin*, 21. On the distribution of textiles as special marks of favor, see Kinoshita, "Almería Silk and the French Feudal Imaginary," 169–70.

21. Captives taken in northern Spain were typically transported to Andalusian markets and sold for redistribution to other parts of the Muslim world (Constable, *Trade and Traders*, 207). In the early centuries of Islam, wars of conquest assured an abundant supply of slaves; by the eleventh and twelfth centuries, slaves "had to be imported from faraway countries and were expensive" (Goitein, *A Mediterranean Society*, 1:130–47, at 131).

22. Burns notes, however, that Floire is described through botanical metaphors—skin "white as lily" (2864), hands "white as nuts" (2865)—while Blancheflor is described in metallurgical terms: "eyes that sparkle like gems" (2878–79), "skin clearer than glass" (2885–86), and "teeth whiter than fine silver" (2895–96)—for Burns a sign of Eastern opulence (*Courtly Love Undressed*, 224).

23. Jocelyn Price, "*Floire et Blancheflor*: The Magic and Mechanics of Love," *Reading Medieval Studies* 8 (1982): 17, cited in Lynn Shutters, "Christian Love or Pagan Transgression? Marriage and Conversion in *Floire et Blancheflor*," in Classen, 85–10, at 96.

24. Shutters, "Christian Love or Pagan Transgression?" 86, 101.

25. Bulliet, *The Case for Islamo-Christian Civilization*, vii, 10, 15. Compare Amin's characterization of medieval Christianity and Islam as "twin siblings" as well as "relentless adversaries" (*Eurocentrism*, 26). On the continuities between late antiquity and early Islam, see Al-Azmeh, "Muslim History: Reflections on Periodisation and Categorisation."

26. Manuscript V (Vatican, Palatinus, lat. 1971). See "Choix de variantes," *Floire et Blancheflor*, ed. Leclanche, 113. On the medieval reception of Ovid, see Swanton, *The Twelfth-Century Renaissance*, 47–49. In the prologue to *Cligès* (2–3), Chrétien de Troyes claims to have put Ovid's *Art of Love* "an romans." The presumed date of *Floire et Blancheflor* places it a good century and a half before Dante's literate lovers, Paolo and Francesca.

27. Compare the ninth-century bishop of Cordoba, who complained that while few Christians could write passable Latin, many could compose poetry in Arabic "with greater art than the Arabs themselves" (Hillenbrand, "The Ornament of the World," 115).

28. See Burnett, "The Translating Activity in Medieval Spain," and Fierro, *Al-Andalus*.

29. Burnett, *The Introduction of Arabic Learning into England*, 31–32.

30. In historian Bernard Hamilton's words, the western imagination was "infiltrated by the world of Islam" ("Knowing the Enemy"). On Ibn Ḥazm (994–1064), see Guichard, *Al-Andalus 711–1492*, 135–40, and Giffen, "Ibn Ḥazm and the *Ṭawq al-Ḥamāma*." On the *Hadīth Bayāḍ wa Riyāḍ* (Rome, Biblioteca Apostolica, Vat. Ar. 368), see *Islam: Art and Architecture*, ed. Hattstein and Delius, 270 and *Al-Andalus*, ed. Dodds, 312–13. Compare *Khamsa* by the twelfth-century Persian poet Nizami, in which a ten-year-old boy and girl who meet at Qurʾānic school "embark on a chaste romance lasting the rest of their lives." A fifteenth-century manuscript illustration shows the hero and heroine sharing a Qurʾān. John Rylands Library, Manchester (Ryl Pers. 36, folio 107), figure 4, in Cook, *The Koran*, 57.

31. Caliph ʿAbd al-Raḥmān III (912–961) had a Christian grandmother (daughter of a Navarrese prince who had come to Cordoba as a hostage), mother (a Christian slave named Muzna), and daughter-in-law (a Navarrese Christian captive named Subh, favorite wife of al-Hakem II). Fletcher, *Moorish Spain*, 53, 73. For other examples of liaisons between Andalusian rulers and Christians, see Boase, "Arab Influences on European Love Poetry," 463.

32. Compare Floire's *planctus* over his supposedly dead sweetheart (717–92).

33. On the use of faux Arabic inscriptions in France, see Watson, *French Romanesque and Islam: Andalusian Elements in French Architectural Decoration c. 1030–1180*, British Archeological Reports, International Series 488 (Oxford: BAR, 1989), 1:63–108. "Completely nielloed" (661) (Toute . . . neelee), the tomb's Islamic flavor is further enhanced by its niello inlay (a technique in which a black

alloy of sulfur is poured into designs etched in silver or gold). See Atal et al., *Islamic Metalwork in the Freer Gallery of Art*, 87. For more on niello, see note 40, below.

34. Goitein, *Mediterranean Society* 1:139. For more on medieval slavery, see Chapter 6, p. 183. In the twelfth century, "gold marks" meant Byzantine *bezants*, *dinars* from Muslim Spain or Fatimid Egypt, or coins minted in the crusader states or Norman Sicily in imitation of Arabic designs. In 1184, Alfonso VIII of Castile began issuing *maravedís* (named for the Almoravids), which bore a Christian cross on one side while identifying the king, in Arabic, as Alfunsh ibn Sanjuh (Alfonso, son of Sancho), "the emir of the Catholics," on the other. Michael L. Bates, "The Islamic Coinage of Spain," in *Al-Andalus*, ed. Dodds, 384–85, 390. The Florentine *florin* and the Genoese *genovino* were not introduced until 1252, the *écu* of Saint Louis in 1263–65, and the Venetian *ducat* in 1284.

35. See Goitein, "Unity of the Mediterranean World," 296–98, and Sanders, "Robes of Honor," 229. Along with the slave trade, the textile industry was one of the main enterprises bringing Christian and Muslim traders together (Abulafia, "The Impact of the Orient," 40). In the *version commune*, Blancheflor is sold for "Mil onces d'or" and "une coupe bien ouvree," with no mention of textiles (*Floire et Blancheflor*, ed. Pelan, 1354, 1356). Benevento was a papal enclave in the Norman kingdom of Sicily, a crossroads for traffic leading from Rome to the ports of Otranto and Brindisi. See also Kinoshita, "Almería Silk and the French Feudal Imaginary."

36. Lesser grades came from Palestine, Yemen, and Egypt. An eleventh-century letter from the Cairo Geniza describes the gullibility of Christian merchants who "do not distinguish between first class and inferior" crops. Balfour-Paul, *Indigo in the Arab World*, 19–26.

37. Later in the tale, Paris's love for Helen is given as the explicit cultural model for Floire's love of Blancheflor: when Floire momentarily flags in pursuit of his beloved, one glance at the goblet is enough to reanimate his passion (1693–1702).

38. See pp. 77–78.

39. Hoffman, "Pathways of Portability," 21–22.

40. Andalusian examples include a silver casket today in the Museo Arqueológico Nacional in Madrid; a perfume bottle in the Museo de Teruel; and a tiny heart-shaped box in the Real Colegiata de San Isidoro in León. See Dodds, *Al-Andalus: The Art of Islamic Spain*, 214, 219, and *Art of Medieval Spain*, 98–99. On technique, see note 33, above. On niellowork's association with Muslim Iberia and Fatimid Egypt, see Marilyn Jenkins, "Al-Andalus: Crucible of the Mediterranean," in *Art of Medieval Spain*, 81, and Goitein, *Mediterranean Society*, 4:212–13. References to niello also appear in the *Pèlerinage de Charlemagne* and the *Charroi de Nîmes*—two epics that treat Latin Europe's contact with Byzantine Greece and the Muslim south, respectively. See entry for "neel, noel, noiel" in Greimas, *Dictionnaire de l'ancien français*, 434.

41. On trade between Egypt and Muslim Spain, see Constable, *Trade and Traders*, 37. Andalusian exports to the East included silks and high-quality dyes (ibid., 156, 158, 173–77).

42. Note the resemblance between this modest baggage train and the *parias* Marsile offers Charlemagne at the outset of the *Chanson de Roland*: "four hundred mules laden with gold and silver" (32) (D'or e d'argent .IIII.C. muls cargez) along with other precious goods.

43. On medieval "innumeracy," see Chapter 5, pp. 144–45.

44. Burns, *Courtly Love Undressed*, 216–18.

45. In the early modern period, to go "a camin francese" meant to sail straight ahead—in contrast to the traditional Mediterranean practice of tramping (sailing from one coastal port to the next, selling old goods and acquiring new ones along the way). Fernand Braudel, *The Mediterranean and the Mediterranean World in the Age of Philip II*, trans. Siân Reynolds (New York: Harper and Row, 1972), 103–4, 107. This is a curious echo of the phrase "camino francés"—the Spanish designation for the Santiago pilgrimage trail.

46. On customs duties in the medieval Muslim world, see Goitein, *Mediterranean Society*, 1:344–45. On the strict control of foreign merchants in Egyptian ports under Mamluk rule, see Abu-Lughod, *Before European Hegemony*, 240–41. Under the Fatimids (969–1171), the Islamic law imposing a double duty on non-Muslim merchants was not enforced, helping make the high medieval Mediterranean a sort of "free trade community."

47. As Shiites, the Fatimids rejected the authority of the ʿAbbasid caliphs of Baghdad. This put them politically and doctrinally at odds with the majority Sunni populations under their rule. For an overview of medieval Cairo, see André Raymond, *Cairo*, chaps. 1–2.

48. The separate halls comprising the Eastern Palace were sometimes collectively called *al-quṣūr al-zāhira* (the brilliant palaces), drawing on the same root used in the Umayyad palatine city of Madīnat al-Zahrāʾ outside Cordoba (see note 76, below). Gülru Necipoglu, "An Outline of Shifting Paradigms in the Palatial Architecture of the Pre-Modern Islamic World," *Ars Orientalis* 23 (1993): 3–24, at 3.

49. This description comes from the eleventh-century Persian traveler Nāṣer-e Khosraw in his *Book of Travels (Safarnāma)*, 45.

50. Dependents included "people of other ranks and stations, such as scholars, literati, poets, and jurisprudents, all of whom have fixed stipends." Nāṣer-e Khosraw, *Book of Travels*, trans. Thackston, 49–50.

51. This phrase is Janina Safran's, in *The Second Umayyad Caliphate*, 10–11. She borrows the notion of "competitive display" from Clifford Geertz, *Negara: The Theater State in Nineteenth-Century Bali* (Princeton, N.J.: Princeton University Press, 1980).

52. Meinecke-Berg, "Le trésor des califes," in *Trésors fatimides du Caire*, 96–98.

53. The treasury was staffed with armies of servants just to clean and look after these objects. Grabar, "Imperial and Urban Art in Islam," in *Colloque international sur l'histoire du Caire*, 183–84.

54. Many of these objects are described in an eleventh-century text called *The Book of Gifts and Rarities (Kitāb al-Hadāyā wa al-Tuḥaf)*, ed. and trans. Ghāda al Ḥijjāwī al-Qaddūmī, Harvard Middle Eastern Monographs 29 (Cambridge,

Mass.: Harvard Center for Middle Eastern Studies, 1996), 229–41 (sections 372–414). In 1068–69 the treasury was looted by disgruntled mercenaries, dispersing countless precious objects onto the markets of Cairo.

55. Goitein, *Mediterranean Society*, vol. 1. For examples of Fatimid material culture, see *Les trésors fatimides du Caire*. On Cairo's place in the "global" economy of a slightly later period, see Abu-Lughod, *Before European Hegemony*, chap. 7.

56. Trading ties had first been established in Ifriqiya (modern-day Tunisia), center of the Fatimids' power before their conquest of Egypt (Cahen, "Les Marchands étrangers au Caire," in *Colloque international sur l'histoire du Caire*, 97–100). On the India trade, see Goitein, "Letters and Documents on the India Trade in Medieval Times," in *Studies in Islamic History and Institutions*, 329–50.

57. Zumthor places "the emir's Moorish palace in *Floire et Blanchefleur*" alongside structures in the *Roman d'Enéas, Cligès, Le Roman de Troie*, and *Le Bel Inconnu*—"cities, palaces, monuments of all kinds"—which he calls central to the development of romance (*La Mesure du monde*, 92).

58. Three gates survive: the Bāb al-Futuh, the Bāb al-Nasr, and the Bāb Zuwaila. The wall was constructed by the eleventh-century vizier Badr al-Jamālī, an Armenian, who imported Armenian masons from Syria for his project. *Islam: Art and Architecture*, 151.

59. Nāṣer-e Khosraw, *Safarnāma*, 54. On the array of spices available in medieval Cairo, see Goitein, *Mediterranean Society*, 2:269–71.

60. Compare the pavilion and pleasure garden outside eleventh-century Cordoba described by Ibn Khāqān. Its courtyard "of pure white marble" was traversed by a stream "wriggling like a snake" and featured a fountain and a pavillion with walls and ceiling decorated in gold and blue. Dickie, "The Islamic Garden in Spain," 92.

61. On Egyptian rock crystal, see Contadini, *Fatimid Art at the V&A Museum*, 16–38.

62. Compare the Castle of Women in Chrétien de Troyes's *Perceval* (7520 ff.).

63. In twelfth-century Egypt, the regularity of Fatimid coinage "had accustomed everyone to *face values*." Thus, after Saladin overthrew the Fatimid caliph in 1171, he distinguished his "orthodox" Sunni regime from that of the "heretical" Ismailis by resorting to a new *irregular* dinar—"economically paradoxical but religiously necessary." Claude Cahen, "Monetary Circulation in Egypt at the Time of the Crusades and the Reform of Al-Kamil," in *The Islamic Middle East, 700–1900: Studies in Economic and Social History*, ed. A. L. Udovitch (Princeton, N.J.: Darwin Press, 1981), 326 (emphasis added).

64. Compare the great *baraka* (blessing) to be had from the cast-off robes (*khilʿa*) of the Fatimid caliphs, highly prized as burial shrouds. Sanders, "Robes of Honor," 225–27.

65. Hoffman, "Pathways of Portability," 25.

66. Compare the "custom" of the Joie de la Cort in Chrétien de Troyes's *Erec et Enide* (5378–6406), which combines an obsessively possessive love relationship with a series of decapitated *knights*.

67. On the changing marriage laws of the twelfth century, see Duby, *The Knight, the Lady and the Priest.*

68. A similar logic structures Marie de France's "Equitan." See Kinoshita, "Royal Pursuits." On literary representations of serial polygamy, see Kinoshita, "Two for the Price of One."

69. The brideshow was an odd tradition mentioned by the Byzantine writer Niketas in his *Life of Philaretos* (822–23). In the previous century, he reports, imperial officials were ordered to bring "the most beautiful young girls in the empire" to the Great Palace in Constantinople so that the empress-mother might select a bride for her son, Constantine VI. The winner was a girl named Maria from the "rural backwater" of Amnia (in Byzantine Armenia); runners-up were given gifts and sent home. Similar accounts exist for the marriages of Emperor Theophilos to Theodora (orphaned daughter of a minor official from rural Anatolia) in 830 and Emperor Michael III to Eudokia Dekapolitissa in 855. All were probably literary fabrications—a "Byzantine adaptation of the Judgement of Paris." For our purposes, two points stand out. First, in the Byzantine empire, a bride of obscure lineage was sometimes preferred to a bride from a powerful family that might meddle in the affairs of empire. Second, the brideshow was a way of managing the loyalty of local elites by keeping them "looking towards Constantinople as the most important centre of patronage and self-advancement, . . . where fortunes could be gained overnight." Judith Herrin, *Women in Purple: Rulers of Medieval Byzantium* (Princeton, N.J.: Princeton University Press, 2001), 137.

70. Compare the medieval Islamic post of the *ḥājib* (often translated as "chamberlain"), etymologically derived from the Arabic root meaning "to veil, cover, screen, shelter, seclude." Originally, the *ḥājib* was a kind of gatekeeper controlling access to the caliph or sultan. (The term is etymologically related to *hijāb*, the curtain used since pre-Islamic times "to conceal the sovereign from the gaze of courtiers or visitors.") In Muslim Spain, he became, by extension, a kind of prime minister supervising the entire civil administration. This was the title adopted both by al-Manṣūr (see above, p. 81) and by the eleventh-century *ṭāʾifa* kings who came to power after the fall of the Caliphate. In Fatimid Egypt, the chief chamberlain bore the title *ṣāhib al-bāb* ("lord of the gate"), likewise emphasizing his gatekeeping function. See O'Callaghan, *History of Medieval Spain*, 140; "Hadjib," *Encyclopaedia of Islam*, 3:45–49; and Wehr, *A Dictionary of Arabic*, 184–85.

71. In later "popular" versions of our romance, Floire gains entry into the tower by defeating its guardian in single combat. On chess as a form of battle, see Michael Holquist, "How to Play Utopia," *Yale French Studies* 41 (1968): 108. Chess is also associated with a gatekeeping function in Chrétien de Troyes's *Perceval* (5893–98, 6000–6003), where Gauvain fends off an attack of unruly townsfolk by hurling chess pieces down from a high tower. See Kinoshita, "Les Echecs de Gauvain ou l'utopie manqué," *Littérature* 71 (1988): 108–19.

72. For example, the so-called Charlemagne set, long considered a gift to Charlemagne from the ʿAbbasid caliph Hārūn al-Rashīd. Recent scholarship places its manufacture in southern Italy (possibly Salerno) in the late eleventh-century.

Michel Pastoureau, *L'Echiquier de Charlemagne: Un jeu pour ne pas jouer* (Paris: A. Biro, 1990), 30–36.

73. For the Palermo painting (c. 1143), see Giovanni Curatola, ed., *Eredità dell'Islam: Arte islamica in Italia* (Milan: Silvana Editoriale, 1993), 189; for the William of Tyre illumination, *L'Orient de Saladin*, 96.

74. Manuscript A lacks the lengthy interchange during which Floire wins at chess but gives his winnings to the porter nevertheless. Leclanche supplies this scene from manuscript B (BNF fr. 1447).

75. On the verb *amer* and its derivatives as a quasi-legal term with feudal resonances, see Jones, *The Ethos of the Song of Roland*, 36–38.

76. Nor is Floire's the only name laden with polysemic possibilities. Though destined to become the conventionalized name for some otherwise rather featureless romance heroines (like Perceval's beloved in Chrétien de Troyes), Blancheflor resonates suggestively with the Arabic name Zahrā'. Derived from the triliteral root z-h-r (to shine, be radiant, blossom, flourish), it is related to *zahra* (pl: *zahr*), the generic word for flower but more specifically used for orange blossoms, which are white (as in Blancheflor). In the mid-tenth century, Caliph ʿAbd al-Raḥmān III named the great palatine complex he constructed just outside Cordoba "Madīnat al-Zahrā'," reputedly in honor of his favorite wife. In medieval poetry, Zahrā' signified a woman with a "white, fair, bright, shining face"—like Blancheflor, whose skin was "whiter than any flower." Etymologically related words occur in the names of two central monuments in medieval Cairo, the al-Azhar ("shining, luminous") mosque, and the great palace complex, *al-quṣūr al-zāhira*, mentioned above. See Wehr, *A Dictionary of Arabic*, 446; Henri Pérès, *La Poésie andalouse en arabe classique au XIᵉ siècle* (Paris: Adrien-Maisonneuve, 1937), 183–84; and Hamid Triki, "Al-Andalus, ce jardin des poètes," in *Les Andalousies*, 212–15. On the legend of Madīnat al-Zahrā', see Ruggles, "Mothers of a Hybrid Dynasty," 83–84.

77. William of Tyre, cited in Heng, *Empire of Magic*, 38–39, 323–24nn. 42–44. On the beardlessness of the Franks, see Usamah ibn Munqidh, *An Arab-Syrian Gentleman*, 165–66.

78. The phrase "touch of the queer" is Carolyn Dinshaw's, in "Chaucer's Queer Touches / a Queer Touches Chaucer," *Exemplaria* 7:1 (1995): 75–92.

79. Bloch, *Medieval French Literature and Law*, 54–58. The lovers' position "bouce a bouce et face a face" is more highly compromising than that of Tristan and Iseut, whom Marc discovers with "their mouths not even touching" (la bouche o l'autre n'ert jostee). Béroul, *Le Roman de Tristan: Poème du XIIᵉ siècle*, 4th ed., ed. Ernest Muret and L. M. Defourques (Paris: Champion, 1979), line 1997.

80. Compare Robert de Clari's *Conquête de Constantinople*, in which historical crusaders encounter the *Christian* king of Nubia. See Chapter 5, pp. 159–60.

81. In the twelfth century, Usāmah ibn Munqidh, lord of Shayzar (Caesaria) in northern Syria, took it as a curiosity that among the crusaders, "not even the king nor any of the chieftains of the Franks can alter or revoke" counsel or judgment. He sees this as evidence of the great esteem in which knights were held in Frankish society. *An Arab-Syrian Gentleman*, 93–94.

82. Greimas translates "franchise" as "liberté," "condition libre," and "noblesse de caractère, générosité." The related word "francheté" is "action noble, généreuse" (*Dictionnaire de l'ancien français*, 298).

83. Compare the legend that Richard the Lionheart offered his sister Joan in marriage to Saladin's brother al-ʿĀdil (see p. 197.).

84. "Riche roiame vos donroie / et d'or fin vos coroneroie. / . . . / car remanés en cest païs! / Vos serés mes confanoniers [standard-bearer] / et mes plus privés consilliers" (3243–45, 3246–48).

85. This conversion of an entire people is typical of the pagans on Latin Christendom's northern and eastern frontiers, while in conquered Muslim lands, conversion was gradual, sometimes taking centuries.

86. See Chapter 1, pp. 19–20.

87. Examples include William Tronzo, "The Mantle of Roger II of Sicily," in Gordon, 241–53; and Karen Rose Mathews, "Reading Romanesque Sculpture: The Iconography and Reception of the South Portal Sculpture at Santiago de Compostela," *Gesta* 39 (2000): 3–12.

88. In the prologue to *Floire*, the narrator details Floire's inheritance of Hungary from a maternal uncle as well: "then he became king of Hungary and all Bulgaria (trestoute Bougerie). An uncle of his who was king of Hungary died without heirs (sans oirs). Floire was his sister's son; that's why he became lord of the honor (sires de l'onour)" (25–30). On medieval Hungary as a contact zone, see Berend, *At the Gate of Christendom*.

89. This is María Rosa Menocal's characterization of the Middle Ages constructed by nineteenth-century philologists ("Signs of the Times," 499).

90. This is Lisa Jardine and Jerry Brotton's appraisal of the long sixteenth century in *Global Interests: Renaissance Art between East and West* (London: Reaktion Books, 2000), 7–8. Similar assessments occur in Deborah Howard, *Venice and the East: The Impact of the Islamic World on Venetian Architecture, 1100–1500* (New Haven, Conn.: Yale University Press, 2000); Rosamond E. Mack, *Bazaar to Piazza: Islamic Trade and Italian Art, 1300–1600* (Berkeley: University of California Press, 2002); and Jill Caskey, *Art and Patronage in the Medieval Mediterranean:Merchant Culture in the Region of Amalfi* (Cambridge: Cambridge University Press, 2004).

Chapter 4. Colonial Possessions

1. Mary Louise Pratt, *Imperial Eyes: Travel Writing and Transculturation* (London: Routledge, 1992), 6–7.

2. Duby, *The Knight, the Lady and the Priest*, 222.

3. Among Marie's *lais*, "Guigemar" and "Equitan" feature married women who commit adultery but remain childless. In "Bisclavret," the lady remains childless within the tale itself, but we are told that her descendants all bear the snub-nose of their ancestress's punishment for her disloyalty. In "Fresne," the protagonist's first marriage goes unconsummated; the day after the wedding, he divorces his wife and marries her twin sister. See Kinoshita, "Two for the Price of One."

4. Marie de France, *Les Lais*, ed. Rychner, l. 9. Moreau, in "La Citez," argues for the *lais'* deep connection to a Celtic world spanning Brittany, Cornwall, and Wales. Rupert Pickens also links these two *lais* but with a focus on the alternation between the voices of male and female internal narrators. See Pickens, "The Poetics of Androgyny in the Lais of Marie de France: 'Yonec,' 'Milun,' and the General Prologue," in *Literary Aspects of Courtly Culture: Selected Papers from the Seventh Triennial Congress of the International Courtly Literature Society, University of Massachusetts, Amherst, 27 July–1 August 1992*, ed. Donald Maddox and Sarah Sturm-Maddox (Cambridge: D. S. Brewer, 1994), 211–19.

5. Ernest Hoepffner, for example, minimizes the significance of Celtic proper names in "Yonec" and "Milun." In *Les Lais de Marie de France*, ed. Hoepffner (Paris: Nizet, 1971), 79, 109–10, cited in Moreau, "La Citez," 497, 503.

6. R. R. Davies, *Age of Conquest*, 127.

7. On his mother's side, Gerald was descended from both Gerald of Windsor, the Norman castellan of Pembroke, and Rhys ap Tewdwr, the powerful eleventh-century king of Deheubarth (South Wales). Examples of this criticism include Cohen, "Hybrids, Monsters, Borderlands"; Rollo, *Historical Fabrication*, chap. 11; and M. Warren, *History on the Edge*.

8. In the prologue to "Laüstic," for example, Marie names the *lai* in three languages: "Its name is 'Laüstic,' I think; That's what they call it in their country; That's 'russignol' in French and 'nightingale' in pure English" (3–6) (Laüstic ad nun, ceo m'est vis, / Si l'apelent en lur païs; / Ceo est "russignol" en franceis / E "nihtegale" en dreit engleis).

9. Peter Haidu situates Marie "geographically at the Anglo-Norman colonial margin of French culture and semiotically at the borderlines of a male-dominated textual culture," seeing her *lais* as a "minor literature" in (for example) their play on "double sign construction" (in numerous *lais*, including "Yonec" and "Milun") and "constitutive alterities" (as in "Guigemar" and "Bisclavret"). See *The Subject Medieval/Modern*, chap. 6.

10. R. R. Davies, *Age of Conquest*, 92.

11. These were Hugh of Avranches, Robert of Montgomery, and William Fitz Osbern, respectively. They were accorded rights—generally retained by the king—to found boroughs, wage war, administer justice, keep chanceries, and exploit the forest. See R. R. Davies, *Age of Conquest*, 28, and Nelson, *Normans in South Wales*, 24.

12. "The history of the area for the next 150 years was to be one of transient political hegemonies established across this line by one side or the other. It was also to be the story of the complete failure of Anglo-Norman society to establish itself in the highland moors" (Nelson, *Normans in South Wales*, 117). On the division between mountains (*mynydd*) and lowlands (*morfa*) in the Welsh imaginary, see R. R. Davies, *Age of Conquest*, 11–12.

13. Bartlett, *The Making of Europe*.

14. In contrast, the Norman church was strongly marked by eleventh-century reforms, including the spread of the universal monastic orders and the strict delineation between clerical and secular spheres. R. R. Davies, *Age of Conquest*, 176.

15. Nelson, *Normans in South Wales*, 159. In 1081 Rhys ap Tewdwr paid homage to William the Conqueror at Saint David's, in exchange receiving Deheubarth as a feudal "fief." From this moment, the Welsh chronicle *Brut y Tywysogion* styles William "king of the Britons" (brenhin y Brytanyeit) (Nelson, *Normans in South Wales*, 35, 39). The ensuing stability allowed Rhys to reconstitute Deheubarth as a political power. R. R. Davies, *Age of Conquest*, 33–34.

16. R. R. Davies, "Henry I and Wales," 138.

17. Royal "latimers" included Bledhericus Latemeri, prince of Dyfed, who served Henry I, and Iorwerth ap Maredudd ap Bleddyn ap Cynfan, prince of Powys, who served Henry II. Bullock-Davies, *Professional Interpreters and the Matter of Britain*, 18.

18. See above, note 7. For examples of Norman-Welsh marriages, see R. R. Davies, *Age of Conquest*, 102.

19. R. R. Davies, *Age of Conquest*, 59.

20. Nelson, *Normans in South Wales*, 9–14.

21. On Henry's use of his grandfather's reign as a point of reference, see W. L. Warren, *Henry II*, 62–63.

22. R. R. Davies, *Age of Conquest*, 41–51. Earlier in the century, Deheubarth was eroded by Norman advances. The success of Lord Rhys (ruled 1155–97) resulted in part from the diversion of Anglo-Norman attention to Ireland in 1170. Allied by marriage with both Anglo-Normans and the native Welsh, Rhys presided over a cultural renaissance, exemplified by the great assembly (*eisteddfod*) of poets and musicians held at Cardigan in 1176 to demonstrate the cultural preeminence of his court. After Henry's death (1189), Rhys and his sons launched raids on Anglo-Norman South Wales, culminating in their victory at Radnor (1196), on the border of England itself (ibid., 217, 221–23).

23. Walker, *Medieval Wales*, 50. Justiciar was an honorary title signifying Rhys's jurisdiction over all the princelings of the south—often bound to him by ties of kinship and matrimony. R. R. Davies, *Age of Conquest*, 51–55, 213, 217, 222.

24. Nelson, *Normans in South Wales*, 6.

25. This is José David Saldívar's description of *la frontera* between the United States and Mexico, inspired in part by Raymond Williams's work on the Welsh-English border (*Border Matters: Remapping American Cultural Studies* [Berkeley: University of California Press, 1997], 13–14, 202n. 3). Compare Cohen's call for "an alliance . . . between medieval studies and . . . borderlands theory," focusing on the "overlap among a multitude of genders, sexualities, spiritualities, ethnicities, races, cultures, languages" ("Hybrids, Monsters, Borderlands," 86).

26. Nelson, *Normans in South Wales*, 152.

27. Tales traveled in the other direction as well. The early thirteenth-century Welsh translation of the *Chanson de Roland* survives in ten manuscripts. It appears as chapter 22 of the Welsh translation of the *Pseudo-Turpin Chronicle* (possibly from Llanbadarn Fawr in Ceredigion) made for Reginald, king of Man and the Western Isles (1188–1226) (Annalee C. Rejhon, *Can Rolant: The Medieval Welsh Version of the Song of Roland*, University of California Publications in Modern Philology 113 [Berkeley: University of California Press, 1984], 68–69, 88–89).

28. Chrétien's patron, Count Philip of Flanders, was Henry II's first cousin, their interests linked by the Flemish cloth industry's dependence on English wool. Flemish immigrants settled in southwest Wales from the time of Henry I (R. R. Davies, *Age of Conquest*, 98–99, 159–60). On anti-Welsh sentiment, see J. Davies, *History of Wales*, 131.

29. The new men who came to power under Henry I (1100–35) included Robert of Gloucester (the king's illegitimate son), Miles of Gloucester, Brian Fitz Count, and (in Caerleon and Usk) Gilbert of Clare; by 1200, these families had all failed in the direct male line, bringing to power yet another group, including William Marshal (R. R. Davies, *Age of Conquest*, 84).

30. See Kinoshita, "Royal Pursuits."

31. Duby, *The Knight, the Lady and the Priest*, chaps. 9–10.

32. On the role traditional Welsh kinship groups played in marriage (*o rodd cenedl*, kin investiture), see R. R. Davies, *Age of Conquest*, 125.

33. R. R. Davies, *Age of Conquest*, 214.

34. Its name derives from the early tenth-century king of Deheubarth, to whom it was attributed (Pryce, *Native Law and the Church*, 89, 93). On the Welsh tradition of legal writings, see R. R. Davies, *Age of Conquest*, 133–34, 221.

35. Gerald of Wales, *Journey through Wales*, 263 (emphasis added).

36. R. R. Davies, *Age of Conquest*, 127–28.

37. William and Maurice FitzGerald played important roles in the Cambro-Norman conquest of Ireland; David (d. 1176) became bishop of Saint David's, in Pembroke.

38. Henry FitzHenry was killed during Henry II's 1157 expedition against Owain of Gwynedd. Robert succeeded his father as constable of Cardigan. Taken captive by his cousin Rhys ap Gruffydd, he was released three years later on promising to support Rhys's campaigns against Henry II. Caught between his oath to his Welsh kinsman and his allegiance to the Anglo-Normans, Robert solved this "problem of divided loyalties" by enlisting in the Irish expedition of 1169. Nelson, *Normans in South Wales*, 135; Lloyd, *History of Wales*, 499, 502; Gerald of Wales, *Journey through Wales*, 189.

39. Lloyd, *History of Wales*, 418.

40. Gerald of Wales attributes the political defeat of Dafydd of Gwynedd and his brother, Rhodri, to the fact that both were "born in incest" to Owain Gwynedd and his first cousin, Cristin. Owain died excommunicate for refusing to relinquish this "incestuous" wife. *Journey through Wales* II.8 (192–94).

41. Davies, *Age of Conquest*, 173–74, 177; Nelson, *Normans in South Wales*, 161. Clerical marriage and clerical dynasties were common across western Europe before the Gregorian reforms of the late eleventh century; however, their persistence in Wales became a mark of Welsh otherness.

42. R. R. Davies, *Age of Conquest*, 177.

43. Ibid., 181–82. The highlands, in contrast, were dominated by the Cistercians, whose introduction of sheep raising created a viable economy that helped incorporate them into the European mainstream. Cistercian monasticism "became the first institution fully shared between the Cambro-Normans and the native Welsh" (Nelson, *Normans in South Wales*, 160–64).

44. See Kinoshita, "Two for the Price of One," 50.

45. Pryce, *Native Law and the Church*, 93. On the manuscript tradition of the Welsh lawbooks, see *The Law of Hywel Dda: Law Texts from Medieval Wales*, ed. and trans. Jenkins (Llandysul: Gomer, 1986), xxi–xxiii.

46. Yonec is a Cornish or Breton diminutive of the popular Welsh name Iwon or Iwein. See Moreau, "La Citez," 497–98. On the importance of names in the "europeanization of Europe," see Bartlett, *The Making of Europe*, 270–72

47. Pryce, *Native Law and the Church*, 97. This custom, called *cynnwys*, survived in parts of Wales until the end of the Middle Ages (R. R. Davies, *Age of Conquest*, 128). The Welsh tolerance of illegitimate children undoubtedly played a part in the Angevins' dynastic alliances with two princes of Gwynedd: Dafydd, who married Henry II's illegitimate sister, Emma (a reward for supporting Henry in the civil wars of 1173–74), and Llewelyn ab Iorwerth, who married John's illegitimate daughter, Joan, in the early thirteenth century. W. L. Warren, *Henry II*, 167, and Walker, *Medieval Wales*, 53.

48. On Grufydd ap Llewelyn (d. 1063), who briefly united all of Wales just before the Norman Conquest, see R. R. Davies, *Age of Conquest*, 24–27; on Bernard of Neufmarché, see p. 86.

49. Gerald bears a grudge against Earl Milo's son Mahel for his treatment of Gerald's maternal uncle David, bishop of Saint David's. See Gerald of Wales, *Journey through Wales* II, 2, 89, 90–91, 94n. 99, 94–95, 100, 109.

50. Years later, he still claimed to remember the language of the little people (Gerald of Wales, *Journey through Wales*, I.8). Other curiosities paralleling elements in Marie's *lais* include the antlered doe (as in "Guigemar"), shot and sent to Henry II (I.1); the pharmaceutically inclined weasel (I.12), as in "Eliduc"; the preoccupation with the metropolitan status of Dol (II.1), as in "Fresne"; and the chance accident that becomes an inherited trait (II.7), as in "Bisclavret."

51. On anamorphosis, see Stephen Greenblatt, *Renaissance Self-Fashioning from More to Shakespeare* (Chicago: University of Chicago Press, 1980), 18–23.

52. Nelson, *Normans in South Wales*, 76.

53. These were Walter of Clare (d. 1138), granted the lordship in 1119; Walter's nephew Gilbert Fitz Gilbert (d. 1148); and Gilbert's son Richard Strongbow. R. R. Davies, *Age of Conquest*, 41 and 278 (diagram 6).

54. R. R. Davies, *Age of Conquest*, 467.

55. Ibid., 100.

56. Iorwerth raided the town in retaliation, but the castle withstood the siege and was specially provisioned against further attacks. Lloyd, *History of Wales*, 540–41.

57. R. R. Davies, *Age of Conquest*, 93. The previous year, Hywel's brother Owain had been killed by the earl of Gloucester's men, in an example of the Norman-on-Welsh violence that threatened Henry II's peace with the native princes (Davies, *Age of Conquest*, 291). For the relationship between Morgan ab Owain and Hywel ab Iorwerth, see Walker, *Medieval Wales*, 31, figure 2A.

58. R. R. Davies, *Age of Conquest*, 217, 271, 275, 277.

59. Geoffrey of Monmouth, *History of the Kings of Britain*, trans. Lewis Thorpe (Harmondsworth: Penguin, 1966), 226–27; *La Geste du roi Arthur*,

ed. and trans. Emmanuèle Baumgartner and Ian Short, Bibliothèque Médiévale (Paris: 10/18, 1993), 100–120; and Chrétien de Troyes, *Perceval, Oeuvres complètes*, 4003, 4606.

60. R. R. Davies, *Age of Conquest*, 181. On the role of castles in the Norman conquest of Wales, see ibid., 89–92.

61. Contrast Caerwent, where the cult of Saint Stephen had replaced that of Saint Tathan (R. R. Davies, *Age of Conquest*, 179–82). Saint Aaron's feast day is July 3. In Gerald of Wales's time the church of Saint Aaron's had a "distinguished chapter of canons" (*Journey through Wales* I.5, 115). The church of Caerleon is still dedicated to him (Moreau, "La Citez," 495).

62. The community of Strata Florida was endowed in 1164 as part of the "triumph of Cistercian monasticism in Wales" between 1131 and 1201. It soon attracted the patronage of the Lord Rhys, king of Deheubarth, and became the center of the tradition of Welsh historical writing that produced the *Brut y Tywysogyon* (R. R. Davies, *Age of Conquest*, 197, 273, and Walker, *Medieval Wales*, 81–82). Contrast the nearby abbey of Margam—also Cistercian but associated with Anglo-Norman interests. Cowley, *Monastic Order in South Wales*, 26–27.

63. R. R. Davies, *Age of Conquest*, 201.

64. Ibid., 123–24.

65. Ibid., 175.

66. This supersedes my previous view of "Yonec" (in Kinoshita, "Cherchez la femme") as a normative tale in which even adultery is conscripted to serve the feudal politics of lineage.

67. Compare the Count Milon (2433) (le cunte Milun) mentioned in the *Chanson de Roland* or Milon de Nanteuil, the dedicatee of Jean Renart's *Roman de la Rose ou de Guillaume de Dole*. In Marie's "Chievrefoil," Tristan is also described as having been born in "Suhtwales" (16).

68. Compare the "internationalism" in "Guigemar," whose titular hero proves himself in wars in Flanders, Lorraine, Burgundy, Anjou, and Gascony (51, 53–54), and "Chaitivel," in which a tournament held at Nantes draws knights from France, Normandy, Flanders, Brabant, Boulogne, Anjou, and Hainault (77–79, 92).

69. On youth, see Duby, "Les 'jeunes' dans la société aristocratique."

70. R. R. Davies, *Age of Conquest*, 85–86, 95. Compare Gerald of Wales's grandfather, the younger son of the constable of Windsor, who demonstrated his prowess in defense of Pembroke castle (1096) before marrying the daughter of Rhys ap Tewdwr. Gerald of Wales, *Journey through Wales* I.12, 148–49.

71. R. R. Davies, *Age of Conquest*, 271. For the dating of Marie's *lais*, see Glyn Burgess, introduction to *Lais*, ed. Alfred Ewert (Oxford: Blackwell, 1965), ix.

72. Throughout this discussion of "Milun," I use "girl" rather than "lady" to translate Marie's designation "dameisele" (ll. 24 et passim), indicating that she, unlike the heroine of "Yonec," is unmarried.

73. Contrast the alternate reality of a romance like Chrétien de Troyes's *Erec et Enide*, where a king's son weds the daughter of an impoverished *vavassor*.

74. Since Milun makes his living with his sword, he can ill afford to leave it behind. Compare "Fresne," in which the foundling girl is abandoned with a ring and blanket of Byzantine silk. The fact that the lady's sister is married in

Northumbria confirms the family's Anglo-Norman connections. In 1136, the ancient kingdom of Northumbria was revived as an earldom for the son of King David of Scotland; in 1149, during the English civil war, David seized it for Scotland. After David's death, his great-nephew Henry II reclaimed it for England—part of his campaign to recover the prerogatives held by his grandfather, Henry I. See W. L. Warren, *Henry II*, 180–82.

75. R. R. Davies, *Age of Conquest*, 128. Reparations included the payment of a "virginity fine" (*amobr*) for a daughter's sexual lapses—its amount determined by the status of the family in question (116).

76. The messenger claims to have captured the swan "outside Caerleon" (183), providing an intertextual link to "Yonec."

77. Tristan and Iseut resort to writing only once, in seeking to return to court: a hermit takes down Tristan's dictated message; Marc, in turn, summons a clerk to read the letter once he receives it. There is no indication the protagonists themselves are literate (*Tristan et Iseut*, ed. Lacroix and Walter, ll. 2355–2434, 2510–2620). Contrast Marie's "Chievrefoil," in which Tristan (from Suhtwales, like Milun) makes an inscription on a branch of hazelwood and Iseut successfully decodes it. See also Chrétien de Troyes, *Lancelot ou le chevalier de la Charrete*, *Oeuvres complètes*, 5338–51.

78. The diffusion of court chanceries is associated with the "europeanization of Europe." Using "European-style Latin charters" as an index of degree of "europeanization," twelfth-century Wales (with 60 extant) falls between Ireland (with 10) and Scotland (with 160). See Pryce, *Literacy in Medieval Celtic Societies*, 3. On clerks and literacy in native Wales, see R. R. Davies, *Age of Conquest*, 263.

79. *The Lais of Marie de France*, trans. Hanning and Ferrante, 180.

80. Illegitimate children were typically legitimized by their parents' subsequent marriage, except in England, where Henry II rejected church policy. See Pryce, *Native Law and the Church*, 98, 101.

81. "Cil ki ceste aventure oïrent / Lunc tens aprés un lai en firent / De la pitié de la dolur / Que cil suffrirent pur amur" (555–58).

82. "Chievrefoil," as noted earlier, is also set in South Wales. Its epilogue names the *lai* in French and in Anglo-Saxon—"The English call it Goatleaf" (115) (Gotelef l'apelent Engleis)—but not in Welsh.

Part III. Crisis and Change in the Thirteenth Century

1. Dunbabin, *France in the Making*, 371–72.

2. See Susan Crane, *Insular Romance: Politics, Faith and Culture in Anglo-Norman and Middle English Literature* (Berkeley: University of California Press, 1986), and "The French of England," Anglo-Norman Studies at Fordham http://www.fordham.edu/frenchofengland/.

3. Kittay and Godzich, *The Emergence of Prose*, xiii. Baldwin VIII of Flanders was, as count of Hainault, Baldwin (Baudouin) V.

4. Spiegel, *Romancing the Past*, 14.

Chapter 5. Brave New Worlds

1. Villehardouin, *maréchal* of Champagne, was one of six envoys entrusted with negotiating passage with the Venetians. Clari's *Conquête* survives in one manuscript, MS 487 of the Royal Library of Copenhagen (late thirteenth or early fourteenth century), Villehardouin's in six.

2. Andrea, "Essay on Primary Sources," 303. Suzanne Fleischman contrasts Villehardouin's critical distance, typical of medieval chroniclers, with Robert's "vivid *personal* reactions to events in which he took part, and the almost childlike wonder with which he depicts the splendors of the Orient" ("On the Representation of History and Fiction in the Middle Ages," 297). In *Early Prose in France*, Beer devotes a chapter to Villehardouin but none to Clari.

3. Micha also contrasts Clari's digressive style to Villehardouin's linear one (introduction to *La Conquête de Constantinople*, 20, 21, 22). Compare Dufournet, *Les Ecrivains de la IVe croisade*, 343, and Hartman, *La Quête et la croisade*, 2.

4. Spiegel, *Romancing the Past*, 7–8. The sole manuscript containing Robert's chronicle also contains a copy of the *Pseudo-Turpin* translation commissioned by Michel de Harnes. Robert of Clari, *Conquest*, trans. McNeal, 8.

5. Note Jonathan Riley-Smith's call for a collaboration between crusade historians and "scholars of vernacular literature, who for far too long have been virtually ignored by historians," in order better to understand "the roots of crusading and the motivation of crusaders" before 1200 ("History, the Crusades and the Latin East," 16–17).

6. Given the church's repeated condemnations of tournaments, Villehardouin's anecdote illustrates how strongly the venture was compromised from the beginning by the ambivalence surrounding Georges Duby's category of "youth." See Bernard of Clairvaux's letter to Suger in Evergates, *Feudal Society in Medieval France*, 106–7, and Duby, "Youth in Aristocratic Society" in *Chivalrous Society*, 112–22.

7. Robert de Clari, *La Conquête de Constantinople*, ed. Lauer, my translation. I have consulted the translation of Edgar Holmes McNeal.

8. It was Hugh's wife, Yolande (sister of Count Baldwin of Flanders), who commissioned Nicolas of Senlis's 1202 translation of the *Pseudo-Turpin*, the first known example of vernacular prose (Spiegel, *Romancing the Past*, 12). For Simon de Montfort's role in the Albigensian Crusade, see Chapter 7.

9. "Clari" has been identified as Cléry-les-Pernois in Domart-en-Ponthieu (place-names important in *La Fille du comte de Pontieu*, as we will see in Chapter 6). Robert de Clari, *La Conquête de Constantinople*, ed. Lauer, v.

10. That is, knights rich enough to lead a company of their men outfitted in their colors. See Crouch, *William Marshal*, 43.

11. Toward the end of this list, Robert mentions Pierre of Amiens a second time, together with his brother Thomas, a cleric and a canon of Amiens.

12. On modern historiography's take on the question of Venetian responsibility, see Brand, "The Fourth Crusade." I borrow the concept of innumeracy

from John Allen Paulos, *Innumeracy: Mathematical Illiteracy and Its Consequences* (New York: Random House, 1988).

13. Godfrey, *1204: The Unholy Crusade*, 40.

14. Dunbabin, *France in the Making*, 310–23.

15. Between 1081 and 1282, the military superiority of the French knight coincided with Italian naval and mercantile dominion over the Mediterranean. In addition to their widespread use of notaries and financial devices like letters of credit and bills of exchange, by the twelfth century Italians had begun "inventing ways of mobilizing private capital for public uses." In Venice "investment in state loans became compulsory; and between 1187 and 1208, magistrates developed methods for determining each family's share and assessing the exact sums due as subscription to each new loan" (McNeill, *Venice*, 2–4, 18).

16. It is in the number of foot soldiers that Robert's figures diverge mostly wildly from those of Villehardouin, who reports contracting for the transport of 4,500 knights, 4,500 horses, 9,000 squires, and 20,000 foot sergeants, at a total cost of 85,000 marks. Even the directive to *arrive* in Venice "between Pentecost and August" (9.3) presumed a more complicated relationship to time and distance than previous injunctions to *set out* by a given date.

17. In reality it was Philip's father, Louis VII, who negotiated the match.

18. French king Philip Augustus's ill-fated marriage to Ingeborg of Denmark, for example, was calculated not simply to secure Danish naval support for a potential invasion of England but to provide ideological justification by resurrecting the Danish king's longstanding claim to the English throne. Sivéry, *Philippe Auguste*, 197.

19. The Old French epic *Raoul de Cambrai* treats the conflict between these two systems, one emergent and one residual: when the titular hero's father dies, King Louis gives his fief to another. Raoul is compensated with the honor of Vermandois—an investiture contested, in turn, by the sons of the late incumbent.

20. On the importance of genealogical thinking in the medieval imaginary, see Duby, "The Structure of Kinship and Nobility"; Bloch, *Etymologies and Genealogies*; and Spiegel, "Genealogy: Form and Function."

21. See Kinoshita, "Poetics of *Translatio*," 325.

22. For French-speaking crusaders, this situation might have recalled the literary precedent of Chrétien de Troyes's *Cligès* (c. 1180). Alexander, the rightful heir to the Greek empire, is displaced by his younger brother Alis. At the end of the romance, Alexander's son, Cligès, with the backing of his maternal great-uncle, King Arthur, is about to launch an attack on Constantinople when Alis conveniently dies, leaving him the throne.

23. Conrad's family had long been involved in the eastern Mediterranean. In addition to the connections mentioned by Robert, Conrad's youngest brother, Ranier, had married Manuel I Comnenos's daughter, Maria Porphyrogenita. Under Alexios II, they opposed the faction of the dowager empress Maria of Antioch; both were eventually executed by Andronicos I.

24. Guy, who had been consecrated king, refused to relinquish his crown until 1192, when Richard the Lionheart agreed to compensate him with the newly conquered island of Cyprus. In 1194 Guy died and was succeeded by his brother

Amalric, who acquired the title of "king" from Emperor Henry VI and subsequently became the fourth husband of the much-married Isabelle of Jerusalem. Edbury, *The Kingdom of Cyprus and the Crusades*, 29, 31.

25. Philip Augustus married Ingeborg in 1193 but repudiated her almost immediately. Resisting the king's attempts to return her to Denmark, Ingeborg lived in virtual captivity for twenty years. Not until 1213 did Philip reinstate her as his wife and queen, bringing about a full reconciliation with Pope Innocent III. See Duby, *The Knight, the Lady and the Priest*, chap. 10; Pernoud and de Cant, *Isambour*; and Sivéry, *Philippe Auguste*, chap. 7.

26. Henry II of Champagne was the son of Count Henry the Liberal and Marie, daughter of Louis VII of France and Eleanor of Aquitaine. Through her mother, Marie was the half-sister of Richard the Lionheart; through her father, of Philip Augustus.

27. Here Robert conflates Baldwin IV's effort (1183) to convince Sibylle to annul her marriage to Guy; his nomination (1185) of Raymond of Tripoli to be regent of the kingdom of Jerusalem; and Isabelle's marked preference for Humphrey of Toron, the young husband she was forced to repudiate, over Conrad of Montferrat, the old husband she was given for reasons of political expediency (1190). Runciman, *History of the Crusades* 2:439, 443, 3:30–32. On Byzantine brideshows, see p. 259n. 69.

28. Runciman, *History of the Crusades*, 3:30–32.

29. This daughter, called Maria "La Marquise," was queen of Jerusalem from 1205 to 1212. The marriage between Conrad and Isabelle was even more problematic than Robert lets on since it was bigamous–"Conrad was rumoured to have one wife living at Constantinople and possibly another in Italy, and never to have troubled about any annulment or divorce" (Runciman, *History of the Crusades*, 3:30)—and "technically incestuous, since Conrad's brother had been married to Isabella's half-sister" (Riley-Smith, *The Crusades*, 115).

30. Chapter 2, pp. 67–72. Kinoshita, "Poetics of *Translatio*." The Greeks returned the favor. In two poems composed shortly after the Second Crusade, the German emperor Conrad is described as "boorish, bestial, greedy, deceitful, and aggressive," while biblical allusions cast Constantinople as the New Jerusalem and Conrad as Sennacherib or Holofernes. Jeffreys and Jeffreys, "The 'Wild Beast from the West,'" 108–11. See also Kazhdan, "Latin and Franks in Byzantium."

31. Pauphilet, "Villehardouin, Robert de Clari et la conquête de Constantinople," 233. He continues: "He loved the anecdote, the curious, picturesque little incident. A number of unexpected figures appear in his book for an instant, little scenes are sketched out; perhaps all that is little in comparison to what such a prodigious adventure should have brought to these crusaders. At least let us be grateful to him for this little that only he has conserved for us" (my translation).

32. Kaykhusraw was the son of a Byzantine mother. Sulaymanshah died in 1204 and was succeeded by his son, Kilij Arslan III, whom Kaykhusraw deposed the following year. Cahen, *Pre-Ottoman Turkey*, 110–15. The Seljuks had conquered Konia (Iconium) from the Byzantine Empire in 1071.

33. On the cosmopolitan nature of the empire, see Brand, "The Turkish Element in Byzantium."

34. On the marriage, see Magdalino, *The Empire of Manuel I Komnenos*, 100.

35. Though the identity of the figure represented in the manuscript has been a matter of controversy, Cecily Hilsdale persuasively associates her with Agnes ("Constructing a Byzantine *Augusta*"). The book in question is Vat. gr. 1851. See also Garland, *Byzantine Empresses*, 201, 203, and plate 27, and Spatharakis, *The Portrait in Byzantine Illuminated Manuscripts*, 210–18.

36. Hilsdale, "Constructing a Byzantine *Augusta*," 461.

37. Maria of Antioch, daughter of Raymond of Poitiers, was Eleanor of Aquitaine's first cousin. Maria Porphyrogenita, Manuel's daughter by his first wife, Bertha of Sulzbach, had long been betrothed to Bela IV of Hungary, whom Manuel (until Alexios's birth) had been grooming to succeed him.

38. *O City of Byzantium*, trans. Magoulias, 153.

39. Robert's description of Andronicos's gruesome public execution (25.52–86) emphasizes the violence inflicted on him by those whose family members he had harmed. In contrast, Choniates—despite his earlier revulsion at some of Andronicos's acts—describes his torturers as "shameless" and "incontinent" and underscores the dignity with which the emperor bore his suffering. See *O City of Byzantium*, trans. Magoulias, 192–93.

40. Agnes was initially Branas's mistress: "ils vécurent une quinzaine d'années en union libre, ce qui n'était pas très scandaleux à la cour de Byzance; il leur naquit une fille, qu'on appela Agnès comme sa mère, qui épousa plus tard un croisé de la seconde génération." Agnes and Branas were married during the reign of Baldwin of Flanders (Colliot, "Images et signes de la femme noble," 109). Agnes's mother, Adele of Champagne, was the sister of Louis's father, Count Thibaut of Blois.

41. On representations of Africans in medieval Byzantine visual arts, see Devisse, *The Image of the Black in Western Art*, 2:96–108.

42. Compare Guibert of Nogent on Urban II's predication of the First Crusade at Clermont in 1095: "He instituted a sign well suited to so honorable a profession by making the figure of the Cross, the stigma of the Lord's Passion, the emblem of the soldiery, or rather, of what was to be the soldiery of God. This, made of any kind of cloth, he ordered to be sewed upon the shirts, cloaks, and *byrra* of those who were about to go." *The First Crusade*, ed. Peters, 15.

43. The plausibility of this account is confirmed by a passage from the eleventh-century chronicler Ibn ʿIdhari al-Marrakushi, who describes Santiago as attracting Christian pilgrims "from the furthest regions, from the land of the Copts, from Nubia, etc." Bresc et al., *La Méditerranée entre pays d'Islam et monde latin*, 21 (my translation from the French).

44. Eventually they converted to Orthodox Christianity and were assimilated into the various populations with which they had contact. Berend, *At the Gate of Christendom*, 68–70.

45. The Latin term *miles*, Duby notes, designates the convergence of a technical fact (the superiority of horsemen in combat), a social fact (the link between the "noble" way of life and the horse), and an institutional fact (the limiting of combat duty to a restricted elite) (Duby, *Chivalrous Society*, 42). Compare the careful distinction between cavalry and infantry drawn in the fateful contract with the Venetians.

46. See *The First Crusade*, ed. Peters, XIII:3. On the crusaders' confusion when confronted by Turkish mounted archers, see *The First Crusade*, ed. Peters, XI:6, and Smail, *Crusading Warfare*, 76, 78.

47. In Chrétien de Troyes's *Perceval ou le Conte du Graal*, Gauvain causes consternation by setting out from Arthur's court with "seven squires . . . seven warhorses, and two shields" (*Oeuvres complètes*, ll. 4804–5). Episodes in the second half of the romance—in which Gauvain is mistaken for a horse-trader, chases after a lady's palfrey, has his mount stolen, and is compelled to mount a lowly packhorse—comically enact the text's literal preoccupation with *cheval-erie*. *Le Conte du Graal* was commissioned by Count Philip of Flanders (d. 1191), uncle of Baldwin IX, the future "Latin emperor" of Constantinople.

48. Spiegel, *Romancing the Past*, 20–23.

49. The nickname referred to Alexios's bushy eyebrows. Queller and Madden, *The Fourth Crusade*, 150.

50. "*A murdered man has been taken unawares*, either *in his sleep* or in a contest without formal challenge or equality in the means of confrontation." Bloch, *Medieval French Literature and Law*, 37 (emphasis added), drawing on sources such as the *Très Ancien Coutumier de Normandie* (c. 1200) and *Le Livre de Justice et de Pletz*. Contrast the very public execution of Andronicos I, recounted above.

51. The assassination of Charles the Good precipitated a succession dispute eventually won by Thierry of Alsace, grandfather of Baldwin IX. See Galbert of Bruges, *The Murder of Charles the Good, Count of Flanders*, trans. James Bruce Ross (New York: Harper and Row, 1967).

52. Kinoshita, "Poetics of *Translatio*," 320–21.

53. "This is not to imply that his contemporary Robert of Clari could not see the forest for the trees; he was simply more attuned to describing trees, as it were" (Fleischman, "On the Representation of History and Fiction in the Middle Ages," 293).

54. Runciman contrasts the behavior of the French and Flemings with that of the Venetians, who "knew the value" of the precious objects filling the city. "Whenever they could they seized treasures and carried them off to adorn the squares and churches and palaces of their town" (*History of the Crusades*, 3:123). On the importance of Choniates's chronicle, see Andrea, "Essay on Primary Sources," 310.

55. On the importance of defining knighthood and nobility "operationally" rather than taxonomically, see Bouchard, *Strong of Body*, chap. 1. On the ideological division between knights and clerics, see Duby, *The Three Orders*.

56. Queller and Madden, *The Fourth Crusade*, 139.

57. *Conquête*, section 82. Robert himself seems to have made off with at least two precious reliquaries of the True Cross, one in silver and the other in crystal, both (now lost) attested in seventeenth-century inventories. Robert of Clari, *Conquest*, trans. McNeal, 5.

58. Boniface of Montferrat had made his own bid for power by marrying Margaret of Hungary, widow of Isaac II. Marrying a widowed empress-consort was a Byzantine practice observable in Nikephoros III Botaneiates's marriage to Maria of Alania, wife of his predecessor, Michael VII Doukas (c. 1078), and in Andronicos I's marriage to Agnes of France (1183).

59. A member of the comital family of Flanders, Henry was related to the kings of England and had briefly been the brother-in-law of Philip Augustus of France.

60. Spiegel, *Romancing the Past*, 8.

61. Michael VIII was the great-nephew of Theodore Lascaris (son-in-law of Alexios III) who, in 1204, established an empire-in-exile in Nicaea. The Palaeologi ruled the renewed Byzantine Empire until the Ottoman conquest of 1453.

62. The Venetians gained control of the western coasts of continental Greece, the whole Peloponnese, Naxos, Andros and Euboea, Gallipoli and the Thracian ports on the Marmora, and Adrianople. In their "realism," however, the Venetians took only what they knew that they could hold: Crete, two Peloponnesian ports, and Corfu; elsewhere, they installed or accepted the homage of Latin or Venetian vassal lords (Runciman, *History of the Crusades*, 3:124–26). Meanwhile, the Genoese (whose maritime empire we will examine in Chapter 6) established themselves in the rival empire of Nicaea–an alliance that paid great dividends after Michael VIII's reconquest of Constantinople in 1261.

63. Bartlett, *The Making of Europe*, chap. 2. The kings of Jerusalem were descended from the counts of Boulogne. Baldwin's IX's great-grandfather, Fulk of Anjou, his grandfather, Thierry of Alsace, and his uncle, Count Philip of Flanders, all had important ties to Outremer. See Kinoshita, "Poetics of *Translatio*," 317.

64. As maternal uncle to the future Louis VIII (son of his sister Isabelle), Baldwin perhaps even stood to exert considerable influence should anything happen to Philip Augustus.

65. Sivéry, *Philippe Auguste*, 171.

66. R. Wolff, "Baldwin of Flanders and Hainaut," 300–301. Baldwin's wife, Marie of Champagne (the daughter of Chrétien de Troyes's famous patron), had come east to join her husband but fell ill and died at Acre. For a more textured view of the reign of Baldwin's daughters, see de Cant, *Jeanne et Marguerite de Constantinople*.

67. A similar series of dynastic accidents weakened the comital house of Champagne. Count Henry II went east on the Third Crusade. After Conrad of Montferrat's assassination in 1192, the count (nephew of both Richard the Lionheart and Philip Augustus) was chosen as Queen Isabelle's new husband. At his death by defenestration in 1197, Champagne passed to his younger brother, Count Thibaut III. Thibaut died, however, in 1201, as he was preparing to lead the Fourth Crusade. He was succeeded by his son, Thibaut IV the Posthumous, under the regency of the dowager countess Blanche of Navarre. Count Henry's daughters by Isabelle of Jerusalem subsequently contested the Champagne succession.

68. Said, *Orientalism*.

Chapter 6. The Romance of Miscege Nation

1. Menocal, "Signs of the Times," 499.

2. The text survives in a single manuscript, B.N. fr. 25462, from the last quarter of the thirteenth century. The editor dates the tale to the end of the reign of Philip Augustus (d. 1223). *La Fille du comte de Pontieu*, ed. Brunel. Translations

are my own. I have consulted Pauline Matarasso's translation in *Aucassin and Nicolette and Other Tales.*

3. My orthography here alludes to Homi Bhabha's deconstruction of fixed national identities in "DissemiNation."

4. Sigal, "Les différents types de pèlerinages." Northeastern French interest in the Santiago pilgrimage route dates back at least to 1090, when Countess Ida of Boulogne wrote to the bishop of Astorga requesting relics of the Virgin's hair. Harris, "Redating the Arca Santa of Oviedo," 92. See also Baiffier, "Relations religieuses de l'Espagne avec le nord de la France."

5. The sites mentioned in the text are all grouped between Rouen and Saint Pol. The dialect and some thirteenth-century notations in the manuscript further localize it to the Boulonnais (*La Fille du comte de Pontieu*, ed. Brunel, vi, ix). Perhaps not coincidentally, the *Pseudo-Turpin*, the Latin "chronicle" first translated into vernacular prose, likewise features the Santiago trail.

6. In 1112, Henry I of England confiscated the Norman holdings of Robert of Bellême, count of Montgommery, and imprisoned him for life. Bellême was given to Count Rotrou II of Perche—Henry I's son-in-law and (as we saw in Chapter 1) a prominent leader in his cousin Alfonso the Battler's Aragonese campaigns. The counts of Ponthieu were descended from Robert and his wife, the countess Agnes (Kathleen Thompson, "William Talvas, Count of Ponthieu, and the Politics of the Anglo-Norman Realm," in *England and Normandy in the Middle Ages*, ed. David Bates and Anne Curry [London: Hambledon, 1994], 169–84, at 169–70). In this chapter I use the spelling Ponthieu to refer to the historical county and Pontieu for its fictional equivalent.

7. For more on Alice, the cast-off fiancée of Richard the Lionheart, see p. 198, below.

8. Malo, *Renaud de Dammartin*, 59.

9. Gaucher married Hugh's daughter Elisabeth in 1196. First established in 1031, the countship of Saint Pol was typical both in its quick rise and in its inability ultimately to resist incorporation in "larger, more uniform political units." Domart, originally in the mouvance of Ponthieu, was lost or transferred in 1209. Fossier, *La terre et les hommes en Picardie*, 2:484, 550, 664n. 208. Robert de Clari, as we saw in Chapter 5, was from Cléry-les-Pernois, in Domart.

10. See Duby, *Le dimanche de Bouvines*, and Baldwin, *Aristocratic Life in Medieval France*, chap. 2.

11. Compare Chrétien de Troyes's *Erec et Enide* (*Oeuvres complètes*, ll. 2838–42), where "custom and practice" (costume et us) demand that a group of brigands should attack a lone adversary one at a time.

12. In Chrétien de Troyes's *Chevalier de la Charrete*, for example, the "Custom of Logres" dictates that any knight happening on a lone maiden is honor bound to treat her with respect; however, if she is under escort, he can challenge her guide and, if he wins, have his way with her "without incurring shame or blame" (*Oeuvres complètes*, ll. 1308–22). On rape as a plot device, see Gravdal, *Ravishing Maidens.*

13. In the twelfth century, forcible rape was punishable by excommunication (under canon law) or execution (in civil law). In practice, of course, there were

asymmetries of class between "the swineherd who ravished a duchess" and "the duke who ravaged a shepherdess." Much canon law, however, focuses on abductions designed to force consent to an otherwise undesired marriage. Brundage, *Law, Sex, and Christian Society*, 249–50, 311–13, 396–98.

14. Chrétien de Troyes, *Le Chevalier de la Charrete*, ll. 3937–99.

15. The maritime route to Flanders was established by the Genoese in 1277. Jacques Bernard, "Trade and Finance in the Middle Ages, 900–1500," in *The Fontana Economic History of Europe: The Middle Ages*, ed. Carlo M. Cipolla (London: Collins/Fontana Books, 1972), 285, 294.

16. The naval base was built to protect al-Andalus from Fatimid attacks and to launch maritime raids against the Christians. "Al-Mariyya," *Encyclopaedia of Islam*, 6:576.

17. Ibn al-Khaṭīb, *Kitāb aᶜmāl al-aᶜlām*, cited in Barrucand and Bednorz, *Moorish Architecture*, 124.

18. Partearroyo, "Almoravid and Almohad Textiles," 105–13. The Almoravids were North African Berbers who invaded al-Andalus in 1086, following Alfonso VI of León-Castile's conquest of Toledo.

19. May, *Silk Textiles of Spain*, 12. On Almería in Muslim histories and geographies, see Serjeant, *Islamic Textiles*, 169–70. Al-Idrīsī was a North African scholar working at the court of the Norman king, Roger II of Sicily (1130–54), for whom he composed his celebrated "Book of Roger." Al-Idrîsî, *La première géographie de l'Occident*, 282 (my translation from the French).

20. Epstein, *Genoa and the Genoese*, 26. An early twelfth-century Latin life of Saint Gilles represents a Genoese merchant ship caught in a storm while sailing home from Almería. *Miracula beati Aegidii*, ed. Ph. Jaffé, MGH Scriptores 12 (Hanover, 1856), 321, cited in Constable, "Genoa and Spain in the Twelfth and Thirteenth Centuries," 637.

21. The Genoese chronicler Caffaro says ten thousand, though Epstein (*Genoa and the Genoese*, 31–32, 50–51) calls this an exaggeration. The Genoese had seized Almería for themselves the previous year but were able to collect only a fraction of the exorbitant tribute to which the Almoravid governor had agreed (Epstein, *Genoa and the Genoese*, 31–32, 49–51). The Castilian side of the 1147 victory was celebrated in the "Poem of Almería," 372 lines of Latin verse appended to the *Chronica Adefonsi Imperatoris*.

22. See Kinoshita, "Almería Silk and the French Feudal Imaginary."

23. Chrétien de Troyes, *Cligès, Oeuvres complètes*, ll. 6314–17. As we saw in Chapter 1, Alfonso I of Aragon conquered Tudela in 1119.

24. Constable, "Muslim Spain and Mediterranean Slavery," 264.

25. Some were used as prostitutes, but others were treated as virtual family members (Phillips, *Slavery from Roman Times*, 72–73). Male slaves were used as soldiers and administrators, often rising to high office. During the period of the ṭāʾifa kings (eleventh century), several states—including Almería—were ruled for a time by Ṣaqāliba, former slaves. Kennedy, *Muslim Spain and Portugal*, 140.

26. Constable, "Muslim Spain and Mediterranean Slavery," 264–84. The regular sale of slaves in Genoa itself is documented from the 1190s. Epstein, *Genoa and the Genoese*, 103.

27. See Chapter 3, note 31.

28. On the ethos of "youth," see Duby, "Youth in Aristocratic Society."

29. Compare Ibn Jubayr's account of the way conversion (in this case, of Muslims under Norman Sicilian rule) could be used as a means to escape familial control: "Should a man show anger to his son or his wife, or a woman to her daughter, the one who is the object of displeasure may perversely throw himself into a church, and there be baptised and turn Christian. Then there will be for the father no way of approaching his son, or the mother her daughter." He adds, "The Muslims of Sicily therefore are most watchful of the management of their family, and their children, in case this should happen." *Travels of Ibn Jubayr*, trans. Broadhurst, 359.

30. de Weever, *Sheba's Daughters.* As for the conventionalized description of the queen's beauty, Steven Epstein's fascinating study of Italian slavery suggests that individuated physical descriptions may have first originated at the other end of the social scale: in the case of slaves, the ability to distinguish individuals was important in sales contracts and the tracking down of runaways. See *Speaking of Slavery*, 103–14.

31. Fletcher, *Moorish Spain*, 53. During the *ṭāʾifa* period, it became politically expedient for ruling Berber lineages to claim Arab origins. Guichard, "The Social History of Muslim Spain," in Jayyusi, 2:679–708, at 686.

32. Canon 68 from H. J. Schroeder, *Disciplinary Decrees of the General Councils: Texts, Translation and Commentary* (St. Louis: B. Herder, 1937), 78–127, emphasis added. Cited in the *Medieval Source Book*, http://www.fordham.edu/halsall/basis/lateran4.html, October 2001. The effort to shore up this and other category boundaries was a telltale symptom of the emergence of what historian R. I. Moore calls a "persecuting society."

33. Significantly, the Council of Lleida (1229) reinterpreted the Lateran canons by mandating distinctive dress for Jews but not for Muslims. Catlos, "Four Kidnappings in Thirteenth-Century Aragon," 173–74 and n. 29.

34. The first quotation comes from Bouchard, *Strong of Body*, 67; the second from Bartlett, "Medieval and Modern Concepts of Race and Ethnicity," 42.

35. A version of the story interpolated into *L'Histoire d'outre-mer et du roi Saladin*, a thirteenth-century prose chronicle in the tradition of the continuations of William of Tyre's history of the Third Crusade, is characteristically more expansive and explicit: "When she had renounced and relinquished her faith, the sultan took her to wife *according to the customs and practices of Saracen lands*" (359–61). On *L'Histoire*, see Brunel's introduction to *La Fille du comte de Pontieu*, ix–xi.

36. My play here on the notion of the "felicitous" speech act refers to Austin, *How to Do Things with Words.* On the importance of genealogy in the medieval imaginary, see Chapter 5, p. 269n. 20.

37. Baronial resistance to the accession of Mathilda (daughter and designated heir of Henry I of England) resulted, for example, in a long civil war between her and her cousin, Stephen of Blois. For genealogical crises in the ruling houses of Jerusalem, Flanders, and Champagne, see Chapter 5, pp. 149–52, 174, 273n. 67.

38. Texts in Old French are less likely to note linguistic difference than, for example, those in Occitan. Schulze-Busacker, "French Conceptions of Foreigners and Foreign Languages," 40.

39. Compare the linguistic handicap faced by Ingeborg, the Danish princess whom French king Philip Augustus married in 1193 and then tried immediately to repudiate. Unable to protest in French as her marriage was (falsely) being declared consanguineous, the resourceful Ingeborg appealed for papal intervention in broken Latin: "Mala Francia! Mala Francia! Roma! Roma!" Pernoud and de Cant, *Isambour*, 44–45.

40. The manual, describing the proper regulation of weighers, bakers, butchers, food vendors, perfume sellers, druggists, and other merchants, was authored by Al-Saqati, the *muḥtasib* (markets inspector) of Malaga. The *muḥtasib* was a Muslim official charged with maintaining *ḥisba* (the two words are etymologically related), which in its larger sense designates proper moral behavior. "Hisba," *Encyclopaedia of Islam*, 3:485–89.

41. Constable, *Trade and Traders*, 207. For other examples of trickery in the Iberian slave trade, see Catlos, "Four Kidnappings in Thirteenth-Century Aragon."

42. Hillenbrand, " 'The Ornament of the World,' " 1:115. In 1178, the archbishop of Toledo issued a *Latin* act which included a note *in Arabic* indicating the act had been repeated in *Roman* for the benefit of two of the parties involved (Burnett, "The Translating Activity in Medieval Spain," 2:1036–37). Even in the north, the prestige of Arabic was such that King Pedro I of Aragon (1094–1104) was known to sign himself Bitr b. Shanja (Peter, son of Sancho). Fletcher, *Quest for the Cid*, figure 10.

43. In the medieval Islamic world, slaves and former slaves, employed as soldiers and administrators, could occasionally wield great power, like the *Ṣaqāliba* (Slav/slave) *ṭāʾifa* kings of eleventh-century al-Andalus or the Mamluks who overthrew the Ayyubid dynasty in Egypt in 1260.

44. Spivak, "Can the Subaltern Speak?"

45. On the Temple as a place of penance as a motif in medieval epic and romance, see Nicholson, *Templars, Hospitallers and Teutonic Knights*, 87–88.

46. The *Histoire d'outre-mer et du roi Saladin* adds an emphasis on duress (minimized in our "primitive" version) to help rationalize the lady's conversion: "I am a Saracen (who) renounced (Christianity), *because otherwise I could not have survived, for I was almost dead*" (in *La Fille du comte de Pontieu*, ed. Brunel, 34, emphasis added).

47. On chess as a means of representing cross-cultural negotiation, see Chapter 3, pp. 00.

48. See Chapter 1, p. 96.

49. Usāmah ibn Munqidh, *An Arab-Syrian Gentleman*, trans. Hitti, 159–60. Usamah was a soldier, poet, and sometimes advisor to Saladin whose memoirs are often quoted for their representation of twelfth-century Frankish-Muslim relations. Though (as in this instance) he formulaically curses the Franks, he also records friendly interactions with King Fulk of Jerusalem and various Templars and other knights.

50. If the merchants who originally convey the count's daughter into slavery are strongly suggestive of the Genoese, her return to Latin Christendom through Brindisi evokes the sphere of influence of their principal rivals, the Venetians. See Abulafia, *The Two Italies*, 144.

51. As James Brundage notes, while Innocent's decretals clarified some un-
certainties, "they failed to supply a reliable guide for handling other situations
where the law remained unclear." Innocent's rulings modified those of his predecessor, Celestine III (1191–98), who ruled that a Saracen who converted to Christianity might marry a Christian woman even if he had a Saracen wife at the time of
his conversion. Earlier, Gratian (in his *Decretum*, c. 1140) had ruled that if two pagans married and one of them subsequently converted to Christianity, the convert
could remarry only if deserted by the non-Christian spouse. Brundage, *Law, Sex,
and Christian Society*, 244, 340.

52. Donald Maddox ("Domesticating Diversity," 98–100) notes the tale's
strong affiliation to genealogical literature tracing a lineage back to a female
founder, either "historical" (the count of Flanders's daughter in the *History of the
Counts of Guines*) or fantastic (the fairy Mélusine, ancestress of the house of
Lusignan).

53. A case of foreign-born heirs challenging native ones for the right of succession occurred in the early thirteenth century, when Count Henry II's daughters by Queen Isabelle of Jerusalem tried to reclaim Champagne from their
cousin, Count Thibaut IV.

54. *Chronicle of the Third Crusade*, trans. Nicholson, book 4, chap. 28.
William was freed a year later in exchange for ten noble Turks: "The Turks would
willingly have spent an infinite sum of money to keep the said William, but the
king's brilliant and lofty spirit would not condescend to be denigrated in any respect" (book 6, chap. 36).

55. Though Malakin is taken here as a proper name, it closely echoes *malik*,
the Arabic word for king (as in the William of Préaux anecdote, above). Since in
Floire et Blancheflor, Baudas is used for "the port closest to Babylone" (i.e.,
Cairo), Malakins de Baudas may be approximated to the "emir of Babylon" of
Chapter 3.

56. This inaugurates the motif Donald Maddox has called the "Europeanization of Saladin" ("Domesticating Diversity," 102–3). On changes in medieval
representations of Saladin, see Tolan, "Mirror of Chivalry." On the fanciful genealogies ascribed to Saladin in the Muslim world, see the fourteenth-century historian al-Maqrizi in *A History of the Ayyubid Sultans of Egypt*, 35.

57. For a summary and critique of this view, see Hamilton, "Knowing the
Enemy."

58. See Chapter 5, p. 174.

59. The *Pilgrim's Guide to Santiago de Compostela* (see pp. 253–54n. 11) characterized the Navarrese as malicious, depraved, and "in everything inimical" to
the French. See Kinoshita, "Fraternizing with the Enemy," 698–99.

60. On the succession struggle resulting from Richard's death, see Chapter
5, p. 148. In 1199, Berengaria's younger sister Blanche married Thibaut III of
Champagne; at his premature death (as he was preparing to lead the Fourth Crusade), Blanche became regent for their posthumous son, Thibaut IV "le Chanson-
nier," during a troubled moment in the relationship between the French king and
his great barons. See Evergates, "Aristocratic Women in the County of Champagne," 81–85.

61. "The Sicilian marriage," according to W. L. Warren, "made a deep impression on the chroniclers, who record in detail the negotiations, the journey to Palermo, and the marriage settlement" (*Henry II*, 143n. 2). Analyzing a mural discovered in 1963 at the hermitage of Sainte Radegonde in Chinon, the art historian Nurith Kenaan-Kedar identifies the mounted noblewoman depicted in the scene as Eleanor of Aquitaine departing for captivity in 1174 after her unsuccessful revolt against Henry II, and the young brown-haired girl riding with her as Joan. "Aliénor d'Aquitaine conduite en captivité," esp. 320.

62. See Kinoshita, "Almería Silk and the French Feudal Imaginary," 173–74. On al-Idrīsī, see above, p. 275n. 19.

63. On Joan's arrival in Palermo, see Norwich, *Kingdom of the Sun*, 310–11, drawing on the chronicle of Roger of Hoveden. On Norman Sicilian architecture, see Sibylle Mazot, "Fatimid Influences in Sicily and Southern Italy," in Hattstein and Delius, *Islam: Art and Architecture*, 158–63.

64. *Travels of Ibn Jubayr*, ed. Broadhurst, 349–50.

65. Constance and Henry's succession was contested by William II's illegitimate nephew, Tancred of Lecce. In the early thirteenth century, chronicler Richard of San Germano was so "obsessed with the problems created for the kingdom by the failure of William II to leave a son" that he went so far as (falsely) to attribute the king's foundation of the monastery of Monreale (1174) to an attempt to "win the blessings of the Holy Virgin on his sterile wife" (Matthew, *The Norman Kingdom of Sicily*, 203). Constance herself remained childless until 1194, when, at the age of forty, she gave birth to the future Frederick II. Her story is charmingly reconstructed by Mary Taylor Simeti in *Travels with a Medieval Queen*.

66. Bahā ̄ʾad-Dīn, "Sultanly Anecdotes," 287–91, in Gabrieli, *Arab Historians of the Crusades*, 227.

67. Runciman says that while Saladin took the proposal as a joke, "Richard may have been quite serious" (*History of the Crusades*, 3:59). In dangling the prospect of a rich political marriage before al-ʿĀdil, Richard seems to have been trying the same strategy of sowing familial discord that the Capetians had so effectively used against the Angevins.

68. Bahā ̄ʾad-Dīn, "Sultanly Anecdotes," 277–78.

69. Having lost the "opportunity" to make his sister queen of a multiconfessional Jerusalem, Richard does the next best thing, engineering the marriage of his nephew, Henry of Champagne, to Isabelle, the recently widowed queen regnant of the Latin kingdom.

70. McCracken, *The Romance of Adultery*, 132–33. As McCracken points out, this fourteenth-century representation of Eleanor's infidelity replaces the contemporary twelfth-century rumor of an adulterous and incestuous liaison with her uncle, Count Raymond of Antioch. Richard became the object of late medieval legend of a different sort: the Middle English romance *Richard Cuer de Lyon* represents him as a cannibal, gleefully feasting on the bodies of defeated Saracen foes. See Heng, *Empire of Magic*, chap. 2.

71. The claim by Eleanor's paternal grandmother, Philippa of Toulouse, to succeed her father, Count Pons, had been set aside by her paternal uncle, the crusader

Raymond of Saint-Gilles. Joan's marriage to Raymond VI—like Richard's own to
Berengaria of Navarre—exemplifies Richard's interest in the southern border of
the "Angevin empire."

72. Raimondet derived substantial prestige from his maternal lineage.
Though only two when his mother died in 1199, at his own death fifty years later
he requested to be buried at the abbey of Fontevraud, at the feet of his mother,
his grandparents Henry and Eleanor, and his uncle Richard. Macé, *Les comtes de
Toulouse*, 60–61, 213–16.

73. Richard had arrived to find Joan detained by Tancred of Lecce, who was
contesting the succession of Constance of Sicily and her husband, Henry VI.
Richard forced Tancred to release Joan and to pay compensation for her dower
rights. Philip set sail from Messina just hours before Berengaria's arrival. See
Gillingham, *Richard the Lionheart*, 160; W. L. Warren, *Henry II*, 109, 611–12; and
Runciman, *History of the Crusades*, 3:40–45.

74. Simon was the brother of Renaut of Dammartin, who commissioned one
of the early vernacular translations of the *Pseudo-Turpin*. Renaud had become
count of Boulogne by abducting and forcibly marrying its heiress, Ida (Baldwin,
Philip Augustus, 81). Simon remained in exile until 1231. Malo, *Renaud de
Dammartin*, 222–23. On Robert of Dreux, see Baldwin, *Philip Augustus*, 342.

75. Gerbert de Montreuil dedicated his *Roman de la Violette* to Marie sometime between 1225 and 1237. Robert Bossuat, Louis Picard, and Guy Reynaud de
Lage, *Dictionnaire des lettres françaises: Le Moyen âge*, rev. Geneviève Hasenohr
and Michel Zink, Encyclopédies d'aujourd'hui (Paris: Livre de Poche, 1992), 308,
660. See also Rita Lejeune, "La femme dans les littératures française et occitane
du XIe au XIIIe siècle," *Cahiers de Civilisation Médiévale* 20 (1977): 201–18, at 207.
Joan's first betrothal to Henry III of England was blocked by Louis IX (Simon of
Dammartin had sworn not to marry his children without the French king's per-
mission). She married Fernando III of Castile in 1237; they had three children:
Fernando (c. 1239–63), Eleanor (1241–90), and Louis (c. 1243–76). After Fer-
nando's death in 1252, Joan supported an unsuccessful revolt against her stepson,
Alfonso X; in 1254 she left Castile for Abbeville, in Ponthieu (Parsons, *Eleanor of
Castile*, 8–9, 16). She died in 1279, leaving Ponthieu to her daughter, Eleanor of
Castile, first wife of Edward I of England.

76. Samia Mehrez, "Translation and the Postcolonial Experience: The Francophone North African Text," in *Rethinking Translation: Discourse, Subjectivity,
Ideology*, ed. Lawrence Venute (London: Routledge, 1992), 120–58, at 122.

77. Menocal, "Signs of the Times," 497–98.

78. Maddox, "Domesticating Diversity," 106–7.

79. On the deployment of the Charlemagne legend under Philip Augustus,
see Baldwin, *Philip Augustus*, 370–71, 376–77.

Chapter 7. Uncivil Wars

1. Renan, "Qu'est-ce qu'une Nation?," 887–906 (emphasis original).

2. Anderson, *Imagined Communities*, 199–201.

3. The internal quotation comes from Léon Gautier, *Epopées françaises* (Paris, 1868), 749, cited by Bloch in "842," 11.

4. Cheyette argues that Pedro "the Catholic" of Aragon would have been as logical a choice as Philip Augustus, and that Innocent chose the king of France over the king of Aragon for political reasons. See *Ermengard of Narbonne*, 354–56.

5. Sumption, *The Albigensian Crusade*, 15–17, 77–79.

6. Peter of Les Vaux-de-Cernay, *Hystoria Albigensis*, ed. Guébin and Lyon; Guillaume de Puylaurens, *Chronica Magistri Guillelmi de Podio Laurentii*, ed. Duvernoy.

7. The *Chanson de la Croisade Albigeoise* survives in one complete manuscript (BN fr. 25425, copied in Toulouse in about 1275), one fragment (now lost), and two late medieval/early modern prosifications. Michel Zink, introduction to *La Chanson de la Croisade Albigeoise*, ed. Martin-Chabot, trans. Gougaud, 16–17. Guilhem's part is composed of 130 laisses totaling 2,749 lines (roughly 28 percent of the total), the Anonymous's of 83 laisses totaling 6,811 lines. In this chapter I cite the old Occitan from *La Chanson de la Croisade Albigeoise*, ed. Martin-Chabot, trans. Gougaud, which is based on *La Chanson de la croisade contre les Albigeois*, ed. Martin-Chabot. The English translation is mine; I have occasionally consulted *Song of the Cathar Wars*, trans. Shirley.

8. Cheyette, *Ermengard of Narbonne*, 3–4.

9. Ibid., 42.

10. *The Poetry of William VII*, ed. Bond, 14–17, 64.

11. Most prominently, Guilhem IX's granddaughter Eleanor of Aquitaine married Louis VII of France and Henry II of England in succession. Also important was Raymond V of Toulouse's marriage to Louis VII's sister Constance (the widow of the count of Boulogne). Macé, *Les comtes de Toulouse*, 58–60.

12. Richard's marriage to Berengaria of Navarre and his sister Joan's to Raymond VI of Toulouse make perfect sense in light of these Occitanian interests. See above, pp. oo.

13. See Philippe Martel, "L'Epoque médiévale," in *Histoire de Nîmes* (Aix-en-Provence: Edisud, 1982), 107–44, at 122, and above, Chapter 2, pp. oo–oo.

14. Raymond Roger had fled Béziers just ahead of the crusading army, evacuating the city's Jews with him. See Sumption, *Albigensian Crusade*, 89–90, 93–94; and Roquebert, *Histoire des Cathares*, 134–37.

15. Sumption, *Albigensian Crusade*, 100. In 1209, the count of Saint Pol (who figures as a fictional character in *La Fille du comte de Pontieu*) was the French king's cousin and ally, Gaucher of Châtillon. Son-in-law and succssor of Count Hugh of Saint Pol, he was killed at the siege of Avignon in 1226. The count of Ponthieu also took part in the Albigensian Crusade. At the siege of Termes (1210), Simon de Montfort was forced to accept a negotiated settlement in part because the count (along with the bishop of Beauvais and the count of Dreux) "told him that they had earned their indulgences and, in spite of the emotional pleas of Simon and his wife, . . . intended to leave on the following morning." See Sumption, *Albigensian Crusade*, 124, 219.

16. We have met Simon before, in Robert de Clari's chronicle of the Fourth Crusade. Scandalized by the sack of the Christian city of Zara on the Adriatic, he

was the most prominent noble to abandon the expedition *before* the conquest of Constantinople, making his way to the Holy Land instead.

17. The dynastic union created by the marriage (in 1150) of Petronilla of Aragon (daughter of the monk-king Ramiro II) and Count Ramon Berenguer IV of Barcelona came to be known as the "Crown of Aragon" and its rulers as count-kings. See Bisson, *The Medieval Crown of Aragon*. On the absorption of Carcassonne, see Cheyette, "The 'Sale' of Carcassonne." Cheyette adopts the term "feudal empire" from John Le Patourel's *Norman Empire*, describing this extension of power as "a tale of conquest by gold rather than by siege and slaughter, a startling contrast to the Conquest far to the north that was its exact contemporary" (830).

18. Sumption, *Albigensian Crusade*, 126.

19. Cheyette, *Ermengard of Narbonne*, 360.

20. Sumption, *Albigensian Crusade*, 158–59.

21. Compare "la nostra gens de Fransa" (105.15) who return to the battle-field where they have just defeated the count of Foix to strip the corpses by moonlight.

22. Compare the subsequent arrival of reinforcements "[d]els crozatz d'Ala-manha e dels de Lombardia, / E dels baros d'Alvernhe e dels d'Esclavonia" (111.18–19).

23. The use of alexandrine rather than decasyllabic verses, and of rhyme rather than assonance, marks our text as "late" in relationship to epics like the *Roland*. Zink, introduction to *Chanson de la Croisade Albigeoise*, ed. Martin-Chabot, 16. For a detailed analysis of the way Guilhem's poetic voice combines "lyric, clerkly, and epic associations," see Huot, "The Political Implications of Poetic Discourse," 134–38.

24. This was especially true in matters relating to inheritance laws and land tenure. Sumption, *Albigensian Crusade*, 154–55; Roquebert, *Histoire des Cathares*, 194–96. Their "colonial" character is revealed in their resemblance to another externally imposed set of statutes, the Assises de Jérusalem (Roquebert, *Histoire des Cathares*, 194).

25. Sylvia Huot speculates that Guilhem de Tudela may have broken off his writing because of his own increasing disillusionment with the crusade ("The Political Implications of Poetic Discourse," 139).

26. Guilhem de Tudela evokes Las Navas de Tolosa in laisse 5 of the poem, saying, "I am still thinking of composing a new song all on good parchment" (5.23–24) (eu ne cug encar far bona canson novela / tot en bel pergamin). On Guilhem's Navarrese connections, see Lafont, "Guilhem de Tudela," 222.

27. Among the earliest such depictions in Europe, these images are iconographically distinct from illustrations of agreements "in which both parties are seated and join one or both hands." Kosto, "The *Liber feudorum maior*," 16, 18.

28. See Chapter 2.

29. Aurell, *Les noces du comte*, 405–6.

30. Sumption, *Albigensian Crusade*, 156–57.

31. The widow of Count Eustace of Boulogne, Constance married Raymond V of Toulouse in 1154. The few mentions of her in comital accounts underscore her royalty: "Constance, the king of the Franks' sister" or "Queen Constance."

Her position at court soon deteriorated, however, and she left Toulouse in 1165, living out the remainder of her life (she died in 1190) at the French court. Macé, *Les Comtes de Toulouse*, 58–60.

32. Wolff, "Epanouissement du Languedoc," in Wolff, 161–63; Sumption, *Albigensian Crusade*, 24. On the commune of Genoa and its influence on Occitanian towns, see Cheyette, *Ermengard of Narbonne*, 93–97.

33. Paterson, *World of the Troubadours*, 70–71. *Paratge* will be discussed in detail on pp. 217–21, below.

34. *The Book of Deeds*, trans. Smith and Buffery.

35. "Faidit"—meaning "exiled" and (by extension) "miserable"—was a resonant cultural term in Occitania. In the case of the hapless Gaucelm Faidit, who (according to one thirteenth-century *vida*) became a troubadour after losing "all his wealth" in a game of dice, it refers to his various misfortunes and amorous sufferings. Boutière and Schutz, *Biographies des troubadours*, 167. After the Albigensian Crusade, it comes to signify the whole generation of nobles disinherited by Simon de Montfort.

36. Raimondet was the grandson Henry II of England on his mother's side and great-grandson of Louis VI of France on his father's. The crusader Alain de Roucy later accounts for Raimondet's military successes by reminding his allies, "he is certainly of a lineage that advances its standing, for Lord Richard was his uncle and Bertran (of Toulouse) his relation" (160.38–39) (es ben de lhinatge que·s milhor'e s'enans, / Qu'en Richarz fo sos oncles e sos parens Bertrans).

37. Pedro's death spelled the end of Aragonese influence north of the Pyrenees. In the mid-thirteenth century, Jaime made his reputation as "the Conqueror" against Iberian Muslims.

38. On the importance of the papal *curia* under Innocent III, see Sayers, *Innocent III*, 38.

39. Lord of Cavaillon, east of the Rhone, Gui originally moved in the political orbit of Count Alfons II of Provence. At Alfons's death (1209), Gui joined the entourage of the counts of Toulouse. He attended Lateran IV with Raymond VI and served as Raimondet's ambassador to Philip Augustus (1222); around 1225 he gained permission to style himself viscount of Cavaillon. Macé, *Les Comtes de Toulouse*, 106, 111, 141, 142, 249.

40. Compare the famous poem by Bertran de Born: "I love the gay Easter season, when leaves and flowers appear; I like hearing the merriment of birds when their song echoes through the woods" (30.1–5) (Be·m plai lo gais temps de pascor, / que fai fuoillas e flors venir; / e plai me qant auch la baudor / dels auzels que fant retintir / lo chant per lo boscatge). On lyric imagery in the Anonymous Continuation, see Huot, "The Political Implications of Poetic Discourse," 140–43.

41. As in the continuation of Bertran de Born's poem: "and it pleases me when I see tents and pavilions pitched on the meadows; and I feel great happiness when I see knights and horses in armor ranged on the fields" (30.6–10) (e plai me qand vei per los pratz / tendas e pavaillons fermatz; / et ai grand alegratge / qan vei per campaignas rengatz / cavalliers e cavals armatz). See also Chapter 2, p. 48.

42. Despite modern emphasis on the *canso*, love lyrics make up less than half the troubadour corpus (Harvey, "Courtly Culture in Medieval Occitania," 21). Gui composed one poem exhorting the count of Toulouse to make war to reclaim his lands, and another attacking William of Les Baux (*Song of the Cathar Wars*, trans. Shirley, 84n. 2). A fourteenth-century Italian *vida* makes Gui the lover of Garsenda of Forcalquier, the wife of Count Alfons II of Provence. It also attributes to him a pair of *coblas* composed in the third month of the siege of Castelnau exhorting "Bertran d'Avignon," who had abandoned the Toulousain cause, to return, for "the French are all around us" (li Franceis nos estan d'eviron). Boutière and Schutz, *Biographies des troubadours*, 504–7.

43. Zambon, "La notion de *Paratge*," 10–12, 14–16. See Guiraut's "Mot era dous e plazens," on the disappearance of "paratie" among both men and women. *The Cansos and Sirventes of the Troubadour Giraut de Borneil*, ed. Sharman, poem 72, pp. 460–64. Among Guiraut's patrons was Alfonso II of Aragon, father of Pedro II (ibid., 3–5, 8).

44. Zambon, "La notion de *Paratge*," 16–17. The exemplary poet here is Peire Cardenal.

45. Paterson, *World of the Troubadours*, 20

46. Introduction to *Bertran de Born*, ed. Paden, Sankovitch, and Stäblein, 9.

47. *Bertran de Born*, poem 24, pp. 294–99. Bertran participated in Young Henry's revolt of 1183 (9). W. L. Warren calls Young Henry "everyone's ideal of a fairy-tale prince," the only member of his family to achieve a measure of real popularity. In matters of governance, however, he was "dilatory," "irresolute," and "feckless," demonstrating "neither taste nor desire for responsibility" (*Henry II*, 580–84). Henry died in 1183; Raimondet (son of Henry's sister Joan) was born in 1197.

48. Paden, Sankovitch, and Stäblein gloss *paratge* as "rank, nobility, birth, family" and *pretz* as "worth, merit, virtue; honor, repute, reputation, good name, esteem, fame, glory; reward; money, price" (*Bertran de Born*, 528, 531).

49. Occitania had undergone a generational change in leadership in the mid-1190s with the deaths of Raymond V of Toulouse, Roger of Béziers (both in 1194), Alfonso II of Aragon, and Ermengard of Narbonne (both in 1196). Cheyette, *Ermengard of Narbonne*, 347.

50. In another *tenso* with Raimbaut de Vaqueiras, Gui favors the rude warrior over the courtly but cowardly lover (Aurell, "Le troubadour Gui de Cavaillon," 15–18).

51. Macé, *Les comtes de Toulouse*, 308. This seamless integration of lyric forms into narrative verse may be compared to Jean Renart's *Le Roman de la Rose ou de Guillaume de Dole*. Almost exactly contemporary with the Albigensian Crusade, this "realist" romance, in which the Emperor Conrad marries the humbly born Liénor, offers a vindication of the nobility of person and behavior over the nobility of lineage.

52. Compare the scene in *Le Charroi de Nîmes* in which Guillaume, from atop a tower in Montpellier, sees "The whole land full of devils, cities burning, churches sacked, chapels collapsing, bell towers toppled, and breasts of courtly ladies twisted" (570–73) (Toute la terre . . . plaine d'aversiers, / Viles ardoir et violer moustiers, / Chapeles fondre et trebuchier clochiers / Mameles tortre a cortoises

moilliers). In the epic *Garin de Montglane* (devoted to the exploits of one of Guillaume's ancestors) the inhabitants of Montglane, clearly marked as Saracens by their belief in "Jupin, Mahon et Tervagant," are also described as "tot *Aubigois, felon et mescreant.*" Hendrickson, "*Garin de Monglane* and *La Chanson de la croisade albigeoise,*" 211. Hendrickson refers (215n. 5) to his critical edition in progress, which I have been unable to locate.

53. The phrase *dreitz eretiers* expresses the same appeal to legitimacy as the epithet *droit oir* given to the Byzantine prince Alexios Angelos. See Chapter 5, pp. 146–48.

54. A second *sirventes,* "Si co·l flacs molins torneia," composed during the siege of Toulouse (1217–18), exhorts Occitanian barons not to make peace with Simon de Montfort: "it would be better to fight than to conclude a dishonorable peace" (II.14) (mais valria guerreges que s'avol plag fazia). That same poem contrasts "Proensals" (V.35) with men from "Franssa ni Borgoingna" (VI.39). Frank, "Tomier et Palaizi, troubadours tarasconnais." References are to strophe and line number.

55. Sumption underscores the "psychological impact" of Beaucaire in destroying impressions of Simon's invincibility (*Albigensian Crusade,* 187).

56. Since the beginning of the occupation, Toulouse had been split between two factions. The *cité,* the older quarter now populated by new men and immigrants, supported the church; here the crusader bishop (and ex-troubadour) Fulk of Marseille organized a "White Brotherhood" that attacked heretics and their sympathizers. The newer *bourg* (around the basilica of Saint Sernin) housed the city's old urban aristocracy. Often sympathetic to heresy even when not heretics themselves, they formed a rival "Black Brotherhood" that resisted the crusaders. Local support for Count Raymond began to coalesce as early as 1211, during Simon de Montfort's unsuccessful two-week siege of the city: in addition to casualties incurred and the resources squandered, the siege also "alienated the catholic majority of Toulouse. Simon had affronted their dignity and brutally rejected their claims on his sympathy. They had watched his men tear up their vines within sight of the city walls and cut down workers in the fields . . . . they never ceased, thereafter, to be among Raymond's strongest supporters" (Sumption, *Albigensian Crusade,* 135–37).

57. Dalmas's determination here is prepared by his lament at Pedro's death at Muret; see p. 212, above.

58. Even besieged by enemy missiles, "obret ab gran joya tota la cominaltatz" (204.3).

59. Compare Perceval, whose father was "wounded between the legs" (par mi les janbe navrez) and whose maternal uncle, the Fisher King, was "wounded by a javelin between his two hips" (feruz d'un javelot / Par mi les hanches amedos). Chrétien de Troyes, *Perceval, Oeuvres complètes,* 436, 3512–13.

60. The future Louis VIII (reigned 1223–26) had already participated in the campaigns of 1215; he intervened in Occitania again in 1219.

61. Sumption, *Albigensian Crusade,* 199.

62. Raymond VI had died in 1222. At the same time, sixteen-year-old Raymond Roger Trencavel, on whose behalf Raymond of Roquefeuille had so

eloquently pled at Lateran IV, finally came into his patrimony, the viscounties of Béziers and Carcassonne.

63. Sumption, *Albigensian Crusade*, 215–25.

64. *Aucassin et Nicolette*, ed. Roques, xv-xvi.

65. Roquebert, *Histoire des Cathares*, 41–46.

66. Paterson, *World of the Troubadours*, 115, 118, and Harvey, "Courtly Culture in Medieval Occitania," 12.

67. See Cheyette, *Ermengard of Narbonne*, 354.

Conclusion

1. Ebitz, "Secular to Sacred," 31. For ivory olifants as a nexus between medieval and modern histories of cultural interaction, see M. Warren, "The Noise of Roland."

2. See Grabar, "The Shared Culture of Objects," and Hoffman, "Pathways of Portability."

Selected Bibliography

PRIMARY SOURCES

Aucassin et Nicolette. Chantefable du XIIIe siècle. 2nd ed. Ed. Mario Roques. Paris: Champion, 1982.

Aucassin and Nicolette and Other Tales. Trans. Pauline Matarasso. Harmondsworth: Penguin, 1971.

The Book of Deeds of James I of Aragon: A Translation of the Medieval Catalan Llibre dels Fets. Trans. Damian Smith and Helena Buffery. Crusade Texts in Translation 10. Aldershot: Ashgate, 2003.

Boutière J., and A. H. Schutz. *Biographies des troubadours: Textes provençaux des XIIIe et XIVe siècles.* 2nd ed. Les Classiques d'Oc 1. Paris: A. G. Nizet, 1973.

The Cansos and Sirventes of the Troubadour Giraut de Borneil: A Critical Edition. Ed. Ruth Verity Sharman. Cambridge: Cambridge University Press, 1989.

La Chanson de Guillaume. Ed. Duncan McMillan. 2 vols. Paris: Picard, 1949–50.

La Chanson de la Croisade Albigeoise. Ed. Eugène Martin-Chabot. Trans. Henri Gougaud. Lettres Gothiques. Paris: Livre de Poche, 1989.

La Chanson de la Croisade contre les Albigeois. Ed. and trans. E. Martin-Chabot. 3 vols. Les Classiques de l'Histoire de France au Moyen Age. Paris, 1931–61.

La Chanson de Roland. Ed. and trans. Joseph Bédier. Paris: H. Piazza, n.d.

La Chanson de Roland. Ed. and trans. Ian Short. Lettres Gothiques. 2nd ed. Paris: Livre de Poche, 1990.

Les Chansons de Guillaume IX, duc d'Aquitaine (1071–1127). Ed. Alfred Jeanroy. Paris: Champion, 1967.

Chrétien de Troyes. *Oeuvres complètes.* Ed. Daniel Poirion. Paris: Gallimard, 1994.

Chronicle of the Third Crusade: A Translation of the Itinerarium Peregrinorum et Gesta Regis Ricardi. Trans. Helen J. Nicholson. Aldershot: Ashgate, 1997.

O City of Byzantium, Annals of Niketas Choniates. Trans. Harry J. Magoulias. Detroit: Wayne State University Press, 1984.

La Conquête de Constantinople par Robert de Clari. Trans. Alexandre Micha. Paris: Christian Bourgois, 1991.

Le Conte de Floire et Blancheflor. Ed. Jean-Luc Leclanche. Paris: Champion, 1983.

La Fille du comte de Pontieu: Nouvelle du XIIIe siècle. Ed. Clovis Brunel. Paris: Champion, 1926.

The First Crusade: The Chronicle of Fulcher of Chartres and Other Source Materials. Ed. Edward Peters. Philadelphia: University of Pennsylvania Press, 1971.

Floire et Blancheflor: Seconde version. Ed. Margaret M. Pelan. Association des Publications près les Universités de Strasbourg. Paris: Editions Ophrys, n.d.

Gabrieli, Francesco. *Arab Historians of the Crusades*. Trans. E. J. Costello. Berkeley: University of California Press, 1969.

Gerald of Wales. *The Journey through Wales/The Description of Wales*. Trans. Lewis Thorpe. Harmondsworth: Penguin, 1978.

Guillaume de Puylaurens. *Chronica Magistri Guillelmi de Podio Laurentii*. Ed. and trans. Jean Duvernoy. Paris: CNRS, 1976.

Guillaume d'Orange: Four Twelfth-Century Epics. Trans. Joan M. Ferrante. New York: Columbia University Press, 1974.

Idrîsî, al-. *La première géographie de l'Occident*. Ed. Henri Bresc and Annliese Nef. Trans. le chevalier Jaubert, rev. Annliese Nef. Paris: Flammarion, 1999.

The Itinerary of Benjamin of Tudela. Ed. and trans. M. N. Adler. *Jewish Quarterly Review* 16 (1904): 453–73, 715–33.

Joinville and Villehardouin. *Chronicles of the Crusades*. Trans. M. R. B. Shaw. Harmondsworth: Penguin, 1963.

The Life and Works of the Troubadour Raimbaut d'Orange. Ed. Walter T. Pattison. Minneapolis: University of Minnesota Press, 1952.

Lyrics of the Troubadours and Trouveres. Trans. Frederick Goldin. Garden City, N.Y.: Anchor Press, 1973.

Maqrizi, al-. *A History of the Ayyubid Sultans of Egypt*. Trans. R. J. C. Broadhurst. Library of Classical Arabic Literature 5. Boston: Twayne Publishers, 1980.

Marie de France. *Les Lais*. Ed. Jean Rychner. Paris: Champion, 1983.

———. *The Lais of Marie de France*. Trans. Robert Hanning and Joan Ferrante. New York: Dutton, 1978.

Nāṣer-e Khosraw's Book of Travels (Safarnāma). Trans. W. M. Thackston, Jr. Persian Heritage Series 36. Albany: State University of New York Press, 1986.

Peter of Les Vaux-de-Cernay. *The History of the Albigensian Crusade*. Trans. W. A. and M. D. Sibly. Woodbridge: Boydell, 1998.

———. *Hystoria Albigensis*. Ed. P. Guébin and E. Lyon. 3 vols. Paris, 1926, 1930, 1939.

The Pilgrim's Guide: A Critical Edition. Ed. Alison Stones and Jeanne Krochalis. London: Harvey Miller Publishers, 1998.

The Poems of the Troubadour Bertran de Born. Ed. William D. Paden, Jr., Tilde Sankovitch, and Patricia H. Stäblein. Berkeley: University of California Press, 1986.

The Poetry of Cercamon and Jaufre Rudel. Ed. and trans. George Wolf and Roy Rosenstein. Garland Library of Medieval Literature, series A, vol. 5. New York: Garland, 1983.

The Poetry of William VII, Count of Poitiers, IX Duke of Aquitaine. Ed. and trans. Gerald A. Bond. Garland Library of Medieval Literature, series A, vol. 4. New York: Garland, 1982.

La Prise d'Orange: Chanson de geste de la fin du XIIᵉ siècle. Trans. Claude Lachet and Jean-Pierre Tusseau. Paris: Editions Klincksieck, 1972.

La Prise d'Orange: Chanson de geste de la fin du XIIᵉ siècle. 7th ed. Ed. Claude Régnier. Paris: Klincksieck, 1986.

Raoul de Cambrai. Ed. and trans. Sarah Kay. Oxford: Clarendon Press, 1992.

Renart, Jean. *Le Roman de la Rose ou de Guillaume de Dole.* Ed. Félix Lecoy. Paris: Champion, 1979.

Robert de Clari. *La Conquête de Constantinople.* Ed. Philippe Lauer. Paris: Champion, 1924.

Robert of Clari. *The Conquest of Constantinople.* Trans. Edgar Holmes McNeal. Toronto: University of Toronto Press, 1996.

The Romance of Floire and Blanchefleur: A French Idyllic Poem of the Twelfth Century. Trans. Merton Jerome Hubert. Chapel Hill: University of North Carolina Press, 1966.

The Song of Roland. Trans. Glyn Burgess. Harmondsworth: Penguin, 1990.

The Song of Roland. Trans. Frederick Goldin. New York: Norton, 1978.

The Song of the Cathar Wars. A History of the Albigensian Crusade. William of Tudela and an Anonymous Successor. Trans. Janet Shirley. Aldershot: Scolar Press, 1996.

The Travels of Ibn Jubayr. Trans. R. J. C. Broadhurst. London: Jonathan Cape, 1952.

Tristan et Iseut: Le poème français—La saga norroise. Ed. and trans. Daniel Lacroix and Philippe Walter. Lettres Gothiques. Paris: Livres de Poche, 1989.

Usāmah ibn Munqidh. *An Arab-Syrian Gentleman and Warrior in the Period of the Crusades: Memoirs of Usamah Ibn Munqidh.* Trans. Philip K. Hitti. Princeton, N.J.: Princeton University Press, 1987.

The Vidas of the Troubadours. Trans. Margarita Egan. Garland Library of Medieval Literature, series B, vol. 6. New York: Garland, 1984.

Le Voyage de Charlemagne à Jérusalem et à Constantinople. Ed. Paul Aebischer. Textes Littéraires Français. Geneva: Droz, 1965.

The World of the Cid: Chronicles of the Spanish Reconquest. Trans. Simon Barton and Richard Fletcher. Manchester: Manchester University Press, 2000.

SECONDARY SOURCES

Abou-el-Haj, Barbara. "Santiago de Compostela in the Time of Diego Gelmírez." *Gesta* 36:2 (1997): 165–79.

Abulafia, David. "The Impact of the Orient: Economic Interactions between East and West in the Medieval Mediterranean." In *Across the Mediterranean Frontiers: Trade, Politics and Religion, 650–1450,* ed. Dionisius A. Agius and Ian Richard Netton. Turnhout: Brepols, 1997, 1–40.

———. *The Two Italies: Economic Relations between the Norman Kingdom of Sicily and the Northern Communes.* Cambridge: Cambridge University Press, 1977.

Abulafia, David, and Nora Berend, eds. *Medieval Frontiers: Concepts and Practices.* Aldershot: Ashgate, 2002.

Abu-Lughod, Janet L. *Before European Hegemony: The World System A.D. 1250–1350.* New York: Oxford University Press, 1989.

Amin, Samir. *Eurocentrism.* Trans. Russell Moore. New York: Monthly Review Press, 1989.

Les Andalousies de Damas à Cordoue: Exposition présentée à l'Institut du monde arabe du 28 novembre 2000 au 15 avril 2001. Paris: Hazan, 2000.

Anderson, Benedict. *Imagined Communities: Reflections on the Origin and Spread of Nationalism.* Rev. ed. London: Verso, 1991.

Andrea, Alfred J. "Essay on Primary Sources." In Queller and Madden, 299–313.

The Art of Medieval Spain, A.D. 500–1200. New York: Metropolitan Museum of Art, 1993.

Atal, Esin, et al. *Islamic Metalwork in the Freer Gallery of Art.* Washington D.C.: Smithsonian, 1985.

Auerbach, Erich. "Roland against Ganelon." In *Mimesis: The Representation of Reality in Western Literature,* trans. Willard R. Trask. Princeton, N.J.: Princeton University Press, 1953, 96–122.

Aurell, Martin. *Les noces du comte: Mariage et pouvoir en Catalogne (785–1213).* Série Histoire Ancienne et Médiévale 32. Paris: Publications de la Sorbonne, 1995.

———. "Le troubadour Gui de Cavaillon (ca. 1175–ca. 1229): Un acteur nobiliaire de la croisade albigeoise." In *Les Voies de l'hérésie,* 2:9–36.

Austin, J. L. *How to Do Things with Words.* 2nd ed. Ed. J. O. Urmson and Marina Sbisà. Cambridge. Mass.: Harvard University Press, 1975.

Azmeh, Aziz al-. "Muslim History: Reflections on Periodisation and Categorisation." *Medieval History Journal* 1 (1998): 211–19.

Baer, Eva. "The Suaire de St. Lazare: An Early Datable Hispano-Islamic Embroidery." *Oriental Art* 13 (1967): 36–48.

Baiffier, Baudouin de. "Relations religieuses de l'Espagne avec le nord de la France: Transfers de reliques (VIIIe-XIIe siècle). *Recherches d'hagiographie latine.* Subsidia Hagiographica 52. Brussels: Société des Bollandistes, 1971, 7–29.

Bakhtin, Mikhail. *The Dialogic Imagination: Four Essays.* Ed. Michael Holquist. Trans. Caryl Emerson and Michael Holquist. Austin: University of Texas Press, 1981.

Baldwin, John W. *Aristocratic Life in Medieval France: The Romances of Jean Renart and Gerbert de Montreuil, 1190–1230.* Baltimore: Johns Hopkins University Press, 2000.

———. *The Government of Philip Augustus: Foundations of French Royal Power in the Middle Ages.* Berkeley: University of California Press, 1986.

Balfour-Paul, Jenny. *Indigo in the Arab World.* Richmond, Surrey: Curzon, 1997.

Baraz, Daniel. *Medieval Cruelty: Changing Perceptions, Late Antiquity to the Early Modern Period.* Ithaca, N.Y.: Cornell University Press, 2003.

Barrucand, Marianne, and Achim Bednorz. *Moorish Architecture in Andalusia.* Trans. Michael Scuffil. Cologne: Taschen Verlag, 1992.

Bartlett, Robert. *The Making of Europe: Conquest, Colonization and Cultural Change, 950–1350.* Princeton, N.J.: Princeton University Press, 1993.

———. "Medieval and Modern Concepts of Race and Ethnicity." *Journal of Medieval and Early Modern Studies* 31:1 (2001): 39–56.

Barton, Simon. "Traitors to the Faith? Christian Mercenaries in al-Andalus and the Maghreb, c. 1100–1300." In *Medieval Spain: Culture, Conflict, and Coexistence.*

Studies in Honour of Angus MacKay, ed. Roger Collins and Anthony Goodman. New York: Palgrave Macmillan, 2002, 23–45.

Beech, George T. "The Eleanor of Aquitaine Vase, William IX of Aquitaine, and Muslim Spain." *Gesta* 32:1 (1993): 3–10.

Beer, Jeanette M. A. *Early Prose in France: Contexts of Bilingualism and Authority.* Kalamazoo, Mich.: Medieval Institute Publications, 1992.

Benton, John. "The *Song of Roland* and the Enculturation of the Warrior Class." *Olifant* 6 (1979): 237–58.

Berend, Nora. *At the Gate of Christendom: Jews, Muslims and "Pagans" in Medieval Hungary, c. 1000–c.1300.* Cambridge: Cambridge University Press, 2001.

Bhabha, Homi K. "DissemiNation: Time, Narrative, and the Margins of the Modern Nation." In *The Location of Culture*, ed. Homi K. Bhabha. London: Routledge, 1990, 139–70.

Bisson, T. N. *The Medieval Crown of Aragon: A Short History.* Oxford: Clarendon Press, 1986.

Blackmore, Josiah, and Gregory S. Hutcheson, eds. *Queer Iberia: Sexualities, Cultures, and Crossings from the Middle Ages to the Renaissance.* Durham, N.C.: Duke University Press, 1999.

Bloch, R. Howard. "842: The First Document and the Birth of Medieval Studies." In *A New History of French Literature*, ed. Denis Hollier. Cambridge, Mass.: Harvard University Press, 1989, 6–13.

———. *Etymologies and Genealogies: A Literary Anthropology of the French Middle Ages.* Chicago: University of Chicago Press, 1983.

———. *Medieval French Literature and Law.* Berkeley: University of California Press, 1977.

———. " 'Mieux vaut jamais que tard': Romance, Philology, and Old French Letters." *Representations* 36 (1991): 64–86.

Bloch, R. Howard, and Stephen G. Nichols, eds. *Medievalism and the Modernist Temper.* Baltimore: Johns Hopkins University Press, 1996.

Boase, Roger. "Arab Influences on European Love Poetry." In Jayyusi, 1:457–82.

Bouchard, Constance Brittain. *Strong of Body, Brave and Noble: Chivalry and Society in Medieval France.* Ithaca, N.Y.: Cornell University Press, 1998.

Brand, Charles M. "The Fourth Crusade: Some Recent Interpretations." *Medievalia et Humanistica* 12 (1984): 33–45.

———. "The Turkish Element in Byzantium, Eleventh-Twelfth Centuries." *Dumbarton Oaks Papers* 43 (1989): 1–25.

Bresc, Henri, et al., eds. *La Méditerranée entre pays d'Islam et monde latin (milieu Xᵉ-milieu XIIIᵉ siècle).* Paris: SEDES, 2001.

Brundage, James A. *Law, Sex, and Christian Society in Medieval Europe.* Chicago: University of Chicago Press, 1987.

Bulliet, Richard W. *The Case for Islamo-Christian Civilization.* New York: Columbia University Press, 2004.

Bullock-Davies, Constance. *Professional Interpreters and the Matter of Britain.* Cardiff: University of Wales Press, 1966.

Burnett, Charles. *The Introduction of Arabic Learning into England.* London: British Library, 1997.

———. "The Translating Activity in Medieval Spain." In Jayyusi 2:1036–58.

Burns, E. Jane. *Courtly Love Undressed: Reading through Clothes in Medieval French Culture.* Philadelphia: University of Pennsylvania Press, 2002.

———, ed. *Medieval Fabrications: Dress, Textiles, Clothwork, and Other Cultural Imaginings.* New York: Palgrave Macmillan, 2004.

Burns, E. Jane, et al. "Feminism and the Discipline of Old French Studies: *Une Bele Disjointure.*" In Bloch and Nichols, 225–66.

Cahen, Claude. *Pre-Ottoman Turkey.* Trans. J. Jones-Williams. New York: Taplinger, 1968.

Catlos, Brian A. "Four Kidnappings in Thirteenth-Century Aragon: Christian Children as Victims of Christian-Muslim Domination." *Scripta Mediterranea* 19–20 (1998–99): 165–79.

———. " 'Mahomet Abenadalill': A Muslim Mercenary in the Service of the Kings of Aragon (1290–1291)." In *Jews, Muslims and Christians in and around the Crown of Aragon: Essays in Honour of Professor Elena Lourie,* ed. Harvey J. Hames. Leiden: Brill, 2004, 257–302.

———. *The Victors and the Vanquished: Christians and Muslims of Catalonia and Aragon, 1050–1300.* Cambridge: Cambridge University Press, 2004.

Cerquiglini, Bernard. "Roland à Roncevaux, ou la trahison des clercs." *Littérature* 42 (1981): 40–56.

Cheyette, Fredric L. *Ermengard of Narbonne and the World of the Troubadours.* Ithaca, N.Y.: Cornell University Press, 2001.

———. "The 'Sale' of Carcassonne to the Count of Barcelona (1067–1070) and the Rise of the Trencavels." *Speculum* 63:4 (1988): 826–64.

Classen, Albrecht, ed. *The Discourse on Love, Marriage, and Transgression in Medieval and Early Modern Literature.* Medieval and Renaissance Texts and Studies 278. Tempe: Arizona Center for Medieval and Renaissance Studies, 2004.

Clifford, James. *Routes: Travel and Translation in the Late Twentieth Century.* Cambridge: Harvard University Press, 1997.

Cohen, Jeffrey Jerome. "Hybrids, Monsters, Borderlands: The Bodies of Gerald of Wales." In Cohen, *Postcolonial Middle Ages,* 85–104.

———, ed. *The Postcolonial Middle Ages.* The New Middle Ages. New York: Palgrave, 2000.

Colliot, Régine. "Images et signes de la femme noble." In *Images et signes de l'Orient dans l'Occident médiéval: Littérature et civilisation.* Sénéfiance 11. Aix: Publications du CUER MA, Université de Provence, 1982, 102–27.

Colloque international sur l'histoire du Caire, 27 mars–5 avril 1969. Cairo: General Egyptian Book Organization, 1972.

Comfort, William Wistar. "The Character Types in the Old French Chansons de geste." *PMLA* 21:2 (1906): 279–434.

———. "The Literary Role of Saracens in the French Epic." *PMLA* 55 (1940): 628–59.

Constable, Olivia Remie. "Genoa and Spain in the Twelfth and Thirteenth Centuries: Notarial Evidence for a Shift in Patterns of Trade." *Journal of European Economic History* 19:3 (1990): 635–56.

———. *Housing the Stranger in the Mediterranean World: Lodging, Trade and Travel in Late Antiquity and the Middle Ages*. Cambridge: Cambridge University Press, 2003.

———. "Muslim Spain and Mediterranean Slavery: The Medieval Slave Trade as an Aspect of Muslim-Christian Relations." In *Christendom and Its Discontents: Exclusion, Persecution, and Rebellion, 1000–1500*, ed. Scott L. Waugh and Peter D. Diehl. Cambridge: Cambridge University Press, 1996, 264–84.

———. *Trade and Traders in Muslim Spain: The Commercial Realignment of the Iberian Peninsula, 900–1500*. Cambridge: Cambridge University Press, 1994.

Contadini, Anna. *Fatimid Art at the Victoria and Albert Museum*. London: V & A Publications, 1998.

Cook, Michael. *The Koran: A Very Short Introduction*. Oxford: Oxford University Press, 2000.

Cook, Robert Francis. *The Sense of the* Song of Roland. Ithaca, N.Y.: Cornell University Press, 1987.

Cowley, F. G. *The Monastic Order in South Wales, 1066–1349*. Cardiff: University of Wales Press, 1977.

Crouch, David. *William Marshal: Court, Career and Chivalry in the Angevin Empire, 1147–1219*. London: Longman, 1990.

Curtius, Ernst Robert. *European Literature and the Latin Middle Ages*. Trans. Willard R. Trask. Princeton, N.J.: Princeton University Press, 1953.

Daniel, Norman. *Heroes and Saracens: An Interpretation of the Chansons de Geste*. Edinburgh: Edinburgh University Press, 1984.

———. *Islam and the West: The Making of an Image*. Edinburgh: Edinburgh University Press, 1960.

Davies, John. *A History of Wales*. London: Allen Lane, 1993.

Davies, R. R. *The Age of Conquest: Wales, 1063–1415*. Oxford: Oxford University Press, 2000.

———. "Henry I and Wales." In *Studies in Medieval History Presented to R. H. C. Davis*, ed. Henry Mayr-Harting and R. I. Moore. London: Hambledon Press, 1985, 133–47.

Day, Gerald W. "Genoa's Eastern Partnership with the House of Montferrat." In *Genoa's Response to Byzantium, 1155–1204: Commercial Expansion and Factionalism in a Medieval City*. Urbana: University of Illinois Press, 1988, 47–69.

de Cant, Geneviève. *Jeanne et Marguerite de Constantinople: Comtesses de Flandre et de Hainaut au XIIIᵉ siècle*. Brussels: Editions Racine, 1995.

Devisse, Jean. *The Image of the Black in Western Art*. Trans. William Granger Ryan. New York: William Morrow, 1979.

de Weever, Jacqueline. *Sheba's Daughters: Whitening and Demonizing the Saracen Woman in Medieval French Epic*. New York: Garland, 1998.

Dickie, James. "The Islamic Garden in Spain." In *The Islamic Garden*, ed. E. B. MacDougall and R. Ettinghausen. Washington, D.C.: Dumbarton Oaks, 1976, 89–105.

Dodds, Jerrilynn D., ed. *Al-Andalus: The Art of Islamic Spain*. New York: Metropolitan Museum of Art, 1992.

Duby, Georges. *Chivalrous Society*. Trans. Cynthia Postan. Berkeley: University of California Press, 1977.

———. *Le dimanche de Bouvines: 27 juillet 1214*. Paris: Gallimard, 1973.

———. "Les 'jeunes' dans la société aristocratique dans la France du Nord-Ouest au XIIᵉ siècle." In *La Société chevaleresque: Hommes et structures du Moyen Age*. Paris: Flammarion, 1988, 129–42.

———. *The Knight, the Lady and the Priest: The Making of Modern Marriage in Medieval France*. Trans. Barbara Bray. New York: Pantheon, 1983.

———. *Love and Marriage in the Middle Ages*. Trans. Jame Dunnett. Chicago: University of Chicago Press, 1994.

———. "The Structure of Kinship and Nobility: Northern France in the Eleventh and Twelfth Centuries." In Duby, *Chivalrous Society*, 134–48.

———. *The Three Orders: Feudal Society Imagined*. Trans. Arthur Goldhammer. Chicago: University of Chicago Press, 1980.

Dufournet, Jean. *Les écrivains de la IVᵉ croisade, Villehardouin et Clari*. Paris: SEDES, 1973.

Duggan, Joseph J. *A Concordance of the* Chanson de Roland. Columbus: Ohio State University Press, 1969.

———. "L'Episode d'Aude dans la tradition en rime de la *Chanson de Roland*." In *Charlemagne in the North: Proceedings of the Twelfth International Conference of the Société Rencesvals*. Edinburgh: Société Rencesvals British Branch, 1993, 273–79.

———. "Franco-German Conflict and the History of French Scholarship on the *Song of Roland*." In *Hermeneutics and Medieval Culture*, ed. Patrick Gallacher and Helen Damico. Albany: State University of New York Press, 1989, 97–106.

———. *The Song of Roland: Formulaic Style and Poetic Craft*. Berkeley: University of California Press, 1973.

Dunbabin, Jean. *France in the Making, 843–1180*. Oxford: Oxford University Press, 1985.

Ebitz, David. "Secular to Sacred: The Transformation of an Oliphant in the Musée de Cluny." *Gesta* 25:1 (1986): 31–38.

Edbury, Peter W. *The Kingdom of Cyprus and the Crusades, 1191–1374*. Cambridge: Cambridge University Press, 1991.

Encyclopaedia of Islam. New ed. Leiden: Brill, 1960–.

L'Epopée romane. Actes du XVe Congrès International Rencesvals, Poitiers, 21–27 août 2000. 2 vols. Ed. Gabriel Bianciotto and Claudio Galderisi. Poitiers: Centre d'Etudes Supérieures de Civilisation Médiévale, 2002.

Epstein, Steven A. *Genoa and the Genoese, 958–1528*. Chapel Hill: University of North Carolina Press, 1996.

———. *Speaking of Slavery: Color, Ethnicity, and Human Bondage in Italy*. Ithaca, N.Y.: Cornell University Press, 2001.

Evergates, Theodore. "Aristocratic Women in the County of Champagne." In *Aristocratic Women in Medieval France*, ed. Theodore Evergates. Philadelphia: University of Pennsylvania Press, 1999, 74–110.

Evergates, Theodore, ed. and trans. *Feudal Society in Medieval France: Documents from the County of Champagne.* Philadelphia: University of Pennsylvania Press, 1993.

Fierro, Maribel. *Al-Andalus: Savoirs et échanges culturels.* Trans. Anne-Marie Lapillonne. Encyclopédie de la Méditerranée. Aix-en-Provence: Edisud, 2001.

Fleischman, Suzanne. "On the Representation of History and Fiction in the Middle Ages." *History and Theory* 22:3 (1983): 278–310.

Fletcher, Richard. *Moorish Spain.* Berkeley: University of California Press, 1992.

———. *The Quest for the Cid.* New York: Oxford University Press, 1989.

Forey, Alan. "The Military Orders and the Conversion of Muslims in the Twelfth and Thirteenth Centuries." *Journal of Medieval History* 28 (2002): 1–22.

Fossier, Robert. *La Terre et les hommes en Picardie jusqu'à la fin du XIIIᵉ siècle.* 2 vols. Paris: Béatrice-Nauwelaerts, 1968.

François, Charles. " 'Floire et Blancheflor': Du chemin de Compostelle au chemin de la Mecque." *Revue Belge de Philologie et d'Histoire* 44 (1966): 833–58.

Frank, Istvan. "Tomier et Palaizi, troubadours tarasconnais (1199–1226)." *Romania* 78 (1957): 46–85.

Friedman, John Block. *The Monstrous Races in Medieval Art and Thought.* Cambridge, Mass.: Harvard University Press, 1981.

Garland, Lynda. *Byzantine Empresses: Women and Power in Byzantium, A.D. 527–1204.* London: Routledge, 1999.

Gaunt, Simon. *Gender and Genre in Medieval French Literature.* Cambridge: Cambridge University Press, 1995.

Geary, Patrick. *Furta Sacra: Thefts of Relics in the Central Middle Ages.* Rev. ed. Princeton, N.J.: Princeton University Press, 1990.

Giffen, Lois A. "Ibn Hazm and the *Tawq al-Hamama*." In Jayyusi, 1:420–42.

Gillingham, John. *Richard the Lionheart.* New York: Times Books, 1978.

Godfrey, John. *1204: The Unholy Crusade.* Oxford: Oxford University Press, 1980.

Goitein, S. D. *A Mediterranean Society: The Jewish Communities of the World as Portrayed in the Documents of the Cairo Geniza.* 5 vols. Berkeley: University of California Press, 1967–88.

———. *Studies in Islamic History & Institutions.* Leiden: Brill, 1966.

Gonzálvez, Ramón. "The Persistence of the Mozarabic Liturgy in Toledo after A.D. 1080." In *Santiago, Saint-Denis, and Saint Peter: The Reception of the Roman Liturgy in León-Castile in 1080,* ed. Bernard F. Reilly. New York: Fordham University Press, 1985, 157–85.

Gordon, Stewart, ed. *Robes and Honor: The Medieval World of Investiture.* New York: Palgrave, 2001.

Goss, Vladimir P., and Christine Verzár Bornstein, eds. *The Meeting of Two Worlds: Cultural Exchange between East and West during the Period of the Crusades.* Kalamazoo, Mich.: Medieval Institute Publications, 1986.

Grabar, Oleg. "The Shared Culture of Objects." In *Byzantine Court Culture from 829 to 1204,* ed. Henry Maguire. Washington, D.C.: Dumbarton Oaks, 1997, 115–29.

Gravdal, Kathryn. *Ravishing Maidens: Writing Rape in Medieval French Literature and Law.* Philadelphia: University of Pennsylvania Press, 1991.

Greimas, A. J. *Dictionnaire de l'ancien français jusqu'au milieu du XIVe siècle.* 2nd ed. Paris: Larousse, 1968.

Grieve, Patricia E. Floire and Blancheflor *and the European Romance.* Cambridge: Cambridge University Press, 1997.

Guenée, Bernard. "Les généalogies entre l'histoire et la politique: La fierté d'être Capétien, en France, au moyen âge." *Annales ESC* 33:3 (1978): 450–77.

Guerreau, Alain. *L'avenir d'un passé incertain: Quelle histoire du Moyen Age au XXIe siècle?* Paris: Seuil, 2001.

Guichard, Pierre. *Al-Andalus 711–1492: Une histoire de l'Andalousie arabe.* Paris: Hachette Littératures, 2000.

Haidu, Peter. *The Subject Medieval/Modern: Text and Governance in the Middle Ages.* Stanford, Calif. Stanford University Press, 2004.

———. *The Subject of Violence: The* Song of Roland *and the Birth of the State.* Bloomington: Indiana University Press, 1993.

Hamilton, Bernard. "Knowing the Enemy: Western Understanding of Islam at the Time of the Crusades." In *Crusaders, Cathars and the Holy Places.* Aldershot: Ashgate/Variorum, 1999.

Harris, Julie A. "Redating the Arca Santa of Oviedo." *Art Bulletin* 77:1 (1995): 82–93.

Harrison, Ann Tukey. "Aude and Bramimonde: Their Importance in the *Chanson de Roland.*" *French Review* 54 (1981): 672–79.

Hartman, Richard. *La Quête et la croisade: Villehardouin, Clari, et le* Lancelot en prose. New York: Postillion Press, 1977.

Harvey, Ruth. "Courtly Culture in Medieval Occitania." In *The Troubadours: An Introduction,* ed. Simon Gaunt and Sarah Kay. Cambridge: Cambridge University Press, 1999, 8–27.

Hattstein, Markus, and Peter Delius, eds. *Islam: Art and Architecture.* Cologne: Könemann, 2000.

Hendrickson, William L. "*Garin de Monglane* and *La chanson de la croisade albigeoise*: A Comparative Old French-Occitanian Study." In *Continuations: Essays on Medieval French Literature and Language,* ed. Norris J. Lacy and Gloria Torrini-Roblin. Birmingham: Summa Publications, 1989, 203–15.

Heng, Geraldine. *Empire of Magic: Medieval Romance and the Politics of Cultural Fantasy.* New York: Columbia University Press, 2003.

Hillenbrand, Robert. *Islamic Architecture: Form, Function, and Meaning.* New York: Columbia University Press, 1994.

———. " 'The Ornament of the World': Medieval Córdoba as a Cultural Centre." In *Jayyusi,* 1:112–35.

Hilsdale, Cecily. "Constructing a Byzantine *Augusta*: A Greek Book for a French Bride." *Art Bulletin* 87:3 (2005): 458–83.

Hitti, Philip K. "The Impact of the Crusades on Moslem Lands." In *The Impact of the Crusades on the Near East, History of the Crusades,* vol. 5, ed. Norman P. Zacour and Harry W. Hazard. Madison: University of Wisconsin Press, 1985.

Hoffman, Eva R. "Pathways of Portability: Islamic and Christian Interchange from the Tenth to the Twelfth Century." *Art History* 24 (2001): 17–50.

Hult, David. "Gaston Paris and the Invention of Courtly Love." In Bloch and Nichols, 192–224.

Huot, Sylvia. "The Political Implications of Poetic Discourse in *The Song of the Albigensian Crusade*." *French Forum* 9:2 (1984): 133–44.

Ingham, Patricia Clare. *Sovereign Fantasies: Arthurian Romance and the Making of Britain*. Philadelphia: University of Pennsylvania Press, 2001.

Ingham, Patricia Clare, and Michelle R. Warren. *Postcolonial Moves: Medieval through Modern*. New York: Palgrave, 2003.

Jayyusi, Salma Khadra, ed. *The Legacy of Muslim Spain*. 2 vols. Leiden: Brill, 1992.

Jeffreys, Elizabeth, and Michael Jeffreys. "The 'Wild Beast from the West': Immediate Literary Reactions in Byzantium to the Second Crusade." In Laiou and Mottahedeh, 101–16.

Jones, George Fenwick. *The Ethos of the Song of Roland*. Baltimore: Johns Hopkins University Press, 1963.

Jonin, Pierre. "Le climat de croisade des chansons de geste." *Cahiers de civilisation médiévale* 7 (1964): 277–88.

Kay, Sarah. *The Chansons de Geste in the Age of Romance: Political Fictions*. Oxford: Clarendon Press, 1995.

Kazhdan, Alexander. "Latin and Franks in Byzantium: Perception and Reality from the Eleventh to the Twelfth Century." In Laiou and Mottahedeh, 83–100.

Kedar, Benjamin Z. *Crusade and Mission: European Approaches toward the Muslims*. Princeton, N.J.: Princeton University Press, 1984.

Kenaan-Kedar, Nurith. "Aliénor d'Aquitaine conduite en captivité: Les peintures murales commémoratives de Sainte-Radegonde de Chinon." *Cahiers de Civilisation Médiévale* 41 (1998): 317–30.

Kennedy, Hugh. *Muslim Spain and Portugal: A Political History of al-Andalus*. London: Longman, 1996.

Kinoshita, Sharon. "Almería Silk and the French Feudal Imaginary: Toward a 'Material' History of the Medieval Mediterranean." In Burns, *Medieval Fabrications*, 165–76.

———. "Cherchez la femme: Feminist Criticism and Marie de France's *Lai de Lanval*." *Romance Notes* 34:3 (1994): 263–73.

———. "Discrepant Medievalisms: Deprovincializing the Middle Ages." In *Worldings: World Literature, Field Imaginaries, Future Practices, Doing Cultural Studies in the Era of Globalization*, ed. Rob Wilson. Santa Cruz: New Pacific Press, forthcoming.

———. "Fraternizing with the Enemy: Christian-Saracen Relations in *Raoul de Cambrai*." In *L'Epopée romane*, 2:695–703.

———. "Heldris de Cornuälle's *Roman de Silence* and the Feudal Politics of Lineage." *PMLA* 110:3 (1995): 397–409.

———. " 'Pagans Are Wrong and Christians Are Right': Alterity, Gender, and Nation in the *Chanson de Roland*." *Journal of Medieval and Early Modern Studies* 31:1 (2001): 79–111.

———. "The Poetics of *Translatio*: French-Byzantine Relations in Chrétien de Troyes's *Cligés*." *Exemplaria* 8:2 (1996): 315–54.

———. "Political Uses and Responses to the Poem: Cultural Studies and Orientalism." In *MLA Approaches to Teaching the Song of Roland*, ed. William Kibler and Leslie Z. Morgan. New York: Modern Language Association, forthcoming.

———. "The Politics of Courtly Love: *La Prise d'Orange* and the Conversion of the Saracen Queen." *Romanic Review* 86:2 (1995): 265–87.

———. "Royal Pursuits: Adultery and Kingship in Marie de France's *Equitan*." *Essays in Medieval Studies* 16 (2000): 41–51.

———. "Two for the Price of One: Courtly Love and Serial Polygamy in the *Lais* of Marie de France." *Arthuriana* 8:2 (1998): 33–55.

Kittay, Jeffrey and Wlad Godzich. *The Emergence of Prose: An Essay in Prosaics*. Minneapolis: University of Minnesota Press, 1987.

Knudson, Charles A. "Le thème de la princesse sarrasine dans *La Prise d'Orange*." *Romance Philology* 22:4 (1969): 449–62.

Kosto, Adam J. "The *Liber feudorum maior* of the Counts of Barcelona: The Cartulary as an Expression of Power." *Journal of Medieval History* 27 (2001): 1–22.

Krueger, Roberta L., ed. *The Cambridge Companion to Medieval Romance*. Cambridge: Cambridge University Press, 2000.

Lacarra, José María. *Alfonso el Batallador*. Saragossa: Guara Editorial, 1978.

———. "La Conquista de Zaragoza por Alfonso I (18 diciembre 1118)." *Al-Andalus* 12 (1947): 65–96.

Lachet, Claude. La Prise d'Orange *ou la parodie courtoise d'une épopée*. Paris: Champion, 1986.

Lafont, Robert. "Guilhem de Tudela, ses origines, les origines de son art." In *Les Troubadours et l'Etat toulousain avant la Croisade (1209)*, ed. Arno Krispin. Annales de Littérature Occitane 1. Bordes: Centre d'Etude de la Littérature Occitane, 1994, 219–28.

Laiou, Angeliki E., and Roy Parviz Mottahedeh, eds. *The Crusades from the Perspective of Byzantium and the Muslim World*. Washington, D.C.: Dumbarton Oaks, 2001.

Langlois, Ernest. *Table des noms propres de toute nature compris dans les chansons de geste imprimées*. Paris: Emile Bouillon, 1904.

Leclanche, Jean-Luc. "La date du conte de *Floire et Blancheflor*." *Romania* 92 (1971): 556–67.

Le Goff, Jacques. *Medieval Civilization, 400–1500*. Trans. Julia Barrow. London: Basil Blackwell, 1988.

———. *Time, Work, and Culture in the Middle Ages*. Trans. Arthur Goldhammer. Chicago: University of Chicago Press, 1980.

Le Patourel, John. *The Norman Empire*. Oxford: Clarendon Press, 1976.

Leupin, Alexandre. "La compromission (sur *Le voyage de Charlemagne à Jérusalem et à Constantinople*)." *Romance Notes* 23:3 (1985): 222–38.

Lloyd, John Edward. *A History of Wales from the Earliest Times to the Edwardian Conquest*. 3rd ed. Vol. 2. London: Longmans, 1939.

Lomax, Derek W. *The Reconquest of Spain*. London: Longman, 1978.

Lot-Borodine, Myrrha. *Le Roman idyllique au Moyen Age.* Paris: Auguste Picard, 1913.

Macé, Laurent. *Les comtes de Toulouse et leur entourage, XIIᵉ-XIIIᵉ siècles: Rivalités, alliances et jeux de pouvoir.* Toulouse: Privat, 2000.

MacInnes, John W. "Gloriette: The Function of the Tower and the Name in the *Prise d'Orange.*" *Olifant* 10:1–2 (1983).

MacKay, Angus. *Spain in the Middle Ages: From Frontier to Empire, 1000–1500.* London: Macmillan, 1977.

Maddox, Donald. "Domesticating Diversity: Female Founders in Medieval Genealogical Literature and *La Fille du Comte de Pontieu.*" In *The Court and Cultural Diversity: Selected Papers from the Eighth Triennial Congress,* ed. Evelyn Mullally and John Thompson. Cambridge: D. S. Brewer, 1997, 97–107.

Magdalino, Paul. *The Empire of Manuel I Komnenos, 1143–1180.* Cambridge: Cambridge University Press, 1993.

Malo, Henri. *Un grand feudataire: Renaud de Dammartin et la coalition de Bouvines.* Paris: Champion, 1898.

Matthew, Donald. *The Norman Kingdom of Sicily.* Cambridge: Cambridge University Press, 1992.

May, Florence Lewis. *Silk Textiles of Spain: Eighth to Fifteenth Century.* New York: Hispanic Society of America, 1957.

McCracken, Peggy. *The Romance of Adultery: Queenship and Sexual Transgression in Old French Literature.* Philadelphia: University of Pennsylvania Press, 1998.

———. "Scandalizing Desire: Eleanor and the Chroniclers." In *Eleanor of Aquitaine: Collected Essays,* ed. John Carmi Parsons and Bonnie Wheeler. New York: St. Martin's, 1999, 247–63.

McNeill, William H. *Venice: the Hinge of Europe, 1081–1797.* Chicago: University of Chicago Press, 1974.

Menocal, María Rosa. *The Arabic Role in Medieval Literary History: A Forgotten Heritage.* Philadelphia: University of Pennsylvania Press, 1987.

———. *The Ornament of the World: How Muslims, Jews, and Christians Created a Culture of Tolerance in Medieval Spain.* Boston: Little, Brown, 2002.

———. *Shards of Love: Exile and the Origins of the Lyric.* Durham: Duke University Press, 1994.

———. "Signs of the Times: Self, Other and History in *Aucassin.*" *Romanic Review* 80:4 (1989): 497–511.

Merceron, Jacques. "Par desoz terre une volte soltive: Etude du cliché narratif du souterrain sarrasin utilisé lors d'un siège ou d'une évasion épiques." In *L'Epopée romane,* 937–47.

Moore, R. I. *The Formation of a Persecuting Society: Power and Deviance in Western Europe, 950–1250.* Oxford: Basil Blackwell, 1987.

Nelson, Lynn H. *The Normans in South Wales, 1070–1171.* Austin: University of Texas Press, 1966.

Nicholson, Helen. *Templars, Hospitallers and Teutonic Knights: Images of the Military Orders, 1128–1291.* Leicester: Leicester University Press, 1993.

Nicol, Donald M. "The Crusades and the Unity of Christendom." In Goss and Bornstein, 169–80.

Nirenberg, David. *Communities of Violence: Persecution of Minorities in the Middle Ages*. Princeton, N.J.: Princeton University Press, 1996.

Norwich, John Julius. *The Kingdom of the Sun, 1130–1194*. London: Faber and Faber, 1976.

O'Callaghan, Joseph. *A History of Medieval Spain*. Ithaca, N.Y.: Cornell University Press, 1975.

Parsons, John Carmi. *Eleanor of Castile: Queen and Society in Thirteenth-Century England*. New York: St. Martin's, 1995.

Partearroyo, Cristina. "Almoravid and Almohad Textiles." In Dodds, 105–13.

Paterson, Linda M. *The World of the Troubadours: Medieval Occitan Society, c. 1100–c. 1300*. Cambridge: Cambridge University Press, 1993.

Pauphilet, Albert. "Villehardouin, Robert de Clari et la Conquête de Constantinople." In *Le Legs du Moyen Age: Etudes de littérature médiévale*. Melun: Librairie d'Argences, 1950.

Pernoud, Régine, and Geneviève de Cant. *Isambour: la reine captive*. Paris: Stock, 1987.

Phillips, William D., Jr. *Slavery from Roman Times to the Early Transatlantic Trade*. Minneapolis: University of Minnesota Press, 1985.

Prawer, Joshua. "The Roots of Medieval Colonialism." In Goss and Bornstein, 23–38.

Pryce, Huw, ed. *Literacy in Medieval Celtic Societies*. Cambridge: Cambridge University Press, 1998.

Pryce, Huw. *Native Law and the Church in Medieval Wales*. Oxford: Clarendon Press, 1993.

Queller, Donald E., and Thomas F. Madden. *The Fourth Crusade: The Conquest of Constantinople*. 2nd ed. Philadelphia: University of Pennsylvania Press, 1997.

Raymond, André. *Cairo*. Trans. Willard Wood. Cambridge, Mass.: Harvard University Press, 2000.

Reilly, Bernard F. *The Medieval Spains*. Cambridge: Cambridge University Press, 1993.

Renan, Ernest. "Qu'est-ce qu'une Nation? (Conférence faite en Sorbonne, le 11 mars 1882)." In *Oeuvres complètes de Ernest Renan*, ed. Henriette Psichari. Paris: Calmann-Lévy, 1947, 1:887–906.

Reynolds, Susan. *Fiefs and Vassals: The Medieval Experience Reinterpreted*. Oxford: Oxford University Press, 1994.

Riley-Smith, Jonathan. *The Crusades: A Short History*. New Haven, Conn.: Yale University Press, 1987.

———. *The First Crusade and the Idea of Crusading*. Philadelphia: University of Pennsylvania Press, 1986.

———. "History, the Crusades and the Latin East, 1095–1204." In *Crusaders and Muslims in Twelfth-Century Syria*, ed. Maya Shatzmiller. The Medieval Mediterranean: Peoples, Economies and Cultures 1. Leiden: Brill, 1993, 1–17.

Robinson, Cynthia. "Arts of the Taifa Kingdoms." In Dodds, 49–61.

———. "Seeing Paradise: Metaphor and Vision in *taifa* Palace Architecture." *Gesta* 36:2 (1997): 145–55.

Rollo, David. *Historical Fabrication, Ethnic Fable and French Romance in Twelfth-Century England.* Lexington: French Forum, 1998.

Roquebert, Michel. *Histoire des Cathares: Hérésie, Croisade, Inquisition du XIe au XIVe siècle.* Paris: Perrin, 1999.

Ruggles, D. Fairchild. "Mothers of a Hybrid Dynasty: Race, Genealogy, and Acculturation in Al-Andalus." *Journal of Medieval and Early Modern Studies* 34:1 (2004): 65–94.

Runciman, Steven. *A History of the Crusades.* 3 vols. Harmondsworth: Penguin, 1981.

Safran, Janina M. *The Second Umayyad Caliphate: The Articulation of Caliphal Legitimacy in Al-Andalus.* Cambridge, Mass: Harvard University Press, 2000.

Said, Edward W. *Orientalism.* New York: Random House, 1978.

Samaran, Charles. "Sur la date approximative du *Roland* d'Oxford." *Romania* 94:4 (1973): 523–27.

Sanders, Paula. "Robes of Honor in Fatimid Egypt." In Gordon, 225–39.

Sayers, Jane. *Innocent III: Leader of Europe, 1198–1216.* London: Longman, 1994.

Schulze-Busacker, Elisabeth. "French Conceptions of Foreigners and Foreign Languages in the Twelfth and Thirteenth Centuries." *Romance Philology* 41:1 (1987): 24–47.

Sénac, Philippe. *Les Carolingiens et al-Andalus: VIIIe-IXe siècles.* Paris: Maisonneuve et Larose, 2002.

Serjeant, R. B. *Islamic Textiles: Material for a History up to the Mongol Conquest.* Beirut: Librarie du Liban, 1972.

Short, Ian. "The Oxford Manuscript of the *Chanson de Roland*: A Palaeographic Note." *Romania* 94:2 (1973): 221–31.

Sigal, Pierre André. "Les différents types de pèlerinages." In *Santiago de Compostela: 1000 ans de Pèlerinage Européen.* Ghent: Centrum voor Kunst en Cultuur, 1985.

Simeti, Mary Taylor. *Travels with a Medieval Queen.* New York: Farrar, Straus and Giroux, 2001.

Sivéry, Gérard. *Philippe Auguste.* Paris: Plon, 1993.

Smail, R. C. *Crusading Warfare, 1097–1193.* Cambridge: Cambridge University Press, 1956.

Southern, R. W. *Western Views of Islam in the Middle Ages.* Cambridge, Mass.: Harvard University Press, 1962.

Spatharakis, Iohannis. *The Portrait in Byzantine Illuminated Manuscripts.* Leiden: Brill, 1976.

Spiegel, Gabrielle M. "Genealogy: Form and Function in Medieval Historiography." In *The Past as Text: The Theory and Practice of Medieval Historiography.* Baltimore: Johns Hopkins University Press, 1997, 99–110.

———. *Romancing the Past: The Rise of Vernacular Prose Historiography in Thirteenth-Century France.* Berkeley: University of California Press, 1993.

Spivak, Gayatri Chakravorty. "Can the Subaltern Speak?" In *Marxism and the Interpretation of Culture*, ed. Cary Nelson and Lawrence Grossberg. Champaign: University of Illinois Press, 1988, 271–313.

Staffa, Susan Jane. *Conquest and Fusion: The Social Evolution of Cairo A.D. 642–1850.* Leiden: Brill, 1977.

Stranges, John A. "The Significance of Bramimonde's Conversion in the *Song of Roland*." *Romance Notes* 16 (1974): 190–96.

Sumption, Jonathan. *The Albigensian Crusade.* London: Faber and Faber, 1978.

Swanton, R. N. *The Twelfth-Century Renaissance.* Manchester: Manchester University Press, 1999.

Thompson, Kathleen. *Power and Border Lordship in Medieval France: The County of the Perche, 1000–1226.* Woodbridge: Boydell Press, 2002.

Tolan, John. "Mirror of Chivalry: Salah al-Din in the Medieval European Imagination." In *Images of the Other: Europe and the Muslim World before 1700,* ed. David R. Blanks. Cairo: American University in Cairo Press, 1996, 7–38.

———. *Saracens: Islam in the Medieval European Imagination.* New York: Columbia University Press, 2002.

Les Trésors fatimides du Caire: Exposition présentée à l'Institut du monde arabe du 28 avril au 30 août 1998. Paris: Institut du Monde Arabe, 1998.

Vance, Eugene. *Reading the Song of Roland.* Englewood Cliffs, N.J.: Prentice-Hall, 1970.

———. "Roland and Charlemagne: The Remembering Voices and the Crypt." In *Mervelous Signals: Poetics and Sign Theory in the Middle Ages.* Lincoln: University of Nebraska Press, 1986, 51–85.

———. "Semiotics and Power: Relics, Icons, and the *Voyage de Charlemagne à Jérusalem et à Constantinople*." *Romanic Review* 79:1 (1988): 164–83.

Les Voies de l'hérésie: Le groupe aristocratique en Languedoc (XI-XIIIᵉ s.), Actes de la 8ᵉ session d'histoire médiévale du Centre d'Etudes Cathares. 3 vols. Heresis 8. Carcassonne: Centre d'Etudes Cathares, 1995.

Walker, David. *Medieval Wales.* Cambridge: Cambridge University Press, 1990.

Wallace, David. *Chaucerian Polity: Absolutist Lineages and Associational Forms in England and Italy.* Stanford, Calif. Stanford University Press, 1997.

Warren, F. M. "The Enamoured Moslem Princess in Orderic Vital and the French Epic." *PMLA* 29 (1914): 341–58.

Warren, Michelle R. *History on the Edge: Excalibur and the Borders of Britain, 1100–1300.* Minneapolis: University of Minnesota Press, 2000.

———. "The Noise of Roland." *Exemplaria* 16:2 (2004): 277–304.

Warren, W. L. *Henry II.* Berkeley: University of California Press, 1973.

Wehr, Hans. *A Dictionary of Modern Written Arabic (Arabic-English).* Ed. J. Milton Cowan. 4th ed. Ithaca, N.Y.: Spoken Language Services, 1994.

Werckmeister, O. K. "Cluny III and the Pilgrimage to Santiago de Compostela." *Gesta* 27:1–2 (1988): 103–12.

Williams, John Bryan. "The Making of a Crusade: the Genoese Anti-Muslim Attacks in Spain, 1146–1148." *Journal of Medieval History* 23:1 (1997): 29–53.

Wolff, Philippe, ed. *Histoire du Languedoc.* Toulouse: Privat, 1967.

Wolff, Robert Lee. "Baldwin of Flanders and Hainaut, First Latin Emperor of Constantinople: His Life, Death, and Resurrection, 1172–1225." *Speculum* 27:3 (1952): 281–322.

Zambon, Francesco. "La notion de *Paratge*, des troubadours à la *Chanson de la Croisade Albigeoise*." In *Les Voies de l'hérésie*, 3:9–27.

Zumthor, Paul. *La Mesure du monde: Représentation de l'espace au Moyen Age*. Paris: Seuil, 1993.

Index

ᶜAbd al-Raḥmān III, 181, 184, 255 n.31, 260 n.76

Abulafia, David, 2

Adelard of Bath, 7, 85–86

al-ᶜĀdil, 8, 195 (tab. 6.2), 197, 279 n.67

Adrianople, battle of, 170–71, 174

Agnes of France (Byzantine empress), 146, 147 (tab. 5.1), 155–58 (and tab. 5.3), 178 (tab. 6.1), 271 nn. 35, 40, 272 n.58

Akbari, Suzanne Conklin, 1

Alain de Roucy, 224, 226, 228

Albigensian crusades (1209–29), 2, 4, 10, 73, 136, 200–235, 236

Aleume de Clari, 143, 167–70

Alexios I Comnenos (Byzantine emperor), 28, 147 (tab. 5.1), 148

Alexios II Comnenos (Byzantine emperor), 146, 147 (tab. 5.1), 157, 158 (tab. 5.3), 178 (tab. 6.1)

Alexios III Angelos (Byzantine emperor), 146, 147 (tab. 5.1)

Alexios IV Angelos (Byzantine emperor) (*droit oir*), 143, 145, 147 (and tab. 5.1), 163–66

Alexios V Ducas (Murzuphlus), 164–66, 167–68

Alfonso I the Battler of Aragon, 6, 19, 21 (and tab. 1.1), 25, 40, 207 (tab. 7.1), 243 n.28

Alfonso II of Aragon, 51 (tab. 2.1), 53, 207 (tab. 7.1), 234, 284 nn. 43, 49

Alfonso VI of León-Castile, 18–19, 79, 243 n.26, 253 n.10

Alfonso VII of Castile, 182

Algeria, 15, 47

Alice of France (countess of Ponthieu), 177, 178 (tab. 6.1), 195 (and tab. 6.2), 198

Aljafería, 20

Almería, 181–83, 186, 242 n.9, 275 nn. 16, 20, 21, 25; fictional representations of, 51, 187, 254 n.13

Almohads, 136, 182, 207, 242 n.18

Almoravids, 6, 22, 82, 182, 241 n.9, 256 n.34, 275 n.19

alterity, 5, 12, 16, 35, 45, 53, 54

amor de lonh, 50, 60, 115, 124, 129. *See also* Jaufre Rudel

Anderson, Benedict, 200

Andronicos I (Byzantine emperor), 146, 147 (tab. 5.1), 157, 158 (tab. 5.3), 271 n.39, 272 n.58

Aragon, Crown of, 3. *See also names of individual kings*

Armenians, 28, 29, 245 n.48

Arnaud-Amaury (papal legate), 203–4, 234

Arthur of Brittany, 136, 141, 148, 150 (tab. 5.2)

Aucassin et Nicolette, 9, 10, 12, 64–66, 78, 87, 138, 160, 233–34, 253 n.5

Aude, 15–16, 34, 41–44, 46, 246 nn. 72, 73

Babylon, 92–103; emir of, 33–34, 278 n.55. *See also* Cairo

Baldwin IX (count of Flanders), 135, 141, 150 (tab. 5.2), 153, 158 (tab. 5.3), 174, 177, 273 nn. 63, 64; as Latin Emperor of Constantinople, 166, 170–71, 173

Bartlett, Robert, 8, 16, 29, 54, 107–8, 174

Basques, 17, 249 n.25

Beaucaire, 12, 201, 217, 221–26, 232–34

Becket, Thomas, 4, 7, 165

Bédier, Joseph, 77, 244 n.34

Berengaria of Navarre (queen of England), 195 (and tab. 6.2), 196 (and tab. 6.3), 198, 217 (tab. 7.2), 280 n.71, 281 n.12

Bertran de Born, 219–21, 283 nn. 40, 41, 284 n.47

Boris (king of Vlachia), 171–72

Bouchard, Constance Brittain, 2

Bouvines, battle of (1214), 2, 4, 137, 138, 178, 198, 204, 234

Acknowledgments

Medieval Boundaries owes much to the unique intellectual environment at the University of California, Santa Cruz. My greatest debt is to past and present members of the Literature Department's caucus in World Literature and Cultural Studies, who taught me, in varied and inspiring ways, what it means to think critically and historically about literary and cultural production: my thanks to Chris Connery, Carla Freccero, Susan Gillman, Kristin Ross, Dan Selden, José David Saldívar, Carter Wilson, Rob Wilson, and the late Roberto Crespi. The Center for Cultural Studies (under its founder, Jim Clifford, and its subsequent directors, Gail Hershatter and Chris Connery) has provided a steady stream of conferences and lectures, making it easy to follow emerging critical trends in a wide range of disciplines. The group in Pre- and Early-Modern Studies has been a welcome presence. Special thanks to Virginia Jansen for her insights on medieval visual culture, and to Brian Catlos for his encyclopedic responses to my queries on medieval Iberia. Brian Miller graciously allowed me to audit his course in introductory Arabic. I gratefully acknowledge the support of the Academic Senate of the University of California, Santa Cruz (in providing research funds) and the Institute for Humanities Research (in affording me precious release time at key stages of this project). Thanks are also due the staff of McHenry Library (especially Beth Remak-Honnef) and Interlibrary Loan for cheerful assistance of various kinds. Not least, I wish to thank my students at UC Santa Cruz, who were in several instances the first audience for the ideas developed in this book. Judy Haas, Valerie Kaussen, Veronica Kirk-Clausen, Hellen Lee, Rebecca Wilcox, and Cathy Yu responded with enthusiasm and insight. Special thanks to Jason Jacobs, who provided extraordinary editorial assistance at the conclusion of this project and who has been a valued interlocutor all along.

In the wider world of academia, I wish to thank the friends and colleagues whose timely invitations allowed me to try early versions of my ideas out on lively and informed audiences: Barbara Altmann and Gina Psaki (University of Oregon), Cynthia Brown (UC Santa Barbara), Lisa

Lampert (University of Illinois), Peggy McCracken and Cathy Sanok (University of Michigan), and Jack Niles (UC Berkeley). Others who have been gracious in giving encouragement, sharing work prior to publication, or providing venues for discussion include Jane Burns, Albrecht Classen, Cecily Hilsdale, Patty Ingham, Karen Mathews, and Michelle Warren. Will Crooke read numerous drafts and contributed many valuable suggestions.

Earlier versions of the material in this book have appeared in " 'Pagans Are Wrong and Christians Are Right': Alterity, Gender and Nation in the *Chanson de Roland*," *Journal of Medieval and Early Modern Studies* 31.1 (2001): 79–111; "The Politics of Courtly Love: *La Prise d'Orange* and the Conversion of the Saracen Queen," *Romanic Review* 86.2 (1995): 265–87; "In the Beginning Was the Road: *Floire et Blancheflor* and the Politics of Translation," in *Traduire au moyen âge*, ed. Rosalynn Voaden et al. (Turnhout: Brepols, 2001), 223–34; "Colonial Possessions: Wales and the Anglo-Norman Imaginary in the *Lais* of Marie de France," in *The Discourse on Love, Marriage, and Transgression in Medieval and Early Modern Literature*, ed. Albrecht Classen (Tempe: Arizona Center for Medieval and Renaissance Studies, 2004), 147–62; "Brave New Worlds: Robert de Clari's *La Conquête de Constantinople*," in *The Crusades: Other Experiences, Alternate Perspectives. Selected Proceedings from the 32nd Annual Cemers Conference*, ed. Khalil I. Semaan (Binghamton, N.Y.: Center for Medieval and Early Renaissance Studies, Global Academic Publishing, 2003), 161–77; and "The Romance of MiscegeNation: Negotiating Identities in *La Fille du Comte de Pontieu*," in *Postcolonial Moves: Medieval through Modern*, ed. Patricia Clare Ingham and Michelle Warren (New York: Palgrave, 2003), 111–31. My thanks to the publishers for permission to reprint.

Finally, for their long years of friendship—for cheerfully humoring my obsession with the Middle Ages, accompanying me to sites they had never heard of, and listening to long, rambling expositions that did not yet have a point—special thanks and heartfelt affection to two honorary medievalists extraordinaire: Monique Young, who is always ready for a new adventure, and Will Crooke, who sees beyond the obvious and always reminds me that the journey is as important as the destination.